Date Due

Ap 19		
MAY 20		
HE NOct89		
AUG 3 1 1999		

THE ONTARIO HISTORICAL STUDIES SERIES

The Ontario Historical Studies Series is a comprehensive history of Ontario from 1791 to the present, which will include several biographies of former premiers, numerous volumes on the economic, social, political, and cultural development of the province, and a general history incorporating the insights and conclusions of the other works in the series. The purpose of the series is to enable general readers and scholars to understand better the distinctive features of Ontario as one of the principal regions within Canada.

The Biographies of the Premiers

J.M.S. Careless, ed., *The Pre-Confederation Premiers: Ontario Government Leaders, 1841–1867*

Charles W. Humphries, *'Honest Enough to Be Bold': The Life and Times of Sir James Pliny Whitney* (Premier, 1905–1914)

Peter Oliver, *G. Howard Ferguson: Ontario Tory* (Premier, 1923–1930)

A.K. McDougall, *John P. Robarts: His Life and Government* (Premier, 1961–1971)

FORTHCOMING

A. Margaret Evans, SIR OLIVER MOWAT (Premier, 1872–1896)
Robert J.D. Page, SIR GEORGE W. ROSS (Premier, 1899–1905)
Charles M. Johnston, HON. E.C. DRURY (Premier, 1919–1923)
John T. Saywell, HON. MITCHELL F. HEPBURN (Premier, 1934–1942)
Roger Graham, HON. LESLIE M. FROST (Premier, 1949–1961)

Robarts speaking to the Western Ontario PC Association, 4 May 1968

A.K. McDOUGALL

John P. Robarts:
His Life and Government

Published by University of Toronto Press
Toronto Buffalo London
for The Ontario Historical Studies Series

ISBN 0-8020-3426-8

Canadian Cataloguing in Publication Data

McDougall, Allan Kerr, 1941–
    John P. Robarts

    (Ontario historical studies series, ISSN 0380-9188)
    Bibliography: p.
    Includes index.
    ISBN 0-8020-3426-8

    1. Robarts, John P., 1917–1982. 2. Prime ministers –
    Ontario – Biography. 3. Politicians – Ontario –
    Biography. 4. Ontario – Politics and government –
    1943–   * 5. Progressive Conservative Party of
    Ontario. I. Title. II. Series.

    FC3076.1.R62M23 1986   971.3'04'0924   c85-099616-3
    F1058.R62M23 1986

This book has been published with funds provided by the Government of Ontario through the Ministry of Citizenship and Culture.

To my parents,
Allan Houliston McDougall and
Elizabeth Ann Kerr McDougall,
and to the memory of
the late Donald Gordon Grady Kerr,
scholar, historian, and friend

Contents

The Ontario Historical Studies Series
  Goldwin French, Peter Oliver, Jeanne Beck, and Maurice Careless ix
Preface xi

PART ONE: LONDON POLITICIAN
  1 'Who's John?' 3
  2 Londoners 16
  3 A Part-time Job 32
  4 The Crossroads 48
  5 Going for the Leadership 58

PART TWO: RUNNING A SMOOTH SHIP
  6 The Robarts Style 75
  7 'Done!' 93
  8 Fighting Grits 101
  9 'Terrible Legislation': Bill 99 112
  10 Modernizing the Government 128
  11 Tending the Golden Goose 142
  12 The Faces of Federalism 161
  13 Centennial: Turning Fifty 177
  14 Centennial: Confederation of Tomorrow 188

PART THREE: THE PASSING OF OLD ONTARIO
  15 New Mood, Old Issues 205
  16 'We Cannot All Be Wrong – Can We?' 223
  17 Entering the Seventies 234
  18 'I'm a Has-been' 251
  19 'My Time Is Finished' 261

Appendices 277
Notes 285
Bibliography 299
Index 307

The Ontario Historical Studies Series

For many years the principal theme in English-Canadian historical writing has been the emergence and the consolidation of the Canadian nation. This theme has been developed in uneasy awareness of the persistence and importance of regional interests and identities, but because of the central role of Ontario in the growth of Canada, Ontario has not been seen as a region. Almost unconsciously, historians have equated the history of the province with that of the nation and have depicted the interests of other regions as obstacles to the unity and welfare of Canada.

The creation of the province of Ontario in 1867 was the visible embodiment of a formidable reality, the existence at the core of the new nation of a powerful if disjointed society whose traditions and characteristics differed in many respects from those of the other British North American colonies. The intervening years have not witnessed the assimilation of Ontario to the other regions in Canada; on the contrary it has become a more clearly articulated entity. Within the formal geographical and institutional framework defined so assiduously by Ontario's political leaders, an increasingly intricate web of economic and social interests has been woven and shaped by the dynamic interplay between Toronto and its hinterland. The character of this regional community has been formed in the tension between a rapid adaptation to the processes of modernization and industrialization in modern Western society and a reluctance to modify or discard traditional attitudes and values. Not surprisingly, the Ontario outlook is a compound of aggressiveness, conservatism, and the conviction that its values should be the model for the rest of Canada.

From the outset the objective of the Board of Trustees of the Ontario Historical Studies Series has been to describe and analyse the historical development of Ontario as a distinct region within Canada. The series as planned will include some thirty-two volumes covering many aspects of the life and work of the province from its original establishment in 1791 as Upper Canada to our own time. Among these will be biographies of several premiers, numerous works on the growth of the provincial economy, educational institutions, minority groups, and the arts, and a synthesis of the history of Ontario, based upon the contributions of the biographies and thematic studies.

In planning this project, the Editors and the Board have endeavoured to maintain a reasonable balance between different kinds and areas of historical research, and to appoint authors ready to ask new questions about the past and to answer them in accordance with the canons of contemporary scholarship. Nine biographical studies have been included, if only because through biography the past comes alive most readily for the general reader as well as the historian. The historian must be sensitive to today's concerns and standards as he engages in the imaginative recreation of the interplay between human beings and circumstances in time. He should seek to be the mediator between the dead and the living, but in the end the humanity and the artistry of his account will determine the extent of its usefulness.

John P. Robarts: His Life and Government describes the formative years of John Robarts, his premiership in the crucial decade of the 1960s, and his later career as a senior statesman, which closed with his tragic death in 1982. The successor to Leslie Frost in the so-called Conservative dynasty, Robarts dealt constructively with the forces of change in his time. His governments took many important initiatives in administrative, economic, social, and cultural matters, whose subsequent impact cannot be accurately assessed at this juncture.

The Editors and the Board of Trustees are grateful to Allan McDougall for accepting the difficult task of writing about a contemporary figure. We are deeply indebted to Professor Michael Bliss for his assistance in giving this volume its final form. We hope that it will enlarge our understanding of John Robarts and his governments and of twentieth-century Ontario.

Goldwin French
Peter Oliver
Jeanne Beck
Maurice Careless, Chairman of the Board of Trustees

Toronto
3 September 1985

Preface

This book is about the life and times of John Parmenter Robarts, Prime Minister of Ontario from November 1961 to March 1971, and especially about his government. The decade of Robarts' premiership opened with a short recession followed by sustained economic growth. Constitutional tensions, fiscal negotiations, and, most of all, changes provoked directly or indirectly by the rising wave of 'baby boomers' left their imprint on his term.

During Robarts' years as premier, the government of Ontario was transformed from the personal, rural-dominated administration of Leslie Frost to the professionally administered, urban-dominated regime of William Davis. The transition was guided by a premier from outside Toronto, intent on extending services beyond the provincial capital to citizens in major regional centres across the province. At the same time, changes in society and in the financial community provoked government responses which challenged Robarts' deeply felt concern for the freedom of the individual. Step by step, government adapted to its new context, and he refined the structures of the state to assert the right of politicians to meet these new challenges. But as he did, he became uneasy about the possible breakdown of the fine distinctions between government intervention and individual self-determination.

The focus of this volume is on John Robarts, his preparation for office, his political friends, his cabinet, and the major economic, political, and structural reforms introduced during the sixties. Changes of lasting significance also occurred in policies related to agriculture, recreational land, and the arts. These subjects await the attention of other scholars and other times. All were important to Robarts.

The text rests largely on interviews generously granted by the persons listed in the bibliography. In addition, the records in the Ontario Archives were used extensively. The size of the collection is staggering. There are twenty-three boxes of personal correspondence, and 566 boxes of general correspondence amassed by Robarts and the Prime Minister's Department alone during the decade. The

Department of Treasury and Economics has stored sixteen hundred cubic feet of paper, and Education has matched it. This study reflects the range and diversity of government activity during Robarts' premiership.

This study was developed as follows. With the help of Bob Tapscott, Gordon Dodds, Alex Ross, Barbara Craig, Larry Weiler, David Russell, and Allan MacDonald, I examined the records of the Prime Minister's Department and the Attorney General's Department in detail. Subsequently, interviews were undertaken with John Robarts, his friends in London, his colleagues in cabinet, and senior personnel in the Prime Minister's Department. John Robarts, in particular, generously gave a lengthy series of interviews, informal consultations and telephone responses concerning problems or questions I had. The Ontario base of the text was set on these foundations. Other departmental records were used as required to complete the account.

Ontario-Quebec issues were explored and analysed with the help of provincial negotiators, their papers, and through conversations with Dale Thomson of McGill University, Jean Lesage's biographer, and Peter White, a former executive assistant to Daniel Johnson. Information about federal politics was derived from federal government documents, and from secondary sources, such as biographies of C.D. Howe, St Laurent, Diefenbaker, Pearson, and Trudeau. These were supplemented by interviews with Robert Coates and brief discussions with or letters from Walter Baker, Walter Gordon, and John Diefenbaker.

My thanks are extended to all those who assisted me with my research. I have not annotated all the debts to interviews in the text; I have only included anecdotes or events remembered and confirmed by three people. However, if an incident related to personal action could not be widely attested to, it is attributed.

The newspapers of the times constitute an important record of public perception of statements and events. The commentaries on Ontario politics of Don O'Hearn, Eric Dowd, Bill Prager, Del Bell, Jonathan Manthorpe, Fraser Kelly and Rosemary Speirs were very helpful.

The writing of the text was interrupted by John Robarts' tragic death. At one point, it had been hoped that he would write his reminiscences to complement this work. When that became impossible, at the request of his friends and the Ontario Historical Studies Series it was decided to describe his personal life in more detail than had at first been planned. Robert and Eleanor Robarts, Robin Robarts, John's step-sister Catherine Eaton, and Katherine Robarts all gave generously of their time and, despite the pain of John's recent death, were most helpful in providing information.

Following the death of John Robarts, which altered the perspective of the volume, the entire text was recast by Michael Bliss. I am grateful to Michael for the assistance he gave me in giving this volume a more historical and biographical orientation than was envisaged at the outset. My sincere thanks go to him and to Jeanne Beck, Goldwin French, and Peter Oliver. The challenge of objectively divorcing oneself from one's own writing, which seemed overwhelming, to say the least, was met in part with their help. Diane Mew, on behalf of the University of Toronto Press, reviewed the final manuscript and, in a genial and constructive way, did an exceptional job of noting and removing inconsistencies and clarifying sections only comprehensible to the author.

Dr J. Keith Reynolds, the secretary to the cabinet in the late 1960s, spent hours helping me understand the relationships between issues and between personalities in the latter years of Robarts' tenure.

At the University of Western Ontario, Dr James J. Talman helped me in the early stages of preparing the manuscript. My wife Barbara has typed the material and unravelled interviews, helped with the proofreading and indexing, and worse, had to put up with me as this work progressed. To her and my children, Allan, Kathryn, and Louisa, who also helped with the proofreading and indexing, my profound thanks. I owe them some time now that it is done.

Any errors that remain are mine. I hope readers will enjoy this account of the formation, the political career and the last years of a prime minister who has a great deal to say to the issues of the 1980s.

AKM
June 1985

Ethel and Herbert Robarts, circa 1936

John Robarts; early days in London

Ordinary Seaman Robarts, 1940

John, Norah, Robin, and Tim, London, 22 December 1961

The change in command: Leslie Frost making a presentation to John Robarts on his assumption of the premiership, November 1961

The 1963 election; Robarts at the victory night celebrations at the Hotel London

Kelso Roberts, attorney general, 1955–62

Robert Macaulay, minister of economics
and development, 1961–3

Fred Cass, attorney general, 1962–4,
Speaker of the House, 1968–71

Charles MacNaughton, provincial
treasurer, 1966–71

Norah, Robin, and John, 1966

Jean Lesage, premier of Quebec, and John Robarts at the newspaper editors' seminar, Toronto, 7 October 1965

The Confederation of Tomorrow conference, 1967

Gordon Walker is nominated to succeed Robarts as the PC candidate in the riding of London North, March 1971

Norah and John arrive at the state dinner for the Queen, London, 26 June 1973

Robarts at the opening of the Middlesex Court Centre, London, 14 October 1974

Governor-General Roland Michener presents John Robarts with Order of Canada medal, Ottawa 1972

Jean-Luc Pepin and John Robarts confer together at a public hearing of the Task Force on Canadian Unity, 1978

Katherine and John share a quiet moment together after his stroke in 1981

John Robarts relaxing at Griffith Island in 1980

PART ONE: LONDON POLITICIAN

1

'Who's John?'

The Robartses were an old family, whose ancestral lands in Cornwall had been given to a John Robartes by Oliver Cromwell. On them he built 'Lanhydrock' in 1657, a stately mansion overlooking the Fowey River. The Canadian branch of the family had been created in the mid-nineteenth century when John's great-grandfather, Thomas Parmenter Robarts, emigrated to Barbados, married the daughter of a prominent British family, the Conliffes, and later came with them to Hamilton, Ontario. When Thomas Parmenter Robarts died shortly after their arrival, his widow and two sons moved to Toronto. George, one of those sons, was a bookkeeper for ten years before moving to Galt in the early 1890s. He married Louisa Job in 1879 and their first child, Herbert Robarts, was born in Toronto on 14 April, 1880.

Herbert Robarts entered the service (as a banking career used to be called) of the Imperial Bank of Canada in 1895, when he was fifteen years old. He started as a clerk in Galt, and then began to move west as the bank grew with the expanding Dominion. He was an assistant manager in Winnipeg and then Brandon, Manitoba, managed his first branch in Estevan, Saskatchewan, then was posted to Nelson, British Columbia. He fell in love with the Rockies, and received the ideal mountain job when he was made manager of the Banff branch in 1912.

Herbert Robarts was an uncomplicated man who liked the outdoor life, and soon was covering the walls of his living room with trophies from his hunting and fishing expeditions. He was readily accepted into the Banff community. One of the young ladies he met there was a recent widow, Florency May Stacpoole Brett. Florency May was the daughter of Frank Stacpoole, a judge in Victoria, British Columbia. The Stacpooles had emigrated from England in 1883, settling in Cypress River, Manitoba. Florency May was born in 1891, lived in Winnipeg while her father apprenticed in law, entered her teens in Dawson City where Frank had followed the prospectors to open his law practice, and then settled in Victoria after his appointment to the bench. In 1910 she had married Earl Brett, the eldest son of a prominent Alberta physician, Dr Robert George Brett, who was to become lieutenant-governor of the province in 1915. Florency May gave birth to her first child, Catherine Brett, in 1912. But that winter Earl Brett suddenly became ill and died of a ruptured appendix. Florency May and her daughter stayed on in Banff with her father-in-law.

Florency May Brett married Herbert Robarts in Banff in September 1914. He was thirty-four years old, she was twenty-three. Their first child, Robert George, was born in June 1915. Their second son, John Parmenter Robarts was born in Banff on 11 January 1917.

Shortly after John's birth, his father was promoted to manager of the Winnipeg branch of the Imperial Bank. The Robarts family arrived in the city just as the Great War ended in late 1918. Unfortunately, it was also just before the devastating influenza epidemic of 1919. Towards the end of that year Florency May came down with the disease. Because she was pregnant her doctors were reluctant to prescribe any very strong medicine; in any case they had nothing to prescribe that would have been particularly effective. She died on 7 February 1920, in her twenty-ninth year. John had just turned three. Herbert Robarts wrote to his sister, Edith Goodall, who lived in London, Ontario, that he had explained to the three children (the two Robarts boys and Catherine Brett) that 'their mummy had gone to heaven to be with her baby since her baby couldn't come down to be with them.' Robert and John seemed satisfied with that explanation, he remarked, but Catherine was very upset.

Edith Robarts Goodall at once went to Winnipeg to help her brother and his children. It was soon decided that a return to Ontario would be in everyone's interest, and the bank obliged by appointing Herbert manager of the branch in his home town, Galt. Edith ('Auntie' to the boys) stayed with the family until they left Winnipeg for Galt in the early summer of 1920.

When the family reached Galt, the children were immediately whisked off to the Goodalls' cottage on East Orchard Beach in the small Lake Erie resort of Port Stanley. There they met their uncle, Alan J. Goodall, a lawyer who had served as manager of the London branch of the Imperial Bank since 1913. 'Unk' Goodall had a marked impact on the Robarts boys in that first summer and the years afterwards. He was a warm but aristocratic man, interested in literature, who loved to recite poetry and tell stories to the boys. The high point in their day would be Unk's bedtime story, an instalment of a tale he developed through the whole summer. 'If we were at Port for two months,' Robert Robarts remembered, 'the story went on for sixty nights, and he never let the side down. If he had to go out for a dinner party ... he came home and did the story and then went back. He had a terrific imagination and we just hung on the ropes waiting for that story.'

The Goodalls did not indulge the Robarts children. The boys were required to do chores at the cottage, putting out the garbage or cutting the grass. Auntie was always strict with them. Still, they were happy at the cottage, playing in the water and sand, doting on Unk's stories. Every Friday evening, Robert and John would run to the top of the hill in town to watch for their father coming from Galt in the bank's Model-T Ford. When he appeared they would race him to the cottage and crawl all over him as he got out. The boys were put to bed early while the grown-ups relaxed over cards – the Goodalls were fanatical bridge players – and a drink or two. Robert and John would be up at six, play outside their father's window in the hope of waking him, and as often as not get invited into his room for a special few minutes together.

Back in Galt, Herbert Robarts hired a series of housekeepers to look after the boys. The housekeeper maintained discipline until dinner, when Herbert returned home from work and, if necessary, resolved the outstanding problems of the day. The young boys were naturally exuberant, loving to spur one another on in mischief. Catherine, who was eight when the family moved to Galt, watched her brothers' pranks from some distance. After she finished her elementary school in Galt, she went on to Branksome Hall in Toronto for her high school education, returning home on holidays and staying with the Goodalls at Christmas. When John was four he started kindergarten, a year early, because of the lack of a mother at home. The boys were not particularly happy in the Galt house, missing the affection of a mother, lacking the opportunity of playing one parent off against the other to relax the rules.

As a bank manager, Herbert Robarts practised one of the most disciplined, regulated, and hierarchical vocations in Canadian life. He expected his boys to adhere to the standards and discipline he set for them. Serious mischief was punished by lickings with his razor strap. Robert remembered John once being taken up to the bathroom, turned over his father's knee, and given the strap across the buttocks for something he had done to the housekeeper. Robert stood outside the door and roared with laughter. 'If you think it's so funny,' his father said, 'you come in here too.' Robert got the second strapping. The strap became the symbol of parental authority; the boys would hide it from time to time, but their father always found it. He did not allow the boys to attend Saturday afternoon movies at the local cinema, forbade gum-chewing, and insisted that they sing in their Anglican church choir.

While Herbert Robarts was a disciplined banker and parent during the week, he introduced his sons to the outdoors he had grown to love on the weekend. He taught them to hunt for rabbits and fish in the streams around Galt. He bought their first hatchets and gave them their first lessons in handling guns. The boys spent a lot of weekends hunting and fishing with their father, and later snared a lot of rabbits and muskrat on their own. In 1927, when John was ten, they set up their own four-trap line, selling their catch to a local fox farm. The Robarts males all loved the outdoors, as anyone realized who saw the stuffed heads of deer and moose and mountain goat and sheep that hung in their hallway, a little moth-eaten as the years passed, but reminders of the wide-open spaces of the Rockies.

Robert and John were healthy, normal boys, close enough in age to do everything together and be great pals. They were classmates because of John's early start in school. John did have a bout of scarlet fever one year, but the disease had no lasting effects, and within a few months he was swimming and skating again. They joined the Galt YMCA and took up competitive swimming. Robert swam in the shorter sprints, while John enjoyed the arduous distance races, the choice perhaps reflecting developing character traits in tenacity and manner.

As lively boys, without a mother to soften and shape the discipline, they got into a fair share of mischief. There were the usual innocent scrapes, such as a memorable rainy Saturday afternoon when father relented about the cowboy movies: John came home from a wild time at the matinee with some of his hair snared with gum and large chunks of it missing altogether, having had it cut out at a friend's house to try to dispose of the evidence. Their father was not impressed. More seriously, the boys managed to drive away several housekeepers with their pranks.

So the boys lived their lives between the poles of discipline and order on the one hand, freedom and good fun on the other. From an early stage, John seems to have shown an ability to distinguish roles or identities, and move easily from one to another. He was a voracious reader, having discovered books largely through Unk Goodall, and enjoyed taking on some character traits of the hero of his latest book. He would argue from that fictitious point of view, until the next book and a new hero came along. Later he seemed to enjoy taking positions purely for argument's sake; the family began to assume he was on his way to becoming a lawyer, like Unk. On his own, young John Robarts changed his identity symbolically and literally by switching from being 'John' to using the alternative 'Jack.'

One Wednesday afternoon the Robarts boys took time after school to help set up chairs in a big tent that had just been raised to house a visiting Chautauqua troupe. They were curious to see the part-circus, part-educational performance, but had to attend a choir practice that evening. They rushed down to the tent right after supper, slipped in, and caught the beginning of the show. Time sped by and Robert suddenly noticed it was time to get to choir. Nudging his brother, he jumped up, ducked under the tent, and turned around outside to find that John had not followed him. He could not get back in, so he called out in a stage whisper, 'John, it's time to go home.' When John still did not appear, Robert dutifully went off to choir practice. Later he learned that John had heard him call, but hadn't responded at all – he had nonchalantly looked at the person beside him and wondered aloud, 'Who's John?' Jack would set his own priorities, a habit which would increasingly try the patience of his father through John's high school years.

He was a Goodall as much as a Robarts. He spent his summers at Port Stanley, and every Christmas the Robartses would leave Galt for the Goodalls' big house on Wolfe Avenue in London. When they arrived, a bare Christmas tree would be standing by the fireplace in the front hall. After supper and a story from Unk the children would be put to bed. Then the adults would decorate the tree. On Christmas morning Unk, Auntie, and Herbert would blindfold the children in their rooms. Then Auntie would lead Catherine into the dining room, Unk and Herbert would carry the boys on their shoulders. In the dining room they could take off the blindfolds and eat breakfast, but the children were not allowed to peek at the tree in the hall. There was the discipline, the routine to follow, even on Christmas morning. When breakfast was finally finished, the doors to the hall would be flung open and the tree revealed in all its splendour beside the roaring fire. Then the children amused themselves with their presents, staying out of the grown-ups' way until dinner.

Herbert Robarts, who was sociable and popular wherever he went, began to court again in the mid-1920s, seeing a great deal of Ethel McIrvine, daughter of a popular mayor of Galt. They were married in the summer of 1927. For the three children, the adjustment to a new life took time. On the morning after their father and new mother returned from their honeymoon, for example, John and Robert bounced into their bedroom at six o'clock, jumped onto the bed, and began to argue about the coloured socks they wanted to wear. That afternoon they tried to raid the kitchen where Ethel had accumulated a spectacular array of snacks, brought all the way from Toronto for the reception the Robartses were holding for their friends. Then, as the guests began to arrive, the boys were found perched up on the gable over the roof, watching. Neither father nor stepmother could persuade them to come down.

Ethel McIrvine appears to have adjusted reasonably well to the lively brood. She cut out the early morning bedroom invasions, but relaxed some of the other rules, such as church choir. John had no trouble getting on with his new mother; Robert was miffed for a while at having lost his privileged claim to the front seat of the car. Summers were now spent at the McIrvine cottage at Southampton on the shores of Lake Huron. The boys made friends readily at the new beach. Hunting and fishing trips introduced Herbert and his sons to the attractions of the Bruce peninsula. The family flourished, and a few years later the boys were joined by a half-sister, Marion.[1]

Three years after his remarriage, Herbert Robarts was posted to London to succeed his brother-in-law, Alan Goodall, as the Imperial Bank's manager. During their first year in London the Robarts family lived in a rented house on Elmwood Avenue in the city's south end, and Robert and Jack took their second year of high school at South Collegiate. It was an uneventful year. That spring, Catherine graduated from Branksome Hall.[2] For the boys, the end of the school year meant a summer of fishing, hunting, and swimming in Southampton. The next fall they moved into a big Victorian brick house at the corner of Waterloo and St James streets in the north end. The boys now were in the catchment area for London Central Collegiate, about a mile south of them on Waterloo Street. Priding itself on its academic reputation and the subsequent careers of its graduates, London Central served the wealthier areas of the city and the offspring of most of the 'old London' families.

Robert and Jack entered grade eleven of their new school in September 1932. The boys appeared to their teachers as quiet, polite, and verging on shy. They were athletic, with Robert concentrating on rugby while Jack went in for basketball and football. Their circles of friends began to diverge a bit now, as Jack got into a younger, football crowd.[3] He also struck up a friendship with a London girl, Norah McCormick, which developed into a teenage romance. Jack was a good student, getting his first-class grades almost effortlessly because he was able to go a long way on a quick mind and sharp memory.

Jack also developed an interest in cards and petty gambling. Quite early on, he and a circle of friends regularly gathered at someone's house after school for a little game. The games stretched on, until Jack was coming in as late as three in the morning. His father, confronting him with the late hours just before exam time, got a revealing answer: 'Come and complain to me when I fail or get failing marks.' All his life John Robarts would see no reason not to enjoy himself so long as he got his work done the next day. He continued his card-playing. 'It used to drive Father nuts,' Robert remembers, but you couldn't use a razor strap on a sixteen-year-old football player. Jack also sampled liquor for the first time while he was in high school.

There was nothing particularly memorable about John Robarts' high school years. He was a popular, above-average student, neither brilliant nor a trouble-maker. Neither an egghead, nor just a jock. He would do all right in life, but no one would have singled him out as a potential prime minister, even of a province. At the end of his grade twelve year, he did have an interesting short composition published in Central's 1934 yearbook, *The Orbit*. There are two characters: a lone scientist trying to discover the secret of alchemy, and a chattering, 'almost human' monkey. When the monkey's noise distracts the scientist, he beats the little animal unmercifully. Then, just as the scientist succeeds in producing gold from lead, the monkey leaps into the apparatus in a frenzy, smashing everything. At the end of 'Retribution' we have an insane scientist, a dead monkey, and a wilderness of broken glass. The story may not have meant much to Jack at the time – perhaps it came out of Unk Goodall's story-telling – but it may have had symbolic overtones. The scientist is the controlled, disciplined, rational, achieving man – the father-figure, the achieving scholar, later the controlled politician. The monkey is the Dionysian impulse – the mischievous child, the game-playing adolescent, the guy letting off steam, the emotional and irrational. The one has to tolerate the other; you have to allow a little monkey business in life or everything gets smashed.

Jack entered the University of Western Ontario in the autumn of 1935, along with Norah McCormick and many of their friends from Central. Western was a fairly small university in the 1930s, but had reasonably high standards and a beautiful new campus northwest of the city centre. Robarts entered the honours course in business administration in his second year, a program designed to train men ('This course is open to men only,' the calendar reads) for careers in business. There was a sprinkling of humanities options among the program's economics and business courses. As in high school, Jack had little trouble maintaining good grades and had a lot of energy left over for more interesting extra-curricular activities.

Jack Robarts, Stu Carver, George Willis, and Cam Killoran, among others from Central, made the Western Mustangs football team, automatically becoming Saturday's campus heroes. Their girl friends, including Norah, supported the team by selling hot dogs and school colours and cheering them on at games. At a couple of inches over six feet, weighing one hundred and eighty pounds, Robarts was an average-sized lineman for his day. He played both offence and defence, was not particularly fast, would not have dreamed of becoming a professional, but had a good time at football on what was considered to be a winning team.

Naturally he joined Delta Upsilon, the preferred fraternity house of the London Central circle. Robarts and his friends were very much the in-group on campus – and off it as well, for Norah was a McCormick of the biscuit family, and she and many of their friends had ties with the old London community and the London Hunt Club. Fraternity life combined fellowship and fun, with terrific parties after every Saturday afternoon football game. In third year, Jack's friends elected him president of the campus Delta Upsilon chapter, and with an appetite mildly whetted for student politics he served as vice-president of Western's students' council in his final year. Norah, a little shyer and more reserved, made her mark on campus as a member of the women's tennis team and the undergraduate women's council. Once when a fellow student, a non-Londoner, took Norah out on a date, Jack and some of his friends followed them off campus to Norah's house, gathered outside and disrupted the evening by pestering them to come out. It was good to be a member of a group, and Jack and Norah continued their courting.

Robarts liked his little taste of campus politics. But his memories of the experience centred on the challenge of getting things done, making decisions, trying to give leadership. He was not interested in politics as lobbying to gather support, as partisanship, or as backroom organization. There were no political science courses in his business curriculum. He was more the prominent and successful man on campus than a campus politician in the mould of a Mackenzie King or a Joe Clark in their student days.

Jack had become acquainted with the big Great Lakes passenger boats during his cottage days at Southampton and after grade thirteen managed to get a summer job as cabin boy. He spent every summer of his college years working on the lake boats, the old *Huronic, Harmonic,* and *Noronic.* Robarts looked back on these experiences fondly: he was outdoors in a beautiful setting, could gamble to his heart's content in off hours (and for higher stakes than he could afford, he remembered), learned a lot about working with other men, and met a range of people he never would have known as a middle-class student in Galt and London. His summer work made Jack seem a little more worldly than some of his classmates at Western, a little more sure of himself and in command.

Robarts graduated from Western in the spring of 1939. He was elected to the Honours Society and his grades were good enough that some of his professors thought he should continue on to graduate school. He already had decided, however, to follow Unk and make his career in the law. He enrolled at Osgoode Hall in Toronto in the fall of 1939. His first year there was uneventful, with everything eclipsed by the outbreak of war. Robarts did find time to make one lifelong commitment. Partly through an acquaintanceship with an Osgoode classmate, Eddie Goodman, Jack decided that an aspiring member of the legal profession should be active in politics. The Robarts, Brett, and Stacpoole families had all been Conservatives. So Jack naturally joined the Osgoode Conservative Club.

Young men all across Canada were joining the Canadian armed forces in the summer of 1940. Robert Robarts joined the army, Stu Carver the air force, and on 5 July George Willis and John Robarts enrolled as ordinary seamen in the Royal Canadian Navy reserve. Robarts became one of the many volunteers seconded from the Royal Canadian Navy to Britain's Royal Navy for his training, which would include a brief spell as a rating and then courses leading to a commission. He crossed the Atlantic that month as an ordinary seaman – 'as green as grass and loving it,'[4] he wrote home a few months later – and then spent considerable time in training barracks in England.

Robert was already in Britain and an officer, and Jack was not sure his lowly rank would allow them full fraternal status when they got together on leave. A comment to his parents on the situation indicates that he was not unhappy at its development:

There is no doubt of the fact that my experiences here are to be very different from Bob's. First, I shall never be far from the sea and the Coastal towns are used to people from all over the world. Also, being an ordinary seaman excludes one from the middle and higher social levels such as Bob sees. In addition, we are more restricted as regards leave and the distance we may be on leave. If I am to see Bob I imagine he will have to come to me rather than vice-versa ... There are advantages in being an ordinary seaman tho' – you meet scads of sailors and they are all willing to 'spin you a yarn' as they say about themselves. But my life has certainly changed completely – I do not think the change could be more complete. I like it, and when I am through should know this part of navy life fairly well.[5]

Jack had hardly landed in Britain when he began enjoying the off-hour fraternizing among fighting men, and glorying in it. 'I met two men in a pub and they very nearly bought me more beer than I could consume. I struggled thro' it. Also I have been talking to sailors from down under & all over this country – they all talk and I talk – you know how I can keep it up until the small hours of the morning!!' He soon got in touch with Robert, found that even ordinary seamen did get leave to go to London, and saw both his brother and a gang of old football pals for good times together. The difficulty that Robarts the rating had in being unable to enter officer's messes or clubs with his more elevated friends was solved when someone found an officer's uniform for him. They teased Jack a lot about his lowly status; he, of course, insisted that he was too poor to buy anyone drinks, and sometimes even talked the boys into paying for his room at the Park Lane Hotel.

Becoming an officer, he soon realized, was above all else a matter of cultivating intense discipline. 'That is not too bad,' he wrote as the training program began in earnest, 'except that it irks one who has not had too much for the past few years ... It is good to use the old head again – much as I kicked about studying, it seems you establish habits and I find I do miss studying and am glad to get back to it.' He wanted to get back to sea again, but showed what would become a characteristic patience: 'Some of the boys want their commissions fast but I think I would rather wait & find out just what it is all about first.' The characteristics of his teachers that most impressed Robarts in this basic training were, he wrote home, 'that cool optimism and refusal to be worried.'[6]

In many ways he was a typical Canadian serviceman abroad, doing quite a bit of sightseeing on his leaves, writing home for more cigarettes, marvelling at the capacity of the British to endure the German air attacks, getting lost in a London fog. He did not spend as much time as some of his buddies with the English girls they met, once commenting to his parents that he preferred male company to female. He was sort of pledged to Norah McCormick anyway, though whether he should marry her after the war seemed to have been a question of active discussion with his parents. 'As you say, mother,' he wrote after a few months in England, 'she is very ambitious which is a laudable trait, but leads her sometimes into things of which I do not exactly approve, if I am to consider her as anything more than a friend – result, or moral – have her as a friend. Which is an opinion I may have to-day and change to-morrow.' In the same letter Robarts expresses his earliest recorded political opinion, a typical fighting man's disgust of politicians: 'let's get the scrap over and then unscramble the mess. I hope we do not have a bunch of bone-head, money-grabbing selfish punks doing the job [after the war] – they are the ones that got us into this mess all right. Well, lights are out and I am getting hot under the collar when I think of our politics at home so I think I'll cut this off.'[7]

Early in 1941 Jack had just returned from a twenty-thousand-mile training voyage to Cape Town, South Africa, when the reality of war came closer to him personally. Robert Robarts and a girl friend were among a crowd of officers dancing in what was billed as 'London's safest restaurant,' the underground Café de Paris, when it received a direct hit from a German bomb on the night of 7 March. Robert was one of the lucky ones pulled alive from the rubble. He had taken thirteen shrapnel wounds in his back and shoulders, had a foot crushed, an ear-drum burned through, and his sight affected by a damaged nerve. Writing to their parents about his brother's condition, Jack was beginning to develop the coolness of the serviceman who knew how bad the bombing could be:

You will probably think that this is quite a line-up of injuries as indeed it is, but living over here one of necessity expects the worst and when I see what happened to others in the same spot ... I cannot but feel very cheerful about the whole thing ... He spent 10 hrs. on the operating table and definitely his doctors did a magnificent job, so if his eye comes around (as it must, or at least to some degree) it is safe to say he is as good as new. Whether it will affect his future service here I do not know, but all that will come with time.

I think that the picture I present is exactly what the situation is and I am not trying to be ultra-optimistic in order to cheer you up ... He was dancing with 'Peter' at the time and he sheltered her as his back was to the bomb, so that she received only one small cut in the thigh with a piece of shrapnel which missed him – a fact that pleases him. He is a very very lucky man, – if you would see some of the devastation over here you would understand me better.[8]

Robert recovered from his wounds and eventually saw combat in Sicily and Italy. Jack was about to take his final few weeks of training before going to sea as an officer. His reflections on naval service below decks showed remarkable maturity and common sense:

I am an old sea-dog already – its the only place to be despite its discomforts at times – I love it. The idea is to remove the roughness of the lower deck from us during the next 8 wks – damn necessary too, in ways, for its been pretty rough & ready the last four months. But I am convinced it is the only way – I know that it has given me the confidence which I feel is so necessary to be a good officer. Also, the real way to learn the sea is to do it with your hands ...

I suppose you have heard many of the complaints some of the lads have sent home – Mother mentioned it in one of her letters. It's a long and not particularly interesting story which boils down to too-long adherence to the old apron-strings and an upbringing which did not include a little roughage on your own, for some of the 150 of us here. Personally, I never mentioned it. 1) because there was nothing to be done anyway; 2) I rather enjoyed the rough & tough (mainly surface) men we've been with; 3) there *is* a war on and one must expect delays especially when one can look around everywhere & see things which demand more immediate attention and 4) I think it the best way to learn the navy & all the term means in regard to practical work, theories and methods, traditions and personnel. After all, one cannot control 'em if one does not know how they think, and there are several outstanding differences between their mental attitude and ours. So there you have it – its been good & bad, but I think I'd do it again.[9]

Robarts got his commission in May 1941 and spent most of the rest of that year and the next serving as a sublieutenant on routine convoy duty on the North Atlantic. He had hoped to be assigned to a small torpedo boat or corvette and one day command his own ship, but had not done well enough in his courses to get one of the most desired postings. With some of his friends urging him to enter the Royal Navy's air arm, Jack compromised by applying for training as a fighter direction officer. A bout of pleurisy interrupted his service briefly in the spring of 1943, but he finally completed his special training and was assigned to the small destroyer HMS *Palomares;* his job was to guide the pilots of the two aircraft *Palomares* could launch by catapult.

Throughout this period Jack set aside money from his monthly pay cheque, building savings for his postwar life. He and his father consulted about finances, with Jack the sailor being less concerned about the situation than Herbert Robarts the banker. 'I am afraid I do not worry about the future (or *my* future) very much,' Jack wrote in 1942, 'for things always seem to work out when the time comes and there is really very little point in even thinking much about it when everything is so unsettled.'

Palomares was sent to the Mediterranean, where it fought at the landings at Salerno and Anzio. This was Robarts' first taste of offensive action in almost four years of war and he was pleased finally to be doing something more useful than herding drunken seamen back to their ships as a duty officer. He was mentioned in dispatches 'for good service in [the] attack on Salerno. For outstanding skill, resolution, leadership and devotion to duty in HM Ships in Operations which led to the successful landing on the Italian mainland and at Salerno.'

He saw a considerable amount of further action before war's end, and the experiences seem to have completed his development of exactly the phlegmatic coolness that the Royal Navy desired in its officers. It was a businesslike calm, detached from the horror of war that other fighting men had developed from other kinds of experiences:

I suppose I could tell you now about some of the actions I have been in down here but it seems to me that the BBC etc. always put it much better than I can – one's reaction under fire is interesting – it all seems so impersonal somehow and you get used to it ... I have watched aircraft attacking us several times in the past and the surprising thing is that one feels nothing at all except an interest in their speed and evading action from the guns. I have just read a book by H.G. Wells about the last war and the reaction of those that fought it – frankly I thought it a lot of tripe and he generally knows what he is talking about – it may be a matter of different generations with different backgrounds and therefore different reactions.[10]

The combat experience also made him more impatient for his own command, for the war to end, and for his life to move along. Immediately after the Salerno action he began thinking seriously about getting married. In January 1944 *Palomares* was crippled in the Anzio operations and the crew received extended leave. Back in London, Jack made up his mind, formally proposing to Norah and asking his stepmother to choose the engagement ring. He observed conservative proprieties in fully discussing the situation with his parents, and wrote a particularly revealing letter to his father, who he knew was wondering about money. The wedding would take place on his next leave in Canada:

I think I should have about $3500 dollars in the bank then and that I have no intention of touching until the war is over. My pay and allowances will be ample for Norah & me for the duration – in fact, we should be able to save, and I hope to use it for Osgoode after the war. I understand the Gov't is going to help us (students) so I think I can make out – No bed of roses but it can be done & if Bones [his nickname for Norah; she called him 'Jackel'; perhaps they both read H.G. Wells] is willing I'll try it. I know it would have been more satisfactory had I finished first, but things have never worked out as planned and I feel confident that I can carry this thing off. So there it is, Pop.[11]

The opportunity for a wedding presented itself when Jack was posted to North Carolina in June 1944 for a gunnery course. On 6 July they were married at the family's London church, St John the Evangelist. Norah Eva Mason McCormick, the youngest daughter of the late C. Garfield McCormick, was a good-looking brunette, outwardly as controlled and in charge of her life as Jack was of his, ambitious that he do well in law, a fierce Conservative in politics though not particularly traditional in other ways. Instead of having a substitute father give her away, she walked down the aisle unescorted and was given in marriage by her mother. It was a smallish wedding, mainly a family affair, with the reception at the London Hunt Club.

After the wedding John finished his course and then reported to his new ship, HMS *Uganda,* where he continued as fighter direction officer. This was his last posting with the Royal Navy, for *Uganda* and many of her crew were transferred to the Royal Canadian Navy, where they served briefly in the Pacific theatre. John saw ports in Formosa, Ceylon, and Australia before finally being demobilized in October 1945. He had particularly enjoyed *Uganda*'s Canadian months, for then the ship had many fewer stiff-lipped officers, and was much more democratic in spirit and wide-open in off-hours than it had been under British control.

Jack's wartime experiences reinforced the sense of role-playing that John Robarts had already developed and which would become the hallmark of his political career. He saw quite clearly that people expected officers to appear to be in command, to have solutions. It was vitally important at all times to project an image of being in total control of a situation, and to live up to that image Robarts hoped that the introduction to his political biography would contain what he saw as a personal motto, someone's remark that 'Sailors, with their built-in sense of order, service, and discipline, should really be running the world.'

Being off-duty was another matter altogether, for the navy had offered a fellow terrific opportunities to cut loose. Previously Jack had seen the Great Lakes and been a bit of a man of the world at Western for it. Now he had seen London during the blitz, the North Atlantic in winter, invasion fleets in the Mediterranean, men fighting and dying and enjoying bittersweet fellowship, and he knew how much more there was to experience than the Anglo-Saxon pieties of small-city Ontario. The war had reinforced his patriotism, and he shared the veterans' sense that they ought to contribute to the building of a better Canada. 'If we service men do not hang together after this and work out something decent we ought to be shot,' he put it bluntly in one of his last letters home.[12]

His main concern, though, was to get on with the education he had been saving and planning for all through the war. He re-entered Osgoode Hall, worked hard, and graduated in 1947, standing near the top of his class. He rejoined the Conservative Club, and remembered that he was like many of the veterans in despising the colourless Mackenzie King and his spiritless war leadership.

Life in postwar Toronto did not please Norah Robarts, who had very little to do while John concentrated on his studies. They were outsiders to Osgoode's social circles, and John made few friends outside the group of active Conservatives. John and Norah assumed they would return to London, and Norah developed a particularly strong dislike of Toronto as a strange, cold community. She had to stay there one more year, for logistics' sake, while John articled with Harry Braden in Hamilton. Braden was a lawyer in general practice there, whose brother's family lived across the street from Herbert Robarts in London. Articling positions and housing were both in short supply for postwar graduates, so a young couple took what they could get. John thought the articling experience was valuable for him; the extra year in Toronto did not make Norah like the city any better.

After the articling and the perfunctory bar admission course, John Robarts was ready to practise law in London. He and Norah returned there on Labour Day weekend in 1948, renting a small house on Waterloo Street near his father's home in the old neighbourhood. During his Western days John and his university friend, Cam Killoran, had talked about opening a practice together after they graduated from Osgoode. Now they tried to carry out the plans that the war had interrupted.

2

Londoners

London, Ontario, is located at the forks of the Thames River, approximately twenty miles north of the Lake Erie shore and thirty miles southeast of Lake Huron. It is almost exactly halfway between Toronto and Windsor, and is the hub of the province's southwestern peninsula, an area bounded on three sides by the Great Lakes and on the fourth by the Niagara Escarpment.

First settled in 1826, London was to become a regional city with interests distinct from those of the provincial capital, Toronto. It grew rapidly through the middle years of the nineteenth century, as the community changed from an agricultural and administrative centre to a diversified small city of banks, factories, and other growing businesses. The population grew steadily, from 15,826 in 1871 to 37,976 in 1901 and 71,148 in 1931. The elite of well-to-do local families, whatever its political sympathies, was united in its concern to advance the common interest of the city. London had never been a satellite of Toronto, much of its nineteenth-century economy taking shape through business and family ties to Montreal, which was the Dominion's most important metropolis. Through the twentieth century there would be a steady tendency for London businessmen and politicians to resist the growing dominance of the provincial capital.[1]

In the early years of the century, London's political tone had been Conservative, as a native son, Adam Beck, led the fight to harness the electrical potential of Niagara Falls for municipalities in southern Ontario, and then became the powerful head of Ontario Hydro. After Beck left the political stage in the mid-1920s, there was a brief period when Londoners' support for the Liberal and Conservative parties was closely divided, with elections being decided on specific issues or personalities. Then, in 1934, the provincial Liberals under the colourful Mitch Hepburn from Elgin County (just down the road from London) swept into power. They stayed in power until Hepburn left.

In office across English Canada in 1930 and out of office everywhere in 1936, the Conservatives gradually regrouped both nationally and provincially. Among the Ontarians who played prominent roles in the party's revival were Cecil and

Leslie Frost from Lindsay, J.M. Macdonnell, Fred Gardiner, and Harry Price in Toronto, Douglas Weldon in London, George Drew and Alex McKenzie in Guelph. The new Tories redirected the provincial party and rejuvenated its leadership.

Drew and a boyhood friend, Alex McKenzie, who had helped organize Drew's municipal election campaigns in Guelph, became the heart of the new Conservative party. By 1943 the provincial Conservative organization was in place. McKenzie had succeeded Cecil Frost as party president. Drew was party leader and an attractive twenty-two-point platform, promising sweeping economic and social reforms for Ontario, was ready to be unveiled when the weakened Liberals were forced to call an election. On 3 August when the young Conservatives reviewed the results, they had won the most seats (thirty-eight), followed by the CCF (thirty-four). The dispirited Liberals placed third. This was the beginning of what would prove to be the longest period of one-party rule in the history of Ontarian governments, lasting almost forty-two years.

In London, the Progressive-Conservatives had little love for George Drew and were mainly interested in advancing the regional interests of southwestern Ontario. The city, which had narrowly returned Liberals for Hepburn, reverted to the Conservatives, narrowly electing William Webster in 1943. Webster was returned in 1945 and received a minor cabinet position in Drew's administration, with responsibility for the Liquor Control Board of Ontario. His health failed. In the 1948 election, which Drew hoped would consolidate his party's hold on provincial power and/or pave the way for his leadership ambitions, Webster was defeated by a young Liberal, Campbell Calder. The government was returned with a reduced majority, but Premier Drew lost his seat.

This was the political scene in London, when John and Norah Robarts returned after John had completed articling under H. Braden. They entered into a closely knit community of younger Londoners who were building or rebuilding their careers after the war. Many of them lived in the northwestern area of the city, less than ten blocks from the homes of their ancestors of the 1880s. They had attended Central Collegiate together and many of them had gone on to Western, where Delta Upsilon had been their fraternity. While jobs and families were the first order of the day, good citizens could hardly ignore the political issues of postwar Canada. To many of the veterans one of the central questions was simply how much room there would be to get on with life in the new postwar welfare state. The war had seen an enormous growth of government intervention in all walks of life, culminating in new and lasting social welfare programs that had to be paid for by new and lasting taxes. It was impossible to go back to the old, prewar order, and to many idealistic young Canadians there were good arguments for expanding the role of government still further, especially through programs which would increase demand and thus avoid the social disaster of the Depression. With the newly discovered fiscal policy, government could take a supportive role in moulding the new Canada without destroying private property. But at the same time, many of the veterans had no love for Mackenzie King, wanted the state to get off their backs, and shared older Conservatives' fears about the shrinking role of the individual in a highly governed society.

The founding of a Progressive-Conservative Association on the Western campus in 1948 was one sign of the growth of political interest on the moderate right in London. Before World War II there had been only a campus Liberal Club, and student Conservatives such as Gordon Ford, son of London *Free Press* editor Arthur Ford, had been without organized support in their debates with the Grits. Now, on 8 December 1948, more than a hundred students, many of them returned men, gathered at the Hotel London to hear Leslie Blackwell, the attorney general in George Drew's government, talk about the need for a conservative approach to social problems. 'In the midst of a disturbed world we are going someplace and none of us are sure where ... On one side we have Socialism and on the other Conservatism.'[2] Blackwell challenged his audience to support an economic system based on the use of capital in private enterprise, not on state capitalism. To people embarking on private lives, trying to put the war behind them, interested in personal freedom and getting things done, the Conservative position seemed attractive.

At a more private, more establishment level, other Londoners were organizing to discuss social and political issues. Perhaps surprisingly, the internment of Japanese-Canadians during the war served as one of the triggering factors. Mrs Charles Ivey Sr, granddaughter-in-law of London lawyer Charles H. Ivey and a leading member of London society, had a Japanese maid. When her son Peter came back from the war in 1946 he learned through the maid about the treatment of Japanese-Canadians on the Pacific coast. Ivey and several of his friends got interested in the issue, wondering how they could help the Japanese-Canadians, particularly with restitution of their property. Nothing concrete developed on this issue, but with the support of Peter's mother an organization was formed to assist new immigrants to Canada.

Young men talking politics and economics at social functions were a bit of a bore to their wives and girl friends. At one party in 1946 Mrs Ivey again intervened, urging the men to organize monthly meetings for their serious political discussions. The idea was taken up, leading to the formation of ADSEPA, the Association for the Discussion of Social, Economic and Political Affairs. Its charter members included several offspring of older London families as well as such former football teammates and fraternity brothers of John Robarts as Stu Carver, Cam Killoran, Eugene Westendorp, and George Willis. There were monthly dinner meetings at the members' houses, with someone presenting a paper afterwards on a topic of his choice. Attendance was usually about fourteen, by invitation only, and with new members of ADSEPA being chosen only after a discussion of the candidate's suitability. The group thrived and its discussions are remembered as being wide-ranging, serious, and sometimes sharp. It was, of course, an all-male society. The wives were invited on an annual weekend outing to some surprise destination, such as Port Huron. Even the hostess of an evening retired while the ADSEPA men talked; Peter Ivey's wife used to sit at the top of the stairs listening to the discussion and feeling she was like a child eavesdropping on her parents.

On a less serious note, some of the young Londoners who had been active in fraternal societies decided it was time the city had its own Oriental Band. Fred Jenkins, Ted Dampier, Bill Gammage, and Bill Goudy got the idea after attending the Imperial Council of the Shriners in Atlantic City, New Jersey, in 1947. The London band tuned up in 1949. It was non-political, but had an overlapping membership with ADSEPA, and many of its members would become active in London politics and John Robarts' career.

Robarts quickly re-established his ties with the old London crowd. He renewed his interest in Delta Upsilon, soon becoming president of its alumni association – an experience that put him in touch with up-and-coming Western undergraduates. He joined the Vimy branch of the Legion and reactivated his membership in the London Hunt Club. John and Norah slipped easily back into the social life of the community, and he soon joined ADSEPA. After a year in the rented house on Waterloo Street, John and Norah bought a small white stucco house on a large lot well back from Regent Street. They shared a back fence with brother Robert, who lived one street over on Sherwood Avenue. Robert and his wife Eleanor had also settled back in town after the war; Robert resumed his career with the Imperial Bank. Another old friend and fellow naval officer in the neighbourhood was Gordon Gilbride, a local businessman active in civic politics who would often drop in on John to shoot the breeze and share a drink on a Saturday afternoon.

For all his contacts, Robarts did not find it easy to build his law practice with Cam Killoran. He looked back on the two years of their partnership as among the toughest in his life. They started with few clients and little income. Instead of gradually improving, the practice became troubled as it became clear that Killoran was still suffering from a serious head injury he had received during the war. He had managed to get through law school, but was often racked by pain and occasionally suffered lapses of memory. Robarts increasingly found himself dealing with complaints that his partner had missed appointments or neglected some commitment.

One May morning in 1949, Robarts, who had little to do, walked over from his law office to the committee rooms of Park Manross, the Progressive-Conservative member of parliament for London who was trying to hold his seat in the federal election that had just been called. A Conservative by family tradition, sharing his contemporaries' reaction to King's war policies, Robarts felt he could use his talents productively in the campaign, and if his new acquaintances needed a lawyer it might help business.

His initiative was abortive. On entering, Robarts was not impressed by his first view of local Conservative politics. The offices seemed in general disorder, and he noticed partially consumed liquor bottles on a table towards the back. When he volunteered to help in the campaign, the workers in the office went into a huddle and then someone told him that the campaign was under control and they didn't need his help. So he left. His services were eventually used late in the campaign after he told a friend about his experience and he was quickly recruited to help sort brochures.

They ought to have made better use of Robarts and other would-be supporters. In the election, Manross was defeated by the local Liberal candidate, Alex Jeffery. Alex had successfully organized the 1948 provincial Liberal campaign in London when the Liberal candidate, Campbell Calder, had knocked off Tory incumbent Bill Webster. Now Jeffery himself profited from the good organization he had helped to create and a massive advertising campaign he had helped to design. On 27 June the Progressive-Conservatives thus found themselves without a federal or a provincial member in London.

Robarts thought the sorry state of Manross' campaign, partly symbolized by his own first experience, aided Jeffery's victory. Manross himself blamed everyone, writing to Leslie Frost:

We had a bad defeat here due to the national trend and the local organization. Our national advertising was terrible and our campaign was all big stuff instead of what the common man appreciates or realizes what he is going to get.

The Western Ontario organization needs a complete revamping and strengthening, and this can be done if we get together and put the proper men in office and make sure that the Ontario government recognizes the political angles in every department. We have been very lax in mending political fences when we had the power to do so.[3]

The old Conservative organization in London had not changed substantially since the glory days of Adam Beck. It operated on three levels. Certain prominent individuals, such as Colonel Douglas Weldon and Arthur Ford, worked directly with party leaders in Toronto and Ottawa. Provincially, a full-time secretary of the Western Ontario PC Association, Gordon Reid, had his office in London and co-ordinated relations between the southwestern Ontario constituencies and party headquarters in Toronto. Reid, who was popular in London, took a leading role recruiting party workers. Finally, the London Progressive-Conservative Association was the focus of local Tory politics. The members of its executive, the ward chairmen, and the poll captains were the visible troops at election time.

Party fundraisers were a fourth group, much more visible in the business community than among the general public. They had an important voice at both local and provincial levels in the party, and at one time or another included the heads of many of the older Conservative families in London. As treasurer of the

London Progressive-Conservative Association, William A. Jenkins had acted as link between the official organization and those who supplied the money. This made him the linch-pin of London Conservatism.

New faces appeared in the London organization soon after the 1949 defeat. William Jenkins' death that year led to his job being taken by his son, Fred, who ran the family hardware and seed store. Fred Jenkins had known Robert Robarts from high school, and his younger sister, Marion, had known John and introduced him to the family. Fred had been groomed by his father for the treasurer's job, knew the party thoroughly, and was strong enough in his own right not to be shunted aside as a novice. The year after his election, Robarts' neighbour Gordon Gilbride was elected president of the association. Robarts himself now started attending the meetings, and there was a distinct sense of a younger generation taking over in the aftermath of defeat.

Gilbride was the sales manager for London Concrete Machinery, and was appropriately aggressive, dynamic, and personable. After returning to London from the war, he had become interested in local politics and in December 1948 won election as one of the eight aldermen representing London's four wards. Gilbride's Ward 1 in the northeastern section of the city had contained a high proportion of servicemen and their families. He saw himself as new blood on London's city council, and in 1949 persuaded another young businessman and fellow Conservative, J. Ronald Chapman, to run in Ward 4, an area of small businessmen and working people in south London. Chapman, a member of a well-known London bookbinding family, was popular and easily elected, joining Gilbride as more new blood.

One Saturday morning in September 1950, Gordon Gilbride and John Robarts got talking politics in Robarts' kitchen over a bottle of rye. Gilbride was complaining about all his responsibilities – his job, city council, his new duties as president of the London PC Association – and mentioned he was not going to seek re-election as an alderman. Robarts urged Gilbride to reconsider, arguing that it was important to have a younger group on council. Gilbride may have been baiting Robarts; if so, John had taken the hook. 'If you think it is so important, why don't you run?' Gilbride asked Robarts. They kept on talking, and finally agreed that they would both run.

Gilbride had mentioned that one of the incumbents in Ward 2, Dr J. Cameron Wilson, an old Londoner, a provincial member from 1926 to 1934, and a leading Tory, was thinking about retiring. That would open up a spot for a new man to represent northwestern London, the neighbourhood John and Norah Robarts and many of their friends had lived in for years. So the chances looked good. Even if Wilson did not retire, Robarts reasoned, he had nothing to lose: 'If Dr Wilson does not run, I may win. If Dr Wilson runs, I have the time to run, and by the end of the election people will at least know there is a lawyer in London by name of Robarts.'[4] So he decided to run in the December 1950 municipal election.

A lively mayoralty race dominated the campaign. The incumbent mayor, Allan Johnson, was being challenged by a former mayor, George Wenige, and by Allan Rush, a detective who had been fired from the London police force over a disciplinary incident. The aldermanic candidates got little attention, having to rely on their personal popularity and whatever contacts they could make with the voters. Dr Wilson finally decided at the last moment to retire. With the one remaining incumbent, Norman Bradford, favoured to head the polls, the race in Ward 2 was for the second seat. Robarts' opposition came from J. Stewart Killingsworth, the personable son of an active local Liberal and former mayor of London.

John Robarts recruited a handful of his friends to help with his campaign. Bill Shortreed, a neighbour and the assistant general manager for Labatt's breweries, effectively managed the effort. Robarts was running as an individual, not as a member of a party, even though he and his family were known to be Conservatives. His campaign literature mentioned the schools he had attended in London, his football experience, his military service, and the fact that he had graduated from Osgoode Hall. If elected, John Robarts promised to provide 'progressive active civic administration.' His speeches were nothing if not succinct: at an all-candidates' meeting after everyone else had spoken at length, Robarts got up and said, 'I'm John Robarts, a candidate for alderman. I'll try to do my best and I'd like your support.' He got the biggest applause from the crowd.[5]

Robarts and his friends found time to canvass door-to-door in the ward, handing out Robarts blotters, a form of campaign 'literature' soon to disappear with the triumph of the ball-point pen. They were more innovative, at least for London municipal politics, in organizing a car pool to drive voters to the polls and advertising it in the *Free Press*. The weather was not good on election day, but because of the interest in the mayoralty race there was a high voter turnout, resulting in the car pool being kept busy. Robarts and his friends worked through the day getting acquaintances out to vote. The effort paid off in the result: Robarts, 1,760 votes; Killingsworth, 1,753. Victory was attributed to the car pool and was a lesson in the virtues of a good organization that Robarts never forgot.

The nine-member council (eight aldermen and the mayor) convened on 18 December 1950. Allan Rush, the deposed detective, had won the mayoralty. Now serving his third term, Gordon Gilbride was a senior alderman. Ronald Chapman had been re-elected, and Robarts was a new boy. All three were prominent in the committee work of council, with Gilbride and Chapman chairing its two principal committees (romantically named Committee One and Committee Two) and Robarts acting as the spokesman for the London and Suburban Planning Board, on which he served as one of council's appointees. He sat on a number of other standing and ad hoc committees, including the Labour Management Committee (where he acted as a kind of business spokesman who balanced A.E. Bettam, the veteran labour spokesman from Ward 3), and the Civil Defence Committee.

Planning Board meetings introduced Robarts to fundamental issues of regional water supply and conservation, urban transportation, and city planning. On council he was active in negotiations with the province to raise money to build a new wing for Victoria Hospital. These first provincial contacts, he remembered, soon came in useful.

There were no ideologically divisive issues in London's affairs that year, and nothing significant in the pattern of Robarts' votes on council. He and Gilbride and Chapman did not always vote the same way on such issues as annexation or the regulation of store hours. But the trio did share a belief that new organizational techniques and new ideas were needed in municipal administration. They became known as the 'three young lions,' a new breed taking the place of the old-style local politicians.

Robarts enjoyed the year on council. He had tested his interest in government and found the experience more satisfying than the frustrating work of scrambling to get himself established in the law. His faltering partnership with Killoran was wound up this year, and Robarts became part of a new and larger grouping, Carrothers, Fox, Robarts, and Betts, which gave him greater financial security. His appetite may already have been whetted for a larger political role. He was over at his brother's one day having a few drinks, Eleanor Robarts remembered, when her mother dropped in for a visit. John got talking with Mrs Thomas about municipal politics, and – lubricated a bit – proclaimed, 'You know I've always been a leader, never a follower. At university I was a leader. And before I'm through, Mrs Thomas, I'm going to run this province.'

Mrs Thomas was not impressed. 'He doesn't think much of himself, does he?' she said to Eleanor.

A major Tory event in southwestern Ontario was the annual meeting of the Western Ontario PC Association. This umbrella organization, bringing together provincial and federal Conservatives from all the ridings in the region, was a prime source of contacts, local intelligence, and organizational ideas. At the May 1951 meeting held in London, association president Elmer Bell recognized John Robarts in the hall outside the meeting room. Bell, a lawyer from Exeter who combined good political instincts with a dry wit, was becoming a moving spirit in the party. He called the young alderman aside and quietly suggested to him that, as a municipal politician who might want to make a mark on the provincial scene, he should be more visible in the meetings – sitting in the front row, taking part in the debates, speaking on behalf of London, that kind of thing. Surprised a bit at the suggestion, Robarts went along with it. An opportunity presented itself when Mayor Rush had to miss the final banquet and asked Robarts to represent the city at the head table. He dined there with Premier Frost, George Drew, now federal party leader, and the members of the association executive. In his after-dinner speech Bell introduced Robarts to bring the city's greetings to the convention. Robarts conveyed the best wishes of London, saying that he did so not just in his capacity as alderman, but also as 'a damn good Tory.' Liking the partisan touch, the crowd applauded. People began to notice John Robarts, a fresh face on the London scene.

Gordon Reid had also noticed the young man. As secretary of the association and its one full-time employee, Reid was the link with Toronto and the leadership. One day in early September 1951, several months after the meeting, Robarts ran into Reid on the street. Reid stopped Robarts and out of the blue, as it were, told the young alderman he was going to be the next provincial candidate for the Conservatives in London. Reid later told a friend that Robarts looked stunned at the suggestion.[6]

As he thought about it, Robarts realized that offering the candidacy to a relative unknown was not so far-fetched, if only because Liberal Cam Calder held the seat and was likely to retain it. Nobody else was rumoured to be seeking the Tory nomination. Bill Webster, who had held the seat for the Conservatives from 1944 to 1948, probably would have first claim on the nomination if he wanted it. But Webster's poor health surely made it unlikely that he would run again. To Robarts, the prospect of running provincially was an interesting challenge. He was a competitive guy. Why not compete here?

He put the idea to Gordon Gilbride, his fellow alderman and president of the London PC Association. Gilbride encouraged him and said that if he was serious about running he should talk to Fred Jenkins. Robarts knew Jenkins only indirectly. He visited the party treasurer at his store, and they had a cautious preliminary conversation along the lines of:

'It seems there's a chance to get the nomination.'

'I've had intimations of that.'

'I don't see anyone else on the horizon; seems like it could be a golden opportunity.'

'Could be.'[7]

Jenkins agreed to give Robarts the names of thirty or forty influential London Conservatives, people whose support Robarts would need if he were going to be the candidate. He also told Robarts he would have to speak to Webster. Over the next few weeks Robarts visited everyone on Jenkins' list. The group included influential fundraisers such as Colonel Weldon; leaders of the local Orange Order, such as Grand Dame Mrs Ruth Day; small businessmen and insurance agents who were active in the party; and members of prominent Conservative families. In most cases Robarts was asking for support from much older, much more experienced party people. All he could promise was to give Calder a good fight in an election. A number of the people Robarts visited told Jenkins they were favourably impressed. The treasurer's response was a $5,000 cheque to finance Robarts' nomination campaign: the young man had been accepted by the organizers. Robarts, comparing the sum with his own meagre income, was shocked.

Robarts' friends and family were less impressed with the idea of his candidacy. His father, who was a good friend of Bill Webster, thought John had 'lost his marbles' in wanting to get involved in someone else's game and wanting to do it before he had established himself financially. Norah was also surprised at her husband's proposal, but politics was part of her heritage – her grandfather had been a popular mayor of London – and she loyally supported her 'Jackel.' Robarts had made the transition from the navy to law and had performed well on council. His legal foundation was still shaky, but he felt the risk of politics would do it no harm. The war was over, they were together, and life lay ahead to be savoured.

For a time it seemed as though Webster would challenge Robarts. His health had in fact improved since 1948 and he was seriously thinking of running again to avenge what he saw as a personal defeat by Calder. Before Jenkins got around to talking to Webster, Webster learned of Robarts' inquiries and phoned the treasurer to find out what was going on. It was not a pleasant conversation. Webster was upset and became more upset when Jenkins suggested that the party needed a fresh, young candidate if it was going to beat the Liberals. The call ended abruptly.[8]

Nobody in the association wanted to see an open fight for the nomination. It could create so much divisiveness that the comeback attempt would be doomed from the start. When Jenkins reported the situation to the executive, they asked Gilbride to talk it over with Webster. Gilbride was on his way to smoothing things over when Webster's mind was made up for him by another relapse into poor health. His options closed, Webster decided to give Robarts whatever support he could behind the scenes, and to help in that way to erase the stigma of 1948. The path to the nomination was clear for Robarts.

All summer there had been rumours that Premier Frost would soon go to the people. It would be his first election since replacing Drew in 1949. The Liberal Toronto *Star* had been campaigning against Frost for months, its natural partisanship turned into red-hot fury by legislation the Tories had brought in affecting the ownership of newspapers by charitable foundations. By fall of 1951 an undeclared provincial campaign was well under way. Late in September, for example, when Frost announced an extension in pension benefits to the disabled, the CCF promptly offered more. On 4 October the premier announced the dissolution of the legislature, with voting to be on 22 November. There were ninety seats at stake, fifty-three held by Frost's PCs, twenty-one by the CCF, and thirteen by the Liberals under the new leadership of Walter Thomson. Frost pledged that the Conservative campaign would not begin until after 14 October when Princess Elizabeth and the Duke of Edinburgh made the last Ontario stop of their royal visit.

The underdog Tory in London, John Robarts was already at work building the nucleus of his campaign organization. He had Bill Shortreed with him from the aldermanic campaign. In the fraternity pub after Delta Upsilon's alumni association fall meeting, Robarts approached Eugene Westendorp, a fellow member of ADSEPA and a first-rate publicity man, to help with his campaign.

Westendorp readily agreed to handle Robarts' advertising, telling him, Robarts later claimed, that he would package him exactly like a box of Kellogg's cornflakes. Westendorp, Shortreed, and John and Norah Robarts met frequently at the Robarts home to discuss the campaign and plot strategy. Jenkins joined them from time to time. R.W. Facer, who worked for the London Printing and Lithographing Company and had experience printing campaign literature for local Conservative campaigns, soon joined the little team.

The London Tories scheduled their nomination meeting for 11 October. On the ninth John Robarts publicly announced that he would seek the candidacy. That night ADSEPA happened to be holding its monthly meeting at Westendorp's home. Some of his ADSEPA friends had helped in the aldermanic campaign the year before, but Robarts had assumed that the group was apolitical and had not presumed to ask for its support. When he arrived at the meeting this night, chairman Westendorp announced that the regular agenda had been suspended. The group had already decided that since one of its members was seeking political office they should all help get him elected. There was a rambling discussion, leading to the conclusion that they had no political experience and that ADSEPA thus had no role to play in the election as an organization, but that members would help as best they could. Some would work through Robarts' organization; others, notably the Liberals in ADSEPA, would do what they could to help in less visible ways. In the meantime, many of the group would show up at the nomination meeting.

The ADSEPA support was important. It was the first clear sign of Robarts' ability to mobilize new people, especially his friends in the London establishment, regardless of their political affiliation. He seemed to be not just another Tory, but a candidate of the younger generation of ambitious and energetic Londoners. A lot of ex-servicemen, including many friends from the Legion, also rallied around John.

The nomination meeting was a well-orchestrated passing of the Tory torch. The chairman, Fred G. McAllister, called for nominations. Fred Jenkins, who was sitting at the back of the hall, nominated Bill Webster. Then Gordon Gilbride, the president, rose from his seat at the front of the hall and nominated John Robarts. There were no further nominations. The chairman read a letter from Webster, sent from his bed in St Joseph's Hospital, thanking the party for nominating him, but withdrawing from the contest in favour of a younger man. Webster concluded his letter by pledging 'to work to return London to the Conservative Party.' Robarts became the PC candidate for London by acclamation. In his acceptance speech he urged everyone to support Leslie Frost, thanked Webster for standing aside, and pointedly reminded the audience that Webster had told them 'that the young Conservatives in number and vigour are the backbone of the Party.'

At the same time, Robarts was shrewd enough to draw on the expertise and experience of the old guard. Bill Webster's support was welcomed, and as

Robarts' official campaign manager he reconstructed lists of past workers who had recently been inactive, sent letters to his friends urging support for Robarts, and advised the younger man on strategy and organization. Robarts moved swiftly to follow up Webster's suggestions with personal visits and requests for help. His campaign organization grew much more quickly than local Liberals realized. Drawing on his ADSEPA and Delta Upsilon and Legion ties, attracting some support from fellows who played in the Oriental Band, building bridges through Webster to the old party faithful, Robarts breathed new life into the London party.

There was a deliberate, almost systematic blending of old and new. In three of the four London wards the established Conservative ward chairmen were given assistants who were young friends of Robarts. In Ward 3, the working-class area, where the Tories had no established chairman, Robarts recruited Richard Dillon, a friend from Western, who had risen rapidly to the rank of Brigadier during the war. To maintain the balance of experience and youth, Chris Hawkins, a well-respected Tory organizer who had been passed over in recent years, came in as his assistant. The dualism worked well, with the experienced people getting their workers active while the newer Conservatives added a host of canvassers, many of whom had never worked in a campaign before. The new people also manned the car pool for election day, carrying on the device that had been so important for Robarts in the municipal election.

The advertising campaign tended to be separate and run by the newcomers. Westendorp directed it, with Facer handling the literature. There was some friction when Webster and other members of the old guard tried to supervise the details. Robarts himself was drawn in, went over the approach with Webster, Jenkins, and Westendorp, and with a little persuasion managed to work it all out in Westendorp's favour. The result was a much more innovative Conservative advertising campaign than in the past. Westendorp made extensive use of radio, drawing on the ADSEPA friends to broadcast carefully prepared endorsements of Robarts in one-minute commercials. A heavy newspaper advertising campaign featured elaborate statistical analyses of Conservative success and Liberal failure, headings such as 'Fable or Fact,' and 'Balance Your Outlook,' and frequent references to the issues and the candidate's service record. Robarts at first objected to what seemed to be an exploitation of his war service in a political cause, but was persuaded that this was one of those things you had to do in politics – part of the packaging in a sense, and perhaps not totally unreasonable at a time when the media were incessantly discussing national security.

The traditional organizers handled fundraising. Liquor licence holders, party faithful, and a number of businessmen and professionals made their usual contributions. The campaign was not expensive, costing $7,000 to $8,000, Robarts remembered, mostly for advertising; Robarts insisted that he would never use paid campaign workers. He broke with a tradition by also insisting that liquor not be available in campaign headquarters, certainly not because he had any objection to drinking per se, but because he did not think liquor mixed well with public committee rooms.

The night after Robarts' nomination, London's Liberals acclaimed Cam Calder, the sitting member, as their candidate. The guest speaker, George Bagwell, a colourful Toronto lawyer, equated the CCF with the Communist party and concluded by charging that a vote for the CCF would be a vote for the Conservative party. A noisy crowd cheered him on, and the Liberal campaign started on an upbeat note. The Conservative strategists in Toronto and the Conservative candidate in London began the campaign believing that London would probably stay Liberal.

Inside the Liberal camp there were already serious organizational problems. The new provincial leader, Walter Thomson, had tried to persuade Alex Jeffery, the federal MP from London who had supported his leadership bid, to run provincially in Middlesex North. That Tory-held riding included the most northerly and westerly portions of the city of London. Disenchanted with Thomson's abuse of his supporters since the leadership convention, Jeffery not only declined to run but spent most of the campaign in Ottawa, effectively depriving Calder of the best organization man the local Liberals had. The internal disagreements were also rippling through the business and professional communities, dampening the enthusiasm of many traditional workers, making it easier for Liberals who liked John Robarts to ignore party labels.[9]

In one sense a vote for the CCF was a vote for the Conservatives, for the third party split the anti-government vote in the riding. The London CCF candidate in 1951 was Pat Daley, president of the London Labour Council. Through the campaign he concentrated on the rising cost of living and the need for better labour legislation. He did not attack the Conservative government, arguing instead that regardless of the Frost government's record, the CCF would do better.

Leslie Frost knew he had an attractive record to stand on. On 16 October the government issued a manifesto entitled 'A Report to the People.' In it, and in his early speeches, Frost reminded Ontarians that their taxes were the lowest in Canada, pointed to rising housing starts, and instanced increasing grants to municipalities. He dangled a vision of the economic benefits that the coming of the St Lawrence Seaway would create and implied that his government deserved credit for the development of cobalt bombs to treat cancer.[10] Using a new radio technique, the premier interviewed his cabinet ministers about the achievements of their departments. Frost presented the Progressive-Conservatives as the party 'of all the people,' promising to work with whatever party was in power in Ottawa for the good of Ontario, in sharp contrast to the divisive partisanship of the old Hepburn Liberals.

Jolliffe of the CCF attacked the government for its failure to support municipalities, to control racketeers, to provide an adequate housing policy, and to formulate a farm policy. The Liberals under Walter Thomson pressed for lower taxes, reduced government expenditures, and a contributory hospital insurance plan. The Toronto *Star* ran its own campaign of absurd eulogies of the Liberals combined with editorials and slanted news stories attacking the Frost government. Robarts later judged that the *Star*'s contribution to the election was probably counter-productive for the Liberals. It did not help a great deal, either, when Mitch Hepburn came out of retirement on 1 November to speak in favour of Walter Thomson and the local Liberal candidate in Elgin County. Frost had endless statistics to hand comparing the depressed Ontario of Hepburn's day with the prospering Progressive-Conservative province. Then when T.C. Douglas, the CCF premier of Saskatchewan, came to Ontario to support Jolliffe, Frost had the opening to compare economic conditions in Ontario with those in Saskatchewan.

Having reported that John Robarts was an excellent candidate, Gordon Reid had asked the premier to visit London in the last days of the campaign, and Frost agreed to wind up his southwestern Ontario tour with a rally at Beal Technical School on 6 November. Not expecting a Conservative victory in the riding, Frost gave it no special attention, but with hard work the Tories had managed to draw the same size crowd of six hundred as the Liberals had for their nomination meeting in the same gym. In a spirited speech, Frost skilfully drew attention to his government's recent spending in the area – the Fanshawe Dam; the new wing at the Victoria Hospital; more than $1 million in provincial grants to London in 1950, which was four times higher than the Liberal grant in 1943 – and slipped over the same message as the Robarts campaign, that the area really ought to have a representative in government.

John Robarts had liked Frost's down-to-earth, low-key style, avoiding extreme positions, not promising more than he was likely to be able to deliver. To a degree he imitated Frost in his campaign, talking in generalities about working for the benefit of London and being a man who would do his best. But there was the harder edge to the Robarts campaign, including a fairly explicit suggestion that London would be in a better position to benefit from Conservative largesse if its members sat on government benches. The implication was of the foolishness of a region sending someone to Queen's Park who, as a Liberal, wouldn't even be a member of the official opposition, let alone share in the job of governing.

By the end of the campaign, the opposition parties had shifted from policy questions to attacks on the Conservatives' competence. The CCF tried to emphasize its own capacity to govern, but was not in a position to do much local advertising. The Liberals enriched their platform with more promises to reduce taxes, government spending, and the price of milk. As well, Walter Thomson undertook to unveil his 'cabinet in the making' as he toured Ontario. The scheme fizzled out in charges that he was offering office to people for electoral considerations rather than on the basis of their ability. Frost kept on advertising his party's record and its goals for the future, while taking occasional swipes at the irresponsibilities of the Liberal *Star*.

Robarts' advertising peaked in radio endorsements and major newspaper spreads in the last week of the campaign. Appeals to 'Balance Your Outlook – Vote John Robarts' were obviously aimed at Londoners who voted Liberal federally. As expected, the Tories got the endorsement of the London *Free Press,* which attacked the inconsistencies in Thomson's promises and the excesses of the Toronto *Star*. Robarts' canvassers were coming back with good reports on the situation. In the weekend before the election ten inches of snow fell on southwestern Ontario. When the Conservatives drew four hundred people to their penultimate pre-election rally at South Collegiate, while the Liberals could only muster three hundred and fifty at the London Public Library, Robarts admitted to himself for the first time that he might win.

Frost broadcast a final election appeal on the CBC, asking the voters to give him a 'good edge,' since the paramount issue in the campaign was 'good government.' On election day, 21 November, the ward organizers were regrouped into platoons of drivers who systematically and vigorously canvassed known Conservatives. As the day wore on they became more and more insistent on delivering certified Tories to the polls. John Robarts remembered his brother Robert practically ordering a fellow to stop sipping beer in his living room and come with him to vote. 'Well, I guess if you want the vote that badly, I'll come,' the Londoner grumbled.

The polls closed at 7 PM. By 8 the Robarts people knew they were going to win. John was leading most of the polls in Ward 3, taking away votes from the CCF. In his own Ward 2 he was picking up support at the Liberals' expense. Cam Calder conceded at 8.10, thanking his workers and telephoning Robarts to congratulate him. Westendorp sent Frost a telegram to report the upset. Soon after Calder arrived at Robarts' Dundas Street headquarters to congratulate him personally. The Tories piped the defeated Liberal into the room. The *Free Press* reported that as he proceeded toward Robarts, Calder commented to Webster, 'Bill, you did it, you old rascal.' Webster replied, 'I promised Frost I'd return this seat to him. This is my swan song and it's got a happy tune.' The humiliation of 1948 had been erased. Standing on a table, Robarts thanked his supporters and congratulated Calder on both a hard-fought campaign and his good record in the legislature. Calder led cheers for Robarts and left.[11]

Across the province, the CCF's percentage of the popular vote dropped from 27 per cent in 1948 to 19 per cent in this election; the Liberals went up from 29 to 31 per cent, and the Conservatives increased by 7 per cent to 48 per cent of the total. The trend in London was slightly more marked, with both the Liberals and the CCF dropping sharply and the Conservative vote going up by 19 per cent. The final tally in London was 13,926 for Robarts, 10,814 for Calder, and 4,655 for Daley of the CCF. Calder blamed the relatively low voter turnout on the bad weather of election day for his defeat. In his recollections of the campaign Robarts was extremely proud of his organization, believing it was far ahead of its time and particularly effective in bringing in young people and former Liberals. Certainly the appeal to

Robarts' friends in Ward 2, the redevelopment of the Ward 3 organization, and the determined effort to get out the Conservative vote are all evident in the result.

But John Robarts also looked back on 1951, accurately, as the election in which Leslie Frost emerged from George Drew's shadow and became a highly effective leader and vote-getter in his own right. To a certain extent, Robarts believed he had been swept into office on Frost's coattails. Big coattails they were, for 1951 was arguably the most impressive of all the Tory landslides in twentieth-century Ontario; Leslie Frost's party won seventy-nine of the ninety seats in the legislature. The CCF was almost destroyed, reduced to two seats, and Jolliffe was defeated in his own riding. So was Walter Thomson of the Liberals, though his party became the official opposition with seven seats. If Leslie Frost had any problem arising from the 1951 election, it was how to keep all of his able backbenchers busy.

3

A Part-time Job

Robarts had run and won. Leslie Frost sent him a congratulatory telegram on election night, and then nothing happened. Robarts devoted his energies to his growing practice and completed his term as an alderman. Throughout, as he recalled, 'there was a deafening silence' from Toronto and Queen's Park. On 17 January Robarts read in the London *Free Press* that the legislature would open in Toronto on 21 February. It was disconcerting to have worked so hard for the party, apparently achieved something important, and then be completely ignored. Later Robarts realized that the experience prepared him for life as a backbencher in the Ontario legislature.

For ordinary members of the provincial assembly, governing Ontario was still very much a part-time job. Normally the legislature began sitting a few weeks after the beginning of the calendar year. Its sessions always lasted for at least forty days, the minimum sitting time necessary if members were to receive their $2,000 annual indemnity, paid to them on 31 March. As April progressed it became increasingly difficult to hold farm-based MPPs, who wanted to get back to their land, in Toronto, and the assembly soon prorogued. The burden of constituency work was not very great during the rest of the year, certainly not enough to require members to keep any kind of separate office in their ridings. In fact MPPs did not have offices of their own at Queen's Park either. Nor did they have private telephones. During sessions it was possible to get secretarial help from the steno pool, and when the assembly was not actually sitting it was often convenient to dictate from your desk in the chamber, often before the curious stares of touring school children.

The real business of governing was handled by the premier, his cabinet, and a small group of top political aides and bureaucrats. A little attention to these is necessary for an understanding both of Frost's system and of the changes John Robarts was to make after he became prime minister.* All of the threads of

* The head of a provincial government is often called 'premier' to distinguish the office from the federal prime minister. However, it is just as correct to call the provincial leader 'prime minister' and this is the title Robarts was to assume despite objections from Canadian centralists.

government merged in Frost's office; not the least of these was party affairs which were the special province of A.D. McKenzie. As semi-permanent president of the Ontario PC Association (though he still retained his law practice), McKenzie monitored the political pulse of Ontario through reports coming into party headquarters from the regional secretaries. These reports provided a mine of information; much of it filtered up to Frost, on deaths, marriages, anniversaries, internal grievances, promising Tories, and the machinations of the opposition parties. McKenzie was very much Frost's sounding board and confidant. When the legislature was in session they met every morning over breakfast in the Venetian Room of the Royal York Hotel to discuss the politics of current issues. The premier often sent outlines of statements or speeches to McKenzie for review and final polishing. Together they led the Conservatives in the political game.

Colonel Ernest J. Young, who had become Drew's executive assistant in 1945 and stayed on with Frost, was the gatekeeper in the premier's office. He handled routine affairs at the centre: arranging communications between party people and civil servants; keeping backbenchers in touch with policy-makers; summarizing reports and submissions to Frost, often with extra background information and his own comments. Frost would scribble a note on documents coming up through Young, who would implement the directive. More complex policy questions might be referred 'sideways' from Young and Frost to a group of advisers in the Treasury Department under the direction of deputy treasurer and chief economist George Gathercole. Gathercole, members of cabinet, and a few important party figures worked directly with Frost. Otherwise, Young was the man to see.

On purely administrative and interdepartmental issues, it would be better to talk to Lorne R. McDonald or his successor in 1953, W. Malcolm McIntyre, who served as deputy minister to the prime minister as well as secretary of the cabinet. They had little to do with politics, monitoring and briefing Frost on administrative and interdepartmental issues. They supervised the preparation of most answers to questions in the legislature, for example, routing the drafts through cabinet for final consideration before presentation to the House. The legislature's own timetable was planned by Frost, meeting with his budget committee, then with Young, then with L.R. McTavish, the legislative counsel. Day-to-day operations of the assembly were handled by the clerk of the legislative assembly, Major Alex Lewis, and later by his son Roderick.

Until 1955 Frost himself held the most important cabinet position outside of the prime ministership, serving as his own provincial treasurer. While he always listened carefully to what his ministers had to say in cabinet meetings, he was somewhat of the autocrat both in cabinet and the legislature. Nothing happened in either arena without Frost's knowledge and approval. Ministers would try out legislative proposals before the Conservative caucus, and if they ran into serious opposition might go back to the drawing board. But Frost did not allow caucus any more substantial role in the formulation of policy.[1]

Did he have his eye on John Robarts from the beginning? Possibly, at least in a small way. Robarts' first letter to Frost was a routine request that the premier meet with a delegation from London's city council to discuss provincial subsidies for municipal services in territory London wanted to annex. The request went through the normal channel: it was referred to Colonel Young, who was to arrange the meeting after consulting the ministers responsible for the relevant services. Young dealt with Robarts in setting up the meeting for early in February. Robarts and the London delegation had a fruitful talk with Frost and his ministers of education, highways, and municipal affairs. As Robarts was leaving the meeting Frost called him into his office and asked him to move the Address in Reply to the Speech from the Throne.

Robarts was not sure what he was being asked to do, but readily agreed. The job was largely a formality – to give a speech eulogizing the government's plans and performance – which customarily was given to a new and promising young backbencher. At thirty-four, Robarts was the youngest Conservative MPP from outside Toronto, and a natural candidate to move the Address. Giving a speech right at the beginning of the legislature would not be onerous, Frost advised Robarts, as Harold Robbins, the party's research officer, would help him to write it. Robarts went over to party headquarters at 85 Richmond Street, found Robbins amid piles of paper in his backroom office, and was briefed on what he had to do. Robbins wrote a draft of the speech for Robarts and mailed it to him. Robarts revised parts of it and mailed the speech back to Toronto for final approval.

The other Conservative backbenchers had their first post-election contact with Frost when they received a letter, mailed on 5 February, welcoming them to the legislature, encouraging them to participate in debate, and urging them to generate publicity in their local media. Frost also asked the members to provide a list of their committee preferences and topics on which they would be willing to speak. Robarts was cautious, replying that he 'did not want to speak until he became better acquainted with the Legislature,' and mentioning an interest in the Committee on Municipal Law. Other new members were more forward. Robert Macaulay, just elected in Toronto-Riverdale, for example, whose father, Leopold Macaulay, had served in Henry's cabinet, and who had known Frost since childhood, submitted a detailed list of topics and committees.[2]

The usual receptions and much of the ceremony surrounding the opening of a session were cancelled because Ontario and the British Commonwealth were still mourning the death of King George VI. On the first morning of his first legislative session, Thursday, 21 February 1952, John Robarts visited the clerk to take his oath of office, and then went into the chamber to see where he had been assigned to sit. The seating plan showed that John Robarts, MPP for London, shared a desk in the back row.

That afternoon the Robarts family were on hand for the opening of the assembly, and had dinner together in Toronto. John stayed in the city for a caucus meeting at

10.30 the next morning. There Frost told his MPPs what was planned for the session. That afternoon the legislature created its striking committee to nominate members for their committee duties, and then adjourned for the weekend. Robarts went home to London.

The following Monday he was back to Toronto in time for the 3 PM beginning of the day's sitting. Committee memberships were announced, and Robarts found himself on five standing committees, the most important of which were municipal law, legal bills, and public accounts. He stayed on these three committees for most of his years as a backbencher. The next day, 26 February, Robarts gave his first speech in the Ontario legislature, moving the Address in Reply to the Speech from the Throne. It could hardly be called an important maiden speech.

The night before had probably been more important for the future of his career. It was the first of many occasions on which John Robarts and Robert Macaulay killed a bottle of rye together as they talked about the provincial scene and the course of politics. Macaulay had introduced himself to Robarts as the legislature was rising and the Londoner was on the way to the Royal York to get a room for the night. Robarts' first comment to Macaulay was that he'd heard a lot about him. He probably had heard that Macaulay, the son of a former Ontario cabinet minister and a personal friend of Frost, was an up-and-coming figure on the Ontario political scene. Robarts and Macaulay had been at Osgoode at the same time, where young Macaulay had been highly visible. They had not struck up a friendship then, perhaps because of the four-year gap in their ages. Now Macaulay invited Robarts over to his apartment where they had a few drinks and got to know each other. It was decided that Robarts would use the second bedroom the nights he had to stay in Toronto.

There were not a lot of these nights during Robarts' early backbench years. His first priority was still to become established in London, and he found it possible to carry out his legislative duties conscientiously while averaging only about two nights a week in Toronto during sessions. He could get a good three hours' work in at his law office during the morning, be picked up by Norah at 11.30 and delivered to the CPR station in time for the 11.45 train to Toronto. He would have lunch on the train, get off at West Toronto at 2.30 PM, and catch a cab to Queen's Park in time to be in his seat for the 3 o'clock opening. If there were no committee meetings after the assembly rose, he would catch the 6.30 train back to London and be in his office again at 8.30 the next morning.

Like most backbenchers, Robarts spoke little in the legislature. The party nabobs did not want the new boys to have much to say there unless it was the approved party line, and even then they were mainly called on as a way of filling time. There were two more important arenas in which Robarts cut his political teeth. One was committee meetings: select committees, where backbenchers could sometimes be influential in helping shape legislative proposals, and such standing committees as private bills and legal bills, in which Frost allowed free discussion and debate. Robarts remembered learning a lot about provincial politics from the Legal Bills Committee. He was on it, for example, when London's attempt to annex large chunks of London and Westminster townships came up. The townships opposed the proposal, and Robarts' more experienced colleagues from the affected areas, Harry Allan and Tom Patrick, lobbied so effectively to kill it that, despite Robarts' support for the proposal, annexation was delayed for a decade. He was seldom again caught off guard on what seemed like routine issues.

The other forum for heated political discussion was the Macaulay apartment, where what started as two-man sessions gradually developed into almost organized Tory gab fests. John and Bob and their friends would talk about the issues, the government's policies, the policy-makers themselves. On a crowded evening someone might be asked to serve as Speaker to keep order, but as the drink flowed the decorum deteriorated. Often by the end of an evening the exuberant Macaulay would be threatening to speak out bluntly on some issue in the legislature, while Robarts tried to cool him down. They were a couple of self-confident and aggressive young legislators, but Robarts was markedly quieter than Macaulay, less innovative, less impulsive, and less likely to get himself in hot water.

The focus of his life, of course, was back in London. Robarts knew he dared not become dependent on the whims of politics (a 'professional politician' as the term was often used, usually scornfully). He was a lawyer first. His legal work at Carrothers, Fox, Robarts, and Betts was developing satisfactorily, a pleasant contrast from the difficult time in the Killoran partnership. Robarts' calm competence quickly built up a substantial list of clients in a general practice which gradually evolved into specialization in corporate law. His friendships with his partners, especially Peter Betts, lasted throughout his career.

In his capacity as an MPP, Robarts saw constituents in his law office. His legal and legislative personas would sometimes get mixed up in the minds of Londoners bringing to their member what were really legal matters. Determined to keep the roles rigidly separate, Robarts would bluntly draw the line, telling the constituent that the problem required legal help, and stating what the fee would be for his professional as opposed to his political services. Both Robarts and his visitors immediately knew where they stood. To some observers, Robarts' methods seemed too brusque and insensitive; they caused one of the articling students who observed Robarts in action to become an active Liberal.

John and Norah were able to afford their first car in 1952. The year before that they had had to borrow Robert's Pontiac for a holiday trip in New York State. Robert's condition was that John and Norah look after their niece, three-year-old Andrea, the next spring while he and his wife Eleanor had a holiday. Norah, who had never cared for an infant, blanched at the suggestion, but Andrea's visit was a great success. John fell naturally into a fatherly role. The couple were unable to have children; so in 1953, after considerable soul-searching, they decided to adopt a baby girl, Robin Hollis Robarts, who grew into a lively, precocious little redhead. She was joined by Timothy, who was adopted in 1956. Tim's babyhood was not easy, for he developed a severe case of eczema that required treatment for several years. The bee's jelly prescribed to salve the sores cost $50 a jar. Often the baby was on tranquillizers. Both parents devoted themselves to Tim and Robin, and the two months of the year that John spent commuting to Toronto were not a particular drain on the time spent with his family. Politics was not shaping his private life. Not yet.

Far from worrying about how to hold public life at bay, Robarts was actively involved on the local scene in reshaping the PC organization to ensure that his 1951 victory would not be a fluke. The main problem was how to keep the newcomers, especially the younger set who had come out to work for Robarts. Most of them were not died-in-the-wool partisans, were tied up with careers and families, and saw their political involvement as a cross between a hobby and occasional public service.

Robarts and Fred Jenkins presented a general outline of the future of their organization to the London PC Association in January 1952. The hard and visible core of the party would be Robarts and the members of the executive. As president, Gordon Gilbride would lead the association and its traditional membership in their normal activities – the Blossom Tea and the euchre and bridge parties thrown by the women's association, the committee work and the annual meeting. Jenkins as treasurer of the association had his traditional responsibilities for fundraising, but would also maintain a list of workers who would not be expected to become involved in the routine affairs of the London PC Association. For this group of sometime Tories a couple of special functions would be held every year to maintain interest and a certain level of enthusiasm. Often Jenkins would throw a huge beef barbecue, a special enough event in years before everyone barbecued all summer long. Robarts would ensure that some senior Tory, usually a member of the cabinet, would be on hand to bring the group up to date on some aspect of the political scene. These affairs grew in popularity in London until they became reasonably important social events, the kind of gathering to which the upwardly mobile liked to be invited as an indication of credentials or achievement. It was a skilful way of keeping the non-political Robarts supporters involved.

Fred Jenkins became the central figure in London Conservatism. His hardware and seed store was near Robarts' office, and when John was not commuting to Toronto, he would often park in Jenkins' lot and talk politics with him before going in to work.

The first test of the new organization's effectiveness came in the 1953 federal election. Whatever might happen to George Drew and the Conservatives nationally, there seemed a good chance to move London back into the Tory camp because Alex Jeffery, quarrelling with his party's establishment over the extension of C.D. Howe's emergency economic power, decided not to seek re-election for the Liberals. The replacement candidate, Dr S. Floyd Maine, who was head of the extension department at the University of Western Ontario, was popular with a broad spectrum of society but something of an outsider to the London business and professional community.[3] If the kind of Londoners who had put John Robarts over the top in 1951 continued to vote for the party, it seemed possible to defeat him.

Getting a suitable PC candidate became the critical problem. Robarts, Jenkins, and Gilbride came to agree on Robert W. Mitchell, a young lawyer in practice with William E. Dwyer, a prominent local Tory. Mitchell had not grown up in London, but he was respected professionally, enjoyed financial security, and was popular with members of the London PC Association. It happened, however, that the people connected with the party's Ontario campaign headquarters in Toronto had concluded that Mayor Allan Rush might be a good candidate and were encouraging him to seek the nomination. Robarts intervened, warning headquarters that the local association would not take kindly to having outsiders thrust a candidate on them. Colonel T.L. Kennedy, the former premier, was sent to London to check out the situation. Robarts brought him to the annual meeting of the London PC Association just as the question of an outside candidate was being put to the group. The reaction was overwhelmingly negative, and the Rush candidacy never materialized.

It seemed as though the nomination meeting would be a formality, but another candidate appeared at the last moment, James H. Currie, the CPR conductor on the businessman's special from London to Toronto. Currie was signing his friends up as new members of the association, and suddenly the established group had to mobilize its forces. The Mitchells brought their friends to the nomination meeting; Jenkins brought in his people from the Oriental Band; Robarts mobilized the Legion and ADSEPA. Six hundred people appeared for the selection of a Conservative candidate. In an important milestone for the 1950 group, Mitchell won. Later Jenkins, Robarts, Gilbride, and the new president of the London PC Association, Jack Thompson, prepared amendments to the rules of procedure for London nomination meetings, introducing written advance nominations and a ten-day period of closed membership before each nomination meeting.

Mitchell met with Robarts and Jenkins to organize his campaign. Robarts did not feel that a provincial member should be visible in a federal election campaign, so he would only be available to help in the backrooms. Jenkins suggested that Ernest G. Halpenny, who was a popular and dynamic member of the Kiwanis and had expressed an interest in the Conservative party, might make an excellent campaign manager. As president of his own pharmaceutical firm, Halpenny would have time to do the job. Jenkins and Robarts approached him and he readily agreed, on condition that they give him some help. Robarts drafted an organization chart for Halpenny and they filled in the names together. Just as Robarts had expanded the old organization in 1951, so Halpenny and Mitchell now added their friends to the campaign team, swelling it still further.

Halpenny repeated the advertising and campaign techniques Robarts had used in

1951. During the campaign the London PCS declined an offer to have George Drew, the national leader, spend time in the city. The results showed that they knew what they were doing. Despite Drew's failure to make significant gains nationally, Mitchell was elected for the Conservatives in London. The local people had rejected the advice and suggestions of outsiders, done it their way, and won again.

With these two uphill victories to their credit, the London Tories began to see themselves as significant players on the Ontario political stage. Those who worked downtown started meeting regularly for morning coffee at Woolworth's, discussing the political scene and considering further roles. It was decided that London should take a high profile at the November 1953 annual meeting of the Ontario PC Association, and that Fred Jenkins ought to be elected an auditor of the provincial organization.

A large delegation of Londoners descended on the Toronto convention. They rented a wing on one floor of the King Edward Hotel, kept a hospitality suite open throughout the convention, and began to get a reputation as a hard-drinking, hard-playing crowd. Also a flute-playing crowd, as some members of the Oriental Band serenaded other delegates at breakfasts. Ontario PCs could not help but notice the Londoners; even Frost visited the enclave to assess what was happening. The London group held their own strategy meetings, lobbied for Jenkins for auditor, and were visible as an organized group. The vote for auditor occurred late in the proceedings. As earlier ballots for the vice presidents were completed, delegates left, but the London group stayed on, and Jenkins was elected. The Toronto organizers, sensitive to the strength and enthusiasm of this new political entity, dubbed them 'the London mafia.' The label stuck, a reference to Ontario's recurring concern for organized crime. The Londoners were an exclusive, organized group outside the orbit of the Toronto backroom. As their leader, Robarts gained significance, but only a decade after the demise of Hepburn. The group's style also was remembered in the halls of Tory power in Toronto.

Through his first term as a legislator, Robarts was content with his part-time duties. In 1953, during one of the interviews that Frost held annually with each of his backbenchers, Robarts told him that he did not want increased responsibilities at Queen's Park until he was financially self-sufficient. In retrospect, Robarts thought this posture had been politically as well as economically important to him. It gave him a good apprenticeship, and time to understand the rhythm of Queen's Park and the Ontario political process. By the time his political involvement deepened, Robarts already knew the system well enough to minimize his mistakes. On the other hand, Frost did not offer him any position of significance.

Robert Macaulay got married in 1954, ending the evening sessions at the apartment. Now Robarts roomed at the Royal York, as did Frost and the majority of the non-Toronto MPPs. The move to the Royal York drew Robarts further into the social life of the legislative fraternity. He joined the Reverend A.W. Downer's non-partisan poker game, and often went out with colleagues to Toronto nightspots – Carman's or the Franz Josef for dinner, the Colonial for jazz. A lot of the backbenchers had time on their hands when they were in Toronto, and through the 1950s the city came to offer more and more diversified ways of spending it. Robarts was usually at the centre of the action.

At the same time that Robarts moved, the pace in the legislature began to pick up, without any particular effort on Robarts' part. The death of Charles Gordon MacOdrum, MPP for Leeds, left the Legal Bills Committee without a chairman. Robarts was appointed as the replacement for the balance of the session, his first position of authority in the legislature. The by-election in Leeds also led to one of the most important political friendships in Robarts' life, when a concerted campaign by Frost, A.D. McKenzie, and George Drew finally persuaded the popular Brockville alderman, James Auld, to run. He took the seat with ease and, through mutual friends, became close to Robarts.

As the term drew to a close, many of the backbenchers were starting to become impatient about their lack of influence in the government. Macaulay was the most outspoken. As soon as he stopped living with the restraining Robarts, he began bombarding Frost with letters and briefs. In January 1955 Macaulay sent one such letter to the premier congratulating him on selecting William F. Nickle for a cabinet post. Typically, he went on to advance the cause of John Robarts: 'I am of course keeping my eye peeled and hope that you will direct your attention towards the City of London and in one of your more expansive moods select my good friend and very able colleague John Robarts.'[4]

Macaulay also pressed Frost to give backbenchers in general a larger share in the policy-making process. Frost was not particularly interested, seeing the backbencher as a link between the government and the constituencies; they could register their reactions to policy proposals at caucus.[5] Several backbenchers, including Robarts and Auld, finally joined in a little Macaulay-organized pressure on the premier when they all signed a petition in March 1955, asking Frost to set up a select committee to study air pollution problems in Toronto.[6] Three weeks later Frost responded with his usual political shrewdness. He announced that several select committees would be established to work between sessions. A Select Committee on Toll Roads would be chaired by John Robarts. A Select Committee on Questions Related to Titles of Motor Vehicles would be chaired by Robert Macaulay. The committee they had wanted, a Select Committee on Smoke Control and Air Pollution, would be chaired by Alfred Cowling, the Conservative whip who sat for High Park in Toronto. Macaulay would be one of its members, Robarts would not. Five weeks after creating the new committees, Frost called a provincial election. With the dissolution of the legislature the select committees ceased to exist.

Leslie Frost effectively neutered the Liberals in his first speech of the campaign. The Tories had managed to obtain an advance copy of the Liberal platform, which would not be announced by their new leader, Farquhar Oliver, until 3 May. On 30 April Frost tailored his own kickoff speech, delivered to eight hundred delegates at the fiftieth annual meeting of the Western Ontario PC Association in London, to anticipate the Liberal attack. The Conservatives favoured giving Ontario exactly the same improvements the Liberals would urge: better water delivery systems in the southwestern peninsula, better education, more financial support for municipalities, more overall economic development. Knowing the opposition would attack his highway program, Frost blamed his problems on federal-provincial disagreements. The Tory record was good, the opposition was irresponsible, the Ontario government was always willing to cooperate with Ottawa for the benefit of the people of Ontario. The Conservatives would move Ontario into a new era of Trans-Canada highways, atomic energy, and the St Lawrence Seaway. Of course, the premier concluded, 'the party of the people of Ontario' would 'welcome to our ranks the good Liberals who want good government, together with those CCF interested in the same thing – prosperity for the province.'[7] Three days later, the Liberal platform sounded like a repetition of Conservative initiatives.

It was a much quieter election than 1951 had been. Both the Liberals and the Toronto *Star* avoided the extremes and hoopla that had been so counter-productive four years earlier. Unfortunately for the Liberals, this quieter strategy gave the impression that there was not much difference between the major parties, except in experience at governing. The Liberals pressed on with their largely pre-empted platform, trying to make mileage with promises of more money for highways, better health care, and increased municipal relief programs. Highway contract over-runs, which had led to a considerable scandal and a minister's resignation, made it possible to accuse the government of mismanagement or worse, and the opposition was not impressed with its costly plan to convert the province's electrical system from 25 to 60 cycles. Even the *Star,* however, realized that the initiative was long overdue, a necessary step to bring Ontario in line with the rest of North America. Frost counter-attacked with his usual sweeping identification of the opposition with the federal Liberals, accusing the former of trying to encourage the latter to meddle in Ontario, and equating Farquhar Oliver's people with the party that had been in office 'during the dark days of Liberal [Hepburn] government in Ontario.'[8]

The CCF had a new leader in Donald C. MacDonald, an experienced political organizer who had replaced Jolliffe in 1953. He had concentrated on building up CCF riding organizations and increasing the party's ties with organized labour, a strategy that started to bear fruit during the campaign as a number of local labour councils resolved to support CCF candidates. The CCF offered a twelve-point program stressing better education, hospital services and housing, along with economic security and consumer protection for the ordinary citizen. The party also made much of the $28 million in over-runs on highway contracts in northern Ontario.

The London electoral map had been changed by a 1954 redistribution of ridings. Robarts' old London constituency was split more or less in half, becoming the two ridings of London North and London South. As Robarts and others had recommended, the dividing line along Dundas Street corresponded to the municipal ward boundaries. Robarts chose to stand for London North, which comprised Gilbride's and his old wards, 1 and 2, the heart of the business and professional and servicemen's communities. In London South the Tories accepted the offer of Ernest G. Jackson to run for the legislature. A tall, athletic young man who had been program director of the London YMCA after serving as a captain in the Royal Canadian Regiment during the war, Jackson had entered the insurance field. His family was active in the PC party and his mother was an acknowledged leader in local party councils. Ernie had been district chairman in Ward 3 in Robarts' 1951 campaign and Mitchell's 1953 effort. He lived in Ward 4 and was a member of the Oriental Band and the Legion.

The two Conservative candidates ran a joint campaign, sharing finances, advertising facilities, and workers, effectively using the organization that had been built in 1951 and strengthened since. The local Liberals were still in disarray, and although they managed to match the Tory style with an equally aggressive advertising campaign, they had neither the machine nor the policies to make inroads. Robarts' Liberal opponent in London North was Clarence Peterson, a widely respected businessman who had signed the original manifesto at the formation of the CCF party in his younger days. Social issues and politics were well discussed at the Peterson home, and two of his sons went on from their own professional and business careers – one to be an MP and the other to end the Conservative dynasty in Ontario as the first Liberal premier since Harry Nixon in 1943. Clarence remembers the 1955 London North campaign as almost a family affair. In the election on 9 June 1955, Robarts and Jackson won their seats without difficulty.

An Ontario Conservative dynasty seemed clearly in the making as Frost's party won its fifth straight election, increasing its share of the popular vote from 48 to 49 per cent. In a slightly expanded house, the PCs would have eighty-four members, the Liberals eleven, and the CCF three. A majority of the opposition members would be new to the legislature, but only a handful of Conservatives were rookies. Once again the election posed for Frost the problem of how to handle a surfeit of backbenchers. By now most of them, including Robarts, had already served a full term of apprenticeship.

Frost reconvened the legislature on 8 September 1955, for the sole purpose of re-establishing the three select committees that had been appointed in April, partly to appease backbenchers' restlessness. Robarts again was to be chairman of the Toll Roads Committee, and now would have a job to do. Other members of his committee included CCF leader Donald MacDonald and Jim Auld from Leeds. Donald J. Collins, an executive officer in the premier's office, served as the committee's secretary – or, as the press claimed, quite accurately, the premier's 'informant' on the committee.

Robarts got his committee to work quickly. Its job was to recommend the best way of financing major highway construction for the province. As well as holding public hearings, the Toll Roads Committee had to do a considerable amount of travelling, both in Ontario and to study toll road systems in the United States. Robarts found himself meeting a lot of local Tory organizers as the committee toured Ontario, with good discussions of a subject, roads and highways, dear to the hearts of old-line party people. Serving and travelling on this kind of committee also led to better fellowship and understanding across party lines. There was a memorable overnight train ride from Atikokan to Fort Frances, for example, when Robarts, MacDonald, and Collins all had to squeeze into the same compartment, but with the aid of a couple of bottles managed to turn a potentially horrible trip into a rollicking session of political argument, transportation expertise, and prophesying about the great northwest. The men got off the train as friends, members of the same 'club,' whose informal contacts and mutual assistance would lubricate the job of governing Ontario in later years. Bonds like these among politicians have always been vital to the efficiency and civility of the political process. Becoming part of and getting to know his way around this network was a crucial aspect of Robarts' apprenticeship.

On their own ground, Robarts and his fellow London PCs were no longer apprentices at the political game. They were beginning to expect due respect, and to flex organizational muscles when it seemed necessary. Late in 1955 a simmering bit of unpleasantness boiled over at the London PC Association centennial dinner in a somewhat alcoholic argument between Robarts' people and the federal member, Robert Mitchell. The local Conservatives had not been particularly impressed by Mitchell's reports on the Ottawa scene. They tended to discount his problems of commuting between London and Ottawa as well as the handicap of being in opposition, and were not pleased that Mitchell had become a friend and protégé of Drew, who had never been highly rated in London. Now Mitchell was drawn into a heated argument about Drew's leadership, the federal Tories' poor performance on policy matters, and Mitchell's capacity to represent London Conservatism in parliament. Mitchell was furious and hurt. A few weeks later, when it became apparent that Drew would be retiring as leader, Mitchell called Jenkins and Robarts to inform them that he would not run again.[9]

Robarts and Jenkins decided to ask Ernest Halpenny to stand for the federal seat. He had the time and the financial independence to undertake the job, and had become well respected in London for his work in the 1953 and 1955 campaigns. Halpenny was one of twenty-four top London Tories Robarts and Jenkins invited to Toronto for the opening of the legislature's winter session. While scurrying around picking up food and drinks for their party that night, Jenkins suggested that Halpenny become London's federal PC candidate. Halpenny said it would be a great idea. At the Londoners' party after the opening of the Ontario legislature, John Robarts announced that Ernest Halpenny would run in the next federal election. The quest was over; there was the excuse for a party – not that one was really needed. The London group again lived up to their 'hard drinking' reputation. When it was over, Halpenny had to wait almost a year before the election was called.

Robarts and Jackson stayed at the Royal York while they were in Toronto that winter of 1955-6. They saw a lot of Auld, who served with Robarts on the Toll Roads Committee and knew Jackson from cadet camp back in the thirties. The three MPPs had a common taste for good dining and good jazz when they were in the city together. That was a fairly irregular coincidence, though, for both Jackson and Robarts were commuting to London whenever possible, while Auld travelled on weekends to Brockville. Robarts was still interested in developing his law practice, Jackson in building up his insurance agency. Neither was committed to politics as a life's work.

But each year drew Robarts a little further into the Toronto scene. At the start of the 1957 session, he, Jackson, and Auld decided to try to save money by renting an apartment together. They found a suitably Tory building in the old Mayfair Mansions on Avenue Road and settled into rooms full of heavy old furniture under high ceilings. One of the fortuitous contacts Robarts made from this move was with Harry Price, an influential party fundraiser and confidant of Frost, who lived in the same building. Fortunately Price's apartment was far enough away in the building to leave him undisturbed by the backbenchers' rowdiness. The evening sessions Robarts used to have in Bob Macaulay's apartment resumed, as wide-ranging and as loud as ever. One night the backbenchers concluded that the Tory caucus was so big that it could stand being split and an independent Conservative party established to be the official opposition. Its leader could then claim the extra allowances paid to the Liberals and they could be used to fund the evening sessions. Often these MPPs thought they were acting as a kind of friendly opposition: several cabinet ministers, including even one of Frost's senior ministers, accepted invitations to have drinks in the apartment and endure a robust grilling. Those who refused to respond to the backbenchers' invitation, on the other hand, were remembered as aloof.

Bob Macaulay had largely dropped out of the boisterous backbench group since his marriage. But he was easily the most restless member of Robarts' circle, effervescing with ideas, never afraid to put them to Frost. In a long letter to Frost on 19 January 1956, for example, Macaulay suggested how the Department of Labour could improve its handling of strikes, proposed a way of financing the TransCanada pipeline, and offered advice on negotiating federal-provincial transfers. All of this before warning, 'I contemplate going over the budget as best I can and in a way which I think the Leader of the Opposition should have been doing for years and has never done.' 'Is he on the right side of the House?' E.J.

Young added at the end of the summary of Macaulay's letter to Frost.[10] They were all on the right side of the House; there were just not enough jobs to keep them busy.

Robarts' Toll Roads Committee submitted its interim report to the legislature late in the 1956 session. It concluded that the construction of limited access toll roads, which were fairly popular in the United States, would not meet the needs of the people of Ontario, especially in the Toronto area. Another year would be necessary to study alternative methods of highway financing. Frost gave the committee the extra year, and they resumed their work in the summer of 1956, studying toll roads in Ohio, New Jersey, and Pennsylvania. When Robarts asked for money so his committee could study the freeway systems in California and Oregon, Frost drew the line, apparently worrying that his boys were proposing a pleasant but unnecessary junket. So the committee had to be content with written reports on the West Coast freeway system.

Robarts submitted the final report of the Toll Roads Committee on 19 February 1957. It recommended that toll-free super-highways be constructed in Ontario, but not along the Lake Erie shore as had been originally suggested. Instead they should be built inland to draw growth away from recreational areas.[11] This was a significant report in the history of Ontario highway planning. Not only would the super-highways, notably 401, be free to motorists, but they would be used as instruments to help guide the urban and rural development of the province.[12] The recognition of these important policy foci for highway planning led to the creation of a Department of Transport in 1958 and the appointment of the Toll Roads Committee's secretary, Donald Collins, as its first deputy minister.

Once its report was accepted the committee disbanded, and Robarts reverted to his backbench idleness. His experience chairing the committee had given him some visibility across the province, especially with Tory organizers, and had extended his friendships in the legislature. But it did not at first cause Leslie Frost to give him more work. There appear to have been two reasons for Robarts' relatively slow advancement. One was that Frost was careful to respect the Londoner's desire to build up his law practice, and would not burden Robarts until he was sure he was ready. Frost once wanted to see Robarts on a political matter, for example, and asked him to drop into his office. Robarts told the premier he was due to appear in court, but would try to get an adjournment. Frost told Robarts the problem could wait, that it was more important for Robarts to make a living.

The second reason for Frost's hesitation about Robarts was the stories he was hearing about the Londoner's interest in having a good time after hours. Frost was not as certain as Robarts that an MPP could separate his on-duty and his off-duty deportment. Mitch Hepburn had not been able to, a memory that coloured the premier's reactions to his young colleague's approach to the job. Frost was tolerant of part-time backbenchers, but was leery to a fault about bringing a hard-drinking, fun-loving fellow into his cabinet, however able he might be. A cabinet minister ought to be more serious, purposeful, and discreet than the sometimes boisterous Robarts seemed to be.

Robarts himself was becoming hesitant about the cost of the Toronto apartment and the lifestyle that went with it, and by the end of the 1957 session he and Jackson had decided to cut back. The apartment trio broke up; Jackson and Robarts moved into the newly opened Westbury Hotel, a few blocks from Queen's Park, which would become their Toronto base for the rest of their careers as legislators.

By the end of the 1950s Leslie Frost's problems with his inner political circle were more worrisome than the antics and ambitions of his backbenchers. In April 1956 Colonel Young, the right-hand man in his office, suffered a severe heart attack. In August the key organizer, Alex McKenzie, had a heart attack. The former premier and national leader, George Drew, who had continued to be influential in Ontario Tory politics, was sick with meningitis and in September 1956 announced his resignation. When Young and McKenzie came back on the job they had far less energy and stamina than in the good years. Frost appointed a young Lindsayite, H. Glen Gordon, to assist Young, and Hugh Latimer, the PC regional director for Toronto, to help McKenzie. Then he had to turn to problems within his cabinet, where both ill health and scandal were starting to exact a toll. The central issue, which infected Ontario politics for several years afterwards, was revelations that cabinet ministers had profited from having obtained stock in the Northern Ontario Natural Gas Company before it was available to the public. In the spring of 1958 three of Frost's ministers, Phillip T. Kelly in Mines, William Griesinger in Public Works, and Lands and Forests minister Clare Mapledoram, had to resign. Fletcher S. Thomas, the minister of agriculture, resigned for health reasons at the same time.

Both Griesinger and Thomas sat for southwestern Ontario ridings, and their exit from the cabinet opened up the prospect of promotion for members from that region. Both Robarts and Jackson wondered if they would be selected. Nothing happened.

In the meantime, the Progressive-Conservative Party of Canada had selected a new national leader, John Diefenbaker, who came to power with a minority government in 1957 and won a landslide majority in 1958. In London, Ernest Halpenny became an active and visible supporter of Diefenbaker during the leadership campaign, establishing a rapport with the new chief that would last through the early Diefenbaker years. Halpenny had no difficulty carrying the federal seat for the Conservatives in London in both elections.

The primary allegiance of the London Tory organization remained with Robarts. Early in 1957, when Diefenbaker was building his electoral organization, he and Allister Grosart, the party's federal organizational genius, visited London and met with the leading figures in the Robarts organization. Would they become active in the new federal campaign team? The answer was a polite negative, with several of the Londoners making clear that their main interest was in provincial politics. Relations between Grosart and the London group remained strained. As the federal member of parliament Ernest Halpenny was left to straddle the gulf, not unlike Mitchell before him. His predicament was sweetened somewhat by his being made a parliamentary assistant in the Diefenbaker government. .

Robarts had the London organization, but apparently had little power or influence at Queen's Park. He was not asked to chair any committees during the 1958 session. Leslie Frost appointed two members of Robarts' 'Class of '51,' Robert Macaulay and John Yaremko, to the cabinet in the spring of 1958. William Stewart, a gifted politician who won a seat in the Middlesex by-election in 1957, was rumoured to have been offered the new Transport portfolio which, if true, might close off opportunities for other members from the London area.[13] The government was close to disarray, with Young and McKenzie both ill again (Young died in 1959, McKenzie the next year), Frost himself tired, and both the highways accusations and the NONG scandal refusing to go away.

John Robarts, watching his friends' careers outpace his own, wondered seriously whether there was any point staying on in politics. For seven years as a backbencher he had been able to handle without much difficulty the dual demands of his law practice and the legislature, while still maintaining a satisfactory private and family life. Starting to gain weight at forty, with a softer expression than in his youth, Robarts now had to prepare for the long haul. In a descriptive phrase, Jonathan Manthorpe perceptively captured Robarts' quality, 'looking and being rather like an untormented political version of Ernest Hemingway.'[14]

John had had a good time. Now it seemed time to make a commitment to one career or the other. He could either get on with the law practice in London or get into the cabinet and become one of the men who really governed Ontario. As the months passed with no summons from Frost, Robarts had pretty well made up his mind not to stand for re-election.

4

The Crossroads

Frost's neglect of Robarts was largely a product of the difficulty he was having getting anything done in the confusion of 1958. It was in fact only a matter of time that year before an offer would be made. The replies to Frost's annual request for his backbenchers' list of policy interests were now being reviewed with an eye to cabinet placement. Robarts had said he was interested in highways, and that he thought the Ontario Water Resources Commission was doing an interesting job in southwestern Ontario.[1] Frost was still hesitant about promoting him because of the reports he had received about Robarts' penchant for lively night life in Toronto. He scouted around for others' opinions, getting a largely favourable response from insiders who knew of Robarts' restlessness. Frost's final discussion was with Donald Collins, who assured him that Robarts was well able to keep his partying separate from his work. On 6 December 1958, Frost called Robarts in London and invited him to join the cabinet as minister without portfolio. His primary duty would be to serve as the link between the cabinet and the Ontario Water Resources Commission.

Robarts asked Frost for a weekend to decide. He was at a crossroads in his life. A return to London meant a virtual guarantee of financial security as a lawyer, as well as ample time for his family. An increased commitment to public life would place him at the centre of Ontario politics, facing the challenges of governing.

The decision had to be his. Norah continued to dislike Toronto, and believed the children should be raised in London. John did not see that as an insurmountable problem; although his new responsibilities would require more time, he could commute on weekends at least. His law practice would suffer, but his family time would remain almost intact. Moreover, he enjoyed the freedom of the occasional evening in Toronto during the week. The increasing pressures of raising a family could be left and then returned to after a break. John struggled with the choice all weekend and boarded the train on Monday morning still unsure of his position.

As he approached the capital, the excitement of politics, the challenge of governing, and the freedom won. He did not relish being just another London lawyer. Maybe he could juggle both sides of his life, the legal and the political, a while longer and thus not close off the challenges of public life. He went directly to Frost's office on his arrival and asked if he could continue to practise law as a minister of the crown. Because he was not independently wealthy, Robarts told Frost, he had to have some insurance against political ill-fortune. Frost assured him he could. On that understanding, John Robarts agreed to enter the cabinet.

His appointment was announced on 22 December as part of a larger cabinet shuffle. John Root, a backbencher like Robarts since 1951, and James Maloney, winner in a 1956 by-election, were also moved to the front benches. Frost had now brought in five young men in the most significant cabinet shuffle since 1943. These were the new faces he would show to the voters in an election likely to be called in 1959.

Robarts' specific duties in this first cabinet position were not onerous. Whereas the aggressive and imaginative Bob Macaulay had been given responsibility for Ontario Hydro and was embarked on wide-ranging studies of nuclear power, Robarts' main job was to oversee the rapidly changing relationship between the Ontario Water Resources Commission, the municipalities, and the provincial government. His experience as an alderman, his willingness to work with people of widely differing views – as illustrated by his performance on the Toll Roads Committee and the London and Suburban Planning Committee – all seemed to qualify him for duties that had the attraction of being somewhat outside the norm of departmental administration.

The OWRC, established in 1956, was responsible for sewage treatment and pollution control throughout the province. Because of the low water table throughout southwestern Ontario, it also had the politically sensitive task of developing and deploying a water supply system throughout the region. The commission was administered by the Department of Public Works, but Robarts was the minister who handled its affairs in the legislature and with other politicians.

During his year on the commission, Robarts maintained a low profile. In the assembly he brought in an amendment to the Ontario Water Resources Commission Act that increased the OWRC's size and changed its fiscal powers to enable it to enter into direct contracts with municipalities. There was no fanfare to the change and little debate. As he learned to field questions in the legislature, Robarts naturally fell into an obliging, explanatory style rather than the aggressiveness of the partisan. Less than a month after his appointment, Robarts wrote Frost that his duties were nebulous and suggested he assume responsibility for the administration of the OWRC. He also asked if a minister without portfolio was eligible for the extra allowance of $2,000 paid to departmental ministers.[2] Frost responded that it was cheaper to have the OWRC administered by Public Works. In recognition of the ambiguous financial position of ministers without portfolio, he promised to introduce a bill to give them an extra $1,800. Robarts got the money without the added responsibility.

He took care to have the relationship between his role as minister of the crown and partner in a private law firm clarified. He asked Frost if his partners could appear before boards and commissions even if he could not. A legal opinion, sought from the attorney general, held that a minister could maintain a private law practice, but he would have to maintain an arm's length relationship with those of his partners who were performing public duties.[3] It would be possible, then, for Robarts to maintain his position in Carrothers, Fox, Robarts, and Betts, but his relations with his partners were now more remote, the beginning of his disengagement from the practice.

The first year in cabinet had not challenged Robarts' belief that he could continue in politics and in the law. Primarily concerned with sewage treatment and water supply problems in southwestern Ontario, the OWRC thus brought him closer to London and his family. He was required to spend more time in Toronto, but the shift was not onerous. Norah participated in regional political functions and was delighted with the new status ascribed to her husband. At home, Robin remembered Norah as a delightful friend who could empathize with her and share her fantasies. In the community, Norah was the disciplined lady who kept her life private except to a few close friends. The self-control which had demanded that Norah march down the aisle alone rather than with a surrogate father had not faded. And it would not see her leave her London.

John continued to stay at the Westbury while in Toronto, and to relax with Jackson and Auld. Not a lot had changed in his life, except that he was on the first rung of the cabinet ladder and could reasonably expect to climb higher. It was Ernie Jackson, the other London member, for whom Robarts' promotion caused a major change of course. Jackson obligingly agreed to handle routine constituency problems in both ridings to help free Robarts for his cabinet duties. At the same time, he realized that his own political future had been subordinated and severely limited. It was highly unlikely that a second London MPP, no matter how able, would be given a cabinet position. Although he thrived on politics, Jackson was not willing to keep on mixing a backbencher's life with his commitments to his business and family. He decided not to run again.

Jackson's decision coincided with Frost asking him to move the Address in Reply to the Speech from the Throne. He told the premier that someone else ought to do it because he was not planning to seek re-election. Frost and McKenzie encouraged Jackson at least to do all that he could to keep the seat Conservative. In London, Robarts, Jenkins, and Halpenny all urged him to reconsider. They managed to persuade him to delay his announcement, but at the London PC Association's spring picnic, held at a cottage north of the city in Denfield, a subdued Jackson told his friends that he planned to retire. He would not change his mind, so the London Conservatives had to turn to the problem of quickly finding a new candidate.

In fact, a name already had been put forward through the informal network of influence in London. John White was a descendant of the Whites who had settled in London in the 1850s, had attended Western, and belonged to Delta Upsilon fraternity. He came back to the city in 1954 after working briefly in Hamilton and established a capital equipment leasing company, the Canadian Industrial Supply Company, in partnership with a fellow Londoner, John Croden. White was an energetic, outspoken young businessman. He enjoyed confrontation and thrived on debate. In 1957 he agreed to stand for the presidency of the DU alumni association on condition that he could advocate a new fraternity house, and that someone would run opposing his position. During the fundraising campaign which followed his successful bid, White was asked to approach a fellow alumnus, Walter Blackburn, who owned the London *Free Press*. Over lunch at the London Club, Blackburn agreed to contribute at once, and with a whole lunchtime stretching ahead of him, John White turned to other topics. In the ensuing small talk, White casually mentioned that he thought he might like to enter politics some day. Blackburn was noncommittal, but surprisingly he remembered the comment.

A little over a year later, at the Christmas dinner of the investment club to which both Blackburn and Ernie Jackson belonged, Jackson mentioned his plan to retire. A week later, at the London Club's Christmas party, Blackburn found himself sitting beside Fred Jenkins. He mentioned hearing about Jackson's plans, wondered if anyone had a successor in mind, and suggested the Tories take a look at John White. In the meantime, he had told White about the situation, and a low-key campaign had begun.

Jenkins, who was surprised by the approach, told Robarts about it the next day. The exciting prospect was that Blackburn would probably endorse White, nailing down the *Free Press'* support for the party. Robarts and Jenkins met White to discuss his candidacy, but made no commitment for several months while White worked hard at building local support. Rumours that other candidates were being considered gradually faded away. At the London South nomination meeting on 27 April 1959, Ernest Jackson announced his retirement and John White was acclaimed as the new candidate. Robarts paid tribute to Jackson and introduced the guest speaker, the Honourable James Allan. A week later at the London North nomination meeting, Robarts was acclaimed again. His friend Bob Macaulay was the guest speaker.

Leslie Frost, still at the height of his popularity, led his rejuvenated government into the 1959 provincial election. With the Diefenbaker administration still riding high in Ottawa, it was a good time for Tories. Frost had blunted the impact of the Northern Ontario Natural Gas affair by getting rid of the most obvious miscreants. Although CCF leader Donald MacDonald tried to keep the issue at the centre of Ontario politics, the Liberals were not nearly so enthusiastic, in substantial part because their new leader, John Wintermeyer, had himself naively dabbled in NONG stock as the result of tips from one of the disgraced ministers. Wintermeyer had a full plate of problems with his party as well, which was disorganized, poorly funded, and hopelessly behind the Tories in the standings at dissolution. In an uneventful campaign, Wintermeyer managed to double his party's representation, from eleven to twenty-two seats, and gain a few percentage points in the popular vote. The CCF made only minor gains, increasing their seats from three to five. After a decade in power, the premier they called 'The Silver Fox' and, increasingly, 'Old Man Ontario,' was unbeatable. The Conservatives won seventy-one seats.

Robarts and John White had no serious trouble carrying London North and London South, but the campaign did mark a turning point in the history of the London PC Association. Following the model of the 1955 election, it had been decided to run a joint campaign in the two ridings, which would be chaired by Jackson and include common advertising, a central financial pool, and common campaign literature. Friction gradually developed, though, as it became apparent that John White and his group, a new, younger crowd, chafed at what they saw as the restraints imposed by the need to work together. White wanted to run a far more aggressive campaign than the laid-back, established Robarts. Possibly he ran a little more scared because the *Free Press* did not support him after all, as one of its senior employees ran for the Liberals in London South. Although the PC organization did not formally come apart, White had his way, largely through the activities of broadcaster Ward Cornell, who informally managed the London South campaign. This was the first slight cracking of the London organization Robarts had created. It hardly seemed significant at the time.

Leslie Frost had watched Robarts carefully during his year as minister without portfolio. The new fellow seemed to be businesslike, pragmatic, and conscientious. He had managed to create a better financial position for the Ontario Water Resources Commission and clarify its relationship to levels of government without inciting any conflict. He was still known to be a bit of a hell-raiser when off duty, but Frost saw how effectively Robarts compartmentalized his on- and off-duty behaviour. Robarts was hardly a shining star like Macaulay, but he was a talented, promising minister who seemed ready for a more challenging position.

Soon he had all the challenge anyone could want. The Department of Education was experiencing the full brunt of demands generated by the movement of the postwar baby boom through the Ontario school system. Every year through the 1950s the province's primary schools had had to accommodate an increase of fifty thousand students in their enrolment. Now the flood was poised at the gates of the secondary school system. The resources available to teach and house these students were strained to the limit, and had to be increased as quickly as possible. Costs were soaring. The public was worried about quality of education following Russia's launching of 'Sputnik,' the world's first space satellite. North Americans had begun to fret that communism was somehow more effective than the West in training scientists. Local employers were claiming that European countries were much more effective than Ontario in training skilled tradesmen. Their preference for hiring these well-trained immigrants over Ontario graduates was a volatile political issue in a time of recession and growing unemployment.

William J. Dunlop, who had held the Education portfolio since 1951, had done yeoman service and enjoyed considerable personal popularity. But his health had failed, forcing Frost to try to assume some of the load. The premier was already saddled with responsibility for federal-provincial negotiations relating to education, which were becoming increasingly complex. With all the problems of his own office, particularly the disorganization following Colonel Young's death, Frost simply could not do more. Within the Department of Education there was considerable demoralization as proposals for reform and change seemed to be positively discouraged.[4] The Department of Labour, on the other hand, was developing and extending training programs to fill the void created by the lack of flexibility in the Department of Education. Altogether, it was time for a new minister.

But not any normally promising young minister would do. A minister of education had to deal with locally elected school boards which were responsible professionally to his department yet were politically autonomous. Ham-handed or unduly aggressive or authoritarian leadership from a minister could spark sharp, hard-to-control reactions in a highly visible policy area. A good minister of education encouraged and coaxed, soothed ruffled feathers, and led by consensus as often as possible. John Robarts had shown he had the temperament and the political skills for this kind of job. In the legislature he had been pragmatic, not partisan. On the Ontario Water Resources Commission he had negotiated new financial terms with skeptical municipalities without a public eruption. Moreover, a cautious reflective response was required, given the magnitude of the challenges facing the department.

On 8 December 1959, Frost offered the Education portfolio to Robarts. He accepted, and his appointment was announced on 17 December. When he had decided a year earlier to accept his first cabinet post, Robarts had made his commitment to government. Now government began to change his life, for being minister of education was effectively a full-time job. Instead of commuting to London for a few days each week, he spent five days in Toronto and commuted home on weekends. He became an inactive partner in his firm as he devoted his full time to his ministry. With both Robarts and Halpenny holding cabinet positions in their respective governments, the affairs of the London PC Association were left to the local executive, which included Jenkins, Jackson, R.W. Mitchell, David Weldon, and Richard Dillon. Jackson helped Robarts with his constituency work. Their casual chats at Jenkins' store were replaced by weekend meetings when required.

As minister of education, Robarts was one of the most visible members of the cabinet. His first two years coincided with the peak demand for capital projects in the primary and secondary school sectors. He was endlessly travelling to attend school openings, graduations, and cornerstone-layings around the province, expanding his political acquaintanceships as he went. Educational honours also began to descend on him, such as the honorary LL.D. that Western awarded him in the spring of 1960. This was Robarts' first honorary degree. When he returned to his Toronto office after the ceremony Bob Macaulay phoned and asked for 'Doctor Robarts.' When Robarts answered, Macaulay asked for an appointment to have his teeth fixed. Robarts never used the title again.

Robarts continued to cultivate a businesslike, non-partisan style in the legislature. He received his first serious grilling from the opposition during the presentation of his estimates in March 1960, and responded by answering questions directly while ignoring interjections. In this speech he was proposing extensions of educational opportunities to certain groups, such as the deaf and retarded, who did not fit neatly within the system, and he was also following the recommendations of the Standing Committee on Education by undertaking to decentralize teacher education, creating new facilities in London, Kingston, and the north. CCF leader MacDonald endorsed this latter policy with some enthusiasm, for he was pleased to see the Ontario College of Education's monopoly on teacher training in the province finally broken.[5] Both policies reflected Robarts' interest in extending government services and making them more accessible to people who lived in major centres across Ontario. Both involved the expansion of government activities, one in a program sense, the other in a geographic sense. During the next decade, the introduction of measures leading in the same directions would be a constant theme in Ontario politics.

Two events in Robarts' first year as minister combined to have a major impact on educational policy. The first was a routine visit to a high school graduation ceremony in Wiarton. Noticing that not a single boy was graduating with a grade thirteen diploma, Robarts asked the principal if this low level of achievement was common. 'The boys don't do well – they won't try,' the principal told him. The incident aroused Robarts' interest in the dropout phenomenon.

After consulting with his departmental officials about the dropout rate, particularly among boys, Robarts concluded that academic achievement was not socially valued in the school system. At the same time, students who did not plan to go to university gained little from Ontario's unusual fifth year of high school, grade thirteen. To try to reward and enhance the prestige of academic achievement Robarts launched the Ontario scholarships, giving cash awards to students who obtained more than an 80 per cent grade thirteen average (in an era of province-wide exams and before grade inflation).

Robarts also began to ponder the possibility of expanding the kinds of vocational and trade programs available for students who were not university-bound. He talked about the situation with a friend and neighbour, Bill McHugh, who worked in the apprenticeship training program at the Department of Labour.

The secondary school system was geared to funnelling students into the universities. Robarts wondered how it could be adapted to prepare young people to enter the technical institutes and other trade and technical options sponsored by the government. To McHugh and others in the Department of Labour, the Ministry of Education had always seemed condescending in its lukewarm support for the Provincial Institute of Trades. Now, under Robarts, it was becoming enthusiastic and supportive.

The second key event of the Robarts education program grew out of the federal government's approach to the problem of unemployment in the recession of the late 1950s. Many of the unemployed, who totalled an alarming 8 per cent of the Canadian workforce in 1960, were poorly educated, unskilled labourers. It was widely thought that they were 'structurally' unemployed, in that they lacked the skills necessary to get work in a modern high-technology society. Economic expansion alone would not necessarily mean jobs for the unskilled or unready; they needed proper training.

The problem was discussed in 1960 at a federal-provincial conference on education, Robarts' first taste of Canadian federalism in action. Later that year, the Honourable Michael Starr, federal minister of labour, shepherded the Technical Assistance and Vocational Training Act through the House of Commons. It raised the federal contribution to provincial retraining programs from 50 to 75 per cent of their cost. Most important in the long run, the act instituted a federal subsidy of 75 per cent of the capital costs incurred by a province in building facilities for technical and vocational training. The aim was to help the currently unemployed, attack the roots of the problem by encouraging vocational and technical training, and, in passing, give a little stimulus to the languishing construction industry. The act was passed in December 1960. But, as Robarts would come to know all too well with these shared-cost programs, the details of its implementation had yet to be negotiated between Ottawa and each of the ten provincial ministries responsible for setting educational policy.

Ontario's negotiations, deemed to be a matter of intergovernmental fiscal relations, were handled by the premier, with Robarts and his department formulating details of Ontario's responses for the approval of Frost and the cabinet. It was relatively easy to take advantage of some of the increased federal funds for training the unemployed, because the courses offered by the department-controlled Provincial Institute of Trades could be expanded. It seemed more in keeping with local autonomy, however, to encourage local authorities to develop other retraining programs under guidance from provincial committees, a slower approach but one that would not offend local sensitivities.[6]

Robarts followed a similar path in responding to the federal offer of capital support for building vocational schools. On 20 February 1961 he told the legislature that the government would not act immediately 'because this is something we will have to fit into our present educational system.' There were some projects that readily conformed to Ottawa's specifications, such as the City of Toronto's request for assistance in building Castle Frank high school solely for students seeking to learn a trade rather than go to university. But small municipalities could not build special schools like Castle Frank. Their problem was how to finance much more diversified schools catering to the university-destined as well as to future clerical and blue-collar workers.

Robarts was searching for a formula to make such school-building possible while collecting the maximum number of dollars from Ottawa under the Technical Assistance and Vocational Training Act. Under pressure in the assembly, he acknowledged that his department was exploring several possible grants formulas, none of which was satisfactory, and that it would not act on Ottawa's initiative until the right formula was agreed upon. On 28 March 1961 Ontario did agree to accept the federal plan in principle, but Robarts was still searching for the best way of financing the grafting of a vocational stream onto the secondary school curriculum.

He and his staff hit on a potential solution that spring. Suppose *two* vocational streams were added to the secondary school system. A high school offering these two streams along with the traditional academic stream would be offering two-thirds of its program in the vocational area. Less than 50 per cent of its offerings would be academic. Would it therefore qualify as effectively a vocational school, and be eligible for the 75 per cent federal subsidy? Robarts took the proposition to Frost on 17 May. Frost discussed it with his treasurer, James Allan, and phoned Michael Starr in Ottawa the next day to ask if such 'vocational' schools would fall within the terms of the act. Starr said they would. As Frost noted at the time, this proposal became the basis of 'a deal with the Federal Government to share 75% – 25% with the Province of x million for perhaps 200 vocational schools.'[7]

With this understanding, the Department of Education went ahead to develop what came to be called the 'Robarts Plan' of curriculum reform, the key to which was the creation of three separate streams within the secondary school curriculum: arts and science; science, technology, and trades; and business and commerce. The second and third streams were defined as vocational. Under the act Ottawa was committed to paying three-quarters of the cost of a vocational wing built on a local high school, three-quarters of any new building housing a provincial trades institute, and, best of all, three-quarters of any new high school offering the Robarts Plan. Ontario could afford to cover the remaining 25 per cent, and so was able to offer local school boards 100 per cent support for the capital costs of qualifying projects.

The Robarts Plan was announced late in August 1961, and was widely endorsed by the press, educators, and members of local school boards. It seemed to be a major, creative educational reform that addressed the most pressing curricular and financial problems facing the school system. By December some 202 proposals were being processed by the department under the new granting program. One hundred and ninety-six of them were initiated in the next fiscal year. Trades institutes and teachers' colleges were built or expanded in regional centres across the province, and Ottawa was paying most of the cost of this new educational plant. Because of the Robarts Plan's popularity, the Ontario government, and particularly the new education minister, John Robarts, were getting most of the credit. It would not always be this way with shared-cost programs, but for now the minister could bask in the glow of his success.

John Robarts' personal success turned out to be particularly well timed. It had not been planned that way, but there was no harm at all done to the minister when it happened that the announcement of the Robarts Plan coincided with the start of the contest to succeed Leslie Frost as leader of the Progressive Conservatives and Prime Minister of Ontario.

5

Going for the Leadership

Unless he is defeated or dies in office, a politician's resignation is only a matter of timing. Enjoying good health and continued personal popularity, Leslie Frost might have stayed on as premier well into the 1960s. Even his closest associates were not sure of his intentions about retirement as the decade began.

The most important factor influencing Frost's decision to leave was probably the thinning of the ranks of his closest advisers, the men of his generation who had been at his side through the political wars. When Colonel Young died in 1958 he was succeeded, not particularly effectively, by men who were Frost's juniors by at least a generation. The death of Alex McKenzie in May 1960 left a particular void, for Frost and McKenzie had enjoyed the closest political and personal rapport. The combined efforts of Elmer Bell, Harold Robbins, and Hugh Latimer (the head of the party's staff) were only barely adequate to replace McKenzie. The next spring, in April 1961, Frost lost another friend and adviser and important fundraiser when E.W. Bickle died. The only members of Frost's original group left with him were W.M. McIntyre and George Gathercole, neither of whom was in a directly political office. Increasingly Frost had to fall back for political advice on a group of old Conservative friends outside of Queen's Park who had worked together since the 1930s. It included Harry Price, who took over from E. Bickle as PC party treasurer; Fred Gardiner, the chairman of Metropolitan Toronto; and Oakley Dalgleish, the editor of the Toronto *Globe and Mail*.

The overall political climate did not improve after the 1959 election victory. Frost's cabinet of the fifties had been eroded by the highways difficulties and the NONG scandal and had to be shored up with younger men. The government faced continued scandal-hunting, culminating in sensational (and never-proven) charges by Liberal MPP Elmer Sopha in May 1961 of links between organized crime and a member of the Conservative cabinet in Ontario. Nationally the economic recession had deepened and showed no signs of abating. A strike at the Royal York Hotel, Leslie Frost's Toronto home, caused personal difficulties for the premier when he felt he had to refuse to cross the picket line. He had just introduced the sales tax to

Ontario – it was begun at 3 per cent – and had to worry about five by-elections that should be held soon. Finally, the premier may have been influenced by the reflection that it would be best for the party if the leadership change could be engineered before the situation deteriorated further.

Frost began teasing the media about his retirement, beginning with a speech in Kingston at a ceremony to honour Sir John A. Macdonald in which he reflected on the importance of knowing when to pass the torch of leadership to younger men. When nobody took the bait, he hinted that reporters should reread that speech. Then in late June at a ceremony in Red Rock opening a power station he announced that he was planning to retire.[1] He refused to set the date, however. He saved his announcement for the beginning of August, just when the founding convention of the New Democratic Party was getting a large amount of press coverage. On the eve of the balloting for the election of the first leader of the national NDP, and late enough to make sure the story would break in the next morning's *Globe and Mail,* Elmer Bell held a press conference as president of the Ontario PC Association to announce that the premier of Ontario was resigning. Frost's timing neatly upstaged the NDP convention in the Toronto newspapers of 3 August. In two more weeks, Bell said, the Ontario PC Association executive would set the date for the leadership convention.

The day after the announcement Frost confirmed his plans at the regular meeting of his cabinet and left immediately for a holiday. Preliminary jockeying among the contenders began as soon as they left the room. Bob Macaulay asked John Robarts if he would be running, but Robarts was noncommittal. Shortly afterwards, Macaulay approached James Auld and offered to support him if he chose to run. Auld dismissed the idea. In the meantime, Robarts retreated to Grand Bend for several days to ponder his situation.

From the time of Frost's Red Rock announcement, Robarts had been under pressure from members of his London organization to run, or at least to start cultivating his base in the Western Ontario PC Association. Their regional support was significant. Robarts and his London friends had come a long way in their careers and in the Progressive-Conservative party during the 1950s. Robarts was minister of education for Ontario. Their federal colleague, Ernest Halpenny, was minister without portfolio in John Diefenbaker's government. Fred Jenkins was auditor of the Ontario PC Association. In 1961 Ernie Jackson had become president of the Western Ontario PC Association and a member of the executive of the Ontario PC Association. He had moved up to replace their friend, Elmer Bell, who in 1960 succeeded A.D. McKenzie as president of the Ontario PC Association. Back in London, an ADSEPA member, Ben Baldwin, was prominent in municipal politics, and other members of Robarts' group held senior positions in the London Club, the London Hunt Club, the Chamber of Commerce, the Queen Alexandria Hospital Association, the local Masonic Order, and in their respective professional associations. As its members had advanced and matured, the 'London mafia' had become a force to be reckoned with.

There was not much for Robarts to lose by running for the leadership – he had the energy and stamina and was always attracted by a challenge – and everything to gain if he could get it. But he was not at all sure of his chances, for he was still largely unknown to the Ontario voters. The announcement of the Robarts Plan, and all the favourable publicity it generated, was still several weeks away and could not be a factor in Robarts' decision.

Everyone thought the front-runner for Frost's job was Attorney General A. Kelso Roberts. The sixty-three-year-old Roberts was a member of the victorious Tory caucus of 1943, had contested the leadership in 1949, and served in Frost's cabinet for the duration. Over the years the Toronto lawyer had built up an extensive web of personal and political contacts with PCs across the province, sometimes doing personal favours, sometimes using patronage, always keeping in touch with the executive of riding associations.

Elmer Bell related a typical incident. In 1955 the town of Grand Bend was becoming a popular playground for young people on weekends during the summer. The local detachment of the Ontario Provincial Police was incapable of maintaining the peace, and local residents petitioned the province for more police resources, but with no success. Finally, a local delegation asked Elmer Bell, a well-known local Conservative, to accompany them to Toronto where they had an appointment with the deputy attorney general. An hour after the appointment, they were still in the waiting room when Attorney General A. Kelso Roberts walked through on his way back from lunch. He vaguely recognized Bell, greeted him and asked about the group. Bell explained their concern, and Roberts immediately acceded to their request. That summer the detachment was bolstered by police seconded from other detachments. The action was typical. Roberts maintained contact with such delegations and built a huge store of political goodwill.

In Toronto, on the other hand, he worked on his own. Living in the city, he did not attend the backbench events of Robarts and his friends, nor did he accept their invitations to participate. He was a full generation older than .the young backbenchers and shared few ties with them. He rode his bicycle down Avenue Road to work early, and he often worked late. As attorney general he remained somewhat distant from the cut-and-thrust of politics. The goodwill Roberts held across Ontario was not reflected in the assembly. He was not disliked; he simply was not part of the crowd. His isolation was not a reflection of his age. Dunnville's James Allan was older, but he had great rapport with his young colleagues. Robarts remembered, for example, how Kelso Roberts once asked him for a list of the London executive just before making a trip to that city. Suspecting Roberts' motives, Robarts found a polite way of not providing the list. James Auld had a similar experience, but gave Roberts his list and then found that three members of his local executive eventually supported Roberts for the leadership despite Auld's own support for Robarts. In short, Kelso Roberts was a wily, old-time politician, with many IOUs to be cashed. His predicament was that he might well find himself a lonely front-runner in a long race.

Among the younger contenders, Robarts and Macaulay had been particularly close personally. Unfortunately for Robarts, Macaulay indicated almost immediately his intention of running, to no one's surprise. From the beginning he drew potential support away from Robarts. Having offered to support Auld, for example, Macaulay then asked Auld for his support. Since Robarts had yet to make up his mind about running, Auld agreed.

By 6 August Robarts had decided to go for the leadership, arguing that once he had decided to make politics his career, he might as well seek the top job when it was available. Robarts refused to accept that it would change his life. The only question was whether he could acquit himself well. Norah supported her husband's decision, not with the excitement of 1951 but with acceptance. Education already kept him in Toronto all week. With the family consultation during the weekend at Grand Bend over, Robarts walked to Ernie Jackson's neighbouring cottage to lay plans for the campaign. With the London organization, Robarts thought, they had at least a firm base for their efforts. Jackson liked the thought of the challenge, and agreed to head the campaign. Robarts would be free to spend most of his time trying to recruit supporters.

Robarts and Jackson made two significant decisions that afternoon. First, the campaign would focus exclusively on wooing delegates and editors of local newspapers. Second, they would spend the first six weeks introducing Robarts to the press and attempting to line up support from MPPs and MPs. Then, after the delegates had been selected, they would tour the constituencies, moving westward from the Ottawa River and finishing at the Manitoba border in the last week.

After talking with Jackson, Robarts phoned James Auld and asked him to be his campaign chairman in eastern Ontario. Auld found himself in a delicate situation, having already pledged his support to Macaulay. He phoned Macaulay and extricated himself from his commitment, but at the same time declined his friend's offer, instead limiting his work on behalf of Robarts to the Brockville area. Auld's problem was fairly common in the campaign, as candidates who were themselves close friends competed for support among mutual friends. Robarts recalled that friendship between the contestants occasionally softened the conflict, but that there was a feeling of being abandoned when a good friend would declare support for someone else. It was going to be an unusually open race among strong candidates, and the party would be fortunate to come out of it without serious internal strains.

In a meeting at his home on 13 August, Robarts revealed his plans to the key people in the London organization, and Jackson outlined their campaign strategy. Jackson's plan was endorsed, and responsibilities were divided up under his leadership. John White would be in charge of the convention floor; David Weldon, the son of Colonel Douglas Weldon, would co-ordinate delegate contact during the convention; Fred Jenkins would handle hospitality suites and accommodation; and Ab Shepherd, a prominent London lawyer and Jenkins' brother-in-law, agreed to look after the fundraising. As the meeting broke up, Robarts pulled David Weldon aside and asked him, 'Do you think I'm crazy?' Caught up in the enthusiasm, Weldon said, 'Of course not.' Later he was struck by the realization that this was something more than another political lark. It was a tremendous undertaking for the handful of Londoners to be trying to make John Robarts prime minister of Ontario.

The Ontario PC Association executive held a kind of mini-convention in Toronto on 17 August, when Frost's resignation was accepted and arrangements made for a leadership convention in Toronto from 23 to 25 October. Seven hundred delegates from riding associations across the province were there that day to ratify the executive's decision. So were most of the likely leadership candidates, though none had yet publicly declared. All the delegates were invited to a special party Kelso Roberts' friends threw to celebrate his sixth anniversary as attorney general. John Robarts held a reception for friends from London and across the province. The *Globe and Mail* was able to identify all the candidates plus at least one other hopeful in its coverage of the day's activities. Immediately after the mini-convention, Robert Macaulay announced his candidacy, closely followed by the popular and forthright minister of health, Matthew Dymond, who had just overseen the implementation of hospital insurance in the province. On Monday, 21 August, John P. Robarts announced that he too was seeking the leadership. Being good friends, Macaulay and Robarts agreed that if one of them won, the other would help see through the transition of power, so that the new regime would be securely launched before the loser retired. Ernie Jackson resigned as president of the Western Ontario PC Association to become Robarts' campaign manager.

The Robarts campaign would draw on the London base for manpower and money. Robarts and a couple of advance men would be at large in the province meeting delegates. As well, there would be other teams of Robarts' supporters canvassing delegates in a more specialized way. Two MPPs from constituencies north of London, William Stewart and Charles MacNaughton, did good work touring rural Ontario to court delegates, getting themselves dubbed 'the Bobbsey twins' as they made their rounds. Other Robarts people concentrated on delegates in the legal, financial, and medical communities.

By far the most important development in his early campaign came a week after it began, when the Robarts Plan was unveiled at Queen's Park. The Ontario press was full of reports of support for the plan from educational leaders across the province. The little-known leadership candidate became overnight an innovative, active minister of education, obviously a major figure in the cabinet. Ironically, neither Robarts nor his supporters had foreseen the impact the Robarts Plan would have in boosting his fortunes. Frost himself was not actively supporting Robarts, so presumably the timing of the announcement was not one of his sly signals.

Macaulay and Kelso Roberts hit the campaign trail early. Roberts called in political debts and obtained several early endorsements from delegates, particularly in Toronto and the north. Macaulay won extensive press coverage for a set of policy proposals on the theme of building a new Ontario. Robarts began to find his campaign losing steam as press coverage of his Plan faded. Through mid-September he had little to show for his campaigning except endorsements from the Wingham *Advance* and a past president of the Young Progressive-Conservatives. Concerned about the situation, Robarts approached Bill Kinmond, who was helping him with his speeches, and asked why he was not being provided with material on something other than the Robarts Plan. Kinmond, who had recently returned from China and represented the Toronto *Star* in the press gallery, responded in his usual direct manner that he would provide other material if he could, but the Robarts Plan was all Robarts had done.

On 25 September James Allan, a dairyman from Dunnville who had joined the cabinet in 1955 as minister of highways, entered the race. Allan was an energetic, rural spokesman who had been the only person to contest the presidency of the party since A.D. McKenzie assumed office. Encouraged by friends, and anxious that government recognize the rural base of Ontario, he was talked into seeking the leadership. The lateness of his decision caused him serious problems, for many of his friends were already in other camps. He tried to recruit Stewart and MacNaughton, for example, but they would not change horses in mid-stream. This was the first of several conflicts over support between Robarts and Allan, who were both after delegates from rural southwestern Ontario. Despite his handicaps, Allan managed to get the endorsement of two cabinet ministers, Fred Cass and Ray Connell, and was thought by some observers to have moved quickly into a first-place struggle with Roberts. Macaulay was judged to be next, Robarts a fading fourth.

The dim view of Robarts' prospects was apparently based on the comparative lack of success of his first major campaign appearance, in Ottawa on 2 September. Both Robarts and Macaulay were in the city about the same time. Macaulay attracted three hundred people, including eight MPPs and seven MPs, some of them from southwestern Ontario, to a public meeting where he pushed his policy proposals. Robarts held only an informal reception, co-hosted by Harry White and William Thomas, the MP for Middlesex (Ernest Halpenny would have been a host, but Diefenbaker would not let one of his ministers perform this function for fear of implying a lack of neutrality in the Ontario race). Twenty-four members of parliament turned out to look Robarts over. On the surface he did not seem to be doing as well as Macaulay, but in fact his tactics were deliberate, and the Ottawa visit also included careful courting of the local editors, with special attention to Grattan O'Leary, the veteran head of the *Ottawa Journal*.

Within a few days of the Ottawa visit, newspapermen were finding once more that Robarts had quite substantial strength. 'John Robarts has remained at short odds throughout the contest,' a *Globe and Mail* writer noted. 'Why is everyone talking Robarts – I mean what's he been doing?'[2] In fact, Robarts and Jackson had been working effectively in their low-key personal campaign within the party. The strategy paid off again during the first week in October when Robarts was endorsed by three cabinet ministers, Ken Warrender, Allan Grossman, and William Nickle. Then another break occurred when Queen's University announced that it would give Robarts an honorary degree at its fall convocation, which was being held on 20 October. It was nice to be scheduled to give a convocation address at a prestigious university on the Friday before the leadership convention.

Robarts' tour reached southwestern Ontario on 9 October. William Stewart held a reception for him at his farm near Granton. Over a hundred delegates, including MPS and MPPS, came out to endorse his bid for the leadership. On the 13th Stewart, who had been working privately for weeks, became the fourth minister to endorse Robarts publicly. Four days later Robarts was seen to have won another battle for the rural vote when the minister of agriculture, William Goodfellow, not only endorsed him but agreed to nominate him at the convention.

Robarts did not articulate a set of policy proposals similar to Macaulay's, but was content to identify his campaign and his style with the existing regime. Much of the attention he got in the press during October came from comment on the Robarts Plan generated through his appearances and speeches at school openings. When his tour wound up at Fort Frances on 18 October, the *Globe and Mail* was predicting a photo finish between himself and Macaulay. It was significant that he led in the race for cabinet support, with five endorsations to Allan's four, and only one each for Macaulay and Kelso Roberts.

Support at the delegate level was harder to calculate, but two sub-contests had emerged as the campaign developed. Robarts and Allan were competing for delegates, both rural and urban, in eastern and southwestern Ontario. Macaulay and Roberts vied for the vote in Toronto and the north. The visibility of both Roberts and Macaulay in Toronto, combined with Toronto's propensity to equate itself with Ontario, led many from that city, including candidates and workers, to believe that the winner would be either Macaulay or Roberts. Of course all the candidates were trying to find support everywhere in the province. In Toronto, Robarts and a young lawyer friend of his, Richard Rohmer, called at the home of every delegate to solicit support. They did not have much success.

The party's old guard had been watching the campaign with interest. Leslie Frost thought Macaulay, whom he had known and liked since childhood, would probably win. Others of the older and more conservative group in the party were less impressed with Macaulay's impatience to get to the top and the flamboyant forwardness of his style. Harry Price, for one, did not feel the bias toward Macaulay that Frost, Fred Gardiner, and Oakley Dalgleish seemed to share. During a September discussion by the four party barons, Price put forward Robarts' name as a better choice, arguing that the minister of education was open to the views of others, was stable, and was not likely to bankrupt the province with wild spending schemes.[3]

Allan's entry into the race, and his obvious strength, prompted Robarts to make an unusual approach to the old guard. He phoned Price, asked to see him on an urgent matter, and arranged a breakfast meeting at the Benvenuto Apartments. There they had a rambling general discussion of the campaign. As Robarts was about to leave, Price asked him what he wanted. Robarts said that if Frost and the old guard wanted Allan to be premier, he would throw his support to Allan and nominate him at the convention. Price told Robarts to keep up the good work in his own campaign – a clear enough hint which sent the Londoner away happy.

By this time Price had decided to back Robarts. He asked James McConnell, a public relations man he knew in Toronto, to estimate the delegate strength of the candidates. McConnell's report suggested that Kelso Roberts was well out in front. This news disconcerted the group around Frost, who considered Roberts inflexible and too easy to bait in the legislature. With the same survey showing that party reaction to Macaulay was sharply divided, the old guard began to move in the direction Price wanted, toward Robarts.

A week before the convention Fred Gardiner called a number of Conservative lawyers across the province, and came away with the same impressions McConnell had reported.[4] During his years as attorney general, Kelso Roberts had built considerable support within the legal community. Now Gardiner, who was himself a leading member of the bar, began using his considerable influence to drum up lawyer support for Robarts. At the same time Harry Price was encouraging Toronto businessmen to take a look at Robarts. These efforts by powerful established Conservatives were independent of the Jackson/Robarts campaign, and were unknown to the Londoners.

Jackson had found the campaign developing about as planned. Because of the emphasis on direct contact with delegates it was considerably less expensive than Macaulay's or Robarts'. This was just as well, for money was scarce.[5] The London community had been supportive, but Shepherd was not having much luck in Toronto. Then, during the week before the convention, a surprising change occurred. The fundraisers began being *offered* donations. According to Jenkins, liquor for the hospitality suites was provided 'by the carload.' Robarts' people thought the new support reflected a realization by the business community that he just might win. It may also have reflected, if not the 'touch of Frost' Robarts and his friends were starting to talk about, at least a pat on the back from Price.

The campaign heated up in the last days, with the candidates turning their attention to finding second-ballot support, and the media hanging on the uncommitteds' every remark, looking for signs of endorsements. Privately Kelso Roberts was trying to get Macaulay, the other candidate from Toronto, to support him. George Wardrope, the minister of reform institutions, who was running himself but largely as a 'favourite son' of northern Ontario, introduced Robarts at a ceremony opening the Lakehead Teachers' College in such glowing terms that some observers interpreted it as an endorsement.[6] And what was Premier Frost saying in that 19 October speech to the Empire Club in Toronto when he urged *young* men to enter politics 'because your country needs you,' and claimed that education was the key to the future? Certainly the competition between the two young candidates was beginning to become strenuous, with Macaulay feeling the weight of Robarts' cabinet endorsements and muttering that while others could publish their lists of Indian chiefs he had the Indians.[7] Neither of them had an endorsement from the retiring big chief, but there is little doubt that Frost wanted one or the other of them to succeed him; he did not support Kelso Roberts.

The Queen's University convocation was an excellent non-partisan platform for Robarts at the end of the campaign. In his speech he harked back to the principles that had led his friends in London to form ADSEPA, championed the right of free speech, and challenged the students and the academic community to confront the government when they felt it was wrong. He was preaching an attractive and not particularly controversial credo of openness and individual responsibility in a free society, and doing so in a forum that set him a little above and outside the tumult of his competitors' campaigns.

The convention opened in the University of Toronto's Varsity Arena on Monday, 23 October 1961. It would last for three days. Frost was to give his farewell address the first night. On Tuesday afternoon Prime Minister Diefenbaker would address the faithful, and his speech would be followed by the nominations of the candidates. Tuesday evening each candidate would address the convention, with a five-minute demonstration permitted after each speech. Voting would begin on Wednesday afternoon. There would be no winner until someone received more than 50 per cent of the votes cast. After an indecisive ballot the candidate with the fewest votes would be dropped, and delegates would prepare to vote again.

The Robarts organization had made two important decisions governing its approach to the convention. David Weldon and Fred Jenkins had agreed that the campaigning at the convention would be entirely positive. Their workers would talk up the merits of John Robarts, not run down any of the other candidates. They were to be polite and respectful of delegates throughout the convention, aiming for second- or later-ballot support from the clearly committed. Although there was to be the usual hoopla, the approach would be fairly low key.

Second, the Robarts demonstration was planned to avoid excess. The planners, John White, Ward Cornell, and Bill Rudd, worked from the model of the U.S. Democratic Party convention that had nominated John F. Kennedy in 1960. They managed to write a Robarts campaign song (to the tune of 'Daisy, Daisy, give me your answer do'), designed a uniform for his demonstrators, organized a one-hundred-person cheering section, and developed such publicity gimmicks as fans inscribed 'I'm a fan of John Robarts.' Back-up work on such details as a convention newspaper was being done by a hired public relations firm. At a review of the committee's work on 7 October, Robarts, Jackson, and White agreed that their demonstration could not hope to compete with those likely to be put on by Roberts or Macaulay, who would have access to their Toronto constituents to pack the floor. It would be just as well to keep it manageable anyway, for fear of offending the sensibilities of the many conservative Conservatives who would be in the crowd.

Fred Jenkins moved to Toronto a week before the convention to organize the hospitality suites and accommodation. On Saturday the 21st the London Conservatives arrived en masse. That night they were briefed on their duties. There were to be the usual Robarts rules of official decorum – nobody on duty at a hospitality suite was to drink, for example – but of course good spirits were encouraged. Oriental Band members had a whole wing of rooms in one of the downtown hotels, and their flutists were commonly in action at breakfasts. The Londoners were in Toronto to have a good time while they put their leader over the top.

As delegates began to arrive on Sunday, Robarts people were in the hotels to greet them and bring their lists up to date. Jackson had decided to move Robarts' headquarters from the Westbury to the Park Plaza, which was just across Bloor Street from Varsity Arena. Halpenny and Jenkins ran the hospitality suite there. A careful if crowded itinerary had been drawn up for John and Norah; Robarts thought that the 'free time' he was allowed just might enable him to catch an occasional meal during the convention.

Robarts' official entry to Toronto was set for four o'clock on Sunday afternoon at Union Station, coinciding with the arrival of trains bringing delegates from both eastern and western Ontario. It was a completely staged event, for Robarts had driven to Toronto earlier in the day. He slipped into Union Station by a side door, and came into the foyer from the train exits just as the train arrived from London.[8] A group of supporters led by young Larry Grossman (whose father was one of Robarts' few Toronto endorsers) broke into the campaign song. A pretty girl pinned a campaign button on Robarts' lapel. A *Globe and Mail* photographer, who had been alerted by Bill Kinmond, Robarts' media lieutenant, snapped a picture. The timing was perfect: as arriving delegates swarmed through Union Station, John Robarts' band played, and his workers handed out literature. No other candidates were on hand. Monday's *Globe and Mail* had a big front-page picture of the arrival, for all the delegates to see and ponder. (The *Globe* itself was editorially supporting youth, with an apparent preference for Macaulay over Robarts.)

Robarts went to his suite at the Westbury, then attended an organization meeting at the Park Plaza early on Monday morning, before going over to Varsity Arena to join the other candidates who were welcoming registering delegates. It was a cold, snowy morning, and the crowds were small. Later in the day Robarts toured his hospitality suites in the various hotels and attended a reception for the Young

Progressive-Conservatives. Norah had her own schedule, visited women's association meetings and met her husband when their schedules overlapped at major events. His campaign workers found they had latched on to a useful gimmick that day, when it turned out that their Polaroid camera was something of a novelty. A delegate could have his picture taken meeting John Robarts and take it home as a souvenir of the convention. Delegates lined up to have their pictures taken.

Leslie Frost's valedictory speech that evening gave no hint of an endorsement. Most commentators on the convention thought the race was close and might take a full six ballots to be decided. Generally, the Toronto candidates and their organizers seemed to be in the ascendant, and both Macaulay and Roberts were confident of victory.[9] Robarts and David Weldon estimated that about three hundred of the approximately seventeen hundred delegates would vote their way on the first ballot – certainly not enough to be in the lead, but likely to be a respectable enough showing. They expected to gain substantially on the second and later ballots.

The nomination of the candidates began after Diefenbaker's speech on Tuesday. As expected, seven members of the Conservative caucus were nominated: Rev. A.W. Downer, the former Speaker; George Wardrope, minister of reform institutions; Matthew Dymond, minister of health; James Allan, provincial treasurer; Robert Macaulay, minister of energy resources; A. Kelso Roberts, attorney general; and John P. Robarts, minister of education. The nomination process was routine until Macaulay's name was put forward, when his followers broke the rules with an enthusiastic demonstration. Chairman Elmer Bell gently rebuked the Macaulay group. There were no other demonstrations. The press thought the loudest applause was for Kelso Roberts and James Allan.[10]

The candidates were to begin their speeches, followed by demonstrations, at 8.00 that evening. By 8.05 all the candidates and their wives had gathered at the entrance to the arena floor – all but John Robarts. Macaulay urged that the proceedings begin, and all the candidates – except John Robarts – took their places on the stage. In Robarts' place there was an empty chair. He arrived several minutes late, having been in his room at the Westbury going over his speech before what he thought was an 8.30 entrance time.

The candidates spoke in alphabetical order. James Allan's large and agrarian demonstration included a big black cow. Up on the platform Kelso Roberts carried signs on his trousers of having been too close to the cow on the way into the auditorium.[11] He was followed by Downer and Dymond, neither of whom were major candidates. Bob Macaulay gave a vigorous, fiery speech, based on his twenty-five point program. Yellow-hatted Macaulayites flooded the floor in a noisy demonstration that went on too long and had to be stopped by Chairman Bell.

Robarts' speech appeared to be a sober, responsible contrast to Macaulay's, or a dull, unimaginative presentation, depending on one's viewpoint; he adhered to what had now become a Robarts slogan, 'A Touch of Frost,' paid tribute to the retiring premier, and promised to do his best if elected leader. The most impressive part was his control of his demonstration. As the Robarts people pranced around the floor, waving signs in both English and French, singing their campaign song, Richard Rohmer sat in a front seat timing them. As the five-minute mark approached. he signalled Robarts, who was standing at the front of the stage. Robarts raised his arms like an orchestra leader. Jack Leighton, leading the demonstration, blew a whistle and the Robarts crowd cleared the floor. Discipline, control, a return to order – a fine symbolic contrast to the Macaulay display. The delegates broke into spontaneous applause.

Kelso Roberts followed with what the Toronto *Telegram*, which was enthusiastically supporting him, described as 'one of the most fighting, knock-down-drag-out speeches of his career ... He was the only candidate to come right out and predict victory for himself.' His demonstration was also raucous, and again Bell had to intercede to get the demonstrators off the floor. Fed up by now with the pseudo-glitz of the demonstrations, the delegates were glad to see them go. After George Wardrope's presentation, the evening was over. Robarts and friends carried on in the Park Plaza hospitality suite well into the morning.

The Toronto candidates and their organizers were still confident on Wednesday morning as the delegates registered and had their credentials checked prior to the voting. Fred Jenkins, who was serving as Robarts' man on the credential committee, got into a row with the Toronto-based people over the timing of the accreditation process. 'They didn't believe anyone from outside Toronto was serious about the thing,' he recalled. Voter registration finally closed at 1 PM, half an hour before the voting was to begin.

The Robarts organization marshalled its resources for the final act. The Park Plaza had become the organizational centre; a telephone-equipped trailer just outside the arena served as on-site headquarters. Delegate contact crews had been organized for work in the arena. The Londoners gave themselves a useful head-start on other candidates when Jenkins, who was to serve as Robarts' scrutineer in the room where the ballots were counted, noticed that the transom over its door was kept open. There was a pay phone in the corridor just outside. After each ballot was counted, Jenkins wrote the results on a piece of paper and, while the others were checking the figures, sidled over to the door, crumpled up the paper and tossed it through the transom. Shepherd was outside pretending to use the phone. He picked up Jenkins' pieces of paper and phoned the results of each ballot to Weldon in the trailer. The information was relayed to the floor workers, who became the first to swoop down upon the supporters of the eliminated candidate.

The results of the first ballot were known on the floor by 2.50 and announced from the stage at 3.05. They were:

Roberts	352
Robarts	345
Macaulay	339
Allan	332
Downer	149
Dymond	138
Wardrope	45

The four leading candidates were remarkably close. In his memoirs Kelso Roberts admitted that the margin of his lead was considerably less than he expected, and he began to sense the spectre of defeat. Some of Robarts' supporters, including Harry Price, were surprised at his strength. They saw a clear prospect of victory for a candidate sitting only seven votes behind the leader.

George Wardrope, who was now eliminated, had been friendly toward Robarts during the campaign, and it was thought that many of his northern Ontario supporters accepted Robarts as a second choice. On the second ballot John Robarts moved into the lead, having gained more support than Roberts and Macaulay combined:

Robarts	423
Roberts	385
Macaulay	363
Allan	324
Downer	104
Dymond	93

Everyone turned to Matthew Dymond's delegates. His supporters split between the two leading non-Toronto candidates, Robarts and Allan, with Robarts again making the largest gains on the third ballot:

Robarts	498
Roberts	380
Macaulay	372
Allan	344
Downer	93

Downer was eliminated, leaving the four principals to fight it out. 'I have the feeling I am the last person in the arena to know the results,' the chairman said in announcing the results of the fourth ballot. It was clear on the next ballot that the freed delegates were now moving towards Kelso Roberts rather than Macaulay, and John Robarts rather than Allan:

Robarts	533
Roberts	419
Macaulay	377
Allan	336

Despite their competition for delegates, Robarts had maintained close ties with Jim Allan throughout the campaign, as a fellow non-Torontonian, as an old friend, and as part of his courting of the old guard. Now he profited immensely from their relationship, garnering the vast majority of Allan's delegates on the fifth ballot, and becoming almost unstoppable:

Robarts	746
Roberts	479
Macaulay	438

The last chance to defeat John Robarts was for the Roberts and Macaulay delegates to combine against him. Roberts had made repeated approaches to Macaulay during the campaign and the convention, and many Toronto Tories felt there was a natural regional alliance between the two.[12] During the fifth ballot there had been rumours of a Roberts-Macaulay pact. Proponents of a Toronto-versus-the-hinterland strategy did not take into account other factors affecting political loyalties such as ties of youth and friendship.

When the results of the fifth ballot were announced, just before 7 PM, Robert Macaulay got up from his seat and started toward an exit. Then he changed directions and made his way to where John Robarts was sitting in the stands. Robarts stood to greet him; Macaulay took Robarts' button from his lapel and pinned it on his own.

To Kelso Roberts' supporters it was a betrayal and the end of their man's chances. Macaulay did not in fact carry all his delegates into Robarts' camp; a substantial minority moved to Roberts, but the attorney general had needed a huge majority of Macaulay's people and in the final ballot he did not come close. Robarts received 976 votes against Roberts' 633.

John and Norah Robarts had spent the last six hours with their family in the stands, conferring occasionally with Jackson and others, but mostly watching and waiting. John had consumed one hot dog and a lot of nervous energy. Elmer Bell, his Exeter associate who had encouraged him to run for the Ontario legislature ten years before, took the podium and announced that John Robarts was the new leader of the Progressive-Conservative party in Ontario. As fate would have it, the announcement was made quickly and just at the moment Norah, who had been present throughout, was taking a break. After a few anxious moments, she was found and John and Norah made their way to the stage where a beaming Leslie Frost raised John's hand in the traditional victory gesture. Kelso Roberts came on stage to move that the vote be made unanimous. Robert Macaulay seconded the motion, to a few jeers from some of their defeated followers. Robarts made a short victory speech that was at once subdued and yet characteristically confident in his pledge to begin the next day to give Ontario 'the finest administration it ever had.'

John Robarts won the 1961 leadership convention for several reasons. From beginning to end, his London organization had run an effective, imaginative, but controlled campaign, adding to Robarts' support without alienating anyone. Without the fortuitous publicity and success of the Robarts Plan, the minister of education probably could never have overcome his relative obscurity. Without the support of Harry Price and other members of Frost's generation – which his campaign did not know he had – he could not have beaten Macaulay. He was given that support partly because the old guard were still determined to keep Kelso Roberts out of the premier's office. But he got it also because of his particular blend of personal qualities. He had been a quiet, mediating, conservative politician, who could move easily in a wide range of circles – generational, regional, ideological. John Robarts seemed safe and competent. Sometimes the mixed metaphor is best: Robarts could carry the torch without rocking the boat. Finally, it had helped him considerably to come from a prosperous, growing urban community that was in the heartland of the province but was not Toronto.

By the time Robarts had finished greeting all the well-wishers on the stage at Varsity Arena, the audience had disappeared. He had to go on to the King Edward Hotel for a press conference. Now he began to feel the exhaustion. Norah took the family back to the Westbury where a small private party was held in their suite. The Robarts organizers had not thought to prepare for any general victory celebration. Kelso Roberts' group had, and many delegates travelled across Bloor Street to enjoy the reception at the Park Plaza. John White and his workers had their party in the Robarts hospitality suite at the Royal York. Late that evening after his press conference, when the prime minister-designate finally returned to the Westbury Hotel, he was pleased to find that Norah had arranged to have a hot meal waiting for him accompanied by six bottles of champagne.

PART TWO: RUNNING A SMOOTH SHIP

6

The Robarts Style

On the morning after his victory, John Robarts emerged from the Westbury Hotel, chatted briefly with waiting reporters, was driven over to Queen's Park where he met more reporters, and then went into the prime minister's office to see Leslie Frost. Frost summoned his staff to meet his successor, then convened the regular cabinet meeting. The agenda was routine. When Frost and Robarts met the press afterwards, Frost did almost all of the talking, consulting with Robarts only about the date the legislature would reconvene. Robarts encouraged the premier to emphasize that the government would go on as usual and the House would meet as planned on 22 November. Robarts was hoping to make the transition in leadership such a smooth process that the Conservative government would hardly be seen to be breaking stride. After the morning's activities, he and Norah returned to London for more celebrations and then left for a few days' recuperation in Grand Bend.

Frost remained premier while Robarts pondered his cabinet selections. As part of the transitional housekeeping, Frost offered to have his cabinet begin the background preparation for the Speech from the Throne, due in less than a month. Robarts readily agreed; then his cabinet would only have to review the proposals and hammer them into final form.

Robarts intended to slip into the role of premier without disrupting his personal life. He and Norah continued to make their home in London, with John commuting back and forth. His Toronto base remained the Westbury. He was acutely aware of his position in history as one of a series of Conservative prime ministers. He would serve for his time and if all went well would pass the torch on to a successor. In the meantime, he knew he was finished practising law for at least the duration of his leadership, but was still concerned about his financial security. He approached Harry Price to discuss the situation. Price had extensive experience with the financial affairs of other politicians, and arranged to raise a fund to give the prime minister the necessary security. It was a traditional Canadian practice, done for Frost, Louis St Laurent, and Lester Pearson in Robarts' time and many earlier provincial and federal politicians. Robarts never knew the names of the donors.[1] Their assistance provided him with a new winterized cottage at Grand Bend, so that the family could retreat from London throughout the year, and also enough additional resources to free him full time for politics and government.

As a cabinet-maker, Robarts faced the usual Canadian constraints: the need for regional, religious, ethnic, and professional diversity. Added to these were new calculations caused by the leadership campaign: Robarts should reward some of his supporters without being seen to be vindictively punishing any of his opponents. The only person he asked for advice on his cabinet was Frost.

Before fitting names to jobs, Robarts decided that the major issues facing his government would be economic development, unemployment, reorganization of the Department of Municipal Affairs, and reform of provincial liquor legislation. He hoped to fit good names to these jobs. But the runner-up for the leadership, Kelso Roberts, would first have to be allowed to pretty well write his own ticket. When Robarts phoned Roberts to discuss the situation, there was no answer. Roberts' office told Robarts that the attorney general had 'gone south' without leaving a forwarding address. The astonished premier-designate finally called John Bassett, publisher of the Toronto *Telegram,* the one man in Ontario who could tell him where Roberts had gone to lick his wounds. When Robarts finally got through, Roberts set three conditions for continuing to serve: that he remain attorney general, that he be sworn in immediately after Robarts, and that he sit on Robarts' immediate left at the cabinet table. Somewhat bemused, Robarts agreed.[2]

The strengths of Bob Macaulay and James Allan were a useful contrast. Macaulay's energies and ideas could be unleashed on one of the most pressing issues facing the government by making him the minister responsible for commerce and development (which became the Department of Economics and Development). He asked to keep Energy and Resources as well, which was fine with Robarts. By continuing in his position as treasurer, James Allan kept a firm hand on the purse strings. Macaulay would have to get his ideas past Allan before they could be financed.

The rest of the cabinet-making consisted of minor shuffling, as some of Robarts' supporters got additional responsibilities and several ministers who planned to retire before the next election obligingly moved aside. Fred Cass moved from reorganizing the troubled Department of Highways to tackle the problems of Municipal Affairs. Allan Grossman would remain a minister without portfolio, but undertook the liquor review. William Stewart became minister of agriculture, as William Goodfellow agreed to mark time in Highways until retirement. George Wardrope moved into Mines, which had been vacant since the death of James Maloney. Charles 'Ted' Daley, who was on the verge of retirement, finally gave up Labour to Ken Warrender. Two new members were added to the cabinet in minor positions: Charles S. MacNaughton from rural southwestern Ontario, and W. Irwin Haskett from urban eastern Ontario. It was a mark of how uncomplicated the governing of Ontario still was in 1961 (and how much useful publicity the Robarts Plan was still generating) that the prime minister continued to serve as minister of education.*

Robarts reviewed his cabinet selections with Macaulay and then Allan. Macaulay was surprised at how modest the changes had been and commented·that he would have preferred to shuffle the entire cabinet, 'if only for purposes of bringing new ideas to each department.' 'This was the very essence of the difference between Mr. Robarts and me,' he reflected some years later, 'and was of the essence ... of why the party had selected Mr. Robarts and not me. The party did not want change for the sake of change; it wanted to evolve and build gradually.'[3]

Robarts completed the details of the cabinet reorganization during the first few days of November 1961. On Wednesday afternoon, 8 November, Leslie Frost met Lieutenant-Governor J. Keiller Mackay in the music room of the vice-regal suite at Queen's Park, presented the resignations of his cabinet, resigned himself, and then recommended that John P. Robarts be sworn in as his successor. The lieutenant-governor asked Robarts to accept the prime ministership. Robarts agreed and was sworn in by J.J. Young, clerk of the Executive Council. Robarts then introduced the members of his cabinet, each of whom was sworn in. The transition ceremony took about an hour. In two weeks the new government would meet the legislature.

Robarts arrived in the prime minister's office to find files piled in stacks, material almost impossible to locate, and a state of general disorganization. Frost had left him with an experienced cabinet, but did not leave the well-oiled government and party machine that Drew had passed on to him. There was still a large gap at the centre, unfilled since the deaths of Young and McKenzie. It was to become even greater some months later when George Gathercole was appointed a vice-chairman of Ontario Hydro to fulfil a promise made by Frost before he retired. Except for W.M. McIntyre, the deputy minister handling the prime minister's office and serving as cabinet secretary, Robarts had a skeletal staff barely adequate for routine administrative functions. One of his first actions was to ask Don Collins, now chairman of the Civil Service Commission, to review the organization of the prime minister's office and improve its capacity to process information. Collins recommended an immediate increase in clerical staff, and then prepared a more extensive reorganization plan that Robarts could implement between sessions.[4]

On 11 November Robarts invited Ernie Jackson, Elmer Bell, and Charles MacNaughton to his Grand Bend cottage for discussions of the state of the political organization they now controlled. Elmer Bell had succeeded McKenzie as president of the Ontario PC Association, but could not spend a great deal of time in Toronto because of his law practice in Exeter. It was agreed that he would limit his

* The personnel and positions held in Robarts' ministries are listed in Appendix A.

activities to the functions of the presidency, while Jackson would be Robarts' unofficial, unpaid political organizer. MacNaughton and Jackson would handle patronage matters, an area Robarts wanted to avoid. Four men would be doing the jobs McKenzie and Frost had handled. Their division of labour had a certain resemblance to that in Robarts' old London organization.

It was also decided to ask Harry Price to stay on as party treasurer. Price had planned to retire with Frost, but had been active enough getting Robarts into the leadership that he felt obliged to help him out, at least through his first general election. Price's know-how, both in Ontario and across the country, was valuable since Robarts, who had not held an economic portfolio, was largely unknown to most of Canada's business and financial community.

As soon as the nucleus of the political organization had been formed, Jackson invited a larger group to meet with him at the Westbury, principally to plan the handling of by-elections for the five vacant seats passed on by Frost. At this meeting MacNaughton, Bell, Jackson, and Price were joined by Hugh Latimer, George Hogan, the president of the Young PC Association, Robarts' long-time friend Eddie Goodman, who had extensive experience at the national and provincial levels of the party, and Eugene Westendorp. This group became the political brains trust that did for Robarts what McKenzie and latterly the Price-Gardiner-Dalgleish triumvirate had done for Frost. Robarts met with them more or less monthly on an informal basis, consulted freely, and gave them direct access. Sometimes they joked about being his 'inner cabinet.' Keen to flex their political muscles early in the new regime, undaunted by an ominous Gallup poll that showed the Conservatives trailing the Liberals, and anxious to get the five by-elections over before there had to be a redistribution on the basis of the new census, they urged Robarts to move quickly to have the writs issued. Before the session convened, Robarts announced that all five by-elections would be held on 18 January 1962.

By mid November, Frost and McIntyre had finished the background work for the Speech from the Throne, and a list of possible policy and legislative initiatives was ready to be reviewed by the new cabinet. The tendency in this dawning of a new regime was for departments to toss quite a few proposals into the hopper and the new ministers to be agreeable, so the final contents of the speech became more of a collage than a coherent plan of legislative action. One of the new initiatives, for example, which was included without any realization of how important it would become in later years, was suggested by Tom Eberlee, Frost's executive officer who had specialized in labour matters. He urged Robarts to consider introducing a provincial human rights code. The idea of consolidating a number of the existing labour and human rights statutes and giving rights a sharper symbolic focus (as John Diefenbaker's government had with its Bill of Rights) had been floating around Queen's Park for several years but had always been set aside at some point in the review procedure. Robarts liked the suggestion and had it put on the list. Generally, the Speech from the Throne contained a wide variety of proposals affecting most of the spectrum of government activities. The new government was satisfied that it had a good plate of business to put before the assembly.

The legislature opened on 22 November 1961, with John P. Robarts in Leslie Frost's old seat. He was flanked on the right by Macaulay and on the left by Kelso Roberts. Frost sat at the extreme left end of the government front bench. Both John Wintermeyer and Donald MacDonald later recalled that they had not quite grasped the fact of Frost's retirement and the end of the era of his personal domination of the legislature until they saw Robarts sitting in his seat. No one knew whether the Londoner was going to be able to fill the shoes of Old Man Ontario.

The session opened amicably enough, with the expected tributes to Frost and with nothing out of the ordinary in the opposition parties' initial criticisms of the Throne Speech. But suddenly, on 29 November, Wintermeyer opened up on the government with blazing guns.

The issue was organized crime in Ontario. In one sense it was a very old concern; ever since the 1870s Ontarians had worried periodically about U.S. 'criminal elements' spilling across the Niagara or Detroit frontiers into the province, either to take refuge or to expand their nefarious operations.[5] During the prohibition era, illegal activities back and forth across the border had been the very essence of organized criminal activity. By the 1950s drinking was legal in Ontario, but most forms of gambling still were not. It was thought that illegal gambling operations, ranging from corner-store bookmaking through full-fledged casinos disguised as social clubs, was a potentially lucrative source of income for criminals and that such crime was bound to be organized and have links across the border.

Several events in the late 1950s and early 1960s helped bring the question to the top of the Ontario political agenda. American politicians from Senator Estes Kefauver to the new attorney general, Robert Kennedy, had raised enormous political interest in Canada as well as the United States with their racket-busting activities. Closer to home, in neighbouring New York State, a commission of investigation had been established in 1958 to find out the facts on organized crime and racketeering. Early in 1961 it had published two reports which apparently revealed widespread illegal gambling through the state; in the border city of Buffalo there was said to be 'wide open' criminal activity, including substantial police corruption. Just prior to these reports, the anti-gambling branch of the Ontario Provincial Police (OPP) had uncovered a case of bribery of an Ontario police officer by gambling club operators.

As concern about the corruption of Ontario by gamblers and other criminals mounted, the attorney general appointed a special committee, chaired by law professor J.D. Morton, to look into the enforcement of gambling laws in Ontario. Kelso Roberts had Morton's completed report at hand as he prepared for the

November 1961 legislative session, and had decided to meet its principal recommendation by bringing in legislation to establish an Ontario Police Commission. Its mission would be both to reform the administration of policing in the province and to carry out ongoing investigations of criminal activities.

Alarm about organized crime was increasing. On 6 November, for example, Commissioner C.W. Harvison of the Royal Canadian Mounted Police told the Canadian Club of Toronto:

The American syndicates are showing an increased interest in Canada and they are moving to take over direct control of some existing criminal organizations and to expand their criminal activities. They are already active in the field of gambling, narcotics and trafficking, counterfeiting, and in the protection rackets. There are some indications and there is some evidence that the syndicates have already started to treat Canada as an area for expansion of their activities.[6]

In the Throne Speech the government announced that it would establish the Police Commission. The next day it tabled the Morton committee's report, some of the language of which went further than Harvison in raising the spectre of a conspiracy against Ontario society. 'There is a grave danger,' Morton concluded, 'if the present illegal gambling operation is permitted to continue, that either domestic or foreign criminal elements will prosper to such an extent as to undermine the very nature of our society.'[7] On 28 November the government brought its Police Commission legislation into the assembly for first reading.

The *Globe and Mail* had assigned Harold Greer, a member of the Queen's Park press gallery, to investigate some of the rumours about crime in Ontario. On advice from its lawyers the paper decided not to print Greer's findings, which seemed to require more substantiation. Greer then took his story to W.M. McIntyre, who also rejected it as being based largely on gossip. Thoroughly upset and suspecting some kind of cover-up, Greer finally went to Liberal leader Wintermeyer and convinced him that it was in the public interest to force the government to get to the bottom of the issue.

Wintermeyer's two-and-a-half-hour speech to the legislature on 29 November was based on Greer's work. Much of the information had come from the notebooks of an OPP constable who had associated with criminals while gathering evidence for the bribery prosecution the year before. Wintermeyer alleged that a substantial amount of illegal gambling was going on in Ontario, that there were links between gambling syndicates in Ontario and the United States, that Ontario law enforcement officers were complicit in gambling operations, and that the provincial government, through the attorney general's department, was protecting certain gambling establishments. Wintermeyer named names, offered to waive his parliamentary immunity against legal proceedings, and insisted that a royal commission be established to investigate the situation.

Taken by surprise, Robarts promised that the government would study Wintermeyer's charges and then respond. There the matter rested until 7 December when John White, speaking largely for himself during the Throne Speech debate, opposed Wintermeyer's demands for a royal commission and described the proposed Ontario Police Commission as the proper investigatory body. He went on to charge that Wintermeyer's 'hollow offer' to waive parliamentary immunity was hypocritical, and in an exchange with the Liberal leader challenged him to 'step out into the corridor and read the speech again.' Carried away with his rhetoric, White charged that another Liberal speaker's 'crime exposé' was 'almost criminally irresponsible,' and concluded by commenting, 'We are used to hearing irresponsible charges from the leader of the CCF and his supporters. We are not used to the same McCarthy-like approach from members of the Liberal party.'[8]

A furious John Wintermeyer grabbed a copy of his notes, stormed out of the chamber, and, standing in the hallway outside the Liberal offices, read the entire two-and-a-half hours of accusations to members of the press gallery. The effect, of course, was to generate a second round of headlines and convince many newspaper readers and editors that there was surely a sound foundation for the charges. Wintermeyer also brought a simmering division within the cabinet to the crisis point.

As attorney general, Kelso Roberts was responsible for law enforcement in the province. His department was creating a new agency, the Ontario Police Commission, with powers to investigate the kinds of issues Wintermeyer was raising. Roberts and several other members of the cabinet had been advising Robarts to ignore Wintermeyer's request for a royal commission and, as White had argued, refer the whole matter to the new Police Commission. The impetuous Robert Macaulay, on the other hand, who was not aware of Roberts' views, advised Robarts immediately that an independent inquiry, such as a royal commission, was the only way of dealing with the charges. He did not believe that an 'independent' Police Commission, a creature of the government, would be adequate. As the tempest developed, Macaulay decided that the issue was so significant, so fundamental to his beliefs about the public service and public life, that he would resign if Robarts did not establish an independent inquiry.[9]

The cabinet had to make up its mind on the morning after White's speech and Wintermeyer's theatrics. Robarts began by announcing that he planned to refer Wintermeyer's accusations to the Police Commission. Macaulay disagreed, Robarts remained firm, other ministers jumped in, and the debate became heated. Macaulay was ready to resign. Neither Kelso Roberts nor Robert Macaulay had much regard for or confidence in one another after the leadership struggle. The cabinet continued to debate after the bells rang to convene the legislature. As the bells kept ringing, rumours of the cabinet division swept Queen's Park. Robarts finally recessed the cabinet, went into the House and, after prayers, announced that the government would 'make its position on the administration of justice clear on Monday.'

The cabinet reconvened later that morning. Senior government officials were summoned to join the discussion, and eventually a compromise evolved. The Police Commission bill would go ahead, and it would come into existence with the duties planned for it, which included investigations of the state of crime in the province. The allegations of wrongdoing made by Wintermeyer, however, would be investigated by a special royal commission. Kelso Roberts agreed to support the compromise, but warned Robarts that he was concerned about the impact the royal commission inquiry might have on individual rights and reminded his leader in passing that there might be a conflict with some of the provisions of their new human rights code.[10]

On 11 December Robarts announced in the legislature that Mr Justice W.D. Roach, a member of the Ontario Court of Appeal and a former Liberal, would head the royal commission. In his speech he used the crisis as evidence of the need for the kind of permanent investigative body proposed in the Police Commission bill.

The appointment of the Roach Commission ended debate in the legislature for the time being. Robarts had handled the issue about as well as he could have. The terms of reference for the commission, which sounded broad, were in fact limited to the substance of Wintermeyer's speech. Despite the balance, Robarts had not been able to avoid being caught in the middle of the Roberts-Macaulay split. He had given Macaulay enough of his way to alienate Roberts, but had been tough enough with Macaulay that, as Macaulay remembered it, the issue had 'torn at the fabric of a very close friendship.' On his part, Macaulay was content enough to stay in the cabinet, but he had alienated many of Roberts' supporters with the insistence on getting his own way or resigning.

On 15 December the legislature adjourned for Christmas. On the 18th, Robarts, Frost, and the staff of the prime minister's office gathered in Robarts' office. The new prime minister removed Frost's picture from the wall and gave it to his predecessor. Command had now changed. During the recess Robarts had the office redecorated with modern business furniture, a change that his executive secretary, Irene Beatty, considered to have lifted the atmosphere through the whole wing. There would be a new, businesslike tone to government in contrast to the homey traditionalism of the Frost years.

There would also be a new relationship with the news media. Frost had handled the Queen's Park reporters in the traditional, informal, clubby way. Many members of the press gallery had small favours tossed their way from time to time, picked up a few extra dollars by serving as secretaries of select committees, or cultivated the ground for a move into the permanent security and higher pay of the civil service. Normally the premier met informally with the reporters every Thursday morning after cabinet to give them an off-the-record background briefing. Robarts, who was not as relaxed with the press as his predecessor, carried on the tradition. The press tested the new leader in an early encounter, when a microphone appeared on the table. Robarts refused to proceed until it was turned off. The transgression upset Robarts and marked the beginning of the end of the easy chats between the new premier and the media boys.

Robarts and Jackson decided that the prime minister needed a press secretary. They appointed William Kinmond, an experienced journalist who had written speeches for Robarts during the leadership campaign, and encouraged him to reform government-media relations. An early step was the distribution of recorded news clips to small radio stations that did not have representatives in the press gallery. Kinmond saw them as a modern counterpart to the press release. Wintermeyer complained that the messages were simply 'government propaganda,' and there was a certain amount of eyebrow-raising by the bigger stations who had their own reporters in the gallery. The television journalists were catered to by Kinmond's allowing their cameras to appear at press conferences. When the television lights blew fuses wherever they were set up, a specially wired press conference room was set up across the hall from the cabinet office. The formalization of press conferences met the needs of the new technology, but also removed the news media from the inner chambers of government.

Over the Christmas break Robarts began reorganizing his office along lines suggested by Don Collins' review. A new Department of the Prime Minister was to be set up, which would include the Cabinet Office, the Prime Minister's Office, and the lieutenant-governor's staff. McIntyre, as senior deputy minister, would be its administrative head, but would concentrate on his job as secretary of the cabinet. Within the prime minister's office, Robarts would select his own political advisers, his appointments secretary, press officer, and accountant. It was a somewhat bifurcated structure, attempting to separate the administrative from the political, rejecting the unification that had existed under the previous regime. If anything, Robarts' office continued to be under-organized and under-staffed.

Robarts' early reorganization tended to eschew centralization. In party politics, as well, he and Jackson put much less reliance on the salaried regional secretaries Frost and McKenzie had used to knit the party together under Toronto guidance. They preferred to rely instead on local riding associations and active local and regional party executives, partly along the lines of the London organization they had created in the 1950s. Jackson was happy to dispense with the regional secretaries as local and regional associations grew in strength and capacity to handle their own affairs. For co-ordination he was content to go a long way with the list of names in his 'black book,' calling these good party people and friends of Robarts whenever he felt the need to be in touch. If you had good people doing jobs, there was no need to over-organize them. Robarts was trying to take the same approach inside the government, taking a direct interest in getting good people into his cabinet and senior civil service positions, and then giving them their head.

This was a long way from an all-out or even a modest thrust to modernize the government of Ontario. It was the Robarts style to assume that the conventions of political life were valuable until proven otherwise. He had not joined the club to change its rules any more than necessary. Indeed, Robarts as premier was quite happy with the club-like, community atmosphere that still existed in his own office, and especially in the legislature. He and Wintermeyer could spar with each other across the floor and then go off and have a drink after the House adjourned for the day. Members' off-duty fun usually cut across rank and party affiliation, with the premier one of the least formal MPPS in off-hours. Astute observers could catch the by-play now and then in debate, as when the boys would be kidding an NDP member as 'a new capitalist' after he had had a good night at Downer's poker table. Even the press stayed in the family with such informal institutions as their annual dinner and follies, when politicians and reporters would parody each other, all good fun and all off the record. Decorum resumed as heads cleared on the morning after.

Robarts had to get through his five January by-elections before the House resumed for its spring session. Previously Liberal seats were at stake in the ridings of Brant and Kenora, Conservative seats in Renfrew South and the Toronto ridings of Beaches and Eglinton. Eugene Westendorp chaired a committee of representatives from several public relations firms used in the leadership campaign, who came up with some flashy gimmicks for this campaign. The situation was not helped by the rashness of Jackson's group in encouraging the public to see the voting as a mini-election, a kind of vote of confidence in the new premier's administration. The opposition parties rose to the challenge.

The general issues were the 3 per cent sales tax introduced the previous spring, the crime question (Harold Greer had joined Wintermeyer's staff as a special assistant, and co-ordinated Liberal attacks on this issue), and the government's overall performance. The local issues varied as usual. In Kenora there was much discussion of the use of a Conservative to fly ballot boxes to the northern polls. In Brant, where Robert Nixon was campaigning for the seat held by his late father, Harry Nixon, the campaign was fairly quiet. But Donald MacDonald stirred up Renfrew South with charges that the Conservatives were giving out timber rights and cutting licences on a patronage basis. Wintermeyer weighed in with accusations that contracts for road work and public services were being doled out for the same purpose. Although Robarts' organizers produced glowing reports on the party's prospects in Renfrew South, the more experienced Price was getting different information from friends on the spot. He sent one of his own men up from Toronto, who confirmed that the government was in serious trouble in the riding.

Robarts' 16 January appointments were cancelled and he was dispatched to Renfrew South in a last-minute effort to refute the opposition and save the seat. His first adventure travelling as the Prime Minister of Ontario did not go well. When they arrived in Peterborough for the night, the premier's aide could not remember where he had made reservations. Robarts had to have his driver stop at the first telephone booth on the outskirts of the city and told his aide not to come out of it until he had found a place for them to stay. In his first call the hapless assistant announced that John Robarts was in town, needed accommodation, and would be right over if anything was available. 'Sure,' the hotelier replied, 'And Kennedy just arrived and Diefenbaker is on the way!' and hung up. They finally located a place for the night and kept the bumbling away from the press.

Robarts could not turn things around in Renfrew South. It went Liberal along with Brant and Kenora. Government supporters narrowly squeaked in in Eglinton and the Beaches. The Liberals took 44.8 per cent of the popular vote in the five ridings, the Conservatives only 38.2 per cent. It was the first time the Conservatives had lost a by-election since coming to power under Drew in 1943. Were they finally vulnerable under young Robarts? A jubilant John Wintermeyer interpreted the results as proof that the Liberals were now the popular alternative to the Conservatives in Ontario. Robarts argued that the defeats reflected voter dissatisfaction with the sales tax. In the private postmortem, Robarts and his advisers concluded that the campaign organization had to be improved and that, while an unruffled manner might be an asset in the legislature, Robarts needed a higher profile as prime minister.

The by-election results, combined with edginess about the approaching redistribution, caused a certain amount of restlessness in caucus. It became public when a Toronto backbencher, Hollis Beckett, apparently forgot the press was present when he told a group of Young PCs that the Conservatives could only win Toronto by gerrymandering the riding boundaries. It would be necessary, he said, to make sure that the redefinition was not given to an all-party committee or an independent commission, which 'could not be depended upon.' Donald MacDonald promptly charged that the Tories were planning a gerrymander, and Robarts had to hold a press conference to promise that redistribution would be conducted with total impartiality.[11]

A few days later Robarts called an unprecedented inter-sessional meeting of the Conservative caucus. Perhaps as a result of his own backbench experience, he was hoping to increase the role of the elected member in the governing of the province, and now for the first time he gave his caucus a preview of the legislative program and solicited comments. He also made pointed criticisms of 'those who made foolish statements in public.' Jackson talked to the caucus about his interest in rejuvenating the local and regional PC Associations. While the press saw the unusual caucus meeting as a kind of call to arms to prepare for an election and to counter post by-election despondency, it was equally a sign of the new premier's style of trying to broaden participation in the governing process at Queen's Park.

Stepping up his activities toward the beginning of the new session of the legislature, Robarts did much more travelling in the province, including several visits to the north. These included appropriate announcements: on one trip he announced a $7,200,000 grant to the Ontario Northland Railway; on another he outlined the government's plan to encourage economic development in the region. When the session resumed on 20 February, the opposition tried to take the initiative by going after Kelso Roberts for appearing to be a non-believer in the Roach royal commission. The premier had to intervene to make clear that the attorney general was fully committed to the commission.[12] Attempts to make hay from Beckett's gerrymander comments were stymied when the government announced that the details of redistribution would be proposed by an independent commission. An announcement at the same time that the human rights code would be proceeded with during the session gave the government two popular items on one day.

Bob Macaulay, responsible for the government's response to unemployment, economic development and energy, generated many of the programs that highlighted the spring session. Through the autumn of 1961 Macaulay and his assistants, Clare Westcott and James Ramsay, had been at work on a twenty-point program to try to stimulate Ontario economic development in virtually every direction: more manufacturing at home, more exports, increased competitiveness through research and development, and so on. To give him the organizational base for co-ordinating the 'economic, industrial, trade and intergovernmental functions' of his economic program, Macaulay had brought in legislation amalgamating the Department of Commerce and Development with the Department of Economics, to form the new Department of Economics and Development.

The premier helped pave Macaulay's way by an aggressive speech to the legislature indicating that the government of Ontario had a role to play in the world of trade and commerce, which might involve a review of 'our traditional position in relation to the federal government.' The division of powers in the British North America Act notwithstanding, Robarts argued that 'the time has come when we must play a much more vigorous and active role as a government than we have in the past.'[13] His position coincided with, but was independent of, Lesage's Quiet Revolution in Quebec.

At the end of January 1962 Macaulay was ready with the details of his economic strategy for Ontario. It included creating an Ontario Economic Council, which would find ways to improve the efficiency of the provincial economy; a loan fund to support risky business ventures; a strengthened Ontario Research Foundation; a program to introduce Ontario manufacturers to potential world markets; and a manufacturing opportunities conference. Dalton Camp's advertising agency had been hired to design publicity for the program. Before anything could be launched, though, Macaulay had to get his estimates approved by the treasurer, Jim Allan. Old, rural, cautious Ontario would have to agree to spend the money proposed by new, industrial, aggressive, entrepreneurial Ontario. Although Macaulay only wanted about $700,000, he had to go back to Robarts and Allan six times before his considerably toned-down program was finally accepted.[14] On 13 March he unveiled his full twenty-point program for economic development. It came complete with a ubiquitous hippopotamus as the symbol of imports Ontario could do without, as well as fingers pointing down from posters at Ontarians guilty of not supporting home manufacturers.

Macaulay's trade crusade and his other booster-type campaigns went on through the next year, not without causing a certain amount of irritation. Importers were not impressed with scarcely veiled condemnations of their livelihood. The provincial Department of Agriculture was a little put out to find Macaulay's men undertaking to sell Ontario tobacco to the Japanese and the Europeans. The Department of Transport was not impressed when Macaulay unveiled a program to improve communication and transportation in northern Ontario. When Ontario House in the United Kingdom was expanded and provincial trade offices were opened in Europe and the United States, there was concern in the federal government that Ontario was beginning to conduct its own international affairs. Overall, the Macaulay program generated immense activity, no little friction, and the Ontario economy did grow and exports did soar.

While Macaulay and his activities were in the spotlight, Robarts continued to be seen at functions across the province, both as prime minister and as minister of education. As the school system built composite schools funded entirely by federal and provincial grants, Robarts reaped the benefits of his program, opening schools across the province. In Toronto, he managed to open as many as three in one night. By the spring of 1962, twenty centres were offering courses for the unemployed under local advisory committees established in 1961, and the scheme had qualified for the 75 per cent federal subsidy. Continuing to meet the needs of the baby boom, Robarts announced plans to build new universities in northern Ontario, the Niagara peninsula, and Toronto, and to grant independent status to two colleges affiliated with Western, one in Waterloo and the other in Windsor. At the same time, he increased the subsidies to local boards of education.

Labour relations problems gave the government two satisfying successes that spring. Early in April a dispute at Ontario Hydro seemed about to escalate into strike action. Robarts met with both sides on 4 April, the day before a strike was to begin, concluded it was inevitable, and immediately announced that the government would force the two sides to accept binding arbitration. Wintermeyer asked him that night if he had selected an arbitrator, and Robarts admitted he had not. But on the second reading of the bill the next day, he was able to announce the appointment of Carl Goldenberg, a veteran industrial relations expert who had just finished chairing a royal commission on the construction industry for the Frost/Robarts government. The bill received royal assent on 5 April, the strike threat was ended, and Robarts' 'swift but quiet' action was well received by the press.

At just about the same time, the Canadian Pacific Railway asked Tom Eberlee, Robarts' labour relations expert, to see if he could arrange mediation in the festering Royal York Hotel strike. With the premier's approval, Eberlee asked

Goldenberg, who was in Toronto for the Hydro arbitration, to mediate the hotel dispute. He agreed and was able to arrange a successful compromise on 16 April, two days before the legislative session ended. It closed with considerable recognition of the new premier's quiet competence. He seemed to be gaining acceptance in his job, though he still did not have the visibility yearned for by his political advisers.

Robarts was quite unlike Frost in letting his cabinet colleagues carry much of the burden and the higher profile in presenting the legislative program. Macaulay was the guru of economic development and 'minister of everything.' Kelso Roberts was linked with the issue of organized crime, not always in ways he liked. Allan Grossman was working on liquor law reforms, and James Allan handled the budget. Robarts carried out his own ministerial functions and intervened in others' affairs only when necessary. His style was closer to that of a chairman of the board, political commentators noticed, but his board in fact extended beyond the cabinet to include his political group as well as his personal office staff. Whereas Frost had had a few advisers and many acquaintants, Robarts tended to cast his net more widely, having a larger circle of advisers over whom he exercised much less control.

The relative calm in Ontario legislative politics in that spring of 1962 was a considerable contrast to the turbulence of the Ottawa scene where a Progressive-Conservative government led by a highly visible, dominant prime minister was about to face the electorate. The day after the Ontario legislature prorogued, John Diefenbaker announced that a federal election would be held on 18 June. Robarts pledged his support for the Chief.[15] The premier and members of his caucus appeared on election platforms throughout the campaign and helped at the constituency level. The results, however, were dismal for the federal party. The Diefenbaker Conservatives dropped from sixty-seven to thirty-five seats in Ontario, losing 17 percentage points in the popular vote. The national results were similar. Having suffered a disastrous defeat, Diefenbaker barely clung to office in a minority government.

The provincial Tory caucus held a sombre July meeting to review the implications of the election, the second major political defeat they had suffered that year. Jackson continued to hammer away at the need for strong constituency organizations and active local executives. It was also decided that the Ontario Conservatives, if they were going to survive in power, would have to differentiate themselves both from the preceding provincial government and from the crippled regime in Ottawa. To do this they still needed some kind of focus. Ideally it should be in the personality of Robarts, but nothing in his premiership as yet suggested that he had the personality to capture the popular imagination.

Meanwhile Robarts and his team were still trying to up-grade the administrative capacity of the government as well as lay the groundwork for the 1962-3 legislative program. A number of the new ministers and their senior civil servants undertook to reorganize their departments. Both Labour and Agriculture, for example, went through major changes. Almost all Ontario civil servants were being affected by the central personnel classification, recruitment, and training policies that Collins was introducing as head of the Civil Service Commission. With the new Public Service Act of 1962 the important first steps were taken toward permitting collective bargaining as well as partisan political activity (such as running for office) for civil servants.

Another important administrative change in the first year was the strengthening of the Treasury Board. This initiative grew in part out of recommendations of the Committee on the Organization of the Government in Ontario appointed during the Frost regime. It recommended the abolition of the Budget Committee and the shifting of its responsibilities to the Treasury Board. Implementation involved enabling Treasury Board to appoint its own staff, giving it the right to review departmental expenditures, and allowing it to advise departments on questions of administrative structure and procedure. Now Treasury Board became the focus of both government expenditure policy and administrative reform. Its acting secretary, H.H. Walker, signalled this change when he wrote the deputy minister of each department in April 1962 asking for a five-year forecast of departmental expenditures.[16] About the same time Carl E. Brannan, soon to become the first full-time secretary of the Treasury Board, was appointed to the Civil Service Commission in a move to co-ordinate financial controls with personnel decisions. Departmental administrators throughout the government gradually came to feel the effects of the stronger controls and centralized services. The full impact, however, would be several years away when the Robarts government went much further down this road, both in administrative centralization and in starting rigidly to monitor expenditures.

Most of the issues raised in the federal election contained implications for Ontario's agenda. In his May campaigning, for example, Diefenbaker had promised to appoint a federal royal commission on taxation. In endorsing the idea, Robarts decided to launch a parallel provincial study, so that when everyone's recommendations were in it would be possible to rationalize the tax structure from the federal to the municipal level. Late in June he announced the tax review, as well as the government's desire to revise municipal boundaries to reflect shifts in population. A special study would be made of commuter needs in Toronto. With medical insurance and pensions growing as topics of concern at both levels of government, Matthew Dymond, the minister of health, was considering the Ontario Medical Association's views on the government's proposed Ontario Medical Insurance Plan. An Ontario committee was working out proposals for pension portability that might win interprovincial support. In addition, Macaulay was putting the finishing touches on his proposed Ontario Development Fund, while Robarts' own department, Education, approved a new grants formula to be called the Ontario Foundation Tax Plan.

During July and August Robarts stressed economic development and fiscal issues. He told a Conservative picnic in Oshawa that his government would continue to develop markets, create jobs, and expand its technical training programs. At the Ontario Municipal Association conference in August he repeated his commitment to initiate a review of the tax system. On 17 September Gathercole submitted to Robarts the first draft of the terms of reference for the Ontario Committee on Taxation. It was to review all aspects of provincial taxation and co-operate with the federal royal commission.

Macaulay was continuing to throw out ideas and policy proposals like a sparkler. He was already reorganizing his department to separate its economic analysis functions from its policy-oriented activities. He suggested to Robarts that the government present a statement outlining the province's general economic policy during the fall sitting of the legislature. It would be an excellent way of seizing the initiative from the opposition, Macaulay argued:

A fundamental mistake we made last year was letting the session start on the initiative and footing of the Opposition. We have very little chance to obtain the initiative in a fall session. The serious, vital legislation is not ready; important estimates are not presented; no economic statement is available; and the budget is not dealt with; instead this fall we could center our session around the fight over Ontario's economic policies, which, in my opinion, is damn near unassailable.[17]

Robarts liked the suggestion, agreeing that it would be impossible to have a budget ready for the fall. To his suggestion Macaulay attached seven more items for inclusion in the Throne Speech. This brought his total, Robarts estimated, to twenty-six.

Macaulay's proposed Ontario Development Fund was one of the ideas that required considerable discussion. It was conceived as a kind of banker of last resort, helping out promising enterprises that were having difficulty borrowing from the banks. There was some concern inside and outside the government that it would either compete with existing financial institutions or would operate recklessly without the constraints imposed on the private sector. Consulted by Robarts, Harry Price urged Macaulay to take into account the views of the financial community in the planning of the agency. After some hesitation Macaulay agreed to a meeting Price arranged. It helped open communications, and Macaulay later met with a larger group of senior executives from the banks, insurance, and trust companies. They gave the idea their support on condition that the company receiving a loan be placed under the supervision of a retired senior executive and that the Ontario Development Fund itself be administered by a crown corporation. After these consultations, which considerably tempered and improved his proposal, Macaulay was ready to take it to cabinet.[18]

While the ingredients were being prepared for the next session's legislative menu, Robarts tried to increase his government's political popularity by instituting cabinet visits to some of the larger centres. On 7 June, for example, the cabinet visited Hamilton, touring the Royal Botanical Gardens, the Chedoke Expressway, and McMaster University's nuclear reactor, finishing the day by being soundly beaten by the Wentworth County Council in a softball game. Later in the summer there was a visit to Sudbury to review government programs in the north and listen to the concerns of northerners. Robarts tried his luck again with the electorate by holding a by-election in the long-time Tory seat of Huron-Bruce. He spent the better part of a week campaigning in the riding, only to see his political organization keep its record unblemished: Huron-Bruce was lost to the Liberals by seven hundred votes. Robarts and his party were still in difficulty with the voters.

As the first anniversary of his leadership approached, Robarts sent a letter to the party membership thanking them for their support, and alluding to his government's 'bold and well advanced plans for Ontario's next stage of economic development.' The government's aim for Ontario was to give the province 'more industry, more jobs, more wages, more opportunity, and from these more productivity and revenue to do the job.' He urged the faithful to be strong at the constituency level within the party, blending 'the enthusiasm of youth with the wisdom of experience' – as he planned to do, he told them, in the reorganization of the government he was about to announce.[19]

He announced it on 25 October, one year to the day from his winning of the leadership. Three cabinet ministers who had indicated they would not seek re-election – Daley, Nickle, and Warrender – were retired. In a general shuffling of portfolios the most visible change of rank was the demotion of Kelso Roberts from attorney general to minister of lands and forests. Fred Cass replaced him in what at the time was the most delicate portfolio. Three younger members were brought into the cabinet: J.R. Simonett as minister without portfolio; Robarts' friend Jim Auld as minister of transport; and, most surprisingly, young William Davis from Brampton. Davis, who had entered the legislature in 1959, moved the Address in Reply to the Speech from the Throne at the opening of his first session, and managed Macaulay's leadership campaign in 1961, was promoted at Macaulay's urging, and took Robarts' place in the major, sensitive, testing Ministry of Education. Macaulay, Allan, Stewart, and Dymond all retained their portfolios. With a few substitutions and shifts these ministers would comprise the nucleus of Robarts' government through the remainder of his time in office.

How long would he govern Ontario? Robarts was getting ready to face the voters in 1963 with a solid legislative program and with a cabinet of his choosing. The government now bore his stamp. Inside the prime minister's office the courtly formality of the Frost years was gone, the first winds of businesslike efficiency had moderated, and Robarts' informal, relaxed style set the tone. His staff threw a surprise party for him on 8 November, the anniversary of the change of first ministers. When Irene Beatty brought in the anniversary cake with one candle, she commented that she hoped Robarts would last to see his thirteenth anniversary in office, which would be a record for Conservative premiers. Robarts laughingly dismissed the idea, saying that ten years in office would be enough for any man.[20]

'Done!'

A provincial premier's job is never limited to his government's own jurisdiction. The Canadian federal system so thoroughly pervades the business of governing that intergovernmental conferring, negotiating, bickering, and politicking have come to consume enormous proportions of all governments' energies. The 'external affairs' aspects of a provincial premier's responsibilities encompass relations with both the other provinces and with Ottawa. During Robarts' early years in office he had to come to grips with the problems that the Quiet Revolution in Quebec was beginning to pose for the Canadian federal system. At the same time, a Conservative prime minister of Ontario had to be seen to support a faltering Conservative prime minister of Canada, John Diefenbaker, whose regime was on the verge of collapse. Through 1962 and early 1963 Robarts managed to stickhandle through these difficulties reasonably adeptly, while at the same time supervising an impressive amount of activity in the legislature and adding his own initiatives to the intergovernmental brew. The combined record of achievements inside and outside the assembly set the stage for the full-scale struggle with his Ontario Liberal opponents in the election that would be held later that year.

Robarts' first foray into the intergovernmental arena as prime minister was a long weekend visit to Montreal in late January 1962, where he made his first speeches on Ontario-Quebec relations. They contained the usual expressions of good-will and references to 'friendly rivalry' between the provinces, but seemed to some Quebec observers to contain a veiled warning in their reference to the need for two provinces with such similar problems and aspirations not to become too competitive 'to the extent of duplicating industries and services.' Some thought Robarts was referring to the Quebec government's plans to create a Quebec-based steel industry, which would compete with Ontario producers.[1] This initiative was to be part of the Lesage government's determination to expand the provincial economy, modernizing it in order to strengthen the base of the French-Canadian cultural life of Quebec and increase opportunities for French-speaking Quebeckers. Since Lesage had defeated the moribund Union Nationale government in 1960, he had been the symbol and spokesman for the unleashing of new energies and a new commitment to state-led development in Quebec. As Lesage himself emphasized when he returned Robarts' visit that June, the new Quebec that he led was determined 'to fulfill its own destiny ... and to play a greater part in the development of its resources.'[2]

It was possible to see Ontario and Quebec as competitors, with conflicting economic interests. Robarts chose not to pursue these issues, stressing instead the areas in which the provinces had common ground. There were some obvious fields in which co-operation was desirable. In August 1962, for example, Robarts and Lesage announced a joint scheme to thwart sales tax evasion. Later they would share common strategies in some of their approaches to Ottawa. These were grounded in an historic community of interest that Canada's two largest provinces had in limiting the federal power's ability to interfere with their ambitious development plans.

Although the Lesage government's projects were getting most of the media attention in the early 1960s, the Ontario administration was almost as aggressive in expanding the area of its activities. When Robarts unveiled another round of Macaulay's trade crusade program on 5 October 1962, for example, he made no apologies for Ontario going its separate way from Ottawa:

The question that must be running through your minds is why should Ontario embark on an ambitious program of trade expansion – surely this is the responsibility of the federal government. Let me make clear, here and now, that the Government of Ontario does not intend to hide behind the skirts of the Federal Government in matters of trade and economic expansion.[3]

A few weeks later Robarts announced plans to introduce a provincial medical insurance program, dashing hope by the Diefenbaker government that the province would join in a national scheme. Other provincial initiatives were to follow in the areas of economic development and technical training.

In keeping its distance from Ottawa, the Robarts government was not only following the historic logic of Ontario self-aggrandizement, but was dissociating itself from a dying and unpopular federal Progressive-Conservative government. The lack of rapport between the Robarts and the Diefenbaker Tories went back to the Londoners' refusal to join Allister Grosart and the national Conservative campaign team in 1957. In Toronto Harry Price had taken a similar position at the same time. Now that he and Robarts' friends dominated the provincial party there was little cordiality with Ottawa – a marked contrast to the close relations between Leslie Frost and George Drew and a source of tension that would continue until Diefenbaker was ousted from the Conservative leadership.

Both publicly and privately Robarts declared his determination to 'stay clear' of the internal politics of the national Conservative party.[4] He would make no comments on the dissension that wracked Diefenbaker's cabinet in the weeks before the government's final defeat in the House of Commons on 5 February 1963. This was to be the first of many occasions on which reporters asked Robarts whether he had aspirations for the national leadership. The Ontario leader told the press that he was quite happy and satisfied where he was. 'We're not responsible for events at Ottawa,' he insisted when pestered for further comment on the national party's agony.[5]

Robarts dutifully appeared on platforms supporting Diefenbaker in the 1963 election campaign, but the Ontario PC organizers tended to avoid the national scene, leaving Diefenbaker to his fate. Robarts was determined to follow Frost's practice of cultivating a reasonable working relationship with whomever ruled in Ottawa. When Lester Pearson's Liberals formed a minority government in April 1963 they received congratulations from the prime minister of Ontario, who indicated his willingness to co-operate with them for the good of Ontario and Canada.

The provincial Conservatives spent most of their energies in the winter of 1962-3 on their own proposals for the better government of Ontario. The 27 November Speech from the Throne was packed with the results of the new administration's year of preparation. The government announced its medical insurance plan for Ontario (providing backstop assistance to those not covered by private carriers); a portable pension scheme; improved facilities for training the handicapped; a new grant formula for education; its intention to create an Ontario Council for the Arts; its plan to establish committees to study food industries in the province, collective bargaining in the civil service, transportation problems in Metropolitan Toronto, and the tax system. The Ministry of Agriculture was to expand on its land drainage and meat-inspection activities. There would be more road-building. The government was interested in improving physical fitness, the teaching of French, higher minimum wages, increased municipal subsidies, acquiring more shoreline and parks for the people of Ontario, and a host of other subjects. In many cases only studies or review were being proposed, but the programs which came to characterize the decade of Robarts' premiership had their seeds in this speech. It marked the beginning of his government's distinctive contributions to social and economic change in Ontario.

Government restructuring, fiscal reform, and economic development occupied centre stage. Robarts' desire to decentralize service and to enrich the recreational and cultural life of Ontarians remained ancillary but, to him, no less important themes. The acquisition of beaches on the Great Lakes preceded the extensive provincial parks initiatives at the close of the decade. The Ontario Arts Council became the vehicle for significant reforms in cultural policy. Its creation illustrates Robarts' style. Proposed by sponsors of the arts from the Toronto business community, the council was promoted personally by Robarts to co-ordinate government support for the 'province's artistic resources.' Robarts' efforts were encouraged by Lieutenant-Governor J. Keiller Mackay, who had a deep appreciation of the cultural and spiritual underpinnings of society. The two men became friends and, when Mackay retired, Robarts captured his talents for the naiscent cultural policy by appointing him the first chairman of the newly formed Ontario Arts Council. The pattern of selecting individuals and then giving them the freedom to work extended beyond cabinet to include the committees created in the Speech from the Throne, the Arts Council, and the Conservative party.

The government took the initiative early in the session, bringing in a series of bills in the first week, including the proposal for an Ontario Development Agency. Robert Macaulay was the key minister in a far-ranging debate on provincial economic development. Before it ended, he brought in a second bill authorizing a further program of loans for small businesses. Departmental estimates were introduced before Christmas and several of the promised committees established. Lancelot Smith would head a five-man group studying the tax system. The committee to work on the transportation needs of Metropolitan Toronto, with particular emphasis on railway commuter services, was also announced. In mid-December, the legislature received the interim report of the Redistribution Commission, recommending the creation of ten new seats in suburban Toronto. The report went directly to the Committee on Privileges and Elections. Everyone speculated throughout the session about the relationship of the government's activities to the election expected sometime in 1963.

After an uneventful Christmas recess, the legislature resumed on 5 February 1963, the day of the Diefenbaker government's defeat in Ottawa. The government continued to introduce its initiatives. On 21 February Robarts introduced the Ontario Foundation Tax Plan. It was an elaborate reform of the education grants system, which took better account of differences in the fiscal capacities of municipalities as well as attempting to put elementary public and separate school systems on a more equal basis. By effectively providing more money for separate elementary schools without taking money from the public school system, Robarts managed to wriggle through another round in one of Ontario's most sensitive and long-running issues, with only the extremists among separate school supporters expressing their disappointment. Both the opposition and such traditionally Liberal newspapers as the Toronto *Star* seemed pleased with the measure.[6]

By the end of February the government had guaranteed its first loan under Macaulay's development program. It was to the Fairfield Corporation in Owen Sound, which was otherwise faced with closure. The company was placed under a board of management composed of senior businessmen from the city, forty jobs were saved, and the scheme seemed to garner public approval. Macaulay, whose activities always caused their share of controversy, was pleased.

On 5 March the estimates of Macaulay's Department of Economics and Development were scheduled for debate in the legislature. At the last moment the minister and his aides rushed to the chamber loaded down with documentation that might be required during debate. As Macaulay reached the corridor outside the Speaker's office, he gasped, threw his papers in the air, and crumpled to the floor. He was rushed to hospital. The newspapers reported that he had suffered a heart attack. That diagnosis was never publicly confirmed. Some said he had had an angina attack; others said it was exhaustion plus the flu; some said it was a good way to get attention. Whatever had happened to him had occurred on centre stage, a highly theatrical setting in which to begin the process of detaching himself from high political office. He had fulfilled his commitment to his friend, seeing him through the transition.

The pace of government continued. On 19 March a revised Pension Benefits Act was introduced, creating and extending portable pensions for many Ontario workers, and the next week a pilot Medical Services Insurance Program was brought in. In what would become an ongoing refrain, the opposition criticized the government's apparent reliance on the private sector for the provision of both pension benefits and health insurance. It was too soon, however, to make significant political mileage with that point of view in Ontario, and the criticisms did not blunt the fact that important action had been taken. At the same time, the cloud of suspicion hanging over the Attorney General's Department and the whole government was apparently dispelled when the royal commission chaired by Wilfred Roach reported that while Ontario had a certain amount of organized crime, there were no links with the mafia and there was no corruption or cover-up in the Attorney General's Department. Most of John Wintermeyer's specific charges had been shown to be unfounded. After one day's heated debate of Roach's findings in the legislature, the government believed the crime issue had been settled. Ontario's spasm of fear about the mafia seemed to have passed; so had the Liberals' most promising election issue.

In the last month of the session the government restructured the Ontario Securities Commission and brought in a new Representation Act to create the recommended ten new ridings in the Toronto area. One of the session's most commented-upon pieces of legislation, because of its symbolic influence, was the introduction of colouring into Ontario margarine. The Robarts government was even daring to confront the sacred cows of rural Ontario.*

John Robarts was doing well and soon began to see the evidence of popular approval. He had been getting a good press; just how good it was became apparent when on 25 March he received a note from a member of the Toronto *Star*'s staff: 'The Powers at the Star are interested. They don't think much of Wintermeyer and may support you.'[7] Here was the first sign of an important movement of opinion toward the Tories to balance the Liberals' success in the 1962 by-elections. It was needed to balance what seemed to be a general strengthening of national

---

* It was still a muted challenge, however, for the one colour that could not be used in Ontario margarine was buttery yellow.

Liberalism as Lester Pearson's rejuvenated party swept aside the floundering Diefenbaker Conservatives in the 6 April general election. Ontario no longer had an allied government in Ottawa. Did it need one? Some of the reasons for the approval of Robarts' regime at Queen's Park were evident in a summary of the session written by the *Star*'s press gallery reporter:

This spring will be remembered as the time when Robarts, the quiet administrator, blossomed out in public, as a full fledged, canny political animal. He's done it with a fusillade of legislation, largely things that have been hanging fire for years, ranging from a minimum wage law to somewhat-coloured margarine to portable pensions to grants for Toronto subways. It's aimed directly at the heart of opposition strength, the urban areas in which federal Grits took 52 of Ontario's 85 seats this month.[8]

A *Globe and Mail* analyst added a comment on Robarts himself: 'One reason for the psychological letdown on the Opposition side of the House stems from an asset with which Mr. Robarts, like the late British Prime Minister, Stanley Baldwin, appears to be blessed in large measure: his enemies – and, at times his friends – are forever anxious to underestimate him.'[9]

Although Robarts liked to keep a low profile, he was coming into his own. With Macaulay's illness and Kelso Roberts' move to the Department of Lands and Forests, he now stood well above his old leadership rivals in the cabinet. His government's legislative program had swamped the opposition, and the Roach Commission's report seemed to have discredited the Liberals' main accusations of wrongdoing. Many other Liberal suggestions had been anticipated, borrowed, or nullified by the legislative innovations. Outside of Queen's Park, Robarts had avoided being identified with the federal Conservative failure and had begun to forge a good working relationship with Quebec on a number of issues involving federal-provincial relations. Early in May 1963, a Canadian Institute of Public Opinion poll showed Robarts leading Wintermeyer by more than three to one as the voters' choice for prime minister of Ontario.

All of the approval notwithstanding, John Robarts' government still had not won a single seat from either opposition party. Nor had his achievements yet been endorsed by the electorate of Ontario. Neither the prime minister nor the government seemed to be particularly distinctive. Robarts' reasonableness and his distaste for colourful partisanship garnered few headlines. How could his political advisers focus an election campaign?

Robarts gave them a focus when he concluded the Throne debate at the end of the session, on 26 April. He and Bill Kinmond had written and rewritten a speech that simply would not gel. Robarts put it aside until the last moment, which turned out to be sometime after 4 AM on the morning of the 26th. The earlier hours of the evening had been spent drinking and socializing with Jim Auld and other friends. Sitting at his desk wondering what to say, Robarts pulled out a copy of the Speech from the Throne that had begun the session. He reread it, and realized that his government had carried out every commitment they had forecast. In his speech in the legislature later that day he went over the Throne Speech item by item. At the end of each item the prime minister announced in his rich, gravelly voice; 'Done!' His members caught the spirit, and joined in the cadence. A chorus of loud, happy Conservatives thundered 'DONE!' ... 'DONE!' ... 'DONE!' across the floor at the opposition. Liberal and CCF interjections were drowned out. Watching the proceedings from the gallery, Ernie Jackson was jubilant, for he knew they had found the focus. All Robarts had to do was campaign on his record. He had kept his promises. You could *trust* a Robarts government.

But it was not quite time to go to the polls. The Diefenbaker Conservatives had been badly beaten in Ontario, the worst the party had fared in a general election since 1949. Wintermeyer and his Liberals were close to the federal Liberals, and had worked actively for them. Wintermeyer himself was particularly close to one of Pearson's popular new ministers, the member for Niagara Falls, Judy LaMarsh. It would be too risky to take on the Liberals in the flush of their victory, for the federal machine might reciprocate for Wintermeyer's support by pulling out all the stops to help him.

The Ontario PCs decided to wait. Pearson's was a minority government, which had made bold, perhaps extravagant, promises to give Canada 'sixty days of decision.' They were promising action that would be a tall order for even a majority government, not least because many of their social programs trenched on provincial jurisdiction. It seemed tactically wise for the Ontario Tories to bide their time. On 22 April, the day Lester Pearson was sworn in as prime minister of Canada, Robarts proposed that a federal-provincial conference be summoned as soon as possible to discuss the prospective Ontario pension scheme and the implementation of a Canada-wide pension portability plan.[10]

There was another sign of the times that day. Leslie Rowntree, Robarts' minister of labour, and his wife were the representatives of the Ontario government at an Ottawa banquet celebrating the jubilee of *Le Droit,* the city's French-language newspaper. In recent years *Le Droit* had taken moderate editorial positions and was fairly friendly to the Robarts government. A telegram from Robarts was read early in the evening's proceedings congratulating the paper on its record of service to the community and to Canada. The guests had not finished their dinner when an Ottawa policeman entered the room and spoke quietly to the chairman. The chairman got up and asked everyone to leave the room because 'something was amiss.' It was a bomb scare and effectively ended the evening. Rowntree was shaken at the thought of this kind of thing happening in Ontario. It seemed to be related to a rising wave of French-Canadian separatism in Quebec, which only a few days earlier had expressed itself violently in a series of bombings of mail boxes in Westmount, the wealthy English-Canadian dominated suburb of Montreal. The separatists were a new and alarming minority, because of the resort to terrorism on their extreme fringe. Such things were never supposed to happen in quiet, peaceable Canada.

John Robarts made a special point of becoming well informed about the separatist challenge, and about the course of the Quiet Revolution in Quebec. He gathered information that spring and in later years from a wide variety of sources. Carl Goldenberg, the labour relations expert who normally lived in Westmount, for example, briefed him on the political history of Quebec and continued to send him notes on Quebec politics for the rest of the decade. William Davis, the young minister of education, was consulted as being sensitive to the political demands of the 'new generation' which seemed to be taking a leading role in 'activist' politics. Alex MacLeod, a former Communist MPP who had left the party after the Russian invasion of Hungary and become a leading figure in the development of the Ontario Human Rights Commission, was asked to explain the undercurrents of Quebec nationalism. By June of 1963 Robarts was well briefed on politics in Quebec and the aspirations of the newly vocal French-Canadian community.

His interest coincided with a major exchange proposed by members of the Ontario and Quebec press galleries, who were always willing to enjoy a funded holiday, but also were anxious to do what they could for national unity. Approached about the idea, Robarts agreed to have the government pay the Ontario group's costs, agreed to head the delegation, and was happy to have the other party leaders, Wintermeyer and MacDonald, included. Robarts gave the keynote speech on Saturday, 16 June at a formal dinner thrown by the Quebec government for the visiting Ontarians. It was a carefully prepared, landmark expression of goodwill from the premier and people of Ontario to the government and people of Quebec. Robarts described confederation as 'a partnership in fact, in spirit and in purpose,' and, using words loaded with soothing connotations for Quebec nationalists, talked about Ontario and Quebec as contemporary manifestations of the 'two nations' that had made Canada great. More practically, he mentioned how the bonds of union between the provinces included a shared common need for greater fiscal resources, currently controlled by Ottawa.[11]

Robarts' act of interprovincial statesmanship surprised and pleased Lesage and the members of the Quebec press corps. The Ontario premier seemed to have an unusual willingness to work with Quebec and to understand the type of confederation Quebec desired. The visit helped draw Liberal Jean Lesage and Conservative John Robarts together as political leaders of Canada's two most important provinces, and their co-operative attitudes seemed to contrast favourably with the bitter political war already being waged among Liberals and Conservatives in Ottawa. Perhaps Robarts had the potential to be more than just the head of a busy government in Ontario.

8

Fighting Grits

The Ontario-Quebec axis was further strengthened in the summer of 1963 when the provinces met the Pearson government at a federal-provincial conference. It had been called to discuss proposals by Ottawa that would encroach upon fields of provincial jurisdiction. Discussions at the conference were the beginning of a long, complex struggle between Ontario and Ottawa over the province's role in national schemes of social insurance.

Robarts had urged Ottawa to call a federal-provincial conference to discuss ways of implementing an interprovincial consensus, arrived at the previous winter, on pension portability (that is, arrangements to enable Canadians to carry their pension benefits from one private or public plan to another anywhere in the country). The Pearson government was deeply interested in the pension issue, having promised to introduce a national contributory pension plan to supplement the universal old age pension. At the federal-provincial conference on 26-27 July, it announced plans for both a Canada pension plan and a new municipal development and loan fund.

Both were contentious. Municipal governments in Canada are legally subordinate to the provinces, having no constitutional standing in their own right. As to the national pension scheme, according to the 1951 amendment to the British North America Act, the provinces still had the power to forestall any future federal initiative in that area. There was no guarantee that Ottawa would present proposals affecting either municipalities or pensions that the provincial governments would accept as meeting their view of the needs of their citizens. Ottawa could not go ahead on these important issues, on which it had promised to act, without provincial support.

The conference was called before Ottawa had released details of the proposals it wanted to discuss. In fact it was still working out the details. On 18 July Robarts wrote to Pearson describing Ontario's new portable pension legislation and requesting that the federal pension plan – which was being tabled in the House of Commons that day – be made compatible with it. Referring to the municipal loan fund that the Liberals also wanted to discuss, he suggested that lack of capital was not the major problem facing municipalities, rather, it was the lack of adequate sources of tax revenue.[1] When Pearson presented the fund proposal to the conference, both Lesage and Robarts criticized it sharply for intruding on provincial jurisdiction. They insisted that federal money not go directly to municipalities, but pass through the provinces in accordance with constitutional proprieties and in proportion to provincial population totals. Pearson surrendered and rewrote the plan along these lines, whereupon the provinces accepted it. It was an act of unexpected federal flexibility and conciliation that many observers heralded as the beginning of a new era of 'co-operative federalism.'

It was less clear that there would be such easy co-operation on pensions. The issue was extremely complicated, for all pension schemes necessarily have important long-term implications involving patterns of saving, investment, and spending. The Ontario portable pension legislation, requiring private employers to set up portable plans, had been brought in after three years of detailed study. Now, after only three months in power, the federal Liberals were proposing a massive national pension scheme the implications of which were by no means clear. It had been introduced in the House of Commons and then to the conference by the brash, partisan minister of national health and welfare, Judy LaMarsh. By and large, the premiers were not impressed. John Robarts had developed a detailed knowledge of the subject from the provincial experience and the work of his pension advisory committee. He wanted more information about the impact the federal scheme might have on the development of pools of investment capital in Canada, the redistributive principles underlying the program – would it spread Ontario's savings across the rest of Canada? – and its cost and timing.[2]

Like Leslie Frost, who had initiated Ontario's interest in the pension field, Robarts favoured a national pension plan in principle, but it had to be a plan that 'fit' with the Ontario government's approach to the problem. Constitutionally, Robarts reminded Pearson, the federal government could not pass legislation superseding Ontario's pension statutes. Jean Lesage was even less co-operative, making clear that his government was probably going to develop a pension plan of its own rather than go along with Ottawa's proposals. The conference disintegrated as it became clear that discussions based on a nebulous federal plan were bound to be unpromising. It was agreed to meet in September to continue to explore the issue. While Ontario and Quebec did not have identical views on the pension question, they had worked together to make sure there would be no unilateral imposition of Ottawa's plan.

With the federal Liberals experiencing a political buffeting as they tried to force the pace, the Ontario Conservatives prepared for a fall election. If the time was not auspicious, the election could be delayed until spring, but they would follow that course at their peril, since the element of surprise would be lost.

The organizers had already been at work for months. Ernie Jackson, who would head the Conservative campaign, had held a two-day campaign school in June for PC candidates and their managers, briefing them on government policy and giving advice on organization and fundraising. In July the party rented a special campaign headquarters on Bloor Street in Toronto, put together a 'brains trust' to develop ideas for the campaign, and assembled most of the material for its central party literature, advertising, and information booklets. A committee manned telephones to answer questions from constituencies across the province as they developed their local organizations. Volunteers were designated to monitor speeches and feed the information to Bill Kinmond, who would be on the road with Robarts throughout the campaign. The Conservatives made the ten new ridings on the outskirts of Metropolitan Toronto their top priority. By the end of July the poll organizers had been recruited in most ridings, candidates were in place, and campaigning had effectively begun.

Gearing up for elections never goes completely smoothly, and there had been the usual number of problems at the riding level. Jackson and the other leading Tories did not hesitate to intervene. In the Don Mills riding in Toronto, for example, the local association had already nominated a young lawyer named Paul Lee. Lee was ready to start campaigning when he learned that the central party organization had decided to replace him with the chairman of the Ontario Economic Council, Stanley J. Randall. Randall was being groomed by Macaulay, who intended to retire after the election, as his replacement. With Robarts' consent, Macaulay had persuaded him to run. Jackson had to provide the constituency. After discussions between Jackson, Lee, and the local association executive, Lee resigned his candidacy. A new nomination convention in Don Mills selected Randall as the candidate.

In Russell, a riding just outside Ottawa, the local association was also divided. One faction supported the Conservative incumbent, Gordon Lavergne, who was also mayor of Eastview; the other supported a young lawyer, A.B.R. (Bert) Lawrence, who had won the nomination convention. Lavergne's faction refused to accept defeat and appealed to Toronto. As president of the Ontario PC Association, Elmer Bell reviewed the situation, decided the meeting had been in order, and confirmed Lawrence's nomination. The losers promptly held their own convention and nominated Lavergne as the Conservative candidate. This time the appeal to headquarters was directly to Robarts, who confirmed Bell's ruling and endorsed Lawrence. When Lavergne decided to run as an independent, Jackson determined to crush him and had Robarts visit the riding twice in support of Lawrence. The central men in Robarts' organization liked to have things their way.

The Liberals were also ready for the fight, with an organization directed by the former journalist Harold Greer. The party was reasonably well organized, although Wintermeyer later acknowledged having had difficulties raising money. He was much less close to the party's powerful traditional newspaper, the Toronto

Star, than his predecessors had been, but at the same time was much closer to the federal party, which had done so well in the 1962 and 1963 federal elections. Wintermeyer had supported his fellow Liberals in that campaign, particularly Judy LaMarsh, and could reasonably expect a certain degree of reciprocation. Despite the Roach Commission's report, he and his advisers, particularly Greer, felt they could use issues involving crime and corruption to telling effect. It was widely rumoured that the Liberals would run some kind of aggressive 'scandal a day' campaign against the government.

The Ontario New Democratic Party, fighting its first election campaign since changing its name from the CCF, had a spirited, well-integrated political organization, but in fact was not in good shape for the campaign. The party had to stretch slender resources of money and manpower for election campaigns all across Canada. It had spent heavily on its gala founding convention in 1961, then had gone through the national elections of 1962 and the spring of 1963. Now, just as the Ontario campaign began, Premier W.A.C. Bennett of British Columbia called a provincial election. The NDP was the official opposition there and it would have to have first call on whatever resources could be provided. Altogether, the Ontario NDP had to run a campaign which was continually short of money.

Informal campaigning was well under way in August, with Robarts playing the usual games about announcing an election date. He fielded a minor hot potato on 9 August, when Brian Cathcart, his minister of travel and publicity, announced his resignation from the cabinet. With the opposition leaders speculating about a cabinet split, Robarts announced that Cathcart's exit was 'regretfully' accepted as part of a minor cabinet shuffle in the making. In fact Cathcart, a holdover from the Frost era, was disagreeing with his colleagues over a number of minor policy matters and Robarts wanted to replace him. On 14 August Robarts announced the second step in the shuffle, moving Auld from Transport to Travel and Publicity, and Irwin Haskett from Reform Institutions to Transport. Allan Grossman, who had been harassed by conflict of interest charges in his administration of the Liquor Control Board of Ontario, was promoted to Reform Institutions. Two days after the shuffle Robarts asked the lieutenant-governor to dissolve the legislature, setting the election date for 25 September.

The three parties began their campaigns during the last week in August. The launchings were appropriately symbolic. Wintermeyer, the Liberal, began his in Ottawa. Donald MacDonald, an organizer and party man, timed his opening statement to coincide with an NDP provincial council meeting in Toronto. Robarts, the new leader trying to win a seventh successive Conservative victory, launched his campaign at a testimonial dinner for Leslie Frost in Lindsay. Several of his advisers were not so sure that it was wise to seem tied to the old government. When would Robarts develop an image of his own?

Robarts began his campaign with no sense of a central issue. In his 23 August speech at the Lindsay fair grounds he pledged to work with the federal government for the good of Ontario and Canada. He listed the achievements of his eighteen months of government and promised to maintain his record of efficient administration. It was apparently going to be up to the opposition to set the parameters of the campaign.

The Liberals wasted no time in creating the single most important issue. On the same evening when Robarts was speaking in Lindsay, Judy LaMarsh returned to Niagara Falls from a three-week tour of Europe, where she had been studying national pension schemes. She went directly to a Liberal rally for her friend John Wintermeyer. There she announced that her government's proposed Canada pension plan could probably not be implemented if Ontario and Quebec went their own way by setting up their own provincial plans. She talked about the higher benefits citizens would get from the proposed national plan than from the private plans which were basic to Ontario's legislation. Wintermeyer followed her and endorsed the federal plan. He repeated this support at his campaign's official opening, and attacked Robarts for following 'the whims of private insurance companies.'[3]

Judy LaMarsh had been intemperate at best, wildly foolish at worst, in having attacked a government whose co-operation was absolutely essential for the success of her ministry's and her government's plan. She had also distorted Ontario's position. After a chat with Lester Pearson she softened her stand, and admitted that Robarts had offered to co-operate with Ottawa in the development of a national plan. Wintermeyer continued attacking Robarts' position, however. Between them, the federal minister and the Ontario opposition leader had tossed the pension question into Ontario's provincial politics – playing politics, as it were, with pensions.

Meanwhile, the Liberal 'scandal' campaign was launched by Arthur Reaume, MPP for Essex North. Speaking at his nomination, Reaume brought up the debate over organized crime, listed allegations of scandal that Liberal researchers had made during the past three years, and declared that his party was going to turn the election into 'the wildest tea party since Boston.' Wintermeyer joined the attack with charge upon charge: that organized crime existed in Ontario, that the provincial government was squelching evidence of corruption in Eastview, that Allan Grossman through his wife had abused his stewardship of the Liquor Control Board, that a White River Conservative had made money on the location of the Trans-Canada Highway, that the Conservatives were to blame for the deaths of three loggers in labour unrest near Kapuskasing, and more.[4]

Robarts ignored the charges. Sticking to a planned strategy, he spent the last days of August making low-key appearances to small groups of Tories and presenting the usual calm defence of his government's record. There was little hoopla, little to garner headlines. 'Bands just didn't seem to fit,' a local organizer commented about the premier's progress during the early stages of his tour. The trouble was, though, that the Liberals did have bands and were getting headlines.

Many Tories felt Robarts' first week was disastrous. They besieged the headquarters staff with pleas that Robarts fight back. When the leading organizers met in Toronto on Labour Day weekend to discuss the balance of the campaign, Leslie Frost was particularly upset. According to Eugene Westendorp, when Frost entered the meeting he threw his briefcase at one of Robarts' people, shouting that they were 'blowing the whole ———— thing.' Jackson reassured the group that the pace would pick up, that the first week had been deliberately slow while people were enjoying the last of their summer holidays.[5]

Robarts began to counter-attack the day after Labour Day. In a speech in Port Arthur he charged Reaume and Wintermeyer with spreading poison. Newspapers picked up the out-of-character remarks as heralding a tough new stance by Robarts. But he quickly reverted to his pragmatic style, talking about everything but charges of scandal. In a day's campaigning around Toronto he elicited little response. As the premier and his party left the city they were outwardly confident but inwardly depressed.

They had begun to formulate a response on the pension issue. Having seen Wintermeyer and LaMarsh together in Toronto, Robarts had decided that the federal minister was actively campaigning for his opponent. That made both Judy and her pension plan fair game. He raised the matter at his nomination speech in London, where he announced that because of the 'misinformation floating around in the campaign' he would attend the federal-provincial pension conference, scheduled to begin on Monday, 9 September to state clearly Ontario's position on a national pension plan.[6]

This threw the ball sharply back into LaMarsh's federal court, where plans had been made for a meeting solely at the ministerial level; no premiers were scheduled to attend. Pearson and his cabinet were not, on the whole, inclined to force an all-out political battle with Robarts on pensions. They had not been having an easy time of governing since their sixty days had gone sour in the spring (mostly because of Walter Gordon's disastrous budget), and had just been embarrassed by Wintermeyer's people leaking to the press the news that Ottawa was about to raise the existing old age pension by ten dollars a month. It was decided to leave LaMarsh on her own to deal with Robarts. Pearson would not attend the conference, which would go ahead as scheduled.[7]

Robarts campaigned from London into the neighbouring municipalities. Elmer Bell described their progress:

A trail through Stratford, Milverton, Listowel, Palmerston, Durham and Hanover. This is for the most part conservative country. The weather is fine, the crops are good and all is right with the world and the Conservative Party. The P.M. speaks briefly to the faithful at each place, imbibes coffee, eats doughnuts or a cookie and on split second timing proceeds on to the next stop. At each place there are anywhere from 50 to 150 old hands renewing their faith or new converts in need of assurance. The Press are fretting for some fight out of the Prime Minister and think at least he should be giving a few uppercuts but the P.M. proceeds at his own pace. At each stop he expounds a morsel of his programme, and exhorts the workers but pretty well ignores Wintermeyer. It might be interesting to remark how that to the best of my recollection, the P.M. at no time in the campaign acknowledged in any address that the New Democratic Party or its leader existed. I suppose Wintermeyer could also have had this anonymity had he chosen to fight on issues rather than on personalities and innuendo.[8]

The morsels Bell referred to were the PC campaign promises. These included free textbooks for students in grades nine and ten, increases in the pensions Ontario provided to the handicapped and needy (if Ottawa also acted), and other fairly minor inducements to vote Conservative.

Quick field work averted a potential embarrassment in Hanover, where a bitter industrial dispute was raging. The minister of labour, Leslie Rowntree, alerted the Robarts party that their meeting that evening was likely to be picketed. Robarts asked Rowntree to be in Hanover by 6 PM ready to mediate the dispute. Rowntree arrived at the last possible moment to brief the prime minister as he left for the local arena. Angry pickets carrying signs reading 'Mr. Premier will you HEAR US?' and 'Slaves to TORY LEGISLATION' were on hand as expected. Robarts began his speech by talking directly to them, supporting their right of free speech, and telling them that the minister of labour was waiting at the Queen's Hotel to see them and help mediate the dispute. The crowd broke into applause. Some of the picketers left to see Rowntree. Others stayed, and at the end of the meeting Robarts shook hands with striking workers who still carried their signs in the left hand while extending the right in greeting. Tories were so nimble that their opponents forgot the difference between left and right.

Robarts and his entourage, including the members of the Pension Advisory Committee, flew to Ottawa for his appearance at the federal-provincial conference on pensions. He reiterated Ontario's preference for a nation-wide plan, promising to co-operate with Ottawa. The two seemingly innocuous conditions of Ontario's support were that the national plan 'permit the integration of private plans,' and that it not 'inhibit the capital investment necessary for the development of the economy.'[9] As soon as he had given his speech, Robarts turned the Ontario delegation over to Jim Allan and flew back to the campaign trail. The appearance generated headlines across the province about the premier's promise to co-operate with Ottawa.

Judy LaMarsh had been hostess to Robarts' effective little appearance on the pension grandstand. She knew she had been upstaged, and she was also beginning to suspect that there was more to Robarts' pension position than a disinterested concern for Ontario's elderly. Robarts' staff unwittingly gave her ammunition when, in preparation for the conference, they listed the occupations of members of the Pension Advisory Committee. One of its members, Bill Rudd, worked for the

London Life Insurance Company. The Pension Advisory Committee in fact commanded a full range of pension expertise, but to LaMarsh and Wintermeyer Rudd's presence confirmed their suspicion that London Life was lurking prominently in John Robarts' political world. Was the Ontario premier really disinterested, or was he a skilled spokesman for the powerful insurance lobby, which had already come out in blunt opposition to the Liberal plan? At the end of the conference LaMarsh told a press conference that Robarts had been an unwanted visitor at the meetings and had offered nothing new. She apparently also said he did not know what he wanted.[10] Simultaneously, Wintermeyer was attacking Robarts for having an employee of London Life on his delegation.

Leslie Frost realized how effectively Judy had again jammed her foot in her mouth. Through Jackson he advised Robarts, who was biding his time, how to respond. On 11 September Robarts issued a statesmanlike press release, detaching himself and his government from the fury of a fighting Judy:

Since I was the only provincial premier who considered it sufficiently important to attend the conference and since I made a long statement setting out with utmost clarity our position and accepted, in principle, and offered my full support in devising a scheme which would be right for all of Canada, and which at the same time would protect our people in Ontario, I must conclude that I cannot take Miss LaMarsh's remarks too seriously.

It is apparent to me that she is determined to project both herself and this national program into our election campaign ... I cannot believe that she really takes herself too seriously in making these remarks.

However I am quite sure that I will be able to co-operate with Mr. Pearson.[11]

Elmer Bell and many of the reporters following the campaign thought the incident a major turning-point. Robarts had re-established his position on pensions, isolated LaMarsh as a somewhat unreliable partisan minister, and, by inference, put the prime minister in his corner. Wintermeyer kept on flailing away at Robarts' ties to the insurance lobby, eventually accusing the Conservatives of lying in their advertising on portable pensions.[12] In fact he and Judy had been deftly out-generalled on the pension issue, appearing shrill and alarmist in the face of the premier's statesmanship. Nor did the Liberal leader's pension position help him in his home city of Kitchener, one of the insurance centres of Ontario.

The other Liberal charges to be fielded came from the scandal campaign. More fat went into the fire on Friday, 13 September, as the deputy provincial secretary, R.J. Cudney, abruptly submitted his resignation and told the press he was doing so because the government had not responded adequately to the recommendations of the Roach Commission. Cudney had been a star witness before the commission, giving extensive testimony on how charters had been given to clubs implicated in gambling. Campaigning in Sarnia, Robarts responded to the resignation by challenging Cudney or Wintermeyer to present him with specific names and instances of wrongdoing on which he could act. None were received. While Cudney's resignation apparently helped the Liberals, their scandal campaign was not making a great deal of headway, not least because the Roach Commission's findings had taken so much of the sting out of the issue. There was a hint of desperation in the Liberals' scandal-hunting, a kind of frantic mud-slinging at the Conservative armour in the hope of hitting a chink. 'The P.M. was too clever to be caught by this tactic,' Bell recalled. 'He, in army parlance, "refused the flank." He allowed Wintermeyer to storm knowing that his able cabinet ministers could contain any penetration and he personally remained outside and above the war of words, continuing serenely to expound his theory of good government.'[13] Wintermeyer's tactics also eclipsed his party's substantial but unpublicized program on social and economic policy, causing many voters to wonder what the Liberals offered as an alternative.

The organizers did manage to infuse a little life into Robarts' campaign. Bell and Kinmond began trying to warm the premier up for his speeches, baiting him with Liberal charges as they drove along to a meeting, sometimes embellishing the mud with personal accusations. After half an hour or so of this, Robarts would be in a mood to deliver a fighting speech. He was louder, more forceful, less dull than in the first week of the campaign, but always careful to avoid getting down in the dirt to wrestle with Wintermeyer.

Robarts showed his usual stamina on the campaign trail, moving through a gruelling round of driving and speaking, speaking and driving, without showing any visible signs of strain. He seemed to revive himself with fresh fruit, his aides remembered. There was little time for serious unwinding and good drinking, though Bell recalls at least one occasion that is a rare window on John Robarts in off-hours:

We had a very good meeting in Sudbury and we were catching the plane from there to Kingston. We got on the plane and the plane was loaded up with lunch, booze, and this was something the Prime Minister rarely partook of on a campaign at all. But this night he was just dead tired. So we started saying well you've got to have a few drinks here. So we did and we were feeling pretty good. Then we started showing the clippings of what Wintermeyer had said about him, and the clippings of what Judy LaMarsh had said about him and so on. We got them all out and were reading them to him trying to get him mad. We got him a little bit worked up and he told us what the hell he was going to do. He was feeling pretty high. The only time I ever saw him talk about his opposition and he said 'You know what we're going to do?' He said 'That Liberal caucus room, do you know where it's going? It's going way up there in the attic.' He said 'We're fixing up quarters for those people, we're going to fix them so damn high that they'll be shaking hands with their maker.' It was quite a show and he gave us a pretty good rundown on Judy LaMarsh and at last we thought we'd got him steamed up – things are going to happen here it was really a delightful time.

We got to Kingston and ... we went over to Syl Apps' place and of course, Syl Apps is a teetotaler, but the rest of us weren't. And by George, we were at Syl Apps' then for a couple of hours and I was trying to get the Prime Minister out of there, but he was enjoying himself you know. So in the wee hours of the night we finally got him out of there and I thought he's got a breakfast meeting tomorrow morning in Kingston and he'll never make it, but he did make it. From the breakfast meeting he was up and then down to the market and really put on a show there. No problems at all.

He had a remarkable sense of recuperation.

It was Ontario's first widely televised campaign. After long, complicated negotiations it had been agreed that the campaign would include a special leaders' debate, held in a television studio. The Robarts camp had been divided on the wisdom of giving the opposition leaders a platform with the prime minister, but had decided that their man was so much better than the competition that he could hardly lose. Still, the rules had been carefully stipulated: no direct debating between the principals, no shots of reactions when a leader was answering a question. Robarts testily refused to allow his picture to be taken while he was being made up to go on television. Just as the show was about to start the chairman asked if the rules could be changed. Robarts threatened to leave. The taping proceeded according to the agreement and the debate was televised on 17 September. Robarts' friends thought he had done well. Most observers found the video confrontation no event at all. 'The reporters showed no imagination in their questioning,' the *Canadian Annual Review* for 1963 observed, 'nor did any of the leaders betray any brilliance they might have possessed.'

By the last week of the campaign there was little new to say. On 21 September the Liberal Toronto *Star* endorsed John Robarts and, somewhat less enthusiastically, the Conservative party. The editors pronounced Robarts to have all but accepted a national pension plan and decided he was not responsible for whatever substance there was to the scandal charges. In the same edition of the *Star* a special poll showed that 43 per cent of Ontarians thought Robarts would make the best premier. Fourteen per cent chose Wintermeyer and 9 per cent favoured Donald MacDonald. The fledgling NDP had tried to conduct a sober, issue-oriented campaign and had been largely ignored.

John Robarts made only two brief appearances in London North, where his brother Robert handled the campaign against Cam Calder, the Liberal they had beaten in 1951. John White ran again in London South. Local Liberals managed to make themselves appear surpassingly silly by challenging the legality of a tea and cookies reception the Conservatives held at the Hotel London to wind up the campaign. The Elections Act forbade a candidate from wooing voters by giving out favours. When the Liberal complaint about the comestibles was forwarded to Conservative organizers by the returning officer, Robert Robarts announced to the five hundred prominent Londoners in attendance that the food and tea would have to be cleared away because the Liberals had objected. John Robarts and John

White met the press, with the prime minister dubbing the affair 'a tempest in a teapot.' This was what Arthur Reaume's 'wild tea party' of a campaign had come to. The Liberal raid on Tory tea pots was reported across the province. No charges were ever laid. Robarts thought the insult to his guests probably swung another fifteen hundred London votes to himself and White. As the campaign closed, no one believed that the government would be defeated.

Robarts and his family awaited the results in London. The Conservatives were ahead in the earliest returns and stayed there. Within an hour of the polls' closing it was clear they had been re-elected. The governing party increased its share of the popular vote by two points, rising to 48.7 per cent. Both the Liberals and the NDP went down slightly. Robarts and all his cabinet were re-elected. The Liberals made some gains in Windsor, southwestern Ontario, and the north, while the NDP did modestly well in Toronto, Oshawa, and Hamilton. The Conservatives had strength all over the province, particularly in the east (where they won back Renfew South, smashed the dissident Tory in Russell, and lost only Ottawa East), and in Toronto, where they won eight of the ten new ridings in the suburbs. All parties increased their standing in the enlarged legislature, but the Tories made the biggest gains, going from seventy-one to seventy-seven seats. The Liberals went from twenty-two to twenty-four, the NDP from five to seven. John Wintermeyer was beaten by more than two thousand votes in his home riding of Waterloo North. He submitted his resignation as Liberal leader the next day and faded from Ontario's political life.

Robarts gave a bland victory speech, promising his campaign workers that they could 'look forward to a productive four years of government in Ontario.' He had done a good job in the campaign, adhering to the party strategy, avoiding being sucked in by the opposition, out-manoeuvring his opponents with considerable skill whenever they tried to corner him. He had continued to be a phlegmatic politician, who could get more rattled in mock give-and-take with his advisers than by anything the Liberals said. He had not really relaxed on the hustings, and still preferred governing to politicking. The electoral job was over for a while, carried out competently. Robarts had gone to the people in his own right and won their approval as prime minister of Ontario.

'Terrible Legislation': Bill 99

The 1963 election seemed to confirm the course Robarts was taking as prime minister: a low-key, chairman-of-the-board, leader-of-the-team approach to government. The results posed only minor, not particularly unpleasant problems, such as how to handle the influx of new Conservative backbenchers. True, there would be some changes in the cabinet, as those who had stayed on to see the new boy through his first election left. But there was a lot of new talent to bring along. There was also the huge amount of legislative housekeeping to do to keep Ontario well governed, the kind of housekeeping that was starting to become the hallmark of Robarts' administration.

There were thirty-two new faces in the Conservative caucus. The impact of the new blood on the party and the legislature would be reminiscent of the situation after 1951 when Robarts himself had been one of the rookies. One measure of the enthusiasm of the group was the large number of newly elected MPPs, including Liberals and New Democrats, who asked Roderick Lewis, the clerk of the assembly, for an introduction to the rules and customs of the legislature. In the old days Lewis had briefed the handful of interested members in his office or over lunch. Now he had to organize and conduct a seminar; it thereafter became part of the routine procedure for the opening of the legislature. The change was a small straw in a slight breeze.

There were so many Conservatives in the expanded House that it was difficult to seat them all in the chamber. They completely filled the traditional government benches on the Speaker's right and spilled over onto the other side. The need to give the opposition parties adequate front bench room led to a group of five junior Tory members from Toronto having to sit behind opposition members and face their own party across the floor. The five developed a spirited sense of identity, gradually becoming known as the 'Chicago Gang' and raising a little hell with attacks on the opposition from its rear and a little heckling of their own frontbenchers across the floor. One of them, R. Alan Eagleson, got into typical hot water one day when he enraged a chronically verbose Liberal speaker by organizing a lottery with neighbouring Liberals and Tories to guess the exact minute when the windbag would stop. Learning of the lottery, the offended member wanted Eagleson charged with gambling.[1] But if there had been an act of organized crime it was protected by parliamentary immunity.

The major change in cabinet was the departure of Robert Macaulay. Shortly after the election Macaulay reminded Robarts of their agreement at the start of the leadership campaign. He had helped his friend through his first year as premier and his subsequent re-election; now he was ready to resign his ministerial responsibilities at Robarts' convenience. Reasons of health would be the stated explanation. Macaulay's departure would end the Robarts-Macaulay duet that had been so important in the rejuvenation at the end of the Frost years and in the new premier's first legislative sessions. The transition of power to Randall, Macaulay's handpicked successor, was not carried out quite as smoothly as Robarts had hoped, for while he was waiting for Randall to set his business and personal affairs in order, the news of Macaulay's impending resignation was leaked to the press as a result of Macaulay's loose talk to his riding organization.[2] Robarts had to call a hurried press conference to accept the resignation and announce that Macaulay's two portfolios, Economics and Development, and Energy Resources, would be handled temporarily by James Allan and J.R. Simonett respectively. A few weeks later Randall took over Economics and Development; Simonett stayed in Energy Resources. Macaulay returned to backbench life and his old habit of bombarding his premier with suggestions.

Another straw in the breezes of change was the opposition Robarts ran into when he proposed a short fall sitting of the legislature. The 1961 experience had caused him to dislike the prospect of rushing into an autumn session and he would have preferred to have none at all, except that he had promised to introduce legislation to enable municipalities to tap the federal Municipal Development and Loan Fund. So he announced that the legislature would convene on 29 October solely for this purpose, remarking offhandedly that the business would take about two hours. Donald MacDonald and the Liberals' interim leader, Farquhar Oliver, strongly objected that the prime minister's attitude was contemptuous of the public business. There was no Speech from the Throne when the legislature met, and no orders of the day. The premier relented a bit on the two-hour estimate and allowed the session to last for a day and a half – time to pass the necessary legislation, reconstitute a couple of select committees, and allow the opposition to let off steam. As later years demonstrated, Robarts was not going to be able to take the legislature back to the old days of the eight-week winter and the got-to-get-the-crops-in timetable. Sentiment was starting to grow in Ontario that politics should be a full-time job.

It already was for the prime minister and his staff. Still a remarkably small staff, though, and even shrinking slightly as more of the Frost people melted away into other jobs. By 1963 Robarts had only two important executive officers under

McIntyre in his Department of the Prime Minister: Bill Kinmond, his press secretary, and Ray Farrell, who acted as assistant secretary of the cabinet. The one new man whom he used from time to time as a special personal assistant was the Toronto lawyer, Richard Rohmer. Rohmer had supported Robarts for the leadership and worked on the fringes of his organization. He agreed to serve as a part-time assistant to the premier so long as he could maintain his law practice. Rohmer would look into special problems, such as regional government, appear at committee meetings from time to time as Robarts' unofficial spokesman, and sometimes move into the Queen's Park office next to Robarts to get a special job done. But he was never considered a member of the staff, and his somewhat shadowy comings and goings were noticed and resented by the regulars as a usurpation of their responsibilities.[3]

Through the autumn of 1963 the cabinet reviewed a long list of legislative proposals and prepared a massive program to put before the House when it reconvened on 15 January. The Throne Speech promised a deluge of legislative activity, not only in the normally dominant areas of economic development and education, but in broader fields involving social, fiscal, and structural reform. Social issues were being addressed, for example, with the promise to create a women's bureau and a proposal to consolidate youth agencies in a new branch of the Department of Education. Fiscal and structural reforms were to take place in several major areas. First, the government committed itself to a fundamental review of its health expenditures, with particular reference to the adequacy of Ontario's supply of hospital beds. Secondly, a new Department of Energy and Resources Management would be charged with increased responsibilities for protecting natural resources and handling the problem of the low water table in the southwestern peninsula. Thirdly, it was proposed to centralize rural education and welfare services in larger township units. Fourthly, the existing Metropolitan Toronto and Region Transportation Study was to be extended to include consideration of the relationship of transport to land-use planning and community development. Fifthly, coming out of the report of the Select Committee on Consumer Credit there would be legislation to protect consumers from loan frauds, stock swindles, and abuses in the used car business. Finally, the government announced that it was beginning to prepare for Canada's centennial celebrations in 1967.

It should have been another busy, businesslike session, following the pattern of the two previous years. Instead, the whole year's activities came to pivot around the crisis caused on 19 March 1964, when Bill 99, An Act to Amend the Police Act, was introduced into the legislature. Ontarians were outraged at what appeared to be legislation stripping away the age-old protections individuals had against the arbitrary use of police authority. Robarts faced a firestorm of public protest and threats of rebellion from his backbenchers and within his cabinet. Neither he nor the cabinet had foreseen any problem with the legislation, and were taken completely by surprise.

Bill 99 was not an accident, not just the result of sloppy drafting and some underlings' oversights. It had deep roots in the organized crime issue, which had been bedevilling Robarts since 1961. It was badly mishandled largely because of serious administrative problems and conflicts in a major department of government headed by a minister with a confused and conflicting set of responsibilities, the attorney general.

Considering the context first, the problems inherent in the office of the attorney general had been recognized since the 1850s. The attorney general is the chief law officer of the crown, responsible for maintaining the rule of law in the province. It was his duty to champion such legal protections as the right of due process, *habeas corpus,* and trial by jury, even at times when they were threatened by the actions of his colleagues in government.[4]

On the other hand, as the system had developed over generations, the attorney general is the political minister in charge of administering a department of government and a member of cabinet bound by conventions of cabinet solidarity. His department had grown by the 1960s to the point where the minister was not only the chief law officer but also the minister responsible for the Department of Insurance, the Emergency Measures Organization, the Ontario Securities Commission, and the Ontario Provincial Police Force (OPP), among other agencies. Thus there were many departmental responsibilities, but the special legal responsibility of the minister meant that his department was not as closely linked as other departments to the political system through cabinet. This isolation had been strengthened during the long tenure of Kelso Roberts, an outsider and loner in both the Frost and Robarts regimes.

The public's alarms about organized crime had caused the Ontario government to respond in several ways, not all of them consistent. We saw that one of Kelso Roberts' main initiatives, introduced in 1961, was to create the Ontario Police Commission. One of his aims in doing this was to get the management of policing away from day-to-day political influence. Thus, it was hoped, partisan interference with law enforcement would be minimized.

The legislation creating the Ontario Police Commission (OPC) gave it broad and somewhat vague authority over Ontario police forces as well as responsibility for determining the scope of organized crime in the province.[5] To ensure its independence, for example, the commission was required to publish in its annual report any attempt by politicians to interfere in its area of responsibility; the report was to be submitted directly to the legislature. Roberts appointed Judge B.J.S. Macdonald of Windsor as the first chairman of the OPC. Macdonald had an excellent administrative record on local police commissions in Windsor and Leamington. Roberts instructed Macdonald to standardize and modernize police administration in the province and particularly to improve relations between municipal forces and the Ontario Provincial Police. The commission was also given responsibility for the administration of the OPP and in the spring and summer of 1962 went ahead with a broad program of reform in the force. Roberts would have liked the commission to have gone still further that year, for he believed it was the logical body to investigate the kinds of charges John Wintermeyer had made about organized crime and corruption in high places. But his views were overriden in cabinet and the Roach Commission was given the mandate instead.

A second response to the crime problem came some months later when Roberts shuffled his cabinet in the autumn of 1962, replacing Kelso Roberts with Fred Cass. Cass was a proven organizer, and his job was to restore political control to a department that seemed, from the point of view of the cabinet, to have been too lax in supervising its agencies.

The Ontario Police Commission had already been singled out as one of the agencies to be reconsidered. Before appointing Cass, Roberts had asked Don Collins, the chairman of the Civil Service Commission, to draft a proposal to create a new departmental organization to administer provincial law enforcement agencies. As part of his proposal, Collins mentioned the OPC's assumption of 'rather wide powers caused largely by filling the leadership vacuum in the rather free wheeling world of the independent agency in the Attorney General's Department.' Collins argued that the commission should effectively be stripped of its wide responsibilities, most of which should properly be returned to ministerial control. 'It should be an advisory agency only insofar as provincial law enforcement is concerned,' Collins argued. 'The commission should not continue to fulfill line administrative functions. The minister should be solely responsible for the policies and direction of the Department.' He forwarded his proposal to the new attorney general, Fred Cass.[6]

Collins was responsible for yet another response to the crime problem in his decision to recommend that Eric H. Silk be made commissioner of the Ontario Provincial Police. Collins had an interest in the appointment because the OPP fell within the jurisdiction of the Civil Service Commission. Morale in the force was poor and its reputation had suffered from the charges of corruption paraded before the Roach Commission.[7] Collins thought the force needed a strong commissioner, and that he had an ideal man for the job in Silk, currently serving as senior legislative counsel. Silk was blunt, forceful, and experienced at administrative reform. One sticking point was his desire to become deputy attorney general; this was overcome by giving him the rank and status of a deputy minister in his job as commissioner of the OPP. Silk was appointed early in 1963 with a mandate to improve the efficiency and effectiveness of the force.

The result of these responses was that by 1963 three powerful men had been given wide responsibilities to improve policing and law enforcement in Ontario: Macdonald at the Police Commission, Cass the attorney general, and Silk of the OPP. The lines of jurisdiction and co-ordination between them, however, were not clear.

The day he took office, Cass objected to the Police Commission's presumption that it had the legal authorization to direct the commissioner of the OPP in the running of his force. He ordered it to act only in a consultative and advisory capacity to the attorney general in matters concerning the OPP. So far the Police Commission had not really acted in any other capacity, having always cleared its OPP proposals with Kelso Roberts. But in fact it did have the Police Act of 1961-2 on its side in giving it control of the OPP, and Judge Macdonald did not appreciate Cass' apparent determination to enforce political control of policing. His resentment increased when Cass began implementing policy for the OPP without bothering to consult the commission.[8] Robarts sided with Cass in the debate and the Police Act was eventually amended accordingly.

Neither Macdonald nor Mr Justice Roach was happy with the Silk appointment. Both his past experience in the department and his current rank as deputy minister inclined Silk to deal directly with the attorney general, bypassing the Police Commission. Roach entered the debate in an addendum to his royal commission report in which he criticized Silk's rank and urged that the OPP report to the Police Commission. Otherwise the visible distance between politics and law enforcement, which had been deliberately created with the formation of the Police Commission, would be reduced again.

Macdonald and Cass continued to spar over control of the OPP and over Macdonald's jurisdiction. In fact both were anxious to reform policing in Ontario, but each was jealous of his turf. Cass wrote Robarts in October 1963, for example:

You may all have read pronouncements by his Hon. Judge B.J.S. Macdonald ... that he proposed to do away with small police forces and have their municipality policed by the OPP. Of course, in this instance as in certain others, his Honour has greatly exceeded the authority vested in the Ontario Police Commission in making pronouncements on government policy. I must advise you, however, that I concur wholeheartedly in His Honour's views that the small municipal police force must disappear.[9]

In the meantime the vexing problem of uncovering the extent of organized crime in Ontario had refused to go away. When the Roach Commission reported that syndicated crime did not exist in Ontario, Commissioner Harvison of the RCMP publicly and firmly disagreed.[10] This insistence that Roach had not settled the matter enabled Macdonald of the Police Commission to do what Kelso Roberts had wanted him to do in the first place: hold his own inquiry into the extent of organized crime. He proceeded to do this, but almost immediately ran into uncertainties about the commission's powers to gather evidence. As Roach had learned, fear of reprisals from the 'mob' seemed to be a serious factor preventing people from testifying about the real state of crime in the province. How could it be overcome?

Early in his work Macdonald asked the Attorney General's Department whether his commission had the power to hold hearings in private, to give an assurance of secrecy to the witness, and to enforce the attendance of witnesses for testimony before the commission at private hearings. The obvious hope was that more information about crime would emerge if witnesses could feel free – or could be required – to testify in private. The law officers of the department looked into his query and concluded that the relevant legislation, section 48 of the Police Act, did not make 'any of these clear beyond doubt.'[11] Macdonald accepted the advice and did not hold any private hearings. But when he submitted his report, on 31 January 1964, he recommended amending the Police Act to:

(a) permit hearings in private as well as in public;
(b) make it an offence without the permission of the commission to disclose information given in private hearings; and
(c) confer on the commission the power of a superior court to punish for contempt at either public or private hearings.[12]

When the department's law officers received the recommendation, they considered it and agreed

in principle ... (a) that the Commission be given authority to hold hearings in private, if necessary; (b) that it be made an offense to disclose names and testimony given at private hearings without the consent of the Commission; and (c) that adequate powers be given to the Commission that it might obtain information under oath at private and public hearings.[13]

On this basis a draft amendment to the Police Act was prepared.

These events were taking place beyond the minister's ken. Fred Cass was burdened with a number of important issues in the autumn and winter of 1963-4, including consumer protection legislation, the growing responsibilities of the Ontario Securities Commission, proposals for an Ontario legal aid scheme, the reorganization of the courts, and proposals for the creation of a law reform commission. As well, he was attempting to pursue a longstanding interest he had in the rights of the individual who faced expropriation. His several responsibilities led to his presenting a long series of bills to the cabinet in November 1963. Among them was an amendment to the Police Act, unrelated to the crime issue, which would increase the Police Commission's power to enforce 'adequate' police service standards on municipalities. Other changes were also being recommended in police administration. The cabinet reviewed and approved the proposed amendments to the Police Act, with attention focusing on the impact the changes would have on small-town forces.

The key amendment, enlarging the commission's powers to investigate crime, was drafted after cabinet approval of the first package and before any of the bills were introduced in the legislature. The law officers who reviewed the draft before submitting it to the attorney general concluded that its key provision, section 14, 'would not affect the right to have counsel, ... the right of communication and of all legal remedies.' So they presented section 14 to the attorney general 'as clarifying but not enlarging the powers of the Commission to conduct inquiries,' except for the provision 'that hearings may be held in private as well as in public.'[14] The amendments had previously been shown to Eric Silk, who had commented on the provisions affecting the OPP and suggested that the commission's need for investigative powers could adequately be dealt with by reference to the Public Inquiries Act. His suggestion was not followed. On 21 February 1964 the new amendment appeared, having been incorporated into the earlier, approved, draft amendment. The explanatory note for the new section 14 stated: 'The new sections provide the machinery necessary for the Commission to investigate matters relating to the extent, investigation or control of crime in Ontario.'[15] There was to be a final review by cabinet and caucus before introduction in the legislature.

The first two weeks of March were a busy, difficult time for John Robarts. The legislature was in session, the annual press gallery dinner was approaching, federal-provincial negotiations were placing an increasing demand on his time, and his father was dying in London. The morning after the press festivities he drove to Grand Bend for the weekend, stopping to see his father at St Joseph's Hospital in London. Herbert Robarts died on 14 March at the age of eighty-three. John Robarts returned to Queen's Park from his father's funeral just in time to adjourn the House. Once that week Donald MacDonald observed the premier asleep in the chamber during the debate. The pace and trauma were exacting their toll.

As a result of Robarts' brief absence from a chronically short-staffed office, there was a backlog of business before cabinet when it met on the morning of Thursday, 19 March. Fred Cass had eleven bills to introduce affecting mortgages, wages, used car dealers, salesmen, the Law Society of Upper Canada, real estate, and juvenile and family courts, as well as his Bill 99, amending the Police Act. All were on the order paper for the afternoon, many had been discussed previously. In his *persona* as chief legal officer, Cass himself was not happy with section 14 of Bill 99, worrying that it would allow the Police Commission to interfere with individual rights.[16] He was not happy generally with the Police Commission, having earlier that morning criticized Macdonald to some reporters for some of the more sweeping recommendations of his report on organized crime. 'Macdonald's ideas could lead Ontario into a police state,' Cass had told the press in a remarkable attack on the chairman.[17]

In the cabinet review of the legislation, however, Cass did not express his reservations. His law officers had assured him that an individual's personal rights were still protected under the amendments. Time was pressing; there were other issues to talk about, and Cass may have felt the whole question was really

Macdonald's doing anyway. The bill was accepted by ministers who would not have read further than the explanatory notes, if they got that far. At 1 PM it went before a caucus at which only ten of the seventy-seven Conservative members were present.[18] The legislature convened an hour later.

Cass tabled the Report of the Ontario Police Commission on Organized Crime as well as the second annual report of the Ontario Police Commission, and then introduced his bills for first reading. He described Bill 99, An Act to Amend the Police Act

as a series of amendments ... to define more particularly the powers of the Ontario Police Commission, and to give it certain additional powers, particularly with respect to determining the adequacy of policing ... It provides for the issuance of commissions to officers of the Ontario Provincial Police Force ... It also provides for the control and direction of the Ontario Provincial Police Force in a manner similar to that now used by the federal government with the Royal Canadian Mounted Police.

The bill had not yet been printed and first reading was just a formality, so none of the opposition members and none of the members of the press corps knew the actual wording of the proposed legislation. When Cass had finished, Liberal Vernon Singer asked 'if all these bills will be going to committee. There is a lot of new and important legislation here and I think the committee should have a look at all of them.' Cass replied that the bills would be going to committee, 'except perhaps the Police Act which might better be discussed in committee of the whole House.'

Section 14 of Bill 99, which would soon be in print for everyone to see, read as follows:

14. *The Police Act* is amended by adding thereto the following sections:

  39c.—(1)   The Commission may inquire into and report to the Attorney General upon any matter relating to,

  (a) the extent, investigation or control of crime;

  (b) the enforcement of law; or

  (c) its functions under this Act.

  (2)   For the purpose of an inquiry under subsection 1, the Commission may summon any person and require him to give evidence on oath, *in camera* or otherwise, and to produce such documents and things as the Commission deems requisite.

  (3)   Where evidence is taken *in camera* under subsection 2, no person, without the consent of the Commission, shall disclose any information or evidence obtained or the name of any witness examined or sought to be examined under subsection 2, and every person who contravenes this subsection is guilty of an offence and on summary conviction is liable to a

fine of not more than $2,000 or to imprisonment for a term of not more than one year, or to both.

39d.—(1) The Commission has all the powers to enforce the attendance of witnesses and to compel them to give evidence and produce documents and things as are vested in any court in civil cases.

(2) Where a person, being present at an inquiry and being required by the Commission to give evidence,

(a) refuses to be sworn;

(b) having been sworn, refuses to answer the questions that are put to him;

(c) fails to produce any writings that he is required to produce; or

(d) refuses to sign his deposition, without offering a reasonable excuse for his failure or refusal, the Commission may, by warrant, commit the person to prison for a period not exceeding eight clear days.

(3) Where a person to whom subsection 2 applies is again brought before the Commission and again refuses to do what is required of him, the Commission may again commit him to prison for a period not exceeding eight clear days and may commit the person to prison from time to time until the person consents to do what is required of him.

39e.—The chairman of the Commission may authorize one or more members of the Commission to conduct any inquiry that the Commission may conduct, and each member so authorized may exercise the powers and perform the duties of the Commission under section 39b, subsections 1 and 2 of 39c, section 39d and section 48.

On the evening of 19 March, while James Auld was presenting the Department of Travel and Publicity estimates in the House, and John Robarts and other members of the cabinet were entertaining members of the press at the Royal York Hotel, Fred Cass was discussing the legislation he had brought in that day. The interview had been taped at 4 PM at Queen's Park. During the preliminary conversation, Peter Reilly of CBC television happened to ask Cass if the Police Bill threatened individual rights. The question triggered the attorney general's concerns as a law officer. 'Yes, that's what bothers me,' Fred Cass told an instantly alert Reilly, going on to argue that its provisions did seem to be necessary to combat organized crime. Reilly persuaded Cass to repeat his reservations for television, and he was recorded as saying of the bill that 'it is drastic, it is dangerous and it is new and it is terrible legislation in an English common law country.' When he was asked why, then, the legislation was being introduced, Cass continued to self-destruct by saying, 'Don't ask me. Ask Judge Macdonald.'[19] Cass then left for home, and some constituency engagements. His comments about Bill 99 were broadcast on the news that evening and appeared as headlines in the 'bulldog' edition of the *Globe and Mail,* which appeared at 9 PM.

Someone brought the *Globe* to Bill Kinmond at the press party. He took one look at it and showed it to Robarts. In the party atmosphere neither man realized the full impact of the Cass gloss on Bill 99, but they agreed there was a problem and decided to meet in the prime minister's office at eight the next morning to find out what had gone wrong. James Auld, who had come over after the legislature adjourned, tried to find Cass but could not locate him. Kelso Roberts was called at home and told about the story by a reporter for the *Globe and Mail*. Roberts commented that 'if what he told me was correct I would be opposed to the Bill,' a statement prominently reported in the paper's morning edition.

The Bill 99 affair might never have occurred had Cass not talked so freely at his press conference, putting a different interpretation on section 14 than his department's lawyers did, using it as a kind of stick to flail Macdonald and the Police Commission out of his deep-seated concern for individual rights. Journalists love to sensationalize and simplify. Read carefully in the light of common law practices – if anyone would have bothered to read it at all – section 14 might or might not have been interpreted as a menace to individual liberties. But now the attorney general himself had directed everyone's attention to the section and told them it was drastic, dangerous, and terrible. Led by the Toronto newspapers, which were full of front-page stories about 'Star Chamber' legislation (it seemed particularly worrisome that people would be interrogated in private – who would know what wrongs were being done to them?) and editorials condemning the 'Bill of Wrongs,' the media alarmed Ontarians into creating a hurricane of outraged protest.

Perhaps Ontarians would not have been outraged at giving the police drastic powers if there had actually been much substance to all the talk over the years about the menace of organized crime. In fact the crime issue had been largely symbolic, a focus for the public's deep, irrational fears about evil menacing their way of life. Now, virtually overnight, Bill 99 raised a new, powerful symbol to invert and focus that same fear. But the evil menace was not the gangsters, it was the government! A government bringing in terrible legislation that could affect every single person in Ontario, for no particularly good reason. The Bill 99 furor was a sharp, dramatic beginning of the deepening attitude of the 1960s and 1970s that governments were the real menace to the freedoms of the individual.

The government, in the person of the prime minister, had no idea what it was doing. There was 'absolute chaos' in the office, Irene Beatty remembered, with phones ringing incessantly and the telex terminal operating twenty-four hours a day. Robarts, Kinmond, and Richard Rohmer had their 8 AM meeting on Friday. Rohmer argued that the bill should be seen through. Kinmond wanted it withdrawn. Robarts decided to salvage what he could. The legal experts in the Attorney General's Department were still saying that the bill did not challenge the rights of the individual as guaranteed by common law. Fred Cass had gone home to rural eastern Ontario for the weekend and, not reading the Toronto newspapers, was oblivious to events in Toronto. Seeing little use in calling him, Robarts took charge.[20] He faced the legislature later in the morning. Farquhar Oliver tried to get a first statement in, but was ruled out of order and Robarts was given the floor. In a classic 'salvage' statement (drafted in large part by Frost), direct and unqualified, putting his own honour at stake, Robarts pledged: 'I, personally, would not tolerate any legislation which infringes upon or jeopardizes the basic, fundamental, personal rights and freedoms of the individuals of this province ... I can assure the House before any action is taken on this bill it will be completely re-examined in the light of what I have said.'[21] He defended the intent of the bill, as best he could, emphasizing the balance that had to be struck between fighting organized crime and preserving the rights of individuals. He tried to argue the government's belief that study in committee would uphold the experts' view that the bill was not a menace. An angry Farquhar Oliver attacked the government for not knowing the contents of its own legislation. Donald MacDonald was somewhat more restrained. Having grasped the irony of the situation, he attacked the Liberals as well as the government: 'I am just a little saddened by the willingness to play politics on the part of some people who a year ago were desperately disturbed with organized crime and now have forgotten about it completely.'

By noon a crowd of University of Toronto students had gathered outside the legislature to protest the evil bill. They wanted to see the premier. Robarts' first instinct was to refuse to come out. But after meeting some of the students inside and at Kinmond's urging, he went out and gave the students the same pledge he had made in the House. The students went away, seemingly satisfied. Not many others were, as the crisis continued to mount. The greatest political danger to Robarts was that members of his own party would speak out against the bill, as Kelso Roberts effectively already had. Other members, particularly Toronto backbenchers, were making their unhappiness known. Roberts himself spent the weekend preparing a long brief for the premier, tracing the background of the organized crime issue, concluding that there was no need to give the Police Commission further power and that Bill 99 should be withdrawn.

Robarts spent much of Saturday closeted with Kinmond, Rohmer, and Leslie Frost. The lawyers from the Attorney General's Department appeared and tried to explain their views on the amendment.[22] Robarts' advisers were divided. The premier eventually agreed to defend the bill when it came up for debate on Monday. On Sunday Frost drafted a plan of attack. The key to the strategy was to link the need for investigatory power for the Ontario Police Commission firmly to its report on organized crime (in which it complained about its lack of power), and insist that the need to counter the threat of American-style syndicated crime in Ontario be taken into account when reviewing the investigative powers of the OPC. Frost suggested that Robarts accept full responsibility for the bill, thus 'starting on a broad front rather than go on the defensive and be destroyed in detail.'

You can best meet the present fury (which I think will be and could be maintained against Cass but not against the P.M.) by a fresh, dignified presentation of the facts and intentionally drawing fire away from the Attorney General and others. In my opinion this will generate admiration for yourself and will immediately place the whole question on a different plane.[23]

Robarts should then refer the bill, along with the report, to the Legal Bills Committee for study before final government policy was set.

Frost's suggestion would postpone debate on the substantive issues posed by Bill 99. There would be a debate only on procedure. Robarts went along with the idea – which was also a way of continuing to sit on the fence about the bill – but stipulated that he was going to continue to reassure the public about the government's commitment to preserve individual rights. He was not yet ready to sacrifice section 14, but was perhaps a little closer to doing so than some of his advisers. The pressure to scrap it was continuing to mount, as Kelso Roberts weighed in that Monday morning with a letter incorporating his weekend's research and urging that the whole bill be withdrawn.

The public galleries were packed when the legislature met that Monday afternoon. Members screamed at each other, and the gallery observers broke into applause from time to time. Robarts began the debate and, as planned, took full responsibility for the bill and the tabling of the Police Commission's report on organized crime. He linked the report to the bill, then took the accommodating step back:

I want to make it eminently clear, as I have said before, that the government did not at the time this bill was introduced, nor does it now, consider this bill to be the final piece of legislation nor the complete answer to the problems that we are attempting to solve ...

If there is a conflict between the rights of the individual and the necessity for powers to deal with the criminal elements in our society, then the rights of the individual must be supreme, even if it means that in so doing we give to the criminal elements in our society an advantage which we would rather they did not have.[24]

Robarts moved that Bill 99 be sent to the Legal Bills Committee.

Farquhar Oliver could do little but complain about the shabbiness of the procedure.[25] He moved an amendment to Robarts' motion which would have had the effect of withdrawing the bill. Donald MacDonald reiterated the opposition's outrage, and attacked the government as being both unrepentant and in chaos. Like Oliver, he drove home the point that the government had to get the bill out of the House because it had lost the confidence of its own backbenchers.

As indeed it had. Allan Lawrence spoke for the dissident backbenchers in a passionate attack on section 14, accentuating his points by shaking his fist in the prime minister's direction:

I want to publicly castigate the people who introduced that section of this bill. The only way I can do it is in committee. To withdraw it in its entirety is nonsense ... Therefore, sir, I feel that we have to support the motion of the hon. Prime Minister in referring this to committee. I may say that I do this with great regret because I do not want to be tainted in any manner, shape or form with that particular section of that bill and I will fight – even cross the floor of this House – and I will vote against this section of the bill if it is put to this House in this form, sir.[26]

Robarts' motion was being supported by Lawrence and other critical backbenchers, such as the 'Chicago gang', only because it did not imply any endorsement of the offensive proposals.

As the debate progressed, the Liberals attacked with Andrew Thompson giving a highly effective, detailed, emotional dissection of the government's position, a speech that helped to elevate him to the Liberal leadership a few months later. The government members papered over their differences long enough to defeat the Liberal amendment. Donald MacDonald then moved another amendment:

I submit to you, Mr. Speaker, that there is a very simple way to resolve the problem that the House now finds itself in and that the government finds itself in. I do not know why the government wants to rub salt in its own wounds by sticking with section 14. I would think it, more than anybody, would want to get rid of section 14 ... Therefore I move ... that the motion be amended by adding thereto, 'and that the committee be instructed to delete section 14 of the said bill.'[27]

Robarts had by now realized that he could not keep section 14 even on the fence. 'I would say that section 14, if its effect is what it has been interpreted to be,' he told the House, 'is as offensive to me as it is to any other honourable member of this House.'[28] He agreed to support MacDonald's amendment on a slightly face-saving condition that section 14 would be subjected to debate in the committee before it was deleted. There was some debate on Robarts' condition, but eventually MacDonald's amendment was passed unanimously.

Robarts' last responsibility of the day was to read to the legislature the letter of resignation Fred Cass had submitted to him that morning. Cass had realized he had no option but to resign. He tried to explain how his responsibilities as the chief law officer of Ontario had led him into the mess:

In answer to certain questions put to me by the Press with respect to Bill 99, I felt constrained to stress the urgent need of the whole problem, and in my capacity as Attorney General I could do no less. The price of our freedom from the invisible tyranny of syndicated crime is the continuance of the vigilance which has thus far protected us from these infamous agencies. In making these comments, I have unintentionally touched upon the sensibilities of our people. In doing this, however, I was answering the dictates of my own conscience.[29]

The House then adjourned.

Democracy and a vigilant press had had their way. Cass' career as a minister had been ruined, and Robarts himself had suffered a humiliating ordeal. Now he had to face his unhappy caucus. Their meeting on Tuesday, 24 March began in an atmosphere of gloom and recrimination. Possibly its turning point was an upbeat speech by John White, who had been out of the city during the heated warm-up to the debate and missed some of the more emotional reactions. White argued that the incident was relatively insignificant in relation to the government's overall program. He or some of the other members might have added that it had come relatively early in the government's life, years before there would have to be an election. Caucus rallied round the leader, who made clear that Bill 99 would be studied extremely carefully. The crisis seemed to have passed.

Raw nerve ends still jangled. On 25 March the new chairman of the Ontario Police Commission, R.P. Milligan, complained in the *Globe and Mail* that removal of section 14 would undercut his commission's power to conduct investigations. A furious Allan Lawrence demanded to know from Robarts when the government was going to stop trying to justify itself.[30] Through McIntyre, Robarts made his displeasure clear to Milligan. The Police Commission was not going to go on its merry way independent of the government's wishes.

Robarts appointed Arthur Wishart, a first-term MPP from Sault Ste Marie and a personal friend, to succeed Cass. Wishart handled the review and modification of Bill 99, which took place in a far calmer atmosphere both in private and before the Legal Bills Committee. It was finally decided to remove uncertainties about the scope of the commission's investigatory powers by writing the common law protections for individual rights, which the law officers felt had always been implicit in the proposals, into the text of the revised section. As revised, Bill 99 reappeared from committee on 28 April and was accepted by the legislature.

The government went further than just rewriting a bad bill. MacDonald and the NDP were making individual rights a more general issue, calling for a select committee to be established and other machinery put in place to give citizens more protection. Wishart recommended that the first task of the law reform commission the government was setting up should be to review the status of civil rights in Ontario. Robarts adapted that proposal to help meet and deflect the NDP's concerns by announcing the creation of a special Royal Commission of Inquiry into Civil Rights. It would be chaired by J.C. McRuer, chief justice of the Ontario Court of Appeal, who had been one of the strongest advocates of a law reform commission. McRuer's task was to define the status of individual rights in Ontario and recommend changes 'necessary and desirable to safeguard the fundamental and basic liberties and freedoms of the individual from infringement by the State or any other body.'[31]

In addition to the tactic of using procedure to duck a substantive issue, Robarts drew other lessons about governing from the Bill 99 mess. He could no longer be just a relaxed chairman of the board. He had to know more about what his ministers were doing, to take responsibility for the whole range of government actions. The buck stopped at the premier's office. Demonstrably, the office was not adequately staffed to process difficult bucks. A new political style and a new organization to suit that style would eventually emerge. In the meantime, to avoid further embarrassment, the premier spent many hours personally reviewing all the legislative proposals that were awaiting introduction to the legislature.

Modernizing the Government

About the same time as Bill 99 was being mishandled, Robarts realized that his government was not doing a particularly good job in federal-provincial negotiations. The Quebec government of Jean Lesage seemed to be doing all the running on the key issues, and winning important victories that had vital implications for Ontario and the rest of Canada. If Ontario was to have an impact, technical, fiscal, and planning resources necessary to enter the Ottawa-Quebec debate had to be readily accessible to the prime minister of Ontario and his cabinet. Or else, Robarts feared, the spoils of Confederation would be divided between Ottawa and Quebec. The Federal-Provincial Conference in Quebec City at the end of March crystallized his concern. When he returned to Toronto steps were initiated to ensure that another Bill 99 fiasco did not occur and that technical expertise augmented the new policy control system.

Whether, as Robarts sometimes suspected, the old friendship between Pearson and his former parliamentary assistant Jean Lesage had shunted Ontario to the sidelines after its early leadership in the pension field, or the infusion of social scientists and especially economists into the senior ranks of the Quebec civil service had changed the language of fiscal negotiations – and thus dated the style of Ontario proposals – the Ontario delegation had assumed a secondary position supporting one or the other of the major actors depending on its view of what was best for Canada. At a time when the future of Canada seemed in doubt, Ontario's floating role was important, but Canada's largest province, with almost 40 per cent of the national economy, expected a more significant place at the table when the allocation of important public resources was at stake. The problems of federalism soon became a dominant theme of the Robarts years.

At first, pensions continued to be the leading issue. The main fight over a national pension plan was between Ottawa and Quebec City, with Ottawa still working on the details of its proposals while the Lesage government had announced its determination to have its own plan for Quebec. The division reflected not just a growing rift between Canada's 'two nations' as Lesage's modernizing thrust melded with resurgent French-Canadian nationalism. It also flowed out of a fundamental difference in pension philosophy. The Ottawa Liberals were proposing an unfunded, pay-as-you-go national plan, in which current contributions would be spent to cover current benefits, the whole thing being phased in relatively quickly. Quebec was determined to implement a funded plan, in which benefits would flow out only after the funds to provide them had been accumulated. It would take longer to reach the point where full benefits could be paid, but the beauty of Quebec's idea from a public sector point of view was that an enormous pool of capital would build up in the plan. This capital would be controlled provincially, and could be invested in ways designed to further provincial economic objectives.

Robarts was not convinced that Ottawa's proposal was preferable to Quebec's. Even if the federal government went further toward the idea of funding the national plan, it would control the pool of capital, much of which would be generated in Ontario. Robarts thought it likely that the money would then be invested to support the regional development objectives of the federal government, and the scheme would, in effect, be draining wealth from Ontario. By contrast, if Ontario had a Quebec-type plan, it would gain the same economic flexibility and benefits the Quebeckers were expecting. If the ideal of one national plan could not be implemented because Quebec was going its own way, Robarts concluded, it would be in Ontario's interest also to go its own way and stay out of a nine-province plan.

Pensions were discussed again at a federal-provincial conference late in November 1963. Lesage announced that his government would introduce a provincial, funded pension plan in 1964. Robarts stated that Ontario would not enter any national plan that was not 'truly national in scope.' Faced with opposition from the two largest provinces, Pearson announced the postponement of Ottawa's plans in hope that an acceptable compromise could be negotiated. Both Lesage and Robarts were pleased.

The same conference discussed another issue which left Robarts less satisfied. The Pearson government had announced its determination to reconsider the formula under which Ottawa gave equalization grants to the provinces. These grants,[1] which had their origins in Canadians' determination not to repeat the crushing regional inequalities that had appeared during the Great Depression, were designed to help the poorer provinces provide services close to the level the wealthier provinces could afford. Ontario had generally supported the principle of equalization, but had a constant interest in preventing the complicated equalization formulas from working too heavily against Ontario. All equalization policies – indeed all redistributive policies – in Canada had to be watched carefully by Ontario because they seemed invariably to be taking part of the wealth Ontario generated and spreading it around the rest of Canada. To an anxious provincial government, equalization meant that the Ontario economy was constantly required to work for the benefit of all other Canadians as well as the people of Ontario.* Surely it was only prudent not to put too much pressure on the goose that was laying so many of Canada's golden eggs.

Of course the issue tended to pit province against province, often raising fears that Ottawa was siding with some provinces against others. Ontario thought it put forward a reasonable, modest proposal on equalization at the November 1963 conference, but Ottawa adopted a final position which was somewhat different and weighted in favour of Quebec. Quebec would get $34 million of the estimated $55 million in new federal payments under the arrangement. Were the Ottawa Liberals leaning a little too far to appease Quebec nationalists and/or Quebec Liberals?

As the Pearson government found, to its unending frustration, nothing seemed to appease Quebec in these years. The Lesage government condemned the equalization scheme. Lesage was out for much bigger game, demanding that Ottawa make far more money available to Quebec by greatly reducing the amount of direct taxes it collected. These taxes – income, corporation, and estate taxes – could legally be levied by either level of government. Historically, largely because of the demands of the two world wars, Ottawa had pre-empted these vital areas of direct taxation. After the wars, federal dominance had been linked to the redistribution of tax resources (or equalization) to reflect differing provincial tax potentials. Now, at a time when all the provinces were feeling starved for money to meet expanding responsibilities, particularly in the provision of social services which were growing faster than Ottawa's needs, it seemed time to demand more 'tax room' from Ottawa. At the least, as Quebec realized, such a demand would create pressure for Ottawa to cough up more generous equalization payments, thus producing more revenue for have-not provinces.

Ottawa worried that surrendering its control of revenue would make it impossible to carry out broad national programs, including Keynesian macroeconomic management. The ultimate fear was the 'balkanization' of the Canadian economy. As we will see, the prime minister of Ontario during the 1960s worried as much about balkanizing tendencies as anyone in Ottawa. On the tax abatement issue at this time in 1963, however, he firmly but moderately allied Ontario with the demand for more tax room on the one hand, but against more liberal equalization on the other.[2]

Robarts' moderation at the conference was generally well received, but he came away feeling he had achieved little, and that Ottawa was catering to Quebec at the expense of Ontario. In a speech in Hamilton in December he described the new equalization formula as a 'unilateral decision of the federal government,' and promised to oppose 'further attempts by Quebec's Premier Jean Lesage to sift off

---

* In Keynesian parlance, it has been argued that federal fiscal and equalization policies necessarily meant the Ontario economy was generating tax surpluses. Thus a constant contractionary pressure or 'tax drag' was being applied to the province's ability to create wealth.

more revenue at the expense of Ontario.'[3] Robarts was not entirely pleased, either, that Lesage had persuaded Pearson to hold the next big federal-provincial conference, scheduled for the end of March 1964, in Quebec City. Until then all such conferences had been held in Ottawa.

During the winter the federal government neatly mousetrapped Robarts on the pension question. On 11 January Pearson wrote the premiers outlining the details of a revised federal plan. Robarts responded on 14 February that the plan was 'unsatisfactory' because of the lack of consideration of the impact it would have on private pension plans and 'on the formation of investment capital upon which the growth of our economy so greatly depends.' He offered to work with the federal government to find a compromise.[4]

By appearing to be primarily negative, Robarts had left himself open to the headlines: 'ROBARTS SCUTTLES OTTAWA PENSIONS,' 'ONTARIO PM IS BLOCKING PENSION PLAN.' On 20 February, saying nothing about Quebec's complete refusal to participate in the Ottawa scheme, Pearson told the House of Commons that he would not accept Robarts' objections. Everyone knew that even a Quebec-free national plan would have to have Ontario's participation. It was Ontario, it seemed, that was disrupting national unity by not going along with Ottawa.

Robarts' office was flooded with mail demanding that Ontario accept the federal plan in the name of national unity. Eugene Forsey, the eminent political scientist and constitutional expert, charged that Ontario's refusal to join the Canada Pension Plan would generate serious centrifugal forces within the Canadian federation. A beleaguered Robarts tried to hold his middle course, reiterating that Ontario would accept a national plan but that the issues were so serious and long term that it would only be prudent to eliminate some of the inadequacies of Ottawa's proposal. Ontario went into pension debate at the federal-provincial conference in Quebec City in March 1964 in this not very comfortable position.

Robarts solidified his *bonne entente* with Lesage late in February when the Quebec press gallery had its junket to Toronto to reciprocate the June visit from the Ontarians. Lesage, Pierre Laporte, and Daniel Johnson accompanied the reporters. Lesage gave a conciliatory speech to the Ontario legislature, outlining the reasons why Quebec was determined to realize its full potential, and talking about the similarities between Canada's two big central provinces. Both faced increased costs for social services. Both faced the need to overcome internal regional disparities. Both faced problems caused by rapid urbanization. Both needed sources of increasing revenues. Lesage suggested that Canada's constitutional problems could largely be solved by greater interprovincial co-operation. His speech and the apparently statesmanlike and cordial meetings of the two provincial premiers seemed to contrast favourably with the partisan wrangling between Pearson and Diefenbaker. Perhaps the Conservative Robarts and the Liberal Lesage could work out national problems in ways that the Conservatives and Liberals in Ottawa apparently could not.

The atmosphere at the Quebec City conference of 31 March to 2 April 1964 was heavy with a foretaste of some of the ugly aspects of political life in Canada in the decades of the 1960s and 1970s. Very heavy security precautions were in effect to protect the delegates from demonstrators or worse. Like many of the other non-Quebeckers, Robarts chafed at the restrictions and the ubiquity of the security people (Judy LaMarsh later wrote movingly about how she would 'never forget the sense of being an unwanted alien in my own country, my life potentially at stake whenever I moved out of my hotel room or the conference chamber.') One day there was a major nationalist/separatist demonstration outside the legislature. As the delegates debated in a tense, smoke-filled chamber, the police on the barricades kept the demonstrators away. René Lévesque, the minister of natural resources in the Quebec cabinet, would pace nervously to the window to check the situation and whisper reports on it to Lesage.[5]

The Quebeckers staged their coup in the pension discussion. Lesage presented a five-hundred-page outline of Quebec's plan, which seemed to be a better piece of social legislation in almost every way than Ottawa's proposal. Lesage's experts were much more competent than Ottawa's, and everyone from the other provinces could see the appeal of the capital pool created in a funded plan. 'Maybe we should contract into the Quebec plan,' Pearson tried to joke after Lesage's presentation. It was not very funny. Nor was Lesage's threat on taxes – that if he did not get more tax room he would impose new taxes on Quebeckers and stump the province blaming Ottawa for the increased burden, as Maurice Duplessis had done in a similar situation in 1953.

The federal delegation could do nothing but retreat. Literally overnight the Ottawa Liberals abandoned the pay-as-you-go principle of their pension plan. They also backed down on their refusal to give up taxes, agreeing to the creation of a Tax Structure Committee 'to review the nature and extent of federal and provincial taxes in relation to the financial responsibilities which now have to be carried by both federal and provincial governments.'[6] Realizing how far Ottawa was bending, Robarts endorsed the federal proposals on condition that they meant more investment capital for the provinces and that the Tax Structure Committee would be a joint body reviewing the overall tax situation in Canada.[7] Although Quebec did not commit itself, the idea seemed generally acceptable. Pearson quickly brought the conference to a conclusion, and the Ottawa people flew out of the hostile Quebec City world as fast as they could. No more federal-provincial conferences would be held outside of Ottawa. A few days later Ottawa agreed to incorporate the best features of the Quebec plan – including funding and provincial control of the funds – into what became the Canada Pension Plan. It also would give a further two percentage points of tax room in the personal income tax field, while Quebec agreed to participate in the work of the Tax Structure Committee.

During this sparring, Lester Pearson had genuflected occasionally in Ontario's direction for diplomatic, strategic, or rhetorical purposes, but it was clear that the battle had been between Ottawa and the government of Quebec. On pensions Robarts had contributed somewhat to Ottawa's frustrations by sticking to his determination not to accept a national plan that did not satisfy his conditions. But it was the Quebeckers who had been so effective and impressive at the final conference through a combination of determination, élan, threats, and good homework. Now the Tax Structure Committee would delve into the whole technical wasp's nest of tax relations.

Robarts realized that Ontario could not defend its interests in these and future federal-provincial negotiations without more expertise. He had to build a base of new competence in the Ontario government. Otherwise, he recalled, 'Quebec and Canada would decide what would happen to the rest of Confederation and we would lose by default.'[8]

The conference, following hard on the heels of Bill 99, focused Robarts' attention on the need to modernize the government. Bill 99 had showed how casual the review of government policy had become within the Conservative party, while also suggesting the need for more internal party discipline. These reforms became the special job of John White, Robarts' fellow Londoner who was appointed chief whip in July, after he had helped shift the caucus toward Robarts during the Bill 99 disruptions. White was a highly partisan MPP who had the premier's confidence and was cabinet material, except that there was already a full complement of ministers from southwestern Ontario. He was a legislature man, committed to improving the lot of members generally, and became a good friend of Rod Lewis, the clerk of the legislature. In fact, White's most important reforms affected all members, not just Conservatives, as he streamlined the committee structure, introduced pre-scheduling of committee meetings, and had timetables circulated. There was also a noticeable improvement in the accommodation for backbenchers. They still shared offices, but now everyone at least had his own desk and telephone. In addition, higher grants were provided to the opposition parties to help support their staff and research.[9]

Robarts was delighted with the scope of White's work. It was part of a general modernization of the legislator's role to meet the demands of a new and busier agenda. Another sign of the times was the gradual lengthening of sessions.[10] Robarts always had a slight preference for the old, easy-going days of government, and tried to avoid long sessions by allowing sittings to go on late into the night so members would not feel under a time gag. Sometimes the House would not adjourn until two in the morning. Eventually Robarts gave way, allowing the sessions to stretch out until the traditional eight-week sitting seemed a relic of a far-distant past.

Within the caucus John White became more firmly in control, breaking with tradition by serving as both chief whip and permanent chairman, using the powers of his double office to tighten the reins of discipline. He balanced the firmer hand by securing the prime minister's agreement to expand caucus's role in policy considerations. There was a special two-day meeting of caucus in the fall of 1964, for example, to review government proposals and consider new ideas before the drafting of the Throne Speech. During the session caucus met regularly and much more formally on a weekly basis, with extra meetings held to debate government bills before they went to the floor of the House. Backbenchers now were more likely to air their disagreements in the privacy of caucus, not before reporters and public galleries. Robarts continued to act as House leader, with White feeding him reports on the state of committees and caucus. White, in effect, had become his legislative lieutenant, freeing Robarts from routine caucus politics.

Bill 99 and the general pressure of work had convinced Robarts that within his office he needed a full-time staff officer. Richard Rohmer, the part-timer, was recommending this, insisting that he had to put a ceiling on his own commitment, since he also had an active legal practice. Robarts asked Rohmer and Don Collins to work out a plan for his department so as to create the position of chief executive officer, and then go and find one.

The problem was to find room for a chief executive officer in a department already headed by W.M. McIntyre, the secretary of cabinet who enjoyed deputy minister rank. Collins made a special trip to Ottawa to study the structure of the Prime Minister's Office on Parliament Hill in hope of finding a solution, but was disappointed. He and Rohmer finally fell back on the distinction between support of the cabinet and staff support of the prime minister, which had been implicit but submerged in the 1961 reorganization of the office. The idea was that McIntyre would retain control of the organization, staffing, and administration of the Department of the Prime Minister's office, along with his cabinet secretary's duties. Everyone, including the new chief executive officer, would report to him. But the CEO would be the head of the prime minister's personal and advisory staff. In particular, he would co-ordinate the flow of demands on the prime minister, 'in such a way to ensure a minimum demand on the Prime Minister with a maximum result.'[11]

To recruit a man for the job, Collins asked each deputy minister in the government to give him the names of the two best administrators he knew. One of the names put forward by Frank MacDougall, the deputy minister of lands and forests, was that of J. Keith Reynolds, a PH.D. who had come from London and served as district forester in that region before being posted to Toronto. Collins and Rohmer interviewed Reynolds and several other candidates, recommended Reynolds, and Robarts hired him. The appointment met a somewhat cool reception with McIntyre, who pointedly sent *Mister* Reynolds a copy of the department's new organization chart, showing McIntyre's name directly over his. Until he retired, McIntyre took care to guard his perquisites as head of the department, including his right of personally opening the mail.

Reynolds began work in August 1964 and grew into his job quietly and carefully. Beginning as the prime minister's personal assistant, he gradually became the conduit for communication between cabinet ministers and Robarts, after the first year attending cabinet meetings as the prime minister's assistant. Gradually the members of cabinet as well as the senior civil servants began looking to him as the man to see about getting through to the prime minister. In effect Reynolds became the gatekeeper for Robarts just as Colonel Young had been for Leslie Frost. It was not quite a return to the past, though, for the size and complexity of government, along with the demands on the ministers, meant that Reynolds had to handle a far wider range of problems than his predecessor.

Robarts and Collins were also trying to build up the government's expertise to handle the range of problems posed by federal-provincial relations. A particularly glaring weakness was the lack of general economic expertise. Such economists as the Ontario government had were mostly working on the programs Macaulay had launched in the Department of Economics and Development. There were a few others connected part-time with the Pension Advisory Committee, and some in the Treasury Department who tried to monitor federal-provincial negotiations. Rigid demarcation between departments made broad, co-ordinated economic analysis of policy-making extremely difficult. The first step seemed to be to find a new chief economist to fill the job vacated by George Gathercole, who had moved to Hydro in 1963. Collins advertised the position.

The advertisement was noticed by a University of Toronto political economist who was wondering about his future in the academic world. H. Ian Macdonald, a Rhodes scholar and former dean of men at University College in the University of Toronto had become 'tired of sitting in University common rooms listening to how awful the world was.' During the past year he had left the ivory tower to participate in a conference on automation and social change sponsored by the Department of Economics and Development. Then he had been appointed to a committee chaired by J.R. Kimber which reviewed securities legislation for the attorney general. At these meetings Macdonald had discovered 'the tremendous intellectual excitement of applying one's knowledge and understanding of the general economic process to real issues and problems, and working it through while participating in an inter-disciplinary exercise with people of other expertise.' These good experiences, plus his disillusionment with university life, led him to consider the chief economist's job. He had met Gathercole at the university and phoned him to ask about the position. Gathercole encouraged Macdonald's interest and recommended him directly to Robarts.[12]

Macdonald had another important contact with politics in September 1964 when he gave a paper at the national Progressive-Conservative conference on Canadian goals, held in Fredericton. It had been organized by George Hogan, now secretary of the PC Association of Canada, who was interested in fostering links between the academic and political worlds. Before the conference's conclusion, Hogan had begun suggesting to some of the Toronto academics, including Macdonald, that a series of such meetings would help governments develop a sense of trends within the Canadian federation. Richard Rohmer extended Hogan's idea by suggesting that a special group of Ontario experts might be created, who could work with a similar group from Quebec. Pursuing the idea, Hogan recommended through Rohmer 'that the Prime Minister appoint a private committee to examine into and to report to him upon the following matters: Ontario vis-à-vis Ottawa, the future of federation and French demands, etc. etc.'[13] Robarts met with Hogan and others, considered the idea, liked it, and set Hogan to work drafting a list of potential members for the Ontario committee.

In the meantime Macdonald had been one of several people interviewed for the chief economist's position. The next step was a meeting with Robarts himself. Robarts put the challenge of the job to Macdonald this way:

Ian, you won't stay forever; you won't be a permanent civil servant, but I'll guarantee you five or six years of probably the most interesting life you could have if you're interested in the future of your country, because this is where it's going to be, where the arguments and the action and discussions are going to be – right here, and you'll be right in the middle of it and after five or six years if you've had enough you'll be able to write your ticket any place.[14]

The enthusiasm was typical of Robarts' own sense of the challenge of governing. 'Mind you, I was selling pretty hard,' Robarts recalled later, 'because I wanted him to come.' Attracted by the premier's description of the job, Macdonald accepted. He would officially be located in the Department of Economics and Development, but in fact had the same kind of government-wide terms of reference as Gathercole before him. He was also determined that his advice would be heard at the centre of government. Macdonald's appointment was announced at the end of September, to take effect on 1 January 1965.

In the interval George Hogan asked Macdonald's help in recruiting members for the new committee of experts on national issues. Macdonald helped shape its membership (not always to Hogan's liking, for non-academic Conservatives such as Hogan himself were excluded) and in January became chairman of the Ontario Advisory Committee on Confederation. Here was the nub of Robarts' build-up to handle federal-provincial relations: on one hand an advisory committee of outside experts under Macdonald; on the other hand a new group of experts on the inside, also under Macdonald.

During the next twenty-four months Ian Macdonald was at the centre of multi-faceted reorganizations within the government. Most of them were aimed at a single goal: improving the horizontal (i.e., the cross-departmental) consideration of problems and policy. The vertical development of policy (within a department up to the minister) was well enough understood and had been improved by earlier reforms. Now it was time to break departmental barriers to eliminate breakdowns in communication and make it possible for the government to respond to the interdepartmental issues being posed both by the new technically demanding federal-provincial negotiations and by efforts to assume broad planning initiatives in the province. Macdonald began recruiting new people to form an interdisciplinary group of policy advisers that he hoped would generate the kind of excitement he had felt while serving on the Kimber Committee.

One of the issues welling up within the Department of Economics and Development was regional development policy. A major international conference on regional development and economic change was sponsored by the department in 1965 and was characterized by wide-ranging multi-disciplinary discussions that subsumed transportation issues, agricultural problems, and urban development. As the staff considered how to create a regional development policy for Ontario, they realized that the subject and implications extended far beyond their department's jurisdiction, encroaching on policies being worked out in other agencies. There was the distinct possibility of an interdepartmental squabble, aggravated by the resentment Macaulay had touched off while building up his own economics empire. Macdonald argued that the best approach would be to create a cabinet committee on regional development. It would be chaired by the prime minister and include ministers of departments affected by broad regional development policy. Macdonald and his staff would provide its secretarial resources and expertise.

Robarts accepted the proposal with a couple of modifications. His own department would provide the secretarial services. Also a parallel committee of senior public servants, chaired by Keith Reynolds, was set up to review regional development proposals before they reached the cabinet committee. Macdonald was a member of the committee. The regional development policy proposals being worked out under his direction eventually moved through this new structure with only minor changes, and were published in April 1966 as the white paper, *Design for Development*.[15] The more contentious issues it raised became a storm centre during the later years of Robarts' prime ministership.

The budget process was another policy area in which Macdonald became deeply involved. He was invited to join the provincial treasurer and his staff in the preparation of the 1965 provincial budget. He found it a frustrating experience, in which there seemed to be a preoccupation with balancing revenues and expenditures and little attention paid to broader questions of provincial fiscal policy. When the same thing happened the next year, Macdonald concluded that rigid departmental separation was the culprit in this area too. He recommended the creation of a cabinet committee on economics and finance 'to look at broad fiscal policy and what the consequences of individual policies were in the total sense.' As an alternative he wanted his economists to join Treasury so that 'the broader aspects of policy could be integrated with the incrementalist approach of the Treasury staff.'[16]

Macdonald had yet another organizational difficulty with Treasury because of divided jurisdiction in federal-provincial affairs. As chief economist he was responsible for the planning and co-ordination of federal-provincial studies; but the Treasury had responsibility for monitoring changes in federal-provincial financial arrangements and the Treasury Research Branch was to review the tax-sharing arrangements with Ottawa. The answer seemed to be to move Macdonald's division into the Treasury. If not, perhaps a separate department could be created to amalgamate all the groups with similar responsibilities in the area.

The secretary of the Treasury Board, Carl Brannan, was fairly sympathetic to Macdonald's proposals, but some of the executive officers in the Prime Minister's Office were afraid he was trying to go too far. Keith Reynolds received an internal comment that the idea of creating a powerful cabinet committee on economics would 'put too much power in the hands of too few economists.'[17] If there was to be a cabinet committee on economics and finance, what would its relationship be to the present Treasury Board? This became a difficult issue in the administrative reorganization.

Stanley Randall, Macdonald's minister, accepted the need for closer co-operation between the chief economist and the Treasury, but was not in favour of the actual reorganization of the two departments. All of the discussion finally resulted in a careful division of responsibilities.* A special Committee of Economic and Financial Advisors, consisting of the chief economist, the deputy provincial treasurer (Hugh Brown), and the secretary of the Treasury Board (Carl Brannan) was created to advise the provincial treasurer and the Treasury Board on overall levels of government expenditure and to recommend 'the establishment of priorities of expenditure within stated limits.'[18] These arrangements were worked out in the winter of 1965-6.

Suggestions to unite the economists with the Treasury and establish a cabinet committee on economic and fiscal policy did not go away. Asked to study the subject by Robarts, the Ontario Economic Council reported in the summer of 1966 that 'the sheer growth and complexity of governmental involvement in the lives of the citizenry,' along with overlapping federal, provincial, and municipal responsibilities, combined with the lack of time of cabinet ministers, created poor communication across the government. 'With the current limited personnel, no matter how able, too many policy decisions tend to evolve from a vertical sense of emergency and without adequate horizontal or even historical consultation,' the council argued. It doubted the ability and the wisdom of the Treasury Board even to attempt the role of evaluating government policy, and recommended the creation of a senior standing cabinet committee on economic planning and

* Treasury Board was to 'bear primary responsibility for the assessment of long-term forecasts of expenditures of Departments and agencies and for the development of projections of expenditures.' The chief economist was to advise Treasury Board on '(a) the impact of proposed programs and policies on the economy of the province; (b) the economic implications of alternative courses of action; (c) current economic conditions and prospects for the future.'

priorities. The council also wanted the prime minister's staff substantially expanded to maintain communications between groups of ministries.[19]

The council's recommendations were too radical for 1966, but, they did reinforce the direction in which Macdonald wanted to go. One opening to the future came in November 1966 when James Allan retired as provincial treasurer and was replaced by Charles MacNaughton. MacNaughton had developed a healthy appreciation of problems of 'horizontal communications' in government through his experiences trying to develop a transportation policy for the Metropolitan Toronto area as minister of highways. Within six weeks of his appointment, the Cabinet Committee on Economics and Finance that Macdonald had suggested was meeting to take decisions recommended by the Committee of Economic and Financial Advisors.

A year later the opportunity developed for further structural reforms when Hugh Brown, the deputy provincial treasurer, retired, opening the way for a shuffling at senior levels. Robarts knew that the Ontario Committee on Taxation was about to recommend the division of the Treasury Department into a Department of Provincial Revenue and a Treasury Department charged with concentrating on broad fiscal and economic policy. Ian Macdonald and his staff would be bound to join Treasury under the proposal. MacNaughton recommended that the best way to facilitate the blending of the transformed economists would be to make Macdonald the new deputy treasurer.

The reorganization and Macdonald's new appointment were effected in November 1967. With the setting up of the new Department of Treasury and Economics and a strengthened Treasury Board, the co-ordination of economic planning and public administration that Macdonald and Brannan had been urging for several years was complete.[20] Just as the Reynolds appointment had echoes of Frost's use of Colonel Young, now Ian Macdonald was uniting broad economic expertise with the functions of the Treasury in the way that Gathercole had done under Frost. The difference was that Macdonald commanded a large staff; Gathercole had been virtually alone.

Charles MacNaughton summed up the purpose of the reorganization as a realization 'that the government's evolving fiscal role requires the services of a highly expert study and research group. Besides controlling the impact of government taxation and spending on the economy, the Treasury area must be vitally concerned with policy alternatives, spending priorities, federal-provincial financial affairs and now the major taxation reforms proposed for the federal, provincial and municipal levels of government.'[21]

The staff in the Prime Minister's Office had initially resisted the change, fearing that a small group of economists would dominate the formation of government policy. The use of staff from Robarts' department to chair sensitive committees helped erode the fears. So did the ability of Reynolds and Macdonald to work together as they settled into their jobs. Both were powerful men in government;

both had the ear of Robarts. Macdonald later reflected that their relationship 'defied definition organizationally. It was a case of two men getting along; if we hadn't, the system never would have worked.'

What kind of system had Robarts created? In the early years of his premiership he had abandoned the tightly centralist, closely controlled governing structure he had inherited. Instead, he relied on his cabinet ministers, encouraging them to reorganize their departments and bring policy proposals up from the ranks to be discussed in cabinet. His early government was much more of a cabinet-team system than Frost had ever allowed. Yet, as the Ontario Economic Council had suggested, the department-focused approach had been reasonably strong in developing and implementing policies vertically. Nevertheless, Bill 99, plus the problems of federalism, had strikingly demonstrated the need for more horizontal co-ordination if the increasingly complex, constantly growing government of Ontario was to be kept under the control of the elected politicians.

The reforms begun in 1964 had reflected Robarts' realization that he had to re-establish firmer supervision and control at the centre. The focus of power had to be in the Office of the Prime Minister and, to a lesser degree, the Treasury. Cabinet's function in scrutinizing vertically developed policies had to be supplemented with the kind of over-arching horizontal controls supplied by the new Committee on Economics and Finance, in order to liberate politicians from the formulas of specialists.

Robarts also needed much stronger support staff as he assumed a more central position. On the purely political side, he had Ernie Jackson, Elmer Bell, and several others, serving as his McKenzie. Now he had brought in Keith Reynolds to be his Colonel Young, and Ian Macdonald as his Gathercole, with John White performing a new role in relation to caucus. Robarts himself had overseen the reorganizations, but always as a synthesizer and adapter of the ideas that others, such as Don Collins, Richard Rohmer, and Ian Macdonald, brought forward. The effect of it all was to free Robarts from having to become immersed in the details of government so he could attend to its broader challenges. It also meant that he would be less personal in his relations with his followers, necessarily more removed, tending to aloofness.

Had he simply gone over to the old Frost style? In the most important sense he had not, for the support staff he was building up in the key departments and agencies was far larger and far better equipped in many ways to provide the sophisticated guidance that a much larger, increasingly complicated government needed. At least it seemed that way. Later we shall see serious problems develop with the system as it faced the demands Ontarians put on their government in the confused years after 1967. In the meantime, there was already notice being taken in some circles, particularly in Toronto, of the extent to which the prime minister relied on Londoners for advice. Jackson was Robarts' political alter ego. A near Londoner, Elmer Bell, ran the Ontario PC Association. White controlled the caucus. Charles MacNaughton of Exeter was treasurer. Now the most important man in the Prime Minister's Department was Reynolds, another Londoner. Perhaps Robarts and a regional clique really were running this great and growing machine. One of the expressions current at the time was to describe the Ontario government as 'Queen's Park on the Thames.'

Most of these organizations and reorganizations took place well away from the centre stage of Ontario political drama. They were not given a great deal of attention by the press or the voters. Far more interesting and dramatic were the crises that the Ontario financial community had a knack of producing from time to time, and the occasional vivid flare-ups in federal-provincial relations. These will be the highlights of the next two chapters.

11

Tending the Golden Goose

Ontario's economy was responsible for many of the differences between John Robarts and the premier of any other Canadian province. Like every one of his predecessors in Ontario, Robarts presided over a province which was not only Canada's richest by almost every standard of measurement, but contained within its borders a degree of economic diversity and sophistication that made it virtually an industrial nation in its own right. Ontario had abundant raw materials and great primary industries. Ontario was central to markets and had great manufacturing industries. Ontario was the home of most of Canada's great banks and securities companies. The taxation revenue generated by Ontario's private wealth made possible the benefits provided by all of the government's agencies and programs in the public sector. And since so much of Ontario's money went to Ottawa to be redistributed throughout Canada, the state of the province's economy guaranteed a respectful hearing for Robarts and his officials at all federal-provincial conferences. It was extremely important to everyone to keep the goose laying the golden eggs.

It was an axiom of Ontario political life that its Progressive-Conservative governments were committed to economic growth – not simply growth for growth's sake, but because prosperity meant opportunities and choices for Ontarians that less fortunate areas had to do without. The engine of growth in Ontario was a healthy, unfettered, enterprising private sector. The predisposition of Ontario Tories was to encourage the generation of wealth through private activities on free markets. The government welcomed the confidence that non-Ontarians – other Canadians, Americans, anyone who wanted to do business – expressed in the province when they chose to create jobs and stimulate business with their investments. It was the firmly expressed policy of both the Frost and early Robarts governments to further the unimpeded operation of capital markets, and to be suspicious of protectionist or nationalist devices that seemed likely to throw up barriers to the easy movement of capital and capitalists.

Policies designed to maximize the creation of wealth by the private sector did not imply a reduction in government activities. There seemed to be many areas in which government could offer a helping hand to the private sector, particularly in hard times. In good times the private sector as a whole would not need help, but there would always be struggling industries and disadvantaged areas of the province for which something useful might have to be done. At all times the government had important and sometimes very trying jobs to do as an umpire in the fierce competitive struggle of entrepreneurs. It was essential in an open society that all those involved in the game of making wealth and livelihoods have confidence that it was being played fairly. Producers had to be confident they would have a fair chance to offer their goods and services on an open market. Consumers had to be confident that neither the ordinary person nor the disadvantaged citizen would be fleeced by the unscrupulous exploiter. Investors and savers needed to be confident that their money would not be jeopardized by capricious, unforeseeable collapses in market mechanisms.

There was considerable sickness in the Ontarian and the whole Canadian economy in the late Frost and early Robarts years. The recession of 1958-62 was characterized by negative growth, intractable levels of unemployment, and an apparent decline of investor interest in Canadian opportunities. Some broad national economic policies, such as the Diefenbaker government's winter works program, had to be implemented to help the unemployed through several grim seasons. The federal government's technical assistance and vocational training program, which was so important in the creation of both the Robarts Plan and the Robarts leadership campaign, was another recession-inspired initiative rooted in assumptions about the need for upgrading the skills and capacities of young people in a modern industrial economy. Robarts' own ministry, Education, became infused in the early 1960s with the idea that education was a necessary investment in improving Ontario's human capital, that argument was used to justify a wide range of programs and campaigns, from attacks on school drop-outs, through justifications for creating a host of new universities and community colleges, to finally setting up a separate ministry to service them.

Most of Robert Macaulay's trade crusading and other innovations were intended to help the faltering Ontario economy get moving again. It happened that other, macroeconomic forces were working in the same direction by about 1962, so that Canada's recession ended about the same time as John G. Diefenbaker's prime ministership declined, giving way to the remarkable sustained boom of the 1960s, the longest period of uninterrupted growth in Canada's history. From the point of view of the state of the province's economy, there was no better time to be governing Ontario.

Many of Macaulay's programs were still pursued in the mid-1960s. Even in good times there was an arguable need for a lending agency of last resort such as the Ontario Development Corporation to help faltering corporations. The nascent Ontario Housing Corporation provided demand for the construction industry while meeting a social need.[1] The Ontario Economic Council could perform a useful advisory function in good times and bad. Nor do good salesmen slack off in easy seasons; they work harder and sell more. Macaulay's successor, Stanley Randall, continued to pursue trade crusades and manufacturing opportunity conferences so vigorously through one boom year after another that he was dubbed 'Ontario's salesman to the world.'

Economists knew the situation had changed significantly between 1961 and 1965, but they did not believe that the changes had solved all the problems in utilizing Canada's resources. In 1961 the problem had seemed to be one of harnessing the *unused* potential of untrained young men and women. By 1965 it was still possible to argue that there was *under-utilized* potential which was keeping Canada's and Ontario's economies from doing even better. Louis Rasminsky, the governor of the Bank of Canada, explained the situation nicely in his report that year in arguing that

the output of the economy ... could have been even higher if our productivity performance had been better ... This underlies the need for emphasis on policies bearing on the 'supply side' of the economy which enhances our ability to produce ... Unemployment is still high in some areas and output would be greater if the remaining pockets of unused resources were drawn into employment. In present circumstances, however, this is a task for those policies which are aimed at particular areas where unused resources exist; it is not one that can be handled satisfactorily by increasing the general pressure of demand in the economy.[2]

Those areas of unused resources were being targeted by Robarts' economic advisers as the key to future provincial economic policy-making. Some regions of Ontario, particularly the major urban centres, were prospering. Other regions were not, and the idea of smoothing out or eliminating regional disparities through precise regional development policies was moving rapidly to the centre of the planning stage.

One approach to regional development had been in place for a decade, but it had relied on local initiative in a way that became a headache to the elected politicians. Regional development associations composed of local businessmen and community leaders had been encouraged to formulate local economic development plans and present them to the provincial cabinet. Some associations were more active than others (leading to regional disparities in attacking regional disparities). Some of the most active had a chronic tendency to bypass their local MPPs in referring proposals directly to the Department of Economics and Development, thus making the elected member appear unneeded in fostering the economic advancement of his riding. Members would be happy to see an approach to regional development that did away with the regional development associations. Not only the 1965 conference, but also the success of the regional government experiment in Metropolitan Toronto, as well as the Beckett Committee recommendations,[3] all encouraged a more centralized approach. This was formalized in the 1966 white paper, *Design for Development*.

The old regional development associations were to be replaced by regional development councils. Their job was to provide 'informational, educational and promotional' functions on behalf of regional advisory boards, which were the effective executive bodies and had MPPS sitting on them. They advised the cabinet on regional development. Regional plans were to be prepared by the Department of Economics and Development, but routed through the local council and board before returning to the cabinet committee for approval. The cabinet committee would then set development priorities.[4] The design seemed an ingenious blending of central planning expertise with local political needs and realities. This policy, along with the work of the Ontario Development Corporation and the Ontario Economic Council, seemed to mean that the government had the mechanisms in place to organize the under-utilized resources of Ontario for further expansion. But this was a relatively long-term approach to economic policy, and while it was being formulated there were medium- and short-term issues, mostly related to maintaining stability and confidence in the economy, that had to be addressed by the government.

In 1961 the Diefenbaker government had appointed a major royal commission, chaired by Ontario's chief justice, Dana Porter, to examine all aspects of money, credit, and finance in Canada. As the Porter Commission began its work, there was a noticeable heightening of concern in the financial community as to whether the public's interest was adequately protected by the existing system. Early in 1962, for example, the *Financial Post* had published a front-page editorial criticizing the regulation of stock trading in Ontario.[5] That autumn the issue surfaced more dramatically when an unusual volume of the shares of Canadian Oil Companies Limited was traded on a rising market just before Shell Oil of Canada announced the terms of an attractive takeover bid. It seemed that insiders had used prior knowledge of the proposal for their private gain.

The Ontario Securities Commission (OSC) which had been established during the wave of criticism of the workings of unrestrained capitalism during the Great Depression (George Drew had been its first chairman), looked into the Canadian Oil Companies rumours, but little came of the inquiry. In February 1963 Attorney General Cass told the legislature that the retirement of the OSC's chairman was an appropriate occasion for the government to look into the commission itself, reviewing its organization, policies, and practices. The announcement became the occasion for a flurry of opposition attacks on lax securities regulation in Ontario – with charges that the commission was too intimately linked with the Toronto Stock Exchange (TSE), that the TSE was helpless to police corporate organization and reorganization, particularly in mining, indeed that it did not *want* to interfere with the wide-open activities of mining stock promoters. The opposition wanted the OSC's power to protect the public interest greatly strengthened.[6]

In April 1963 the OSC finally reported on the Canadian Oil Companies takeover, finding that a few people had benefited from share purchases before the announcement of the takeover bid, but it could not be shown they had had 'privileged information.' Cass promised the legislature that the general question of corporate 'insider' trading would be considered and protective legislation brought in if necessary. More rumours about the Canadian Oil Companies takeover haunted the government during that year's election campaign. So, to an extent, did an old issue that had come out of the closet again, when new evidence received from the attorney general of British Columbia forced the Ontario government to reopen the Northern Ontario Natural Gas investigation. The crime probes had also raised questions about certain lending practices in Ontario, specifically accusations of loan-sharking carried on by front men for the mob. In April 1963, Robarts had responded to this and other concerns about lending by establishing a Select Committee on Consumer Credit, and during the election campaign promised to bring in legislation to protect the public from exorbitant interest rates.

Yet another impetus to legislative reform developed after the election, when J.D. Arnup, the treasurer of the Law Society of Upper Canada, convinced Fred Cass of the need to establish a law reform agency with a general mandate to review and suggest changes in Ontario statutes. Arnup's work, and subsequent discussions with Chief Justice McRuer, Dean Allan Leal of Osgoode Hall, and Robarts himself, provided the basis for Bill 75, passed in 1964, which established the Ontario Law Reform Commission. Another representative of the legal community who met with Cass about the same time was Eddie Goodman, who presented a recommendation from the Canadian Bar Association urging the attorney general to strike a committee 'to study and make recommendations for legislation on questions of primary distribution, trading disclosures and insiders' trading.'[7] The Bar Association was reinforcing Cass' own inclination to go beyond the earlier commitment to review the OSC and look into the general framework of securities regulation in the province. Indeed, the whole series of events in the past year and a half, including perhaps the possibility that the Porter Commission might recommend a federal takeover of securities regulation, impelled the government in this direction.

Cass asked J.R. Kimber, master of the Supreme Court of Ontario and the chairman of the Ontario Securities Commission, W.B. Common, the deputy attorney general, and three leading members of the bar to draft the terms of reference for a review committee. Then he appointed them all members of the committee under Kimber's chairmanship, with a mandate to look into takeover bids, insider trading, disclosure requirements in securities' issues, procedures governing primary distribution of securities, and the organization of the Ontario Securities Commission. The Kimber Committee's appointment was particularly timely in that it was already at work when the Porter Commission weighed in with its report, published in April 1964. The Porter Commission severely criticized procedures on Canadian stock exchanges, standards of securities regulation, and the Ontario Securities Commission.

The Select Committee on Consumer Credit uncovered some exorbitant interest rates charged by mortgage brokers, sparking an attorney general's investigation which led to the cancellation of the registration of two firms. Otherwise the 1964 session was quiet in the consumer protection area. A useful internal consolidation of agencies in the Department of the Attorney General into a new Department of Insurance was almost complete. The bill to establish the Law Reform Commission had its first reading in March. Another select committee, whose work would eventually be important in the securities area, was proposed by the government to 'enquire into the exploration, discovery and development of our mineral resources.' All of this was before the Bill 99 affair abruptly ended Fred Cass' career in the cabinet, deflecting attention to the Ontario Police Commission and the government's broader problems.

The new attorney general, Arthur Wishart, came from northern Ontario and had the northerner's natural interest in the future of the mining industry. He was alert to the fact that mining promotion and development was at once the area in which the greatest abuses had taken place in the Ontario securities industry (Ontario had been the penny-stock promoter's heaven for decades) and also a field of enterprise extremely sensitive to the intrusion of regulators. Mining men, by and large, did not like securities commissions and government bureaucrats, preferring a climate of wide-open development, lots of penny stocks – and buyer beware. Wishart realized that the recommendations of the new select committee looking into ways of promoting prospecting and mining development would have to be co-ordinated with those of his own department's Kimber Committee on a better regulatory system, so that the result would be legislation 'consistent with all interests.' He alerted Robarts to this need for balance just as all of the careful planning was once again overtaken by events.[8]

On 16 April 1964 the big Texas Gulf Sulphur Company announced that it had made an enormous discovery, a lode of cooper, lead, zinc, and other minerals near Timmins. The following day the Toronto Stock Exchange went wild, with more than eleven million shares changing hands in the first few hours of trading. Mining fever created a classic rush for claims in the Timmins area and the biggest penny-stock boom in Canadian history hit the TSE. Both the president of the exchange, General Howard Graham, and the chairman of the OSC tried to keep the lid on by warning an excited public that investments in the Timmins area were highly speculative. Wishart added his own caution in a speech to the legislature.

Rumours that insiders had profited from the discovery through trading in Texas Gulf shares on the New York Stock Exchange caused the U.S. Securities and Exchange Commission to launch an investigation in May. Texas Gulf did not trade on the Toronto Stock Exchange, so Ontario could not investigate these stories on its own; Wishart could only direct the OSC to co-operate with the SEC investigation. He could also look into Timmins area companies listed on the TSE, and on 11 June appointed a special three-member team to review trading in these companies stocks during the Timmins flurry. It was seen as a fact-finding study, which would complement the work of the existing Kimber Committee.[9]

The speculators, like the regulators, had turned their attention to the smaller companies holding property near the big Texas Gulf find. One of these companies, Windfall Oils and Mines Limited, began drilling on its holdings at the end of June and a few days later rumours began circulating that Windfall was a good buy. On 6 July Windfall shares rose dramatically on the TSE. Worrying about the danger of insiders making windfall Windfall profits, possibly by spreading unsubstantiated rumours, the exchange asked the company for an up-to-date statement, to be released to the public. If it was not satisfactory, trading in Windfall shares would be suspended on Monday, 13 July. When Monday arrived, the TSE officials had not received enough information to be satisfied, but had received repeated assurances of the imminent provision of more complete information. TSE and OSC personnel met with two promoters of Windfall Oils and Mines, George and Viola MacMillan, on Tuesday. It was later reported that the MacMillans 'evaded ... direct answers to questions as to what the drill core disclosed ... They succeeded in creating the impression in the minds of the chairman of the Ontario Securities Commission and others that the very last section of the core already drilled was good.'[10] A carefully worded statement from Kimber denied the validity of any rumours of assay results on the Windfall claim. But trading in Windfall was not suspended, the president of the TSE publicly accepted a Windfall report on its drilling activities as 'reasonably satisfactory' and speculation continued. By late July the OSC was becoming suspicious, in Kimber's words, that 'there was a strong possibility that some individuals were playing on the public interest to manipulate these stocks.' On 28 July Kimber asked Wishart to authorize an investigation into Windfall and two other companies to determine if illegal acts had been committed. Wishart issued the order at once, but to avoid repercussions on the stock market decided not to have it published.[11] After the exchange closed on 31 July it was announced that Windfall's assays showed no discovery. Immediately there was a wild rush to sell Windfall. Its roller-coaster ride that month took the stock from 60 cents a share on 6 July to $5.50 on 21 July and back to 35 cents on 31 July, creating all sorts of opportunities for sharp operators (including, it turned out, the MacMillans) to profit en route.

The crisis of confidence in the Toronto Stock Exchange, which had been getting bad publicity for years, was immediate. Robarts was away from Toronto, en route to an interprovincial conference in Alberta, when he heard the Windfall news. From Jasper on 4 August he announced his intention to appoint a special royal commission 'to investigate, examine, and probe into all the events of the last few weeks, which will include stock market speculation and activities, in relation to recent discoveries in the Timmins area.' The press release contained another of Robarts' direct, personal assumptions of responsibility:

I would emphasize my very strong, and long-held, opinion that public confidence in the financing of our mineral resources is most essential. That confidence can only be retained if the ways and means adopted for the development of those resources are of unimpeachable character and based upon the highest integrity of purpose. I am determined to leave no stone unturned to ensure that this policy operates in Ontario, as the investor must be sufficiently protected against the possibility of manipulation of markets for shares and stocks involved in the development of our natural resources.[12]

There was immediate reaction to the premier's announcement, but from a surprising quarter. In moving so quickly and directly, Robarts had ruffled the feathers of the members of the attorney general's Committee on Securities Regulation. They made their feelings clear to the premier in a remarkable telegram, which began:

We are startled and perplexed to read in the Toronto Press today of an announcement from your office to the effect that it is proposed to appoint a one man royal commission to investigate and study primary distribution of securities through the stock exchange which is one of the topics specifically within the stated scope of the committee of which we are members ... It is neither feasible nor practical to have two independent studies of this important problem being conducted at the same time. We would appreciate your clarification of this matter so that we can assess our position as members of your Attorney General's Committee ...[13]

Eddie Goodman, who had been instrumental in creating the review, added in a personal letter his view of the importance of Robarts' stressing that the new royal commission would look into Windfall alone. 'It would be a great shame,' Goodman warned, 'if the [attorney general's committee's] members were to feel that their hard work for a year is being lightly discarded by the government.' He went on to raise an important point of principle about the inquiry, one which would come up with increasing frequency in Ontario during the next few years:

It should be made abundantly clear that the government cannot make certain that people do not lose money when they make speculative investments in the stock market. Unless it is shown that the only obligation of government is to pass the proper regulations concerning distribution, trading and disclosures, people are going to feel that every time some company goes bust or its stock falls drastically, the government is responsible. So far, no one has made it clear that the government's sole responsibility is to see that people who speculate are protected from improper use of confidential information or fraud.[14]

Robarts conferred with Wishart and Kimber and met other representatives from the attorney general's committee, reassuring them that the two investigations would be complementary rather than overlapping. On 11 August he announced that Arthur Kelly, a judge of the Supreme Court of Ontario, would be the one-man royal commissioner appointed 'to investigate recent fluctuations in the price of shares of Windfall Oils and Mines Limited.' At the same time as he defined Kelly's responsibilities very narrowly, Robarts echoed Goodman's point of principle in warning investors that 'no government can prevent the individual citizen from making speculative investments in the stock market and from either making or losing money on such investments.'[15] It was a neat little piece of quarterback scrambling to complete the play.*

While the investigations into mine financing were proceeding, another incident occurred involving a failure of investor expectations, this time in the agricultural community. In 1960 a group of livestock producers had formed a meat-packing co-operative to attempt to bypass the private packers. It was incorporated as the Farmers Allied Meat Enterprises Cooperative (FAME) and planned to build a chain of seven packing houses across the province. Nothing much came of these plans at first, but in 1964 FAME purchased the F.W. Fearman Company, a long-established Hamilton firm that had run into financial difficulty. FAME itself ran into financial difficulty trying to close the deal, and its board of directors was soon on the doorstep of the minister of agriculture, William Stewart, asking for special help. When Stewart turned the farmer-entrepreneurs down, a special FAME shareholders' meeting, held in Brampton on 15 January 1965, challenged the government's position:

Whereas the Ontario government has seen fit in the past to guarantee a loan of $11 million to the tobacco board ... and whereas there are several times more livestock producers than tobacco producers, therefore be it resolved that the shareholders of FAME request the Ontario government to guarantee to back a loan to FAME equal to the appraised value of the F.W. Fearman plant.[17]

The meeting also asked the Ontario government to conduct a thorough investigation into the affairs of FAME.

There was more to the FAME situation than just another company heading for bankruptcy. The Ontario Flue Cured Tobacco Marketing Board had been offered special assistance in November 1962. More important, since early 1963 it had

---

* One final obstacle had to be hurdled a year later when the various studies were in their final stages. The interim report of the Select Committee on Mining recommended that it be allowed to continue to study issues relating to mine financing, including the raising of risk capital and the primary distribution of mining shares through stock exchanges. Now it was Commissioner Kelly's turn to react, and he wrote the prime minister that he intended to carry on his investigation without regard to the proceedings of the Select Committee. Robarts played the diplomat again, stressing the differences in purpose between the two studies and stating that the government would make its own decisions about procedures after both reports had been received.[16]

been government of Ontario policy, through the Ontario Development Corporation, to subsidize small businesses that needed capital so they could create or preserve jobs in the province. FAME did not qualify for ODC aid, or for support under the Cooperative Loans Act,[18] but it certainly wanted help, and its affairs affected a large number of Ontario farmers who had invested in the new co-operative. Where did fairness lie? How could a government justify subsidizing or bailing out some companies and turning down others? But how could it draw the line so as not to give aid to everyone?

Robarts and Wishart met with FAME shareholders and agreed to keep the question of aiding the company open until the investigation into its affairs was complete. On 11 March Mr Justice Campbell Grant was appointed to conduct an inquiry. He reported in August that the co-operative had experienced a 'rather shaky start' and that the Fearman purchase had been 'a completely unsound business undertaking.' Grant was sympathetic to the plight of the investors and questioned in an aside whether the government should not assume some responsibility: 'One could ask what was the proper role of government in the FAME disaster. With so many Ontario farmers faced with such a loss, would it have been too much to expect the government to place the plant under trusteeship and provide the necessary backing until the organization had found its feet?'[19] Grant's conclusion that the bankruptcy resulted from poor management decisions set the government's response; compensating investors for management error was not a legitimate role for the provincial government.

FAME had always been fairly obscure, having never caught the attention of the urban press. By the time of Grant's report its fate was far overshadowed by the crisis caused by the collapse of a far more important Ontario company, the Atlantic Acceptance Corporation. Atlantic Acceptance was a Toronto-based firm, offering short-term financing to individuals and businesses, with thirty-six acceptance offices and nineteen small loan branches across Canada. It had expanded rapidly, obtaining much of its funds on U.S. money markets that had been flush with short-term corporate savings. Among the risks in this kind of operation was the periodic need for 'bridge-financing,' often only a few days every quarter or so when corporate creditors were meeting other obligations. As well, Canadian borrowers could not be sure that attractive interest-rate spreads would continue to attract U.S. money their way. By late 1964 the spread was narrowing; the pool of available capital shrank further after Lyndon Johnson's February 1965 speech to Congress urging voluntary restraints on capital expenditures abroad. By the spring of 1965 Atlantic Acceptance was scrambling for money, exhausting one line of credit after another and starting to take major losses as high-risk investments it had made fell apart.[20] It needed significant bridge-financing in mid-June, but its bankers refused to go beyond their already extended ceilings. On 14 June Atlantic Acceptance Corporation defaulted on a $5 million secured note.

The failure shook the Canadian financial community. Atlantic Acceptance was far from an unimportant finance company, and these were far from being hard times. Mr Justice Hughes' subsequent report summarized the significance of the default:

For a Canadian company of this size doing business in the field of finance in times of unexampled affluence, in respect of which no sign of instability had been previously detected, and which had then debt outstanding in excess of $130,000,000 owing to lenders which included institutions regarded as the most shrewd and experienced investors in North America, suddenly to default on a routine obligation was an event which astonished the financial world. From it flowed the collapse of Atlantic Acceptance and all its subsidiaries, the bankruptcy of many companies dependent upon it, the ruin of many lives and the searching re-examination of financial practices and legislation of long standing.[21]

Atlantic Acceptance was placed in receivership and its trustees and auditors began trying to find out what had gone wrong. Almost immediately they uncovered serious losses in several companies closely affiliated with Atlantic Acceptance. Earlier that spring investigators for the Ontario Securities Commission had come across some of these affairs which seemed to show that Atlantic Acceptance money had gone into several firms whose operations were not always sound or honest.[22] When the default occurred, the OSC investigation shifted to Atlantic Acceptance itself. The commission began to worry about the possibility that funds had been deliberately siphoned away from Atlantic Acceptance through its loans, but could not begin with this assumption of guilt. Perhaps it was just a matter of desperate businessmen trying to recoup losses by taking greater and greater risks.[23]

Other companies had incurred severe risks in advancing money to Atlantic Acceptance. Towards the end of June, Wilfred D. Gregory, the president of British Mortgage and Trust Company, based in Stratford, realized his firm had drastic problems meeting its obligations. Gregory had been a director of Atlantic Acceptance. He disclosed the grave situation to H.R. Lawson, a member of the British Mortgage and Trust board who was also president of the National Life Assurance Company. Gregory rejected Lawson's advice that he resign as British Mortgage and Trust president, and at a board meeting on 29 June he, Lawson, and the company's general manager were appointed a special committee to carry out a drastic liquidation of assets. They hoped they could keep British Mortgage and Trust above water by meeting its short-term obligations until the Atlantic Acceptance undertow had subsided.[24]

Early in July Gregory came close to concluding a sale of British Mortgage and Trust to Denison Mines Limited. But when the press disclosed Denison's offer to buy control of 'faltering British Mortgage and Trust Company' on 8 July, the bottom dropped out of its stock overnight as investors and depositors suddenly realized that British Mortgage and Trust was very sick. There was virtual panic in Stratford, where anxious depositors rushed to get their money back and take it across the street to the Bank of Montreal. On 16 July the registrar of loan and trust companies, who was monitoring the outflow, informed the attorney general that the situation was critical. British Mortgage and Trust was within hours of collapse unless it received the $6 million involved in the Denison offer. Perhaps if other trust companies purchased $20 million of mortgages from British Mortgage and Trust, the registrar suggested, or if the government lent it $5 million on the security of its office premises and real estate, the company could get through the critical period without the Denison money. But the registrar felt justified at the same time in forwarding a notice to the attorney general cancelling the registration of the company: 'I have proof that the company is unable to pay its debts and is insolvent.'[25] It was decided to hold the cancellation order, however, until the attorney general agreed it should be sent. Gregory, who had been kept informed of the registrar's concern, was sent a copy of the letter, stating it was felt British Mortgage and Trust was insolvent.

At this point a worried John Robarts became involved. He later recalled that his concern was not on behalf of investors in British Mortgage and Trust, but instead for its depositors and for the stability of the other trust companies in Ontario. Could the system withstand the kind of crisis of confidence that seemed to be gathering? Would other trust companies suffer runs on their assets from frightened depositors and follow British Mortgage and Trust down?[26] Robarts asked Richard Rohmer to explore the possibility of getting support from other trust companies through the Trust Companies Association of Canada. It was unsympathetic. To stave off disaster, Ontario Hydro provided temporary liquidity by depositing funds in British Mortgage and Trust. Robarts was now receiving reports four times a day on the balance of funds available at British Mortgage and Trust. Through friends at Canada Trust he tried to persuade other trust companies to rally behind British Mortgage and Trust but had no success.[27] Meanwhile, the value of its shares fell below $10, breaking one of the stipulations in the Denison agreement, which then fell apart.

H.R. Lawson had managed to use his contacts at the National Life Assurance Company to interest its chairman, Senator Wallace McCutcheon, in a rescue effort. Both men were substantial shareholders.[28] They decided that the only recourse was a takeover of British Mortgage and Trust by another trust company. Victoria and Grey Trust Company came forward, offering to buy British Mortgage and Trust for $2.50 a share. Less than a month earlier the shares had traded at $27 and they had been still higher before Atlantic Acceptance collapsed.

Victoria and Grey's directors approved the amalgamation proposal on 26 July. The next day Gregory resigned as president of British Mortgage and Trust and Lawson was elected his successor. McCutcheon appeared at that meeting to explain the alternatives available to the company's board. Effectively there was no choice: they could accept the Victoria and Grey offer or they could decline it and see their registration cancelled. The directors accepted Victoria and Grey's offer.

Meanwhile, the Ontario government announced that it would guarantee loans from the chartered banks to a total of $3 million to maintain the liquidity of British Mortgage and Trust.

Leslie Frost was a member of the board of Victoria and Grey. So was Walter Harris, a former Liberal finance minister. McCutcheon, who had arranged the deal, was a friend of Ernest Halpenny and had close links to Harry Price and the London business community. It cannot be determined whether Price's intervention or these political connections favoured Victoria and Grey, made its directors sensitive to the political importance of maintaining trust in the trust company system, or if the board simply responded to the prospect of a good investment. The board did recognize the significance of the issue for the governments of both Ontario and Canada, and knew it was in a situation that transcended private economic interests. Before the takeover was consummated, Victoria and Grey attempted to limit its risk by asking the federal minister of finance, Walter Gordon, to permit the company to write off losses experienced in the realization of assets of British Mortgage and Trust. Gordon agreed, on condition that the government of Ontario 'make a real financial contribution and that the remission of tax not add value to the shares of British Mortgage and Trust Company.'[29] Then it was Ontario's turn.

Robarts had extensive consultations with Kimber before entering into negotiations with Walter Harris and H.J. McLaughlin of Victoria and Grey. Among the issues the government people had to consider were accusations that the government itself was partly at fault in the whole affair for not having informed the public of its concern about Atlantic Acceptance before the default occurred, and its responsibilities for forcing directors to disclose important information to the shareholders of the companies it regulated. They also discussed the details of the amalgamation and the difficult problem of the value of the British Mortgage and Trust shares. When he met with Harris and McLaughlin, Robarts stressed his concern for the viability of the financial system in Ontario, but balked at their request that his government guarantee any losses Victoria and Grey might incur as a result of the takeover.[30] After further negotiations, and with a 15 September deadline for concluding the takeover looming, Robarts agreed that the Ontario government would remit corporate income tax on losses realized on the various assets of British Mortgage and Trust on condition that 'a substantial portion of the present British Mortgage and Trust business [be] carried on, and that such remission of tax will not add any value to the shares of British Mortgage and Trust Co.'[31] The government would maintain its commitment to support the liquidity of the company up to $3 million, but would not guarantee the loans of the company.

Robarts was not sure that Victoria and Grey would accept his terms, and to the last moment had Rohmer exploring other possibilities if it all fell through. It did not. On 15 September the boards of both trust companies approved the terms of the takeover. By 30 September there were no more liquidity problems. Robarts' personal intervention in the incident had been primarily to protect depositors and maintain confidence (the investors in British Mortgage and Trust had lost most of their money). His government had not been alone in taking action, for not only had Walter Gordon helped ease the takeover, but quite early in the crisis the Bank of Canada had made known its determination to help the chartered banks cover the difficult liquidity situation in the financial system.

While negotiating, Robarts asked for information about the events leading up to the Atlantic Acceptance collapse. The OSC was having difficulty with its investigation, as its scope expanded to other areas of the financial world that were outside its jurisdiction, such as trust companies. The commission suggested that the powers it needed could be obtained if the attorney general declared a special investigation in the public interest under the Securities Act. Robarts rejected that idea in favour of an inquiry open to the public, and on 30 July announced that Mr Justice Samuel Hughes would head a royal commission into the Atlantic Acceptance affair.[32]

By mid September of 1965 the storms in the financial community seemed to have abated. Mr Justice Hughes was at work on his investigation and the savings of British Mortgage and Trust depositors were being honoured by Victoria and Grey. With no new disasters distracting attention, it was time to take action on the reports and recommendations starting to pile up about the state of the system and the government's handling or mishandling of its regulatory responsibilities. Campbell Grant's FAME report was in, as were the Kelly investigation of Windfall Mines, the Kimber Committee's study of securities legislation, the report of the Select Committee on Consumer Credit, and an interim report from the Select Committee on Mining. Most of the recommendations affected the Attorney General's Department.

There had been little doubt for several years that the Ontario Securities Commission was going to have to be strengthened, both by law and in its personnel. During the trust companies' crisis of the summer of 1965 Wishart had consultants at work recommending the changes and the costs necessary to implement the thrust of recommendations coming from the Kimber and Kelly studies. By the spring of 1966 Wishart had his proposals, estimates of their cost, and a draft Securities Act ready to go forward.

At the same time all the turmoil, hard on the heels of the Bill 99 incident, finally provoked action to end the schizophrenic position of the attorney general. Mr Justice McRuer helped to decide the issue by stating that the conflict of responsibilities within the department was so thoroughgoing as to require separation. Robarts concurred, and immediately adopted a McRuer suggestion that the title 'Attorney General' be extended to include 'Minister of Justice.'[33] In addition, Wishart finally came forward with the proposal that the new, improved Ontario Securities Commission, the Department of Insurance, and the administrator of the Loans and Trusts Act be grouped together under a separate department.

From a list of fifteen possible titles supplied by Wishart, Robarts chose the Department of Financial and Commercial Affairs.

As a result of recommendations of the Select Committee on Consumer Credit, a new Consumer Protection Bureau was added. Drafts of the Consumer Protection Act and the Consumer Protection Bureau Act were also ready by March 1966.

Robarts had personally been involved in the development of policies to avoid a repetition of the British Mortgage and Trust incident. He discussed the general situation with Mr Justice Hughes (who would take more than four years to unravel the Atlantic Acceptance tangle, not presenting his report until late in 1969), received detailed suggestions from Wallace McCutcheon, and conferred with Walter Gordon and other federal officials about possible joint action with the federal government. Robarts was eager to work out joint inspection procedures, and throughout these months was deeply involved in interprovincial and federal-provincial discussions about the possibility of standardizing securities, trust company, and consumer protection legislation on a national basis. When Ottawa decided not to act, Ontario had to work out tougher controls on its own. Robarts endorsed a package of new requirements, commenting in a letter to Wishart that it was all 'a pretty big plateful.' 'On the other hand,' he added, 'if we do not have our course of action planned and ready to implement when the next session rolls around, I think we will be highly critized not only by the Opposition, but by the public.'[34] In March 1966 amendments to the Loans and Trust Act were introduced to stiffen capital requirements, reserve requirements, regulations governing trust company investments, and insider trading practices.

All the legislation affecting corporations and securities seemed in the process of being amended that spring, entirely new acts were being brought in, new departments created, and old ones reorganized. On 31 March, about the time when sittings of the legislature had come to an end in former years, Wishart wrote Robarts that he still had twenty-three bills to be considered. The session did not prorogue until 8 July 1966, setting another new record of 110 sitting days. Even at that, an impatient Robarts had often kept the House until after midnight to try to force the pace.

During debates on the new bills and departmental estimates, the opposition parties criticized the Robarts government for not having given stronger protection to the public interest. It should have handled the crises better and it should have had tougher laws and administrative policies in place. Why had the Ontario Securities Commission not done a better job of controlling the situation on the Toronto Stock Exchange? Why had Windfall been allowed to happen? Why wasn't the OSC getting still greater powers? Why weren't the investors in FAME being given more support? But Price, the Progressive-Conservative member from Toronto-St David's, who had chaired the Select Committee on Consumer Credit, offered a good definition of the Tories' view of the role of government in the economy when he argued that the new consumer credit legislation would stimulate greater competition in the industry:

We in no way seek to shackle private enterprise. But the truth is that for some years back the market place has not favoured the consumer. We now seek by legislative means to give full play to competitive forces in the market place.

While attempting by these consumer Acts ... to build in protection for the public we make it clear to the unscrupulous operators that our society finds their activities intolerable and will eliminate them.[35]

The prime minister himself had to explain the situation in attempting to justify his non-support for the investors in FAME. It was true, he argued, that the tobacco producers had been given aid through a loan guarantee. But it had been necessary and reasonable because the producers were required by law to sell to the one marketing board, and aid to it had kept them from being thrown to the mercy of unscrupulous buyers. With respect to the support given to British Mortgage and Trust, Robarts argued:

No assistance was given to that firm, its shareholders or anyone who invested in the company. The strong decline in the market price of the shares of that company from last spring until the British Mortgage and Trust Company was taken over by the Victoria and Grey Trust Company clearly supports this statement.

However, to clarify what did in fact occur ... in order to protect the position of the depositors, not the shareholders ... the government offered the British Mortgage and Trust Company a deposit by which it could meet its obligations to its depositors if this should be required ... Later, when the Victoria and Grey Trust Company had negotiated purchase of the British Mortgage and Trust, arrangements were made for a government agency to deposit a sum of money in the Victoria and Grey Trust Company. This action assisted the Victoria and Grey Trust Company in carrying out its arrangements to take over the deposits and related business obligations of the British Mortgage and Trust Company ... The agency making the deposit is, of course, on the same basis as any other depositor.

Robarts claimed that his government was 'very sympathetic' to the plight of farmers who had invested in FAME, but here he drew the line: 'If any assistance were to be provided in this case the government would be faced with demands for assistance from shareholders who have invested in many kinds of companies and enterprises that had or face probable or imminent failure for one reason or another.' The location of the line was where fraud, unscrupulous dealing, and improper disclosure gave way to the normal risks of the marketplace. Government would try to limit the impediments to free and fair competition, intervening where necessary and then leaving it to the market to determine the winners and the losers. It had no obligation to bail out every company of losers.[36]

The burst of new legislation to implement the recommendations of the numerous investigations and studies ought to have brought the sometimes tumultuous chapter to a close. It did not. One week after the new Department of Financial and Commercial Affairs came into operation, and before the new securities legislation had been proclaimed, another Ontario financial company collapsed. The Prudential Finance Corporation, a medium-sized finance company with assets and liabilities in the $20 million range, was placed in interim receivership on 19 November 1966 and declared bankrupt on 5 December, three days after its president was arrested on charges which included theft and forgery. Prudential brought down several other companies in its wake, including the North American General Insurance Company, which became the first federally incorporated insurance company to fail in many decades. The collapse also brought another, wider storm of criticism down on the Ontario Securities Commission, the attorney general, and the Robarts government.

Arthur Wishart was once again in the hot seat in the legislature, issuing a long statement on 2 December relating the history of the collapse. When he was pressed to explain why the government had not investigated the company after the disputed election of a new board of directors in 1966, Wishart offered another statement of the limits of the regulatory philosophy:

The government concluded the affair had involved a dispute between competing business-men and that the government should not take part in such a matter for the benefit of either side.

Beyond the responsibility of government to supervise and control certain areas of the business and financial world within the framework of existing legislation there is a duty and responsibility on businessmen, particularly officers and directors of companies, to act in the best interests of their companies to make their own business decisions where the government has no authority to interfere.[37]

Wishart was able to argue that the public trustee had taken action in early November and that a full-fledged investigation had been under way before the bankruptcy, but it all seemed too little too late. There seemed to be a growing sentiment on the part of many observers that if the government agencies had been doing their job, failures like this would not take place at all.

There was also bitterness in Ottawa, which had felt the shock waves both in the insurance company failure and because the government had not accepted Dana Porter's earlier invitation to step in and try to clean up inadequacies in provincial regulation of near-banks. In December Mitchell Sharp, now minister of finance, delivered a bitter attack in the House of Commons on the Robarts government's handling of the situation:

Prudential Finance is a provincially chartered company and the Ontario authorities have been aware of its problems for some time. The federal government is concerned when any group of Canadians suffers in this way. We have a particular interest in this case, beyond the general protection of Canadian investors, because a federal company, North American General Insurance, was undermined by the collapse of a provincial company – Prudential Finance. The collapse of Prudential Finance and others that have gone before could only have been prevented by the improvement of provincial laws and administration.

Our jurisdiction is limited: nevertheless, we are not satisfied with the general level of protection afforded the investor in Canada. The provincial authorities must find ways to make that protection more adequate, and the federal government is prepared to assist them. We are already reviewing our laws ... [38]

Although Diefenbaker aimed most of his criticism at the federal government's inaction, he assumed Ontario had bungled the situation, and implied that these matters should be handled by the senior level of government. David Lewis of the NDP perhaps came closest to the heart of the issue when he urged both governments to co-operate 'to find some way of compensating the poor investors and policy holders who have suffered from this tragedy which our government and the provincial government failed to prevent.'[39]

Wishart tried to argue back a couple of days later:

It is surely not the proper role of government to invade the field of corporate management. This is the responsibility and obligation of the directors and officers of each individual company. If they violate the law, they will be prosecuted. This government had not been lax in this field. In Ontario, at the present time, close to 100 charges are pending against officers and directors of companies where the Crown is alleging some violation of the Criminal Code or the Securities Act.

But I must emphasize again that securities legislation cannot guarantee an investor against loss. There is a risk in every investment and the size of the return to the investor depends substantially on the size of the risk ...

The entire legislative program of the province has been directed towards informing the investor and enforcing the existing criminal laws so that his interests will not be abused in the future.[40]

The Ontario PCs were becoming increasingly coherent in explaining their instinctive, pragmatic policy on government intervention, but it was not clear that they could continue to maintain such distinctions in the face of what seemed to be becoming almost seasonal crises. That winter's troubled trust company was York Trust and Savings Corporation. Rumours that it was about to collapse sparked opposition demands to know what Ontario was doing to protect depositors.

Leslie Rowntree, the first head of the new Department of Financial and Commercial Affairs, was ready with an answer: the Ontario Deposit Insurance Corporation Act. It went from first reading to royal assent in three days in February 1967. All loan and trust companies incorporated under Ontario law were required to join the new corporation and pay the cost of insuring depositors in such institutions to a maximum of $20,000 per person. The insurance was to begin the day the act came into force. The government had thus resorted to legislation to do what Robarts had hoped the trust companies could have done on their own with British Mortgage and Trust Company in the summer of 1965 – act as each other's insurers. To some extent Ottawa was already leading the way in the field with an insurance scheme of its own, but this was consistent legislation for a government like Robarts' to bring in. The savings of innocent depositors could be protected by the good capitalist device of insurance; investors would still have to take their risks.

Robarts would have to justify his handling of these economic issues before an increasingly critical electorate late in 1967. Through these years he had stood his ground reasonably well as the government had been buffeted by financial crises on one hand and opposition and newspaper criticisms on the other. He had acted quickly when necessary, refused to act when important principles seemed to be at stake, and shepherded a mass of legislative changes into existence which extended the regulatory activities of the Ontario government while at the same time maintaining a commitment to the free enterprise system. Possibly the greatest single disappointment in the area was that no particularly important agreements had been reached to handle some of the problems on a national level through federal-provincial co-operation. An Ontario proposal for a Canadian Securities and Exchange Commission, responsible to a council of ministers and using the resources of existing provincial agencies, was typical of initiatives that failed.[41] Much of Ontario's new legislation, however, and especially the Ontario Securities Act of 1966, was used as a model by other provinces.

One obvious method Robarts used to handle staggering economic and political blows had been to go into a kind of royal commission clinch to gain breathing space and collective head-clearing. The device was appropriate and useful, and was used to its full effectiveness in Ontario and Canada during the 1960s (and has probably been under-used since, particularly at the federal level). Now enough was enough. Robarts would not appoint a royal commission investigation into the Prudential collapse. Except for listing new names of companies and players there would be little to do but repeat previous inquiries. These had resulted in recommendations which had been implemented, creating new regulatory machinery. Add a quick, permanent bandaid to the system in the form of deposit insurance, and little more was needed. It would never be possible to protect everyone against crooks and frauds. Investors who wanted to be free to make profits had to realize they were free and responsible to take losses. This was Ontario Progressive-Conservative economics. It was how you kept the goose laying the golden egg.

The Faces of Federalism

Robarts occasionally got away from the increasingly arduous demands of his office. The crossroads between law and politics had been passed. Law remained a possibility in the future, but Queen's Park and the continuing struggles of Confederation consumed his energy. The choice had been made, and the political commitment even transgressed on family time. By 1964 Robin was eleven and Tim was eight. Both were in public school in London. Norah remained a supportive and affectionate mother, presenting a tough and 'in control' manner to the community while hiding deepening concerns for her family and her marriage. The couple tried to maintain their private life through trips abroad, especially to England and Ireland. The breaks helped, but the decision to keep the family in London meant the isolation would continue. By this time John felt that the pace of life in Toronto would not permit him to have a stable family life in that city in any event, so London was probably best for the family. Norah at least could be with her friends and the children in their community. Norah might have been willing to move if she had been encouraged, but when she wasn't the memories of her days as a student's spouse kept her at home.

After the session ended in the spring of 1964 Robarts put Bill 99 and the reorganization of his government briefly behind him while he and Norah enjoyed a few weeks in England and on the continent. Of course there was some trade crusading to be done, new government offices to be opened, and the rituals of speech-making, but at least the trip home aboard the *Corinthia* offered a total break from politics. When the ship docked on 25 June John and Norah emerged relaxed and ready to start again.

As soon as John left the gang-plank, a throng of reporters pressed him for his views on the just-released first volume of the report of the federal Royal Commission on Health Services, chaired by Mr Justice Emmett M. Hall. It had recommended the creation of universal compulsory health insurance for Canadians. His private life pushed into the background, Robarts was back into politics.

His first impulse was to be co-operative. He was not strongly wedded to the

Ontario plan that his government had drafted in 1962-3 and which was still being studied by a special committee. Of course he would have to see the details of a federal plan before he would commit Ontario, but in health insurances as on other federal-provincial issues his instinct was to favour a national solution rather than a limited provincial approach, or at least a national solution that would respect provincial rights. It seemed to be a season for federal-provincial co-operation in social programs, for the compromise reached on pensions after the Quebec conference that spring had made possible precisely the kind of federal-provincial co-operation to create a national social program which seemed implied in the Hall Commission's recommendations.

Robarts had strengthened his government's capacity to handle itself in the cut-and-thrust of federal-provincial relations. He had done so partly from seeing how well Quebec had done on the pension fight, partly from a sense of how complicated the intergovernmental discussions were likely to become in the next few years. On the dominant issue of Quebec and its aspirations, Robarts had managed to define a fairly clear Ontario position. He exuded goodwill for Quebec's aspirations, offered real support in areas where the two provinces' needs and interests coincided, and expressed firm resistance on issues where Quebec seemed to be demanding excessive powers.

At the Quebec conference and in the later negotiations, Pearson had turned to Robarts and his positions as offering a kind of national perspective that Ottawa and Quebec might coalesce around. The Tax Structure Committee, which was being established to implement the resolutions of the Quebec conference, seemed particularly promising to Robarts, possibly the beginning of a new era in continuing federal-provincial revenue allocations to meet changing expenditure needs while maintaining one central fiscal and monetary policy. Its work would be preparatory to a major review of the whole Canadian tax structure, which awaited the reports of the federal Royal Commission on Taxation and various provincial committees, including Ontario's Commission on Taxation.[1] In major speeches in the spring of 1964 Robarts had urged an end to adversarial approaches to conflicts in federal-provincial jurisdiction. His was a managerial approach to federalism, characterized by a strong bias in favour of using the institutions of what has been called 'executive federalism' to work out mutually acceptable solutions.

The spirit of co-operation permeated interprovincial relations that summer. When the premiers met at Jasper in their annual conference (in private and without a federal presence) they seemed to make useful progress on methods of standardizing pension portability and education across Canada. The hope was to smooth out interprovincial distinctions likely to impede the mobility of Canadians. There was not so much progress in discussions aimed at ending the barriers that some provinces' preferential purchasing practices represented. Saskatchewan, British Columbia, New Brunswick, and now Quebec were all committed to giving resident businesses an advantage in government contracting. When Robarts raised the issue, opposing the division of the already small Canadian market into regions – he was particularly concerned about the impact of Quebec's preferences on Ontario – he was in a minority.[2] (He did not have entirely clean hands either, for his own government was urging its people to 'Buy Ontario'; the other provinces, however, had moved much further into protectionism.)

When the discussion turned to preparations for the centennial celebrations in 1967 and to the question of constitutional reform there was more harmony. As Canada's leaders prepared to recognize the one hundredth anniversary of the first Confederation conference by meeting again at Charlottetown in September, it seemed time to finish the job by agreeing on the patriation of the British North America Act. The main obstruction was the need for the federal government and the provinces to agree on a formula for making amendments to a Canadian constitution. Without an amending formula there could be no patriation, no significant constitutional change.

The most important area of agreement among the provinces at Jasper was a discovery that all of them seemed to support in principle the Fulton amending formula, which had been worked out during Diefenbaker's tenure at a 1961 conference on the constitution (when Davie Fulton was minister of justice) and had languished since. The premiers now urged Ottawa to make it the basis of discussion for the new Charlottetown conference. Lester Pearson agreed, writing all of the provinces to canvass changes in their positions since 1961, and concluding optimistically: 'Taking into account the results which have already been accomplished, we might reach an agreement in principle at Charlottetown, the detailed formulation of which might then be entrenched at a further constitutional conference ...'[3]

Goodwill permeated the opening of the Charlottetown conference in September 1964. Robarts, in his opening statement, called on 'all governments present at this historic conference to take the final step to make this country truly independent.' Jean Lesage agreed in principle to patriation, though warned that it would be necessary to agree on the amending formula first. Here the discussions began to disclose fundamental differences, for Ottawa and Quebec disagreed over whether powers seized by Ottawa through a constitutional amendment in 1949 should be open to unilateral amendment by Ottawa. The final communiqué contained a carefully worded though still positive announcement of a further meeting: 'The Prime Ministers and Premiers affirmed their unanimous decision to conclude the repatriation of the B.N.A. Act without delay.' Robarts announced that the Ontario legislature would debate patriation at its next session.[4]

Politics periodically called budding statesmen back to reality. Just after the Charlottetown conference two by-elections were held. One was to fill Robert Macaulay's vacant seat in Toronto-Riverdale. The Liberal candidate was the prominent media personality Charles Templeton, who was also an announced candidate for the Liberal leadership, to be decided a week later. It was the NDP, however, that made the running in Riverdale, staging an impressive house-to-house canvass and electing their candidate, lawyer James Renwick. The Conservatives consoled themselves with the other result, in which they regained a traditionally Tory seat in Windsor-Sandwich that the Liberals had held since 1959. Leadership of the hapless Ontario Liberal party fell to Andrew Thompson, MPP for Dovercourt in Toronto, who had worked for Pearson in Ottawa and risen to prominence during the Bill 99 debate.

The next round in federal-provincial relations was a major conference in mid October, which would consider the whole gamut of major issues – constitutional, pensions, taxation, resource policy, and possibly even medicare.[5]

The conference was a resounding success. The federal government introduced acceptable compromise proposals on the amending formula, which now became known as the Fulton-Favreau formula and was unanimously accepted by the first ministers. So were terms of reference for the Tax Structure Committee, including a list of studies to be carried out within the next eighteen months. It was agreed Ontario thought, that the Tax Structure Committee would do the preparatory work for the 1967 renegotiation of the tax-sharing agreements between Ottawa and the provinces. The premiers even had time on their hands to begin discussion of the recommendations of the Hall Royal Commission on Health Services, as well as the simmering problem of offshore mineral rights, before going home a day early. Robarts was particularly pleased, he said, with the mandate that the Tax Structure Committee had to undertake 'a very exhaustive and searching study and review of responsibilities of these Governments, and then to allocate to those governments the sources of revenue from which it has to meet [its] responsibilities ...'[6]

The momentum carried on toward what seemed certain patriation of the constitution in 1965 or 1966. On 3 November Pearson sent the premiers copies of a proposed 'Act to provide for the Amendment in Canada of the Constitution of Canada.' He asked for quick action and for each premier to 'advise me formally of the concurrence of your province in the substance of the proposed Act.'[7] Within a week Ontario had signified its concurrence with the wording. Almost all seemed well in these halcyon months of a new pre-centennial Canadian nationalism. Among themselves the provinces had recently agreed to standardize portability requirements for pensions.

In contrast to these solid steps forward, however, there were the worrisome disturbances involving national symbols. Queen Elizabeth had been given an unfriendly reception in Quebec during her recent visit. John Diefenbaker and his diehard supporters gave the Liberal government's proposal to replace British-derived flags with a new Canadian maple leaf flag an equally unfriendly reception. John Robarts gave a sharp interview to reporters following Quebec's ill-treatment of the Queen. Although he had great sympathy for Quebec, Robarts stated: 'The time has come to say something ... What I seek in return is an understanding and a sympathy for our point of view. And I don't think Quebec has that at the present time.' He had little to say about flags, though he later garnered useful political mileage by having a modified Red Ensign declared the official flag of Ontario.

John Diefenbaker's discontents went far beyond flag-waving. He and his federal party began attacking the constitutional amendment agreements, and on 2 November the Chief gave a particularly partisan speech to the Ontario PC Association annual meeting in which he described the amending formula as a vehicle designed to balkanize Canada. Robarts, who had fully supported the formula (which, as Davie Fulton was trying to tell Diefenbaker, had originated with the Diefenbaker Conservatives), sat on the platform through Diefenbaker's speech and the next night used his time to urge that 'the problems of Confederation must be faced from a non-partisan point of view.'[8] Diefenbaker, who had returned to the convention unannounced, stood outside the hall and listened.

The press played up the differences between the speeches as evidence of a growing rift between the two Conservative leaders, as indeed it was. Diefenbaker and Robarts differed fundamentally in their approaches to constitutional reform, to federalism, and to almost all other matters, and there was no bond of friendship between the men to soften their differences. Some federal Tories blamed Robarts for having caused the tension. Why was he suddenly saying so much about problems of Confederation and national unity? Were there ulterior motives, such as leadership ambitions, behind his positions? A sympathetic Toronto *Telegram* reporter was more accurate in writing of Robarts having been 'deeply troubled by the crisis which is facing the country ... and he insists on putting Ontario's views and opinions on national unity as forcibly as possible. And this he will do – even when it conflicts with the views of the party's national leader.'[9]

The Conservative party could have absorbed these differences had it not been coming apart at the seams over the issue of Diefenbaker's erratic, divisive leadership. By the end of the year the Quebec wing of the party, such as it was, was in open rebellion and so were several of Diefenbaker's former ministers, including Douglas Harkness. Many press observers saw Robarts, whose stature in federal-provincial affairs was constantly growing, as the logical successor to Diefenbaker. Robarts tried to keep clear of the internal bickering by insisting he was interested only in the problems facing Ontario and Canada. The paradox was that the more he appeared to be aloof from the fierce party politics of Tory leadership fights, the more attractive a candidate he was for the Tory leadership.

Work on the amending formula continued. On 22 February 1965 Pearson tabled a white paper on the subject in the House of Commons, and promised to submit the amending proposal for debate after the provinces had approved it. He wrote the provinces asking them to approve the procedure. Ontario's response to the request was a resolution introduced into the legislature by Arthur Wishart on 11 March which read, in part, 'That this House approves and supports the Addresses of the Senate and House of Commons of Canada to Her Majesty the Queen praying that

Her Majesty may graciously be pleased to cause a Bill to be laid before the Parliament of the United Kingdom in the following terms.'[10] It was passed after a day of debate.

One week later John Diefenbaker rose in the House of Commons on a question of privilege, read Ontario's resolution, and then charged into battle:

What has taken place ... offsets the rights and privileges of this House of Commons ... This resolution does not represent the facts nor the state of affairs. There has been no address. We have been asking what would be the nature of the government's plans in this connection, whether we would have the opportunity to examine ... the draft of the proposed act ... We now find ourselves in a position in the Parliament of Canada where one of the legislatures has passed a resolution approving that which has not been put before parliament ... It places parliament in a position secondary to that of any of the legislative assemblies which may approve of a similar form.[11]

Prime Minister Pearson denied that there had been any secret or improper intergovernmental collaboration and promised to look into the matter. The press enjoyed the contretemps, as Diefenbaker seemed to be accusing Robarts' government of having affronted the Parliament of Canada. Robarts stated cautiously that he did not want to get drawn into any fight with the national leader, and that they were still friends.[12] The last remark was not true. Diefenbaker's attempt to make political mileage out of what was at worst a procedural slip by the Ontario government was the kind of offensive manoeuvre that sharply divided him from the far less partisan Robarts. The matter was dropped in the House of Commons, but tension between the two Conservative leaders continued.

The Pearson Liberals now in April 1965 introduced a major set of new proposals for social legislation. The federal government (with provincial support in this case) wanted to consolidate a number of welfare programs into a new Canada Assistance Plan. Programs of economic aid to low employment areas of the country were to be introduced, and the offshore resources question would be referred to the Supreme Court. Most important, the federal government intended to go ahead with a national health insurance scheme, what Canadians commonly called 'medicare,' a term originally coined in the United States.

First reactions to the federal initiatives came from the Lesage government, which was being heavily influenced by a rising tide of nationalist and semi-separatist sentiment in Quebec and was rapidly becoming less inclined to co-operate with Ottawa. Lesage was upset by the offshore reference, annoyed about details regarding pension portability, fighting with Ottawa about the provinces' role in international relations, and becoming skittish about the constitutional agreement. His government made clear its determination to opt out of all the new social programs Ottawa was proposing, including medicare.

Ontario was more cautious, as Robarts' instincts leaned toward the maintenance of national institutions and policies wherever possible. He and his advisers saw nothing in principle that was objectionable in the Canada Assistance Plan, and could live with an economic development plan based on federal-provincial co-operation. They were becoming more worried about the contracting out option Quebec seemed to want to exercise every time Ottawa proposed anything, and felt they should resist this tendency in the hope of bolstering moderate federalist opinion in that province.[13]

They also wanted to scotch the idea that Canada's future revolved around the confrontation of 'two nations' along the Ottawa–Quebec City axis. Partly for that reason Ontario decided to resist Lesage's proposal for a permanent federal-provincial secretariat. Instead of further muddying the waters with more bureaucracy, Ottawa and the provinces should settle down to clarify the existing system, particularly to sort out questions of responsibility and taxes.[14] In several June 1965 speeches Robarts turned to national unity, talking of the need for a stronger sense of national purpose to offset regional loyalties, particularly in Quebec. Then he immediately had to deny that the speeches were an advertisement of his availability for Diefenbaker's job.

Medicare was going to be a crucial issue in federal-provincial relations. Ontario's years of planning for medical insurance had come to fruition in the winter and spring of 1965 with passage of legislation to establish a voluntary medical insurance scheme in the province. The government would insure low-income citizens. The rest of the population would be covered through non-government insurers, with the government setting a ceiling on premiums. Ontario's Medical Services Insurance Act was passed in the teeth of sharp criticism from both opposition parties to the effect that the government was too solicitous of private insurers and doctors and too hard on the needy. Until Ottawa actually announced the details of its proposed national plan, it could not be known whether the two governments would be able to co-ordinate their approaches to medical insurance or would be in conflict. Basic constitutional responsibility for health care services, of course, lay with the provinces.

Lester Pearson announced the basic principles of the federal medicare plan at a federal-provincial conference in mid July. It was a variation on a shared-cost program: Ottawa would pay a major share of the cost of any provincial program that met four conditions. These were: portability with other provincial plans; comprehensive coverage of the services provided by general practitioners and specialists; universality; and government administration of the insurance. As the Ontarians studied the proposal they realized their own plan did not meet the last two conditions. On 27 July Robarts harshly criticized the federal government for having failed to confer with the provinces. Without consultation Ottawa had decided to use its financial muscle to pressure the provinces into establishing medicare on its terms. Criticizing this 'shotgun approach' to health insurance, Robarts would only agree to discuss the Ottawa proposals further. OMSIP, the Ontario Medical Services Insurance Plan, would come into effect in the summer of 1966 as planned.[15]

The more his government studied Ottawa's suggestions, the more Robarts realized how seriously Ontario's plans would be disrupted. All of the private group plans, some of which had been in operation for decades in the province, would disappear. It was not clear that Ottawa knew the cost of its proposals or their impact on health services. Robarts could not understand why it was thought inadequate to proceed with Ontario's practical, far less grandiose and complicated method of having the state cover people who could not afford private insurance. Ontario's doctors, who would be doing the work of providing the health care, supported Ontario's scheme.

The Pearson government was fighting a general election, called for 8 November 1965. Robarts realized that nothing would please the Grits more than being able to tar the Tories as opponents of medicare (which seemed like being opposed to medical care, and not far from being an enemy of motherhood). Judy LaMarsh was reported to believe Ottawa's conditions on the issue were non-negotiable and to be ready to pounce. Through the campaign Robarts kept mum on the issue; he repeated his determination to go ahead with the Ontario plan when it was too late in the campaign to be taken up.[16]

The national Progressive-Conservative party, which Diefenbakerism had driven into a state of near-collapse, closed ranks for the Chief's last election fight. The Ontario Conservatives promised, as Elmer Bell put it, to give 'full throttle support' to the national party.[17] Robarts and Diefenbaker had a highly visible lunch early in the campaign, and the Ontario premier was reported as having promised to add eight new Tory seats from Ontario. Robarts was with Diefenbaker at the campaign's opening rally in Toronto, where he enthusiastically supported the national leader's proposal for a federal-provincial conference that would hold a wide-ranging discussion on Canada's future. His remarks included unusually sharp criticism of Quebec's dominance of the national debate: 'This isn't simply a matter of what Quebec wants – it's a matter of what *we* want ... Up to now it's been a one-way street out of Quebec, which is saying what it wants.'[18]

The premiers of Ontario and Quebec engaged in nearly direct dialogue on Confederation and its needs a week later when both gave major speeches at a seminar in Toronto sponsored by Ontario and Quebec newspaper editors. Lesage had been touring western Canada, and had responded to a climate of suspicion and misunderstanding with increasingly tough talk about Quebec's need for special status within Confederation, partly so it could champion the rights of francophone minorities outside Quebec. Now in Toronto he intimated that there was so much national misunderstanding, except in Ontario (where his friend John Robarts was sitting in the front row), that Canada did not yet have the 'marriage of minds' necessary to proceed with constitutional reform.[19] Speaking the next day, Robarts tried to define the challenges facing the partners in Confederation. Ontario and Quebec agreed on one priority, the need for an adjustment of the revenue/taxation situation. French Canadians' aspirations for recognition of their cultural and linguistic rights within Confederation also were supported by Ontario, but it did not accept Lesage's view that the government of Quebec had special responsibilities for French Canadians across Canada. The most fundamental difference of opinion was over the economy and the role of the central government. 'I doubt very much,' Robarts stated, 'whether Ontario can accept a federal system which is not based on the principle of a single national economy and a single national government which has control over that economy.'[20] Here he was attacking Pearson as much as Lesage, making clear that Ontario would not recognize any bilateral agreements between the federal government and a province that affected human or natural resources in Ontario.

John Robarts considered Jean Lesage a personal friend. At times the two seemed to share a vision of federalism that differed only on the margin of provincial self-interest. In Montreal and Toronto they could relax together and discuss issues directly, out of the spotlight of publicity. But their friendship did not mean automatic agreement on all Canadian issues. In fact they disagreed at least as often as they found common ground, and the area of disagreement was to grow steadily larger during these last months of Lesage's power. By November the Lesage government had scuttled the constitutional accord, based on Fulton-Favreau, in the name of its belief in *statut particulier* for Quebec, and Robarts was becoming more critical of economic nationalism of all kinds, both in Quebec and Ottawa. What was impressive about their disagreements, however, was that they managed to express differences of opinion in a tone of concern, sympathy, and statesmanship. Ontario, in particular, cared about Quebec, and it cared about Canada. John Robarts was rapidly becoming the least provincial of provincial premiers. And all this at a time when the two national leaders, Prime Minister Pearson and former Prime Minister Diefenbaker, were locked in the most rancorous, least constructive of their four electoral confrontations. While Pearson and Diefenbaker fought like aging cats, John Robarts and Jean Lesage had calmly discussed national problems, with Robarts taking a firmer position on the need for a strong central government than the prime minister himself. 'Pearson and Diefenbaker talked about regionalism on the Prairies and exchanged verbal blows over gangland slayings,' one reporter wrote in summary of these days in October, 'while Lesage and Robarts discussed the fundamentals of Confederation and Canadian nationalism.' Perhaps Robarts and Lesage would be the next leaders of the national parties, the newspapers speculated.[21]

The November election results produced little change. The voters denied the Pearson Liberals the majority government they had pleaded for, but they also kept the Conservatives out of power. In Ontario the Liberals gained only marginally, picking up two seats; but of course the Conservatives had done more poorly than in 1963. Robarts' alleged 'full throttle' support for Diefenbaker had not been very enthusiastic and had not translated into extra seats. Nor did the Ontario premier's post-election comment that the results were just as he had expected create more goodwill. Diefenbaker and his supporters had no soothing words for the Ontario Tories, one of them describing the Ontario results as 'another Bay Street stab in the back.'

That impression was shared by Eddie Goodman, the national Progressive-Conservative campaign chairman, and by Diefenbaker. Some years later, Diefenbaker wrote: 'As far as Frost was concerned, he stood. As for Mr. Robarts, he did nothing to help in the 1965 election; indeed he directed various Cabinet Ministers to take no part in the campaign or the result would have been very different. Had he entered into the campaign with even a small percentage of the enthusiasm of Mr. Frost, the Conservative Party would have formed the new Government of Canada. Less than 8,000 votes would have brought about a change of Government.'[22]

After the federal election there was a general shifting and regrouping of fundamental positions in both Ottawa and Ontario. Robarts' government had become convinced that the province was heading towards serious long-term financial problems. The government needed much tighter expenditure controls, more money from Ottawa, and continued strength in its tax base if it was going to maintain a balanced budget. This was no time, Robarts felt, for the province to undertake the kind of major expenditure commitments that would be involved in meeting Ottawa's conditions on medicare. Ottawa could afford to toss its money around, Ontario was beginning to realize, because its taxation revenues apparently gave it a permanent surplus. The interim report of the Tax Structure Committee, released in December 1965, seemed to confirm this view: that Canada's existing tax structure was going to produce long-term surpluses for Ottawa and chronic debts for the provinces. And now, on medicare, Ottawa seemed willing to use its surplus to pressure the provinces into increasing their spending.

Planning for the provincial budget that winter was extremely difficult, with James Allan having to increase taxes in almost every area (including the first increase in the retail sales tax) and still not finding enough revenue to predict a balanced budget. In the midst of this planning Robarts delivered sharply worded speeches explaining why Ontario could not afford to accept Ottawa's medicare proposals, and why it would be better for the whole federation if medicare were put off until the work of the Tax Structure Committee could lead to 'a more effective form of planning and programming than we have ever known before.'[23] Unfortunately the impact of his arguments was blunted by erroneous under-estimates of Ottawa's proposed contributions, and it was hard to get across the message that even on the correct figures Ontario could not afford to make the commitment it was being pressured towards. Surely this was just poor-mouthing by rich, booming Ontario. In February, Matthew Dymond introduced amendments to Ontario's plan which reduced the role of commercial carriers and tightened government controls, but still did not meet federal requirements. Over intense criticism from the opposition – the Liberals favoured the national scheme;

the NDP wanted a more radical one, based on Saskatchewan's lead – the less ambitious Ontario plan was to go ahead. It was a plan, Robarts said, 'geared to meet our financial capabilities at the moment.'[24]

Then in the spring of 1966 Ottawa began showing a new, hard face of federalism. The Liberals had decided that 'co-operative federalism' meant too much weakening of the federal government, perhaps too much catering to Quebec. Now they would stop fudging lines of jurisdiction, stop the haemorrhaging of initiative and money away from Ottawa. Finance Minister Mitchell Sharp made clear that Ottawa was no longer interested in restructuring revenue, expenditure, and equalization policies in a co-operative way. It was moving to a position that started by accepting the existing distribution of powers and responsibilities, and stressed the need for each government to raise the money it considered necessary to meet these responsibilities. Suddenly Ottawa was less interested in potential reforms and revisions rooted in the findings of the Tax Structure Committee or the impending taxation inquiries. It wanted a new equalization formula and a new tax-sharing agreement, but would leave the situation at that. It no longer seemed to recognize that the status quo contained a fundamental imbalance or that the Tax Structure Committee's very existence, at least in Robarts' view, was the result of Pearson's acknowledgment at Quebec in 1964 that something had to be done about that imbalance. Having led the provinces down one road for several years, Ottawa suddenly wanted to turn everyone into a new alley, where it was going to rough them all up a little.

The game changed suddenly, astonishingly, in Quebec too, when the Union Nationale party, led by Daniel Johnson, came out of nowhere to defeat the Lesage Liberals in the June 1966 provincial election. Jean Lesage, who had been courted so carefully in Ontario and seemed to be such a good friend, all things considered, and had become a towering figure in Canadian political life, disappeared overnight. The new Quebec premier, Johnson, was an unknown quantity.

Robarts tried to get to know Johnson very quickly. He and Keith Reynolds met with Johnson and Marcel Faribault, Johnson's constitutional expert, at the Ritz Carleton in Montreal in July for first conversations. Although most observers felt Johnson had won the election because of a reaction against the Lesage government's massive reforms, it was soon apparent that there was to be no backing away from Quebec's assertiveness on the Canadian stage. Indeed, Johnson had used the slogan 'Québec d'abord' in his campaign and had published a book entitled *Egalité ou Indépéndance*. He gave every promise of being more of a French-Canadian nationalist, to the point of flirting with separatism, than Lesage had ever been.

Everyone's gloves were dropped during the summer of 1966. When the provincial premiers gathered for their annual conference, Daniel Johnson made clear that his government intended to 'crash the 50 percent barrier' in the personal income tax field, but at the same time would not accept the expense of medicare even if Ottawa paid half the cost (Lesage had reversed his earlier reluctance and had accepted the federal plan). From Ontario's point of view, Johnson's stance was welcome because Ottawa almost certainly would not be able to go ahead without the support of Quebec and Ontario. A survey taken at the conference showed to the premiers' surprise that seven of the ten of them opposed the federal plan.

Many of them also opposed the new equalization grant formula that Ottawa had proposed in private discussions that spring. The new formula would cost Saskatchewan $35 million. Premier Ross Thatcher was outspoken in condemning it. Daniel Johnson had little to say on the subject, perhaps because his province stood to gain approximately 90 per cent of the $100 million being added to the equalization pot by the federal government. Worried that the formula was another example of pandering to Quebec, Robarts revealed some of its details to the press at the end of the conference, breaking confidentiality. When Pearson made known his displeasure at the breach of protocol, Robarts commented tartly that it was time there was 'wide public knowledge of exactly what these federal-provincial agreements are and how they operate.'[25]

Vital decisions were supposed to be made at two conferences in the autumn – a Tax Structure Committee meeting in September, and a full-fledged federal-provincial summit in October. The federal government removed some of the tension of the medicare debate by announcing a year's delay, until 1 July 1968, in the timetable for the implementation of its plan. But then it formally presented the new hard-line on fiscal federalism. Mitchell Sharp's statement to the Tax Structure Committee spelled out Ottawa's belief that each level of government in Canada should be responsible for raising its own revenue. Tax resources would not be shifted from Ottawa to the provinces – which, if they needed money, could levy new taxes themselves. If Tax Structure Committee projections indicated provincial deficits down the line, the cause would not be lack of access to tax revenue in Ottawa's hands, 'but the reluctance of governments to bear the responsibility for increasing the level of taxation.' Ottawa was going to go ahead with its new equalization grant formula. It was going to begin disentangling federal-provincial responsibilities by withdrawing from several shared-cost programs, in these cases, but only these cases, transferring equalized points of income tax to the provinces. One of the effects of disentanglement would be to end Quebec's unique position as the only province opting out of shared-cost programs.[26]

Robarts was fundamentally opposed to Ottawa's new philosophy. He now spelled out Ontario's clear alternative. It was that there be an agreed-upon ceiling on the levels of major taxes in the country – an agreed-upon size of the pie – and within that limit a division of money based on the projections of needs developed by the Tax Structure Committee. The new federal approach of having each government create its own taxation pie would lead to tax competition among governments, an inability to co-ordinate national fiscal policy, the disruption of federal-provincial planning, and more constraints on private-sector growth. If governments tried to make too many pies, Robarts could have said, there would be a shortage of dough. Queen's Park was not very happy with the equalization formula either, regretting the additional drain Ottawa proposed to impose on 'the paymaster for much of these federal transfers to the poorer provinces,' Ontario. Privately Robarts' advisers guessed that the new equalization money flowing to Quebec was intended to make it possible for that province to afford to opt into medicare.[27]

Daniel Johnson made Robarts look like a paragon of moderation. Basing his position explicitly on a 'two nations' theory of Confederation (the two nations being represented by the Quebec government on the one hand and the Ottawa government on the other), Johnson demanded 100 per cent of the three major direct taxes for Quebec. In the name of the French-Canadian nation Quebec was determined to have control of the linguistic, cultural, social, and now the economic future of French Canadians. At the end of the conference's first day Johnson delivered to the press a threat to hold a referendum on Quebec's place in Confederation. Not many other provinces offered support for Ottawa's proposals either. On his return to Toronto, Robarts told the press that the conference got 'a little out of hand' in some of the consitutional talk, and that Ottawa's determination to scrap the idea of a limit on the taxation the national economy could bear was 'most irrational.'[28]

Kelso Roberts supplied an interlude to planning for the October conference by presenting a long memorandum to Robarts on the fantastic expansion of government spending in the 1960s and claiming that enough was enough. Robarts tried to channel him off in the treasurer's direction, but Roberts decided to become a one-man austerity program. As a member of Treasury Board he took vigorous offence to a proposal to spend $5 million to build the Northern Ontario Institute of Technology at Kirkland Lake. A few days later he resigned from the cabinet.[29] Robarts was not at all sorry to see him go. Roberts might have been correct to be alarmed about the government's financial situation; his proposals for dealing with it seemed irrelevant. There were far greater fiscal fish to fry, as Ontario fought to get the money from Ottawa that it needed to meet its social priorities.

The October federal-provincial conference was characterized by a nearly total collapse of co-operation and civility. Ottawa announced major new proposals to give the provinces unconditional grants to help cover the cost of post-secondary education, while phasing out its grants for vocational and technical training. Taken by surprise, presented with elaborate but poorly drafted initiatives, a number of the premiers, including Robarts, were angry at Ottawa's presumption and bad manners. Robarts became angrier as Ottawa backpedalled and revised; finally he labelled the technical and vocational proposals a hoax. Meanwhile, Mitchell Sharp stood fast on the new determination to have governments raise their own taxes to fund their own programs (with this self-serving qualification to justify intrusion into higher education and health insurance: 'It is only when the federal government acknowledges that certain provincial programmes or expenditures have a higher priority than competing federal priorities, that the government is warranted in asking Parliament to impose taxes to contribute toward meeting their costs').[30] Ottawa was still determined to go ahead with both disentanglement of shared-cost programs and the new equalization formula. Robarts resisted all aspects of these proposals. He challenged Ottawa to permit publication of the studies that had gone into the Tax Structure Committee's prediction of provincial deficits and federal surpluses. Ottawa would not agree. Robarts insisted that Ontario needed five more points of personal income tax in 1967-8 and three points in 1968-9 as 'an equitable sharing of the total government deficit in the years immediately ahead.'[31]

Daniel Johnson was at least as determined as Robarts to get more tax room, and Duff Roblin of Manitoba joined them in an angry confrontation with Pearson and Sharp. Johnson eventually called Sharp 'a one-man British North America Act.' The federal politicians remained adamant. Robarts kept his distance from Johnson's extremism, commenting that he was 'concerned about the position of Premier Daniel Johnson and the latter's demands for Quebec. And I hope Mr. Johnson is concerned about mine.' But he was also frustrated enough at the whole situation to demand, before the meeting adjourned, that the entire structure of Confederation be reviewed.[32] In effect he was saying it was time to sit down and talk about how to remake a country that wasn't working. The conference ended in such total disagreement that it was impossible to draft even a communiqué of clichés. No premier accompanied Pearson to the final press conference. Robarts' parting shot was a description of both the conference and the Tax Structure Committee meeting as an exercise in futility.[33] On the eve of Canada's centennial, federal-provincial relations had all but collapsed.

The situation in the national Progressive-Conservative party was even worse. The movement to terminate Diefenbaker's leadership had crystallized in Dalton Camp's campaign for re-election as party president on a platform calling for the establishment of a regular leadership review. Robarts tried to stay out of the fight. With national leadership the burning issue at the Ontario PC Association's annual convention late in October, for example, Robarts' speech at the closing banquet was about the fiscal challenge facing Ontario. During his speech he announced that he proposed to convene a series of federal-provincial meetings to discuss the future of Confederation. (The proposal had already been endorsed by Johnson, who shared Robarts' concern for the federal government's disregard for the provinces.)

The Camp-Diefenbaker battle intensified as the annual meeting of the PC Association of Canada approached. Every detail in the planning of the meeting, particularly the timing of key events, became important in the struggle. A critical meeting of the national executive was held on 13 November to plan the agenda for the convention. When Robarts, a member of the executive, could not be located for the meeting, Ernie Jackson was phoned in Toronto in the hope that Robarts would be located long enough to have him nominate an alternate to take his place. With Robarts on the road with his family between Grand Bend and London, Jackson agreed to authorize Stanley Randall, who was already in Ottawa, to serve as Robarts' alternate. Jackson did not realize that Randall was identified with the Camp faction. So was Elmer Bell, who had tried vainly to dissociate his personal involvement from that of the Ontario group. The Diefenbaker camp assumed that Robarts shared Bell's and Randall's views. They were wrong. Robarts did not like his federal counterpart, but disliked the character of internal struggles within the national party more. He responded by withdrawing from the fray.[34] Years later, on reflection, he commented that if Jackson could have reached him he would have ordered that no alternate be appointed.[35]

Robarts visited the national convention as briefly as possible. He would arrive in Ottawa for the evening session of the first day of the convention, join other leading federal and provincial Conservatives on the platform for Diefenbaker's speech, and return to Toronto the next morning. Arriving in Ottawa, he went directly to his room in the Chateau Laurier to stay away from the politicking and wait until it was time to appear on the platform. A series of minor contretemps made it seem as if Camp's organizers were orchestrating the timing of Robarts' appearance on the platform – which happened just as Camp finished his speech. Robarts appeared, shook Camp's hand, and took his seat. Diefenbaker arrived later and was given a rude, hostile reception by the convention. 'All I wanted to do was to be in Toronto,' Robarts remembered of the night. As soon as Diefenbaker's speech was over, he got out of the hall and stayed in his room until it was time to go home the next morning.

But the damage had been done. The Toronto *Star* reported, quite incorrectly, that Robarts had thrown his political power behind Camp: 'In a carefully-planned political manoeuvre – Robarts made a dramatic entrance to the convention just as the party's national president – Dalton Camp – completed an emotional speech defending his stewardship as President, ... shook hands with Camp and sat beside him on the stage.'[36] Robarts disclaimed any part in any plan to swing Ontario Conservative support behind Camp and against Diefenbaker. Diefenbaker's supporters did not believe him, and later singled Robarts out as the premier who had given the most obvious support to Camp's 'insurrection.'

Camp was re-elected and got his leadership review. Robarts was announced by the press, as usual, as a leading contender. As usual he denied the rumours. There were other rumours that the Ontario organization was already campaigning on his behalf. Many ardent Diefenbakerites wrote his name near the top of their enemies' list.[37]

To many Canadians on the eve of centennial year, John Robarts did appear to be a credible man to move to Ottawa. Throughout these seemingly endless and endlessly confused discussions, he had spoken firmly for Ontario. He had steered a coherent, consistent, and moderate course, opposing federal interference with Ontario's interests, proposing co-operative, consultative approaches, talking continually about the national interest, befriending and being concerned about Quebec, but insisting on calling a halt when Quebec seemed to be becoming the spoiled child of Confederation.

He had not won notable victories. As 1966 ended, Robarts felt that Ottawa had betrayed the basic agreement of 1964 that had seemed to establish a structure in which co-operative federalism could flourish. A major attempt to patriate Canada's constitution had ended in failure, and there was less unity in Canada in 1966 than there had been several years earlier. The goodwill Robarts and other concerned English Canadians had tried to mobilize to support Quebec's aspirations had not prevented the steady growth of a Quebec nationalism which was not particularly understanding of the rest of Canada. There were major battles ahead with Ottawa over tax revenues and medicare, and the future of his own Progressive-Conservative party at the federal level was still clouded with fallout from the bitter leadership fight. Robarts' early successes in getting along with Ottawa and his own attempts to address national issues had had the effect of further separating his own wing of the party from the Diefenbaker forces.

But paradoxically, the more frustrations and setbacks the Robarts government seemed to experience, the more confidence ordinary Ontarians, and many outside of Ontario, seemed to have in John Robarts' leadership capacities. On the eve of centennial year he was more than one more figure in the line of Tory premiers of Ontario. He was now an elder statesman of a confused, complex confederation – which was now set to celebrate having survived a full one hundred years. A few days into Canada's hundredth year, John Robarts himself would turn fifty.

Centennial: Turning Fifty

The centennial celebrations began on New Year's Eve. On Parliament Hill in Ottawa the centennial flame was lit. Bonfires flared across the country. In Toronto the Governor General's Horse Guards led a torchlight procession from Union Station up University Avenue to Queen's Park, where a stage had been erected across the front of the legislative building. A fanfare of trumpets welcomed the celebrants.

The crowd of happy Canadians grew and grew, eventually reaching forty thousand. The Civil Service Choir sang hymns. John Robarts and the mayor of Toronto, William Dennison, were among the dignitaries and gave short speeches. When Robarts mentioned the bonfires across Canada, someone yelled in jest that Toronto should donate its old city hall. The festivities ended with the lighting of a centennial flame, a fireworks display, and Mayor Dennison ringing a cowbell. As the crowd broke up to go partying (many of them to the new city hall, where police worried that the idea of burning the old one might just catch on), John Robarts and his family left for Grand Bend and a weekend at their cottage.

The year ahead looked like a good and busy one. The Robarts family was planning to move into a bigger house on the prestigious Parkway in London. Robarts' blind trust had grown to $262,500, and its administrator had informed him it could assume the mortgage, ensuring the family's fiscal base was secure. Publicly, there were all the rest of the centennial celebrations, of course, which would reach a climax on Dominion Day and with the summer-long world's fair in Montreal. Politically, the government would almost certainly go to the people in a provincial election sometime in 1967. Robarts was committed to a major initiative in national affairs with his conference to assess the future shape of Confederation. More mundanely, but of deep interest to the premier, the reports of both the federal Royal Commission on Taxation and Ontario's Committee on Taxation were soon to be published, making possible the long-desired reform of the tax system. Robarts' own reforms of the Ontario government were now almost complete, giving the province a new capacity to manage the burdens of public administration. There were troublesome issues ahead, the most vexatious of them being the turmoil within the national Progressive-Conservative party, about to rid itself of John Diefenbaker. The Ottawa scene was vexatious in general, for Robarts had yet to see his desire for constructive co-operation between Ottawa and the provinces implemented in any significant way.

Robarts' preparations for the centennial had involved a major cabinet shuffle at the end of November 1966. Kelso Roberts had already gone; James Allan and Louis Cecile (minister of public welfare) retired. Charles MacNaughton, who had been a close adviser and protégé of the premier, replaced Allan as provincial treasurer. Leslie Rowntree, who had shrewd political instincts, moved from Labour into the new Financial and Commercial Affairs portfolio. John Yaremko, who had been first elected in 1951 with Robarts and had beaten him into the cabinet, was moved to Public Welfare, and George Gomme, from eastern Ontario, took over Highways. Five new members were added: Robert Welch, a lawyer from the Niagara peninsula, became provincial secretary and minister of citizenship; René Brunelle, a tourist resort operator from northern Ontario, was the new minister of lands and forests. Dalton Bales, who had chaired the Borough of York Board of Health, took over Labour, while Thomas Wells from Toronto and Darcy McKeough from Chatham joined the cabinet as ministers without portfolio.[1] Some observers detected a shift to the right in the personnel of the new cabinet. Robarts himself stressed the emphasis on younger men in the reorganization – correctly, it turned out, for in this centennial rejuvenation he created the basis of his government for the next five years as well as his successor's ministries in the 1970s. Some of Robarts' critics in the party noticed how the promotion of MacNaughton and McKeough meant even more power for southwestern Ontario – an expansion of the 'Queen's Park on the Thames' motif.

Robarts, Jackson, and the party's new public relations adviser, Peter Hunter, decided to plan tentatively for a spring election. The timing might be reconsidered in the light of the federal situation, where Diefenbaker was demanding an immediate leadership convention, an event that might well be nasty and damaging for Conservatives across the country. The Ontario Throne Speech, delivered on 25 January, was widely interpreted as a pre-election document. It dealt with a wide range of issues, including farm modernization, urban transportation, home ownership, conservation, and technical training. 'For most holes in the dike Mr Robarts has a finger,' the Toronto *Telegram* headlined its report. To mark the centennial, the Throne Speech announced the creation of the Ontario Heritage Foundation, as well as the government's desire to convene a 'Confederation of Tomorrow' conference. Robarts strengthened election speculation by announcing that the House would begin early afternoon and evening sittings, and that the provincial budget would be brought in early in Febraury.

The government did not expect a particularly fierce election struggle, and was not even sure what the issues would be in a booming, bustling province that had enjoyed 8.5 per cent economic growth in 1966. Neither of the opposition parties seemed likely to be able to cause significant trouble. The strongest reaction to the Throne Speech, it turned out, came not from the Liberals or the NDP in the legislature, but from the Pearson government in Ottawa. On 26 January Robarts received a confidential letter from Lester Pearson expressing his concern about Ontario's plan to convene a federal-provincial conference.[2] The letter and the public statements that soon followed opened up a new level of debate about the role of the federal and provincial governments in the reshaping of Confederation.

Robarts had broached the idea of a conference on Confederation almost in passing and possibly in pique at the conclusion of the disastrous October 1966 federal-provincial conference. At the time, Pearson had seemed to accept the initiative, and Daniel Johnson of Quebec, who shared Robarts' misgivings about Ottawa's stance in federal-provincial relations, was quick to support Ontario's proposal. Ontario's and Quebec's constitutional advisers met for three days in mid January in Kingston to get acquainted and share views.[3] The sessions were not as fruitful as the Ontario people had hoped (Quebec had not gone ahead with anything like a counterpart to the Ontario Advisory Committee on Confederation), but did establish long-term intergovernmental contacts. But, with Johnson's support confirmed, Ontario decided to hold its Confederation of Tomorrow conference.

Lester Pearson wrote Robarts that he thought the October proposal had been for an interprovincial conference – in other words, a meeting of the provinces that Ottawa would not attend. The convening of conferences at which both the federal and the provincial governments attended had always been the sole prerogative of Ottawa, and Pearson was worried that it would be a bad precedent for one province to call a federal-provincial conference. Instead, Pearson suggested that the topic of the future of Confederation be included on the agenda of a conference convened by Ottawa. He made his disagreement with Ontario public when he told the House of Commons on 27 January: 'I can think of nothing more unproductive than the impression that a constitutional conference will be held shortly to review our constitution before all the preparatory work has been carefully worked out.'[4]

Some of the members of the Ontario Advisory Committee on Confederation – indeed, many members of the provincial cabinet – had similar doubts about rushing into such a conference, but Robarts, backed fully by his Quebec counterpart, was determined to persevere. 'I vehemently and completely reject the proposition that there is no room for initiative on the part of the provinces in these matters,' he told his legislature. Replying to Pearson's letter, he outlined his vision of the conference at length:

[At confederation] there was need for unity. Today there is a swelling chorus of millions of voices expressing a similar need. Perhaps once again, in some measure at least, by appropriate discussion in a conference, unfettered by the techniques and procedures in effect at the various types of conferences held over the past several years, achievements might result from representatives of the Governments of Canada sitting down together to examine Confederation and to take stock of the state of affairs ... to take the time to discuss and review, in an atmosphere free from rancour, areas of agreement and disagreement ...

Out of it, in my opinion, can come suggestions for plans to chart our future and to shape the second century of our nation based upon a sure and firm foundation.

No one can justly deny the Provinces, nor prevent them from asserting, the right to assume their proper place and play their proper role in the evolvement [*sic*] of the governmental process in our country. The conference proposed is not to be a forum for decision-making. Moreover, it is not the intention that the Conference would set about to draft a new Constitution ... Rather it would be a meeting of minds, in a relaxed atmosphere.[5]

He concluded by asking for Ottawa's co-operation and goodwill.

Robarts' opponents were not sure what he was up to. Was it an Ontario power play, some kind of adroit counter-attack after the wars of 1965-6? Was it an election ploy? Was it a joint Ontario-Quebec attack on the federal power? In a sense it was all of these things, but more fundamentally it was John Robarts' personal determination that there be serious discussions on the future of Confederation by the spokesmen for equal governments. As with all his support for such federal-provincial initiatives as the Tax Structure Committee, Robarts believed that problems of joint concern had to be settled by Ottawa and the provinces conferring and working as partners, not by negotiations or confrontations between one senior government facing a flock of juniors. 'Sooner or later, the Federal government has to recognize the position of the Provinces ...,' he wrote his constitutional adviser, Ian Macdonald, during the sparring.[6]

Six weeks into the new year, the long sitting hours were in effect in the legislature. Charles MacNaughton was to bring in his first budget on Tuesday, 14 February. Robarts, who had celebrated his fiftieth birthday on 11 January, was in a comfortable routine of escaping from Toronto on winter weekends to relax with his family at the cottage at Grand Bend. On 11 and 12 February he spent most of his time outdoors on a new snowmobile. When the family went back to London on Sunday night he was not feeling well. On Monday he phoned his office to say he had the flu and would not be coming in.

Tuesday was budget day. Robarts' driver, Jack Smith, arrived at the London home that morning to bring him to Toronto for MacNaughton's budget speech. Robarts was still in bed. Smith realized at a glance that the prime minister was very ill. Robarts insisted that he was going to go to Toronto and told Smith to leave him alone for a little while and he would be all right. He tried to get dressed. Big, powerful, determined John Robarts was too ill to tie his tie. Norah Robarts told Smith she had tried to get John to stay in bed but he wouldn't listen. Now Smith's impressions reinforced her fear and she called the family doctor. He came quickly, examined the premier, and ordered him into hospital immediately. An ambulance was called.

Robarts had been determined not to allow mere physical frailty to prevent him from being at his official post for an important occasion. Now he continued to deny reality. He refused to be carried down the stairs of his home on a stretcher. Then he refused to ride in the ambulance. Smith and the doctor had to get him into the limousine instead, which Smith drove to the hospital, the ambulance leading the way.

The doctors could not immediately determine what was wrong, giving rise to instant speculation about illness so serious that he would have to resign. When he met the press in his hospital room, though, Robarts looked reasonably healthy. He thought he might have a bleeding ulcer. The final diagnosis was severe hiatus hernia. It soon quieted down and Robarts was out of hospital before the end of February. He returned to Queen's Park and the session on 6 March.

The incident was the first public occasion when Robarts had been incapacitated. He had been strong enough to hide his chronic ankle and knee problems, a reminder of his football days, although his father had expressed concern over them from time to time. In a similar way, his drinking had not tarnished his public performance. This incident, although relatively minor, marks a threshold in Robarts' career. The continuing health and marital problems in his private life would gradually become more visible in his public affairs.

Throughout his backbench and then his cabinet years, Robarts had succeeded in separating his political and his personal life, commuting back and forth from the Toronto political world to the London circle of family and friends. Norah Robarts was not a traditional political wife; she preferred to be at home with her children or enjoying the social life of her set in London, and was uncomfortable as a supporting actor in unfamiliar political surroundings. As he went from being a backbencher to a junior minister and then minister of education and finally prime minister, the demands of political life on John Robarts' time had grown steadily. During his premiership there had been a dramatic increase in workload as the sessions of the legislature had grown longer, the number of bills to be vetted and put through increased by the score, the federal-provincial conferences became almost a level of governing.

It was harder and harder to get home to London. There would be a crisis at Queen's Park, requiring the premier to stay and straighten things out. He would be off mending political fences, giving a speech somewhere in eastern or northern Ontario. Or he would be in Quebec, or in Alberta, or in Ottawa, meeting with other politicians. Even in London there would be local political business he never had time for in Toronto, people to be met, plans to be made. Politics consumed his time, as it came to consume the time of most Canadian politicians of John Robarts' generation. Now it began to consume his marriage.

Norah remained at home in London. John's trips home became less frequent and less regular. He still had to get some time off-duty, some time to relax, but more and more often he took it on the fly, catching some drinks or a dinner with friends in the midst of politicking. Once Norah heard that John had been seen in Toronto having dinner with a female acquaintance. He was powerfully attractive and attracted to women. Norah decided to make coming home special by putting on an exquisite meal one Friday evening. Robin and Tim and Norah were all beautifully dressed and groomed to meet John. Six o'clock arrived and no John. Then seven, then eight. One lonely aperitif turned into two and then three as Norah waited. John finally arrived, having been delayed by work. He had not called. A beautiful evening turned into disappointment and bitter quarrelling.

Coming home began to mean tension, and suspicion, and recriminations. It was a little better at the cottage at Grand Bend, but even there the family did not escape from politics. Ernie Jackson's cottage was near by. Elmer Bell and Charles MacNaughton lived a stone's throw away in Exeter. Norah Robarts was left on her own to bring up two children and to brood over stories passed back to her about John's life in Toronto. Like millions of lonely people before and after her she began to rely on alcohol to deaden the pain. Her inability to keep her husband in bed at the onset of his hernia was a sign of the shrinking influence she had over his life. Nor did she bother to phone Toronto and tell a world that was foreign to her of the details of her husband's illness.[7]

A few weeks later, after he had recovered, John deliberately undertook a heavy speaking schedule. He was going to prove to the press, and to himself, that he was healthy and capable of leading the government in an election. Outwardly he seemed to pull it off, showing no signs of the hernia or the years in office. But the wear and tear on his marriage was visible to close observers. They also saw signs of physical deterioration; he began to gain weight, his blood pressure gradually rose, knee problems relating to the old football injuries began to make walking painful and slow. Robarts had always been able to enjoy drinks at night and be fresh for work the next day. But now he was fifty, not twenty, thirty, or even forty. An aging body could take only so much punishment. He could no longer always bounce back. Nor was it certain that Robarts always drank purely for pleasure. Like Norah, like so many busy executives and politicians and writers of his generation, he may have been beginning to use liquor as a crutch.

Robarts had accepted one important limitation; he had no interest in running for the national leadership of his party, no interest in becoming prime minister of Canada. Running the government of Canada's wealthiest province was the limit of his political ambition. When things were going well at Queen's Park, being prime minister of Ontario was extremely satisfying. In unguarded moments Robarts would sometimes say that he didn't need to try to run Canada from Ottawa because he already ran it from Queen's Park.[8] Very early in the Conservative leadership contest he was approached about becoming a candidate, by Dalton Camp and

Robert Stanfield among others, and refused. Even if he had wanted the national leadership, he thought his candidacy would goad Diefenbaker into direct personal opposition to him, resulting in an ugly contest. Robarts' refusal was so unequivocal that he did not become the front-runner on the sidelines the way his successor did in the 1983 Conservative leadership contest.

The national leadership convention was scheduled to be held in Toronto the week of 4 September. The main question it posed for the Ontario Tories was how to time their provincial election. Robarts seemed healthy enough to fight a late spring campaign, but it seemed risky to try to pull one off at a time when Conservatives were potentially very divided and distracted by the run-up to the federal gathering. Reliable sources from Ottawa were also reporting that a frustrated and angry John Diefenbaker might lash out and intervene in an Ontario election to try to defeat Robarts.[9] Postponing an election until the leadership convention would serve several purposes. Tory discontents would be settled, Diefenbaker would be gone or at least preoccupied, the convention itself would give the party a lot of publicity and probably draw useful attention to Robarts as the mediating statesmanlike premier of the host province. There were other advantages to waiting for the fall, such as the prospect of having recommendations from the Ontario Committee on Taxation that could be usefully implemented, and perhaps profiting from goodwill spilling over from the centennial summer. So it was decided to call the provincial election as the convention was ending, with the voting to be in mid October.

The Conservatives gradually realized that the election was going to reflect ways in which the Ontario political scene was beginning to change. Some of the most visible changes in the routine of government, such as the extensions of the session, the increased workload on politicians, and the reorganizations of government to try to stay in control of events, have been noticed earlier. Another fairly obvious change in Ontario political life was the decline in the average age of the electorate as the leading edge of the baby boom generation entered its twenties. Perceptions of the importance of youth caused the leaders of the old Tory dynasty to emphasize the youthfulness and vitality of the government, especially after Robarts' cabinet changes. The irony of John Robarts, who had just passed fifty and was starting down a long slope of physical decline, championing the Conservatives as a dynamic, energetic party, was only faintly evident at the time.

It was also a seasonal response to some of the silliness of centennial year. Worrying about 'go-go' politics (named for 'go-go' dancers, most of whom were still innocently dressed) was a superficial response to the beginnings of a deeper, more fundamental metamorphosis in the tone of Ontario politics. Life in the legislature was becoming less of a ritual or game, more of a war, with knives bared and safety catches released, and basic issues being raised about the role of government and the rights of the individual.

Many of the criticisms of government policies during the past several years had tended to move in the same direction. Robarts had seemed to make it difficult for Ottawa to bring in more generous pensions for Canadians. He was still making it difficult for Ottawa to bring in universal medical insurance. In both cases he seemed particularly solicitous of the interests of powerful private insurance companies. When companies that had been growing rich and powerful because they took advantage of the innocence of the small investor, such as Prudential Finance, collapsed, the government seemed to have little regard for the little man's interest. When trade unions in Ontario went out on strike – as they were doing more frequently in these years of growing inflation and a tight labour market – the government's response was to permit courts to grant injunctions limiting the resort to picketing. Throughout Robarts' premiership, Ontario had been growing wealthier by the year; it was the most prosperous province Canada had ever had. Its government, some of the critics said, was doing a fine job of making sure that the established and the powerful got their share and more of Ontario's prosperity. But what about the little man? What about the shareholder impoverished by the collapse of Prudential Finance? What about the sick who needed to be cared for in overcrowded hospitals? What about the average income earner who could not afford to buy a home in Metropolitan Toronto, the farmer bypassed by affluence, the housewife wrestling with rising prices?

Gradually in the years before 1967 the opposition had stepped up its assault inside and outside the legislature on the Tory dynasty. Labour militancy led to tinderbox situations on the picket lines, finally forcing Robarts to appoint a royal commission, chaired by Mr Justice Ivan Rand, to look into Ontario's collective bargaining framework. The Liberal opposition was still not particularly effective, as Andrew Thompson proved to be a sad disappointment and resigned before ever fighting an election. His replacement was Robert Nixon, the son of the last Liberal premier of Ontario, a decent man with little experience. Instead of the Liberals, it seemed to be the New Democratic Party that understood which way the winds were blowing, and gradually began speaking for the ordinary man on the issues that affected him and against the government that seemed to oppress him. The NDP combined the experienced leadership of MacDonald with energetic young organizers such as Stephen Lewis, and had proven how effective it could be when James Renwick had won Bob Macaulay's old seat in Toronto. And it was the NDP that attracted the man whose career best symbolized the new Ontario politics of the late 1960s, Dr Morton Shulman.

Shulman began 1967 serving as chief coroner of Metropolitan Toronto. For several years he had been given widespread publicity – including even a CBC television series patterned after him – because of his strong belief in the historic role of the coroner as the protector of the citizen, not a servant of government. From time to time Shulman had been outspoken in his criticisms of institutions and organizations that crossed the path of his investigations. In early April he began a new investigation into a fire at the Workmen's Compensation Board Hospital in Toronto in which a man had died.

During the reorganization of the Attorney General's Department the government had placed coroners under a new supervising coroner for Ontario. Dr H.B. Cotnam, who held the position, stepped into the Toronto situation by deciding to hold the inquest himself. Shulman reacted angrily, charging that Cotnam's intervention carried with it 'the unpleasant implication that the government does not want all the facts brought out.'[10] He refused to turn the case over to Cotnam, and on 7 April was fired by order-in-council. Here was the crusading coroner dismissed by the big government – and garnering more publicity over the weekend in a struggle over access to his files. To most people the details of the charges and counter-charges hardly mattered. It seemed that Morty Shulman, the people's champion, was being got out of the way.

Robarts could not ignore Shulman's charges that some kind of cover-up was in the works. When the House met on 10 April he announced that a royal commission would be appointed to investigate Shulman's allegations.[11] The leaders of both opposition parties tried to generate an emergency debate, but the Speaker ruled that although the issue was important in Toronto it did not qualify as a matter of general importance. His ruling not to adjourn the ordinary business of the House was challenged, but upheld. MacDonald of the NDP responded by claiming the procedure was undemocratic and marching out of the House to hold a press conference at which James Renwick, the NDP's legal affairs critic, called for Attorney General Wishart's resignation.

The breakdown in legislative civility, perhaps the worst since the Bill 99 debate, carried on for several more days, with Wishart accusing Renwick of being either cowardly or despicable, and the opposition prejudging the royal commission as having been appointed to 'cover up' government mistakes.[12] Shulman and his allegations were grist for the Toronto newspapers that spring, as was the story that both opposition parties were wooing the medical tribune to run in the next election. Early in July Shulman announced that he had joined the NDP and would be a candidate in the election. Ontario politics was going to hear more from Morton Shulman.

First there would be the centennial celebrations, culminating on Dominion Day. The ceremonial centre of the country would be in Ottawa and for the provincial premiers one of the highlights of the year would be a special ceremony on 5 July in which the Queen would swear them in as members of her Canadian Privy Council. Late in April Lester Pearson proposed that the premiers stay on after the 5 July ceremonies to discuss the proposed Confederation of Tomorrow conference. The suggestion sparked several weeks of careful but intense debate between Ontario and Ottawa.

On 3 May Ian Macdonald, Keith Reynolds, and Robarts' adviser on intergovernmental affairs, Don Stevenson, met in Ottawa with Pierre Elliott Trudeau, then federal minister of justice, and Gordon Robertson, the secretary of the cabinet, to discuss the idea of the conference. The federal spokesmen had three major worries about Ontario's proposal. They feared that the conference might precipitate premature discussion of constitutional change. Secondly, if it focused on Canadian *problems* it might generate a negative atmosphere and possibly a sense of the provinces ganging up on Ottawa. Thirdly, Ottawa still did not like the precedent of a province convening a federal-provincial conference.

The counter-proposal by Ottawa was for Robarts to refrain from issuing formal invitations to the conference until after it had been discussed on 5 July. An agreement on that day could be expressed in a communiqué which would 'acknowledge that [the conference] was due to the initiative of Mr. Robarts, even though it would be formally convened by the federal government.' The conference could then be held in Toronto in November or December. Pearson would be chairman. The tenor of the discussion would be positive, and each province could submit two items to the federal government for inclusion on the agenda. The press would be excluded and the federal representatives would speak to an 'agreed federal position' in order to preserve cabinet solidarity. If Robarts did not agree to their proposal, the meeting notes record, '[he] would be quite within his rights to call an interprovincial conference on any subject he wished, but Mr. Trudeau in particular felt that an inter-provincial conference on the subject of Confederation would be most undesirable at the current juncture of our history.' The Ontario delegation agreed to put the proposal to Robarts.[13]

Ian Macdonald thought Ontario should offer Ottawa a compromise. Robarts could ask Pearson to chair the conference and agree to have the agenda set jointly, though with the conference remaining under Ontario's control. If Pearson declined the offer, his government would seem ungenerous. While Robarts was considering his options, Pearson told the House of Commons that the 5 July meeting in Ottawa would offer 'an opportunity for a free exchange of views on how we see the future of our country and confederation,' and suggested that the ten provincial premiers might endorse a national bill of rights to be enshrined in the Canadian constitution. Such an agreement on fundamental values could be the beginning of a review of Canada's constitutional structure.[14]

The *Globe and Mail* interpreted Pearson's announcement as 'an attempt to over-ride a proposal by Premier John Robarts for a conference in Toronto to discuss the goals of Confederation.' Robarts was not pleased with Pearson's ploy and became more determined that Ontario would go ahead with its conference. A week later, in mid May, he introduced a resolution requesting the legislature to authorize his government to convene a Confederation of Tomorrow conference. He assured the federal government that the conference would not invade its jurisdiction and outlined four broad topics for discussion: the shortcomings of the present system; the broad objectives the system should strive to realize; intergovernmental relationships; English-French relations. No one could fail to see that the federal government had a deep interest in all four topics. Robarts expressed his hope that the federal government would attend.[15]

Robarts and Pearson continued their argument through June. Robarts hoped Pearson would agree to chair the Confederation of Tomorrow conference; Pearson refused. Robarts then asked him to send observers, preferably of cabinet rank; Pearson demurred. Robarts tried again, urging that the 5 July meeting end in a communiqué announcing the unanimous support of all heads of government for the Confederation of Tomorrow conference. Pearson's final position, expressed to Robarts on 15 June, was that Ottawa concurred with the idea of an interprovincial conference to discuss confederation, but would only send observers, who would be drawn from the public service.[16] Robarts had retained control of the conference but had lost the prospect of effective participation by Ottawa.

As the summer of 1967 approached, Canada's attention turned to the highlights of centennial celebrations, and particularly to Expo '67 in Montreal. Robarts visited the World's Fair at its opening on 27 April. He was delighted with the Ontario Pavilion and the superb promotional movie and song, 'A Place to Stand.' He would return to Montreal many times during that summer, far more often than his official duties required. Like many other Canadians, he seemed to be struck by the freedom, excitement, and vitality of Expo, a window leading away from the disciplines and constraints and disappointments of everyday life. Often Robarts brought his children, Tim and Robin, with him. It was a summer when the kind of private life away from Queen's Park that the premier craved led him not west to London, but in the opposite direction.

Centennial: Confederation of Tomorrow

Canada's hundredth birthday fell on a Saturday. John Robarts officiated at London's centennial parade in the morning, joined Lieutenant-Governor Earl Rowe in Toronto to watch the trooping of the colour by the 48th Highlanders in Varsity Arena in the afternoon, and travelled to Montreal with Robin that evening. On Sunday morning they welcomed visitors to the Ontario Pavilion. The pavilion was among the great successes of Expo (particularly on Sundays when bars were closed all across Ontario but open in the Ontario Pavilion in Montreal).

Queen Elizabeth and Prince Philip visited Expo and held a reception for the premiers that afternoon. As he was leaving the reception with Robin, Robarts insisted to reporters that he had no intention of seeking the leadership of the national Conservative party. This effectively ended all speculation about his being in the race. On Monday Robarts and James Ramsay, the former Macaulay aide who had guided the development of Ontario's exhibit at Expo, escorted the Queen and her party through the Ontario Pavilion. Robarts was noticeably at ease on occasions like these, seeming genuinely to enjoy meeting total strangers at Ontario's showcase. Acquaintances thought he was becoming a more accomplished politician, having found that he could relax easily in public. From 1967 on he seemed to be a more aggressive, more political prime minister, less the managerial 'stuffed shirt' he had sometimes seemed in his early years.

Norah Robarts flew to Kingston on 4 July to meet John and attend dinner with the Queen and Prince Philip aboard the royal yacht *Britannia,* which had sailed up the seaway. The Robartses, the Pearsons, and the provincial premiers gathered at the Royal Military College quay to await a royal barge which took them out to the yacht. It was a pleasant, relaxed dinner, accompanied by the Royal Marine band. At nine o'clock the next morning a cavalcade of limousines carrying premiers left Kingston for Ottawa. At Government House at noon the premiers were sworn in as members of the Privy Council of Canada. They had lunch with the prime minister, after which they briefly discussed his government's interest in a Bill of Rights and the Robarts government's plans for its Confederation of Tomorrow conference.

Reflecting the Pearson-Robarts stand-off in June, the communiqué of the meeting indicated that the conference would be interprovincial only. The proposed Bill of Rights would be discussed at a federal-provincial conference early in 1968. Robarts announced that the Confederation of Tomorrow conference would be held in Toronto during the third week of November. All of the premiers, except British Columbia's Bennett, had promised to attend.

Robarts next visited Expo during the third week of July. It was part of an annual outing that he, Jim Auld, and Ernie Jackson liked to take with their sons, usually roughing it with home-made meals on Auld's yacht, what the kids called their 'peanut butter cruise.' This year they sailed from Brockville up the Rideau waterway to Ottawa and then down the Ottawa River to Montreal and Expo. They arrived just before noon on 24 July for a day at the World's Fair before Robarts had to fly home.

Robarts' unofficial visit coincided with the regal tour that the president of France, Charles de Gaulle, made the same day along the old Chemin du Roi from Quebec City to Montreal. Arriving in Montreal about the same time as Robarts, de Gaulle spoke to an enthusiastic crowd from the balcony of the Hôtel de Ville. He told them that the atmosphere along the route he had driven reminded him of the Liberation of France, and carried on in the spirit of the Liberation to signify his solidarity with the people of Quebec by shouting the slogans: 'Vive Montréal! Vive le Québec! Vive le Québec libre! Vive le Canada français! Vive la France!'

Oblivious to the outrage he had caused across Canada, General de Gaulle visited Expo the next day. The premier of Ontario stood quietly on a small observation deck at the top of the Ontario Pavilion watching de Gaulle tour the Quebec pavilion, protected, of course, by massive security. Robarts was deeply troubled. He told Jim Ramsay how worried he was about the implications of de Gaulle's statement and how unhappy he was at what de Gaulle had brought to Canada. Robarts was scheduled to attend a dinner in Ottawa for de Gaulle the next night, but now he did not want to go. The decision was taken out of his hands when the general, encouraged by the government of Canada, broke off his trip and sailed back to France. He had done more damage to Canadian unity with one speech than many politicians could manage in a lifetime.

The affair strengthened Robarts' commitment to try to stop the drift towards separatism. He made a special personal effort to guarantee that Ontario Day at Expo, 5 August, would be an outstanding success. He was the leader, cheerleader, key speaker, and most enthusiastic celebrant at the ceremonies, having roared into Montreal with a train full of MPPs, ministers, senior civil servants, ethnic dancers, and reporters. In his speech on the occasion he went out of his way to stress national unity and describe his own province as a mosaic of ethnic communities, not a bastion of the British Empire. He eulogized Expo as the catalyst 'which has brought Canadians streaming back and forth across their magnificent country.'[1]

Robarts hoped the enthusiasm of Expo could be transferred to the Confederation of Tomorrow conference, which Ian Macdonald was in charge of organizing. The premier made a point of having James Ramsay, who had handled Ontario's presence at Expo, placed in charge of the physical arrangements for the conference.

Throughout the spring and summer there had been a gradual build-up for the provincial election. The government had continued to plug all ominous-looking holes in its dikes with announcements of new programs and policies. In May the creation of a special GO commuter transit system to move people in and out of Toronto was announced, along with a redevelopment plan for the downtown area. Concerns about the high cost of housing were countered by a Home Ownership Made Easy (HOME) program, which was to involve twelve thousand units by the end of the year. In June a plan to preserve the Niagara Escarpment from environmental damage was released. In August Robarts added five thousand more lots to the HOME projections and announced that the province would convene a special conference in December to study pollution. And half a million dollars was to be spent on a special project to determine ways of increasing the incomes of Ontario farmers.

The most important document for the development of policy was the long-awaited report of the Ontario Committee on Taxation, which had been five years in the making under the chairmanship of Lancelot Smith. The government had a few weeks' advance reading of the massive, complex document, and was ready with a preliminary response to it when it was formally released on 31 August. There were some 350 recommendations for the modernization of the provincial tax structure, many of which would have to go through the hopper of federal-provincial negotiation because of action Ottawa proposed to take on the basis of its own Carter Royal Commission. The provincial treasurer, Charles MacNaughton, used the unveiling of the report to repeat a promise to convene a provincial-municipal conference to discuss its recommendations, and, not surprisingly, to argue that full implementation would require more income tax room from Ottawa. The two recommendations that the province could implement immediately and usefully involved lifting all remaining costs for the administration of justice from the municipalities and introducing a basic shelter exemption grant payable to the taxpayer. It would mean an immediate, direct saving in property taxes for the average homeowner, and the government thought it could handle the cost without increasing any other tax.

Another important policy announcement had implications for both the impending political struggle and the discussions at the Confederation of Tomorrow conference. Late in August the Ontario Advisory Committee on Confederation recommended that bilingual and French secondary schools be established in Ontario to fill a void in the public school system between existing French elementary schools on the one hand and the French capacity of the universities on the other. Robarts concurred, and in a 24 August speech to l'association canadienne des educateurs de langue française, the prime minister announced that Ontario would establish and fund French secondary schools in the public system wherever the number of students warranted. First reaction to the new policy was mixed, with French-speaking Ontarians greeting it with enthusiasm and a senior educator in Metroplitan Toronto describing it as a waste of money. Robarts had not realized how the new policy would divide and confuse the separate school lobby in Ontario, a group the politicians had always had to handle with kid gloves (and whose votes tended, on balance, to go to the Liberals). The prospect of French-language secondary schools would attract many separate school supporters to the public system, though conversely creating a drain on separate school resources and creating an internal debate on whether or not it was feasible to have two French school systems, one public and one separate. The wider importance of the new policy, of course, was as a symbol of Ontario's willingness to move along a road of recognition of the French fact in the province as part of its commitment to renewed national unity.

Canadian Conservatives gathered in Toronto after Labour Day to replace John Diefenbaker. On the first day of the convention there were inevitable rumours that Robarts might come in as a last-minute candidate. He announced his neutrality as host premier, and most of his cabinet followed his lead. In the early stages of the campaign, Robarts had written letters to leading Conservatives endorsing the qualities of Duff Roblin. With Robert Stanfield's entry, however, Robarts' support was given behind the scenes to his maritime counterpart. In public, there was one last flurry of speculation when Robarts called a press conference for late on Tuesday, 5 September. At it he announced that the Ontario election would be held on 17 October. His announcement got headlines. Conservatives got headlines all the rest of the week, with Robarts often in the limelight (though still apparently neutral) as the delegates chose Nova Scotia's premier, Robert Stanfield, to be the new national leader. The response of the provincial Liberals and the NDP to the onset of the campaign was largely ignored.

Provincial Conservative candidates and their campaign managers stayed in Toronto after the national convention for a two-day training session with Ernie Jackson and other party organizers. There was still no particular issue to worry about or focus on. In announcing the election, Robarts had fallen into the businesslike, chief-executive-officer-of-Ontario stance that came so naturally to him. It was like a report to an annual shareholders' meeting as he reviewed the province's splendid economic record since 1963 and talked of the challenges ahead, including

the revamping and reorganization of our municipal structure of government ... the reorganization of the tax structure ... revision of our fiscal relationship with the Federal Government, the basic question of the future form of our country ... further developments in ... education, continued development in the fields of housing, transportation and power.

What were the governors of Ontario trying to achieve? More of the same, Robarts said, spelling out a creed much like Leslie Frost's and George Drew's before him, the goal of 'which is the heart and centre of the policy of our Party and our Government – namely – more people, more capital, more industry, more wages, more opportunity and a constantly improving life for every one of our citizens.'[2]

The Conservatives tried to add the youthful, swinging touch to their bland competence when they kicked off the campaign at a rally in a Hamilton high school auditorium complete with go-go dancers, bands, and cheerleaders. In an era of great prosperity and weakening restraints on government spending they also added a considerable emphasis on attractive new projects, such as HOME and its offspring, that they continued to announce in timely situations during the campaign. At a Hamilton rally, for example, Robarts promised $2 million for a new civic auditorium if the city could get matching federal support, and announced a $38 million order for steel pipe from the Steel Company of Canada. A few days later in the Lakehead came the announcement of new grants to industries willing to locate in the province's slow-growth regions, such as the Lakehead.

The opposition parties naturally charged the government with trying to buy votes, but mostly they tried to campaign on what they thought were the new issues of the late sixties. Many Torontonians seemed uneasy about the new borough system the government had brought in over the objections (sometimes voiced in its own caucus) of people living in such doomed municipalities as Leaside, Mimico, and New Toronto. Pollution and the hardships caused by inflation seemed to worry the electorate. The new Liberal leader, Robert Nixon, tried to demonstrate his concern for pure water by being photographed taking samples of the water in Toronto harbour. The provincial Liberals' concern for citizens squeezed by the high cost of housing rebounded embarrassingly in the middle of the campaign when the federal Liberal government raised the interest rate on National Housing Act loans to the then-astronomical level of 8¼ per cent. A voice from the past chimed in on the housing issue when the secretary of state, Judy LaMarsh, mentioned a few days before voting that Ottawa might have to step in if Ontario did not provide more leadership on housing. Robarts welcomed her intervention, but claimed that Judy had 'entered this campaign a little late to render the same assistance she did in 1963.'[3] There was virtually no scandal-mongering in one of the dullest Ontario campaigns of the century.

The New Democrats seemed to have positioned themselves to do best at the government's expense. In June they had issued a seventy-seven-page platform explaining their moderate social democratic approach to Ontario's problems, with a particular emphasis on the rights of the individual. They had strong support from organized labour, which believed the Robarts government was not impartial in industrial disputes. The national NDP's full-time organizers were free to work in the Ontario campaign. Most significantly, the NDP seemed to have strengthened its appeal in urban Ontario by attracting some of the most prominent 'victims' of big government and established power to run as candidates. There was the crusading coroner, Morton Shulman, running for the NDP in Toronto. John Brown, who had been fired as director of the Warrendale Treatment Centre, was also running in Toronto, determined to bring the plight of patients 'faced by an insensitive government' to the attention of the public. In Brantford, the campaign of journalist Mac Makarchuk was greatly aided by his being fired from his job at the Brantford *Expositor,* apparently because of his intention to run as an NDP candidate. The NDP seemed to be the haven and champion of the disaffected, the weak, and the powerless. Shulman urged those who had lost money in the Prudential collapse to press their claims on the government. The one discordant note at the Conservative kick-off rally was a demonstration by the Hamilton-Niagara Prudential Finance Creditors Association wanting compensation from the Robarts government.

One incident, which symbolized the new politics of combining concern for the little people with lots of media exposure, took place on 28 September. The wife of a family that had been serving as foster parents to two wards of the Waterloo Children's Aid Society was charged with abduction for refusing to turn them back to the CAS. It was a complicated case in which Anglican foster parents were objecting to the society's desire to separate the two little Roman Catholic girls in new homes, and phoned the media when the CAS worker and the police came to get them. The foster parents literally fought to keep the children; pictures of the affair included a shot of a policeman attempting physically to tear one of the little girls from the arms of the foster parent. An aroused public directed a flood of mail and angry phone calls at the callous authorities – the head of the CAS had to be put under protective custody – and the government and John Robarts' campaign offices.

Robarts interrupted his tour to call John Yaremko, his minister of social and family services, to ensure that the girls would not be separated. He then ordered an inquiry into the events surrounding the girls' removal.[4] Once it was called, the Waterloo crown attorney dropped the charges laid by the Children's Aid Society. Robarts had taken most of the heat out of the issue, but not before government and the authorities had once again become equated with the powerful and the callous. Both Robert Nixon and Donald MacDonald seemed to respond to the incident by accentuating their concern for the underdog.

Otherwise, the campaign was quiet, dull, almost issueless. The harshest blow to the premier was dealt by the manager of Toronto's Yorkdale shopping centre, who literally barred the door to keep Robarts and a local Tory candidate from campaigning on politician-free private property. 'The dead calm of lethargy on the part of the electorate has failed to fan a flicker of opposition fire,' the Sudbury *Star* wrote. Most pundits thought the government would probably lose some support on election day; no one thought it could be beaten.[5] Robarts would not let the opposition parties draw him into debate about his Confederation for Tomorrow conference during the campaign. The opposition parties were equally careful not to let him get away with attempts to make national unity an issue in a provincial election. As the campaign wound down, Robarts made the usual criticisms of 'the opposition's irresponsible charges and promises,' reminded the voters of the government's record, and did begin to address the growing sense of polarization in the province when he commented that 'Government is not a "we" and "they" proposition. Once this campaign is over the Progressive Conservative government that you elect will once more become the government of all the people of this province.'[6]

Robarts spent only two days in London, one towards the beginning and one at the end of the campaign. When he was there for his nomination meeting a fairly routine reception for the press at the Robarts home became a memorable party when an inexperienced caterer was pressed into service as a barman and reversed the usual portion of spirit to mix in the drinks he poured. The reporters lapped it up. So, perhaps, did Robarts' speechwriters, who were still finishing the document as the premier was sitting on the platform waiting to be called to the podium. As Robarts was being introduced, a hand shot out from behind the curtains holding a sheaf of papers. He walked over, took the notes, walked to the podium, and delivered a speech he had not seen before.

Most of the old London gang still had their shoulders to the wheel for the campaign, with Robert Robarts running the London North effort and Ward Cornell looking after John White's organization in London South. Fred Jenkins was still the treasurer and the party's linch-pin for the city. But new members had been added to the executive from London's burgeoning suburbs, and some of the younger generation who had begun to get their feet wet in the federal campaign of 1965 were now moving into important positions. Fred Jenkins' son Bill was Robert Robarts' assistant in London North and Gordon Walker, a local lawyer and protégé of John White, assumed a similar role in London South.

On election day Robarts voted early and then returned home. That evening the Robarts family watched the results with a few close friends at a suite in the Hotel London. The first returns were not encouraging. The Liberal candidate in London North, Frank Cartier, won the first poll to report. On a province-wide basis there were indications that the Tories might slip to a minority government position. Most riding boundaries had been changed in the general redistribution, which had added nine new seats (the total was now 117) making it difficult to assess results on the basis of past voting patterns. Robarts himself, for example, did not know many of the voters in his riding and, while his support still held firm in his old ward, he saw his overall majority considerably reduced. He won handily, of course, in a much less exciting race than John White had in London South against former mayor Gordon Stronach. White won as well, as did enough Tories across the province to guarantee another term in office and with a majority.

A fair number of Ontario voters had drifted away from the Conservatives. The party's share of the popular vote fell almost seven points to 42 per cent. The Liberal share declined by four points to 31 per cent, with the New Democrats making an impressive gain of almost 10 per cent by winning the support of one in four of Ontario's voters. The NDP knocked off two of Robarts' cabinet ministers in northern Ontario, George Wardrope and Wilfrid Spooner, and showed strength across the Golden Horseshoe and in labour-influenced cities such as Windsor, Oshawa, and Peterborough. The three prominent NDP 'victim' candidates, Shulman, John Brown, and Makarchuk, were elected. The Liberals had picked up a little support in the rural southwest, the northeast, and Toronto, and brought in one impressive newcomer, James Bullbrook from Sarnia. The government's slippage was spread fairly evenly across the province, with the smallest drop in eastern Ontario and the largest in London.[7] Robarts thought the lack of an issue was probably the main reason for the losses.

The government had had too thick a cushion to be pounded out of office. The Tories would have sixty-nine seats in the new House, down seven from the standing at dissolution. The Liberals had gained seven, bringing their total to twenty-eight and preserving their role as the official opposition. There would now be twenty New Democrats where previously there had been eight – an impressive growth, but still disappointing to Donald MacDonald, who had hoped to become leader of the opposition. Ontario's Progressive-Conservative dynasty carried on, essentially undisturbed.

Robarts was on the road from London to Toronto before 7 AM on the morning after the election, and spent the day catching up on routine administration. Then he turned his mind to the Confederation of Tomorrow conference.

Planning for the conference had been going on for several months. Topics for discussion had been set – the agenda was to be deliberately wide-ranging – and the Ontario Advisory Committee on Confederation was hard at work producing background papers. Representatives from Ontario had visited the provincial capitals to discuss the agenda and arrangements. Two decisions had been made on seemingly trivial matters which turned out to have great importance. One was to televise most of the proceedings. Television had not so far been present at federal-provincial conferences. Robarts had suggested from time to time that television might be allowed to cover proceedings, and he toyed with the idea for this conference. It got strong support from Bill Kinmond and Bill Rathbun, a former broadcaster who had become a communications specialist in Robarts' office. They wanted the conference to be as accessible to the media and the public as modern communication technology could permit.

The other decision involved the site of the conference. Early in September the planning committee had routinely decided to hold it in the Royal York Hotel. But James Ramsay, seconded to the conference from his triumph at Expo, decided that Ontario should set its sites higher than a venerable ballroom. The Royal York was old Ontario. When Ramsay looked out his office window he saw the first symbol of the new Ontario in the towering Toronto-Dominion Centre, the first of the great erections in downtown Toronto. Why not hold the conference at the top of Canada, on the highest floor of the nation's highest building? Difficult logistical problems had to be worked out to make television coverage in that rarified atmosphere possible, but the technology worked. The Confederation of Tomorrow conference would meet in one of the buildings of tomorrow and be made available to Canadians by tomorrow's technology. Ontario would show the rest of Canada, including Ottawa, how to throw a conference.

The government of Canada continued to be a grumbling bystander. Throughout the summer Pearson's ministry had maintained its hard line on most matters involving federal-provincial relations, particularly the fiscal question and medicare. In November Mitchell Sharp told the House of Commons that Ottawa would act on its own to put its financial house in order, raising some taxes, cutting some spending and lending programs, giving high priority to the introduction of medicare. Ontario continued to be frustrated and annoyed at the reluctance to co-ordinate priorities between the two levels of government, and particularly at Ottawa's assigning a high priority to intruding on provincial responsibilities with medicare, which was one of Ontario's lowest priorities. The Ontario position now had much more effective support in the federal House of Commons from the new Tory leader, Bob Stanfield. Stanfield was one of the government's sharpest critics, too, when it announced that it would be sending only four relatively low-level observers to the Confederation of Tomorrow conference. Some commentators suggested that if Pearson would not go to the conference, perhaps opposition leader Stanfield should.

Some journalists had trouble understanding that the apparent vagueness in the agenda was appropriate to a conference intended to be a forum for wide-ranging discussion, not a decision-making body. Robarts had decided that there would be few limits to the discussion, and underlined this by adding Senate reform and the idea of a constitutional Bill of Rights to the agenda. Not only was he unfazed by objections that the latter topic was to be discussed at the federal-provincial conference on the constitution planned for early 1968, but he announced that he would personally lead the discussion on the Bill of Rights at his conference.[8] Announcing this in a speech in Regina on 20 November, Robarts pointed out that the federal government had effectively and unilaterally changed the constitutional division of powers through the Canada Pension Plan, federal loans to municipalities, family and youth allowances, equalization payments, and now medicare.[9] The idea of getting back at Ottawa was not too far below the surface of Robarts' planning for the conference. He knew that the federal people, on their part, hoped the conference would be a fifty-four-storey comedown for the upstart premier. Ottawa was busy leaking its doubts and prophecies of disaster. There was a real possibility that little good would come from a discussion of the future of Canada in which the government of Canada dared not participate.

W.A.C. Bennett of British Columbia did not think the conference would be worth his time, and sent his attorney general instead. Duff Roblin of Manitoba was in the throes of a provincial leadership convention; his successor would arrive while the conference was proceeding. The other seven provincial premiers were present and well briefed when John Robarts, the chairman, opened the conference on Monday, 27 November. In his opening remarks Robarts criticized the existing state of federal-provincial relations as being too often a set of ad hoc responses to short-term problems, uninformed by any national consensus on principles or purpose. He denied any intention of undermining the federal government and, turning to Quebec's interest in finding a 'special status' within a new confederation, made clear his view of the danger of undermining the federal authority. Ontario preferred to see a consensus on an overall Canadian framework, with certain 'inviolable powers' for the federal government within which each region or province could, on certain matters, negotiate something like special status. The provinces would all be equal, the federal government would be strong, but there would be room for much diversity within the system.[10]

Daniel Johnson followed Robarts and endorsed his concept of regional diversity within a unified country. But the lengthy background paper explaining Quebec's positions vis-à-vis a new constitution went much further in its detailed, radical suggestions. The constitution should be totally rewritten. Quebec insisted that matters involving education, social security, and health services be strictly provincial fields of jurisdiction. Quebec wanted the power to guide its own economic and cultural development. Quebec had a special interest and needed special status in all problems relating to language and culture; perhaps on other issues all the provinces had a shared concern.

Johnson saw himself as answering English Canada's frequent question, 'What does Quebec want?' What would stave off the new separatist movement, now led by René Lévesque, who had come out of the closet after the de Gaulle visit and declared himself a separatist? How much constitutional change was necessary? What kind of 'special status' should Quebec have? In a coincidence that seemed perfectly to underline the urgency of calm discussion about Canada's future, the premiers learned at noon on the first day that General de Gaulle had been at it again. In a Paris press conference he had called for a rewriting of Canada's constitution and the strengthening of the bonds of the French community in Europe and North America. Although the reporters pressed the premiers for their reaction, they tended to leave the matter to Prime Minister Pearson. Even Johnson suggested that it reflected some kind of private fight between Pearson and de Gaulle. The fact remained that the president of France was once again fishing in Canada's already troubled waters.[11]

In their opening statements and in the afternoon discussion, the western provinces and Newfoundland argued that constitutional changes were not a high priority for them. Economic issues were more important, and their concern for economic development inclined several of the premiers, particularly those from the less prosperous provinces, to be wary of any further weakening of the central government. Daniel Johnson continued to argue that the need for French Canadians not to be economically handicapped in Canada and to feel at home everywhere in the country ought to be over-riding national concerns. At a minimum it was time to entrench the rights of the two cultural communities in a new Canadian constitution, though Johnson and other Quebeckers were pleased at the steps some of the provinces had taken to provide French-language instruction in their school systems.

Press coverage of the first day of the conference helped unite the premiers on the second day. The Toronto newspapers had tended to magnify the differences between the provinces, suggesting considerable disagreement and disunity. Now the television cameras gave the premiers an opportunity to reach the people directly while striking back at the old gatekeepers of their proceedings. Joey Smallwood of Newfoundland, for example, whose colourful presentation of his people's problems had received extensive press coverage, stood up and objected to a headline report that he had threatened to leave the conference. 'You couldn't blast me out of here,' he retorted. Daniel Johnson denounced a Toronto *Star* headline that he had warned 'I can't stop separatism,' as well as a report quoting him as saying Quebec could survive as an independent state. Premier Louis Robichaud of New Brunswick gave an impassioned speech contrasting Johnson's views with de Gaulle's advocacy of separatism and reminding everyone, especially the television viewers, that Johnson was 'putting his head on the block by advocating Confederation and declaring himself a Canadian.' Eventually the *Globe and Mail,* in an editorial entitled 'Mea culpa! Mea culpa!' found that the conference was virtually unanimous in agreeing 'that the Toronto press does a dreadful job of mirroring their deliberations.' It was not sure whether to blame the press for not knowing how to cover open conferences or the premiers for expecting ritual coverage of a staged ritual.[12] If it had achieved nothing else, the Confederation of Tomorrow conference was a milestone in the bypassing of print journalism by the immediacy of television.

The premiers found common ground, too, in discussing the steps the various provinces had taken to expand linguistic rights. William Davis, for example, reported to the conference on the extension of French-language education in Ontario, and Robarts declared that Ontario had forever abandoned the old 1912 policy of restricting the use of French in the province's schools. But the fundamental difference between Quebec and the others about the need for constitutional change remained. Ernest Manning of Alberta seemed particularly rigid, saying that the people of Canada would not accept a new constitution and warning strongly against attempts to entrench French-language rights. His neighbour, Ross Thatcher of Saskatchewan, commented that 'if we had a hundred problems, the constitution would be hundred and first.'

Nova Scotia and Ontario took mediating positions, suggesting that perhaps piecemeal amendments to the constitution rather than a wholesale redrafting could meet immediate needs. Johnson appeared to come around to this position, at least as a start, by the third day of the conference, and the premiers finally agreed to carry on continuing discussions of ways of amending the constitution. By the time the conference adjourned, after a final afternoon of cordial Ottawa-bashing, a great deal of goodwill and openness had been generated. In his closing statement John Robarts, who had chaired the conference throughout, praised Johnson's warmth, strength, and skill, and appealed to English Canadians through the television cameras to recognize the need for change and to attempt to understand the feelings of French Canada and French Canadians. No one hid the substantial differences that existed, but in an atmosphere redolent of the *bonne entente* that older generations of Ontarians had often tried to encourage, it seemed more possible to live with them and someday resolve them than it had even a few days before.

The premiers went away happy, with even Daniel Johnson claiming that 'English Canadians have learned to be less afraid of equality.' The press was almost unanimous in judging the conference an overwhelming triumph, 'moving from rigidity to reason and from stalemate to success.' Ottawa was criticized for having by-passed the occasion; Robarts was praised for having assumed 'a truly remarkable leadership role.'[13] Even Lester Pearson telephoned Robarts to congratulate him. Years later, Robarts reflected that the conference had succeeded because of its setting, because of television, and because it consisted of genuine Canadians talking to each other:

It was a first time and it's pretty hard to look out those windows and not have some confidence in your country ... and then that [television] program went right across Canada and we had some very able, very astute men who were able to sit there and talk about the problems of their part of Canada in terms of Mr. Average Guy and Mrs. Average Woman, turning it on and watching it on television, and they understood because they were talking ordinary language. There was no gobbledegook, no economics, no finance. This is how my part of the country works and where we have our problems ... The Alberta people had a chance to look at the East and all of a sudden they weren't just those nameless, faceless people who live a long way away and exploit me, or ... whatever. They were human beings that had problems just like you or me and were trying to cope with them. So anyway, we had some fun with the federal people because they were mad as hell ... They really hoped that I'd fall flat on my face and once I was successful they couldn't leave it there.[14]

Ottawa's view had been that Robarts had staged a premature and probably improper discussion of problems while Ottawa was still working on its more considered strategy for constitutional change. To most observers, however, including a number in Ottawa, the federal government had allowed the quest for

Canadian renewal to become sidetracked through a combination of bureaucratic dithering and rigidity on short-term issues. John Robarts had intervened in a climate of growing national crisis and organized a conference which demonstrated to Canadians that a will to unity still existed. He put the Canadian debate back on track. This was his finest hour as a national politician, an act of great service to his country. It also forced the federal government to commit itself to serious constitutional negotiations as soon as possible if it was to regain the initiative in the constitutional debate.

Paradoxically, the Confederation of Tomorrow conference was followed by a shrinking of Robarts' prominence as the federal government deployed its resources for the counter-thrust. At most times before and after the conference, Robarts' interest had been in advocating gradual change, the tolerance of diversity, and the adjustment of the nuts and bolts of fiscal and economic policy, not in grand constitutional design or redesign. Ontario would continue to be very active and aggressive in promoting its interests in specific policy areas, both interprovincially and in discussions with Ottawa. Robarts' advisers, Ian Macdonald's staff and the Advisory Committee on Confederation, continued to prepare positions on constitutional questions, partly through the continuing committee of four premiers set up by the Confederation of Tomorrow conference, partly to prepare for the February federal-provincial constitutional conference. But proposals to adjust the structure could be easily eclipsed by proposals for sweeping change. The initiatives would come from Ottawa, specifically from the minister of justice, soon to be prime minister, Pierre Elliott Trudeau.

It was Trudeau who, on 1 February 1968, tabled a proposed Canadian Charter of Human Rights in the House of Commons as a starting point for constitutional reform. And while Robarts spoke prominently and effectively on behalf of greater bilingualism at the constitution conference that month (Ontario was lukewarm on the charter issue, not particularly in favour of entrenching rights but willing to go along with further study and discussion), it was Trudeau who leaped into a leadership role, both constitutionally and politically, with his sharp challenges to Daniel Johnson at this gathering – and, in a lesson learned from Confederation of Tomorrow, did it before television cameras. The leadership vacuum Robarts had stepped into had disappeared. Suddenly Canada had a constitutional expert who was ready, informed, and eager to deal with the issues that the Quebec nationalists/separatists were raising. Certainly in Trudeau's eyes, and to many other observers, it was almost as though no one else was needed any more to carry on the debate.

As well, there were starting to be signs that some of Robarts' positions on national questions were more advanced than the views of many in Ontario. After the February 1968 conference he was deluged with mail criticizing his mediating position on language rights, much of it fiercely opposing bilingualism. Having just announced his intention to make the Ontario legislature bilingual, Robarts was forced to backpedal in a speech to the House by reminding the public that Ontario had not been declared officially bilingual, that no person in Ontario was forced to learn a second language, and that he was not trying to appease Quebec or any other province. Nor was he engaged in constitutional discussions designed to turn Canada into a republic, as some monarchists claimed.[15] Then, in the federal election campaign that spring, Robarts could not avoid appearing to support Trudeau's stance in opposition to Quebec's attempts to play a role in international affairs. He was finding it hard to avoid being sucked into the polarization that the Trudeau versus Johnson conflict seemed to be causing in the country.

Robarts' real preference was to work out piecemeal solutions to Canada's problems. In the midst of the federal election he expressed his mature view in this statement (which he then chose not to give in the legislature but which captured his reaction to the new style of constitutional debate):

We in Canada have always been able to resolve the difficulties with which we have been faced by means of consultation and negotiation. This ability to achieve a practical solution to individual problems through the exercise of calm balance and common sense has been the keystone to the strength of the successful relationships between the various governments of Canada. Evolution, rather than revolution, has been a rewarding method of dealing with the challenges we face ...

It is the opinion of the Government of Ontario that the best interests of Canada are not being served when matters of such delicacy and importance to the future of our country become specific issues in an election campaign. It does not serve the best interests of the people of our country to say that an issue of constitutional law will be resolved in the ballot box ... And it may well be that positions taken in the heat of an election campaign will be found to be undesirable, impracticable, even intolerable, when viewed in the calm light of more adequate examination.[16]

Although Robarts was not particularly impressed with Trudeau's a priori approach to constitution-making, at least the machinery was chugging along again, and Robarts could claim considerable credit for that. For the rest of his premiership it would move slowly and fitfully, in fact culminating in failure when Quebec's new premier, Robert Bourassa, refused to accept the consensus reached at the Victoria Conference in 1971.

PART THREE: THE PASSING OF OLD ONTARIO

New Mood, Old Issues

By the mid-1960s Ontarians were enjoying a standard of living far higher than any previous generation of Canadians had ever experienced. As part of their new affluence they expected much higher standards of social service than their grandparents or parents had accepted. It was not just a question of saying farewell to the one-room school and the schoolteacher who taught all the grades. It was a matter of creating the triple-streamed composite school, where teachers were specialists, and where even the minority of students with learning disabilities could get highly-trained help. It was a matter of making the most modern hospital facilities, with specialized doctors and nurses, available to all Ontarians, not simply the fortunate residents of Toronto and one or two other urban areas. It was a matter of replacing the underpaid local constable with trained professional law enforcement personnel, the volunteer welfare worker with a qualified social worker. It was a matter of upgrading the qualifications of all the specialists engaged in providing social services and paying them commensurately. It was a matter of reorganizing municipal governments, reorganizing tax systems, reorganizing the Ontario government itself. The slower, more local, perhaps more individual ways of doing things in the old Ontario in which John Robarts and most of his generation had grown up were passing away. His government had to shepherd the province into the new age of affluence, bigness, specialization, professionalization, and bureaucracy.

But the province was changing in even more fundamental ways than in the improvement of its material base. The affluence and security and peace of the late 1940s and the 1950s, following the carnage of war, had caused Ontarians to participate as enthusiastically as any North Americans in the great postwar baby boom. As minister of education at the beginning of the decade John Robarts had opened many of the elementary and secondary schools Ontario built to educate this horde of children. In the 1967 election he appealed to the advance guard of the baby boomers who had begun voting.

Much of the old moral order in Ontario was passing, as many of the young abandoned the puritanism, the discipline and order and hierarchy underlying so many aspects of their parents' lifestyles. They wanted to liberalize the censorship standards, liberalize the drinking laws, liberalize education, grow their hair long, and smoke some marijuana.

New issues were posed by growth itself. Suppose population growth continued at the rates of the last two decades. Suppose the new people continued to use resources at the same rate. How could Canada feed all these people, let alone support endless increases in their prosperity? How could the environment be protected from all these people and their needs and their wastes? The area of Ontario from Toronto to Windsor was the most populous part of Canada. It also had some of Canada's most fertile soil. How could the farmland be protected from the people and their sprawling cities? How could the recreational land, such as the Niagara escarpment, be preserved for future generations? How could the animals be saved from the people, the people and the animals saved from pollution? How could the people be protected from themselves?

The new Ontario that John Robarts had to govern contained the hippie culture of Toronto's Yorkville and the drug haven of Rochdale College. It was the Ontario of poisoned air, according to the CBC 1967 documentary, 'Air of Death,' which charged that toxic air was a hazard to everyone in the sleepy village of Port Maitland. It was 1,276 letters sent to John Robarts in March 1967 protesting the province's bounty on wolves. Eighty per cent of the letters came from apartment dwellers in Metropolitan Toronto, who had been moved by a television plea for the wolf by the writer Farley Mowat. The fiasco over Bill 99 three years earlier had generated only one-fifth as much correspondence.

It was an Ontario ringing with buzzwords such as 'ecology,' 'quality of life,' 'self-determination,' and 'Stop Spadina.' But it was also an Ontario whose older generation was puzzled and sometimes angered by the new climate. Many of the institutions of the community, including government, were scrambling frantically to adjust. Many individuals, particularly in rural areas, had little sympathy for the demands of those who did not seem to be paying their way or who seemed to be resisting an ethos of economic growth. The political polarization of the community, both regional and generational, was part of the deterioration of the old comity.

Through it all the Robarts government tried to hold the centre. The last years would not be easy. It proved far harder to adapt to change than the government had planned, because it was now apparent that the changes included society's cutting itself loose from its spiritual moorings. Nor was it at all easy for John Robarts to adapt to the new climate. Not only had his own roots been deep in the old Ontario that was passing, but now the deterioration of his personal life meant that he was too often himself adrift, a victim of swirling political and personal winds.

The swollen contingent of twenty New Democrats, fourteen of whom were sitting in the legislature for the first time, best expressed the tone of the new politics.

Although Donald MacDonald still led the party, the young turks were restless. The most restless of all was the deposed coroner, Morton Shulman, who quickly became a new, one-man force in the Ontario legislature.

Consider Shulman's maiden speech on 6 and 7 March 1968.[1] He began on a light note by thanking Robarts for his promotion, since 'were it not for his actions I would be still working in the morgue on Lombard Street.' Then he went on the attack on issue after issue, raking through the government's record on securities regulation, then turning to pollution. The CBC had shown its 'Air of Death' documentary about the Dunnville area a few months earlier. 'It is a sorry fact that in this province the hon. Minister of Health is responsible for air pollution control,' Shulman commented. 'I note with interest that he has followed good Conservative doctrine in connection with the Dunnville disaster by setting up a Royal Commission to stall or subvert the moment of truth.' Not only was a cover-up going to take place, but Hydro was about to construct a new plant in the area to 'burn United States coal at the rate of 720 tons per hour,' generating more pollutants, which would lead to the creation of 'sulphuric acid mist' to kill the vegetation around Dunnville that the current fluorine pollutants had only damaged.

When James Allan tried to interrupt Shulman on a point of order to state that there was no pollution in Dunnville, Shulman replied that when he was in Dunnville the farmers thought there was. During the evening recess Leslie Rowntree, a Shulman target because of his responsibility for securities regulation, vented his spleen in an after-dinner speech by urging the doctor to make his statements outside the privileged chamber of the legislature. When Shulman resumed the next afternoon, he read the report of Rowntree's speech into the record before going on to rehash the Workmen's Compensation Board hospital fire and its effects on injured patients and their families, casting the government as responsible for their suffering. Then he turned to the Prudential Finance Corporation, and linked Robarts to it. On being challenged by Rowntree, Shulman backpedalled briefly to admit that his reference to a meeting 'in the Prime Minister's office' was in Robarts' law office in London before he became prime minister. When Rowntree accused Shulman of smearing the prime minister, the Speaker interjected to ask that Shulman 'should be extended a little more courtesy in view of the fact that it is his maiden speech.' Shulman backtracked a bit more, but maintained that the innocent attachment of the prime minister's name to Prudential justified action being taken to compensate the company's noteholders. He concluded by pleading for Ontario to accept a group of Asian refugees from Kenya, by endorsing the recommendations of the McRuer Royal Commission which related to coroners, and by condemning the government's use of judges 'for political purposes.'

It was a tour de force of muckraking and innuendo, supported by a selective array of apparently precise facts, reminiscent of John Wintermeyer's performance on organized crime years earlier, though considerably more wide-ranging. Shulman appealed to those who had a will to believe. With Wintermeyer, the belief was in sinister criminal forces undermining Ontario. Now it was the sinister machinations, or at least the blunders, of the powerful, who could use the machinery of government to cover up their misdeeds. Shulman's first effort in the legislature heralded the advent of years in which political rhetoric in Ontario became increasingly divorced from rational consideration of specific pieces of legislation, increasingly directed at the new hopes and fears of a confused public and their media tribunes.

Conservative backbenchers were similarly inclined to worry rhetorically about their special demons. A new Tory backbencher, Dr Richard Potter, for example, began his maiden speech with a tribute to Robarts and the government and then turned to the subject of socialism:

I am afraid we are coming closer and closer to one very large problem, one which we must clearly recognize and examine before it is too late.

In Canada today, as in every other country in the world, there is a group of people, ever increasing in size, who unwittingly perhaps and without sinister intent, are determined to destroy all individuality and to establish a state-controlled society.

More and more we see our governments being influenced by this group to offer us increasingly socialistic policies ... Few of us are willing to refuse something that is being given us for nothing and so we close our eyes and allow ourselves to be deluded into supporting these policies.[2]

Here were the deep, dark fears that preyed on the Conservative mind. "Socialists are spreading a bacillus ... scattering the drug that spells the decay of a nation,' John White added, urging his party to rededicate itself to 'the freedom of the individual and freedom of property.'[3]

None of these speeches had much to do with the specifics of the government's legislative program. Occasionally the legislation and the worries would intersect, as in a debate that spring on the government's Act to Amend the Lord's Day (Ontario) Act, liberalizing Sunday observance. First the Liberal opposition showed itself embarrassingly divided on the bill, with Robert Nixon the leader supporting it and one of his backbenchers saying the government was being too liberal. Then the government's own chief whip, Leonard Reilly, rose up and surprised the House by speaking against the bill. 'Some members of this House should get up and say that sometimes we go too far,' Reilly said. 'This is an age of permissiveness ... Maybe we should think in terms of what happened to a decadent society ...'[4] Other Tory backbenchers supported Reilly. Although the bill passed, the government realized it was going to be more difficult in the future to control its own members, let alone force the opposition members to stick to the point in debate.

Robarts' main interest was not in the froth of the legislature anyway, but in getting on with big reform programs which had been in the planning stages for years. His government's main priority was to work out the changes necessary in the political, economic, and administrative structure of Ontario that would enable its citizens to profit fully and equally from the social services they expected a modern state to provide.

None of the planning was easy, for many of the problems led into each other, had complex ramifications, overlapped, or were likely to be resisted by vested interests. The problem of providing modern policing is a good example. The roots of reform went back to the late Frost years, the work of Kelso Roberts, and the mandate of the Ontario Police Commission to raise standards of policing across the province. The OPC's studies concluded that a force of at least ten men was necessary to provide a 'professional' service for a community. The old one-man force or the part-time policeman was no longer tolerable. The problem with making the adjustment, of course, was that a ten-man force had to serve a population large enough to keep its ten men decently employed. Small municipalities could not expect to run and pay for modern police forces. Solutions to the situation would be either to take away responsibility for policing from the small municipalities, or to merge small municipalities into new municipal units large enough to support modern police forces.

Education was almost an exact parallel. Could small communities support modern schools? Could the small, local school board survive in an age of teacher specialization, curricular options, and increased student and parent expectations? Probably not. Therefore should the provision of education be cut loose from its attachment to the local municipality? Or did this again suggest that the local municipality itself might be obsolete?

What were the cost and other implications of modernizing these social services? Certainly small municipalities would not be happy with the prospect of losing either their right to influence key local services, or their very existence. In middle-sized municipalities, which had the capacity to provide the new services, there were going to be heavy costs of modernization. It might be possible to soften the political backlash by 'grandfathering' teachers without degrees or policemen with a grade ten education, but the more highly trained new recruits would certainly demand more compensation. As standards were raised to a provincial mean, there would naturally be demands for standard salaries. In policing, for example, municipal forces in towns such as Pembroke insisted on being paid the same scale as OPP officers. When that fundamental parity was granted, the municipal council of Pembroke found it had lost control of the cost of its police force. When the province raised the salaries of the OPP (who wanted parity with the RCMP), Pembroke's only alternative to spending more money was to reduce the size of its force. The OPC and the attorney general rejected that proposal as regression below the standards of service required by the provincial government. Pembroke needed more money and had a certain moral claim that the money should come from the province. Every other middle-sized community had similar problems.

Of course the police in the big municipalities believed that they ought to maintain a salary differential from those in the middle-sized ones. Or there were special cases, sometimes involving collective bargaining. When Charles Mac-Naughton announced late in 1967, for example, that jail guards and clerks would be incorporated into the provincial public service, the guards at Toronto's Don Jail resisted. They had higher salaries and better fringe benefits than their provincial counterparts and had confidence in their bargaining agent, the Canadian Union of Public Employees. Integration into the public service would bind them to the provincial pay scale and require membership in the Civil Service Association. The result was a bitter, widely publicized strike. The final compromise involved letting the guards maintain an affiliation with CUPE and keep their higher pay scale until provincial salaries caught up.

So reforms could pose serious problems. Often the only solution for difficulties was more money, generating a tendency to raise everyone's costs to those at the highest level of government involvement. A developing inflationary climate in a tight labour market added to the cost pressures. At the same time the municipalities and local school boards were trapped by having to rely on property taxes as the main source of their revenue. Often labelled a regressive tax, the local property tax was certainly a politically unpopular way of attempting to raise revenue. Rapid urban growth meant that some of the big municipalities could raise the revenue they needed on a constant tax rate. But many of the small and medium-sized municipalities could not. Often the communities that most needed more money were the ones with the least ability to find it.

What could the provincial government do? Move slowly and carefully, for one thing, because these problems often had unforeseen political implications. We will see later how even the most careful planning could founder on political shoals. The movement had begun in the late Frost and early Robarts years, particularly in the study of municipal problems. A Toronto backbencher, Hollis Beckett, chaired an important Select Committee on the Municipal Act and Related Matters, which brought in a series of reports during 1964 and 1965 recommending the introduction of regional government, based on county boundaries, as a solution to the problem of local services. Regional municipalities would contain the population necessary for the efficient utilization of specialists and thus be the proper local government unit to provide modern public services. The Beckett Committee's recommendation, which partly reflected the Metropolitan Toronto experience, was widely endorsed, and gained further support in studies of the prospects of regional government in the Niagara peninsula, the Ottawa area, and at the Lakehead.[5]

The tax implications of the municipal situation were tricky enough, however, that Robarts wanted to postpone major reforms until he had the recommendations of Lancelot Smith's Committee on Taxation. These, we saw, were presented in

1967, just before the election. They included a recommendation that regional government be established, though not following county boundaries as Beckett had advocated.

With the idea of larger units in the air, Robarts was ready for the parallel development in education. By 1967 the Department of Education, which had already been encouraging the amalgamation of township boards, was exploring the prospect of introducing county boards across the province. Robarts' interest in moving quickly on French-language schools played into this development, for county units would probably be necessary to provide the base for such highly specialized schools. As Robarts prepared for the Confederation of Tomorrow conference, wanting to highlight the province's progress on French, he seized upon a Department of Education proposal for a 1969 pilot project in county consolidation, and went further with it. On 4 November 1967 he announced that county schools boards would become mandatory across Ontario on 1 January 1969. The new boards would be elected and levy their own education tax, and would 'eliminate inequalities in educational opportunities.' When the change was complete, the number of local school boards in Ontario would be reduced from 1,012 to 76.[6]

The opposition had mixed feelings about the school board reforms. It was hard to criticize a movement that the Smith Committee had also supported, and one apparently in the direction of both equality and efficiency. But there were other sources of resistance that Robarts ought to have listened to more carefully. Local school trustees in rural Ontario complained that the new boards would place the administration of education 'too far from the people themselves.'[7] At the opposite extreme of organization, the provincial teachers' federations, on the verge of a period of extreme militancy, were upset at not being consulted. True, Robarts had minimized the political damage the announcement could do by making it a month after the election. In both Manitoba and New Brunswick there seemed to have been recent sharp voter resistance to school board amalgamation. Ontario voters would not have a chance to resist – not yet anyway.

Before the mass of tax recommendations of the Smith report could be sorted out and a plan of action implemented, the financial squeeze on the municipalities became acute. The years 1966 and 1967 were particularly difficult. The provincial government hoped to meet some of the strain with the Design for Development plan, announced in April 1966. Regional development planning would, in theory, harness under-utilized resources for growth where it was needed while relieving pressure on already-committed resources in currently high-growth areas. At the same time, cabinet decided that it had to establish much better restraint on its own expenditures while also getting more tax room from Ottawa if it was going to keep its deficits from increasing.

Unfortunately for Ontario, the thrust for a larger share of income and corporation taxes ran directly into the federal government's new stone wall of insisting that governments wanting more money should raise it with their own taxes. By centennial year Ottawa was also in a mood of restraint to try to keep the lid on the economy. The national government fortified its resistance to giving the provinces additional tax room by arguing that this would only encourage increased provincial spending which would undermine the need for national restraint. Ontario responded that Ottawa's medicare program was a prime example of unnecessary fiscal burdens and ought to be shelved in the interests of restraint. The closer medicare came to implementation the more it became the focus of acrimonious debate.

The two great tax studies had done nothing to moderate federal-provincial disputes. Ontario's Smith Committee had reinforced the provincial view by recommending that revenues be allocated to the different levels of local government proportionately to their responsibilities and their fiscal capacity. Ottawa's Carter Royal Commission, however, had recommended that Ottawa give away no more points on the income tax, take over the whole of the corporation tax revenues, and let the provinces have more of the regressive sales tax. In November 1967 Ottawa signalled its intention to act unilaterally to raise taxes (through a 3 per cent surcharge on its share of the personal income tax) for the purpose of cooling off the economy and helping fund medicare.[8] Ontario wanted expenditure priorities to be set in consultation with the provinces, particularly in such areas of provincial jurisdiction as medicare. If more money was going to be spent, Ontario would prefer to spend it on housing, which was in desperately short supply, whereas private medical insurance in the province, supplemented by the government's plans, seemed adequate.[9]

Faced with Ottawa's intransigence, about all Ontario could do was try to put its own house in order. Ottawa's medicare program was to come into effect on 1 July 1968. On 24 January Robarts announced that Ontario would not enter medicare for at least a year after that date. 'I reject the federal proposals,' he said, 'as being excessively expensive, unfair to those provinces unable to participate, not consistent with our priorities, and tampering improperly with matters which are directly the responsibility of the province.'[10]

Robarts' housekeeping initiatives melded nicely with the thrust for administrative reform that senior civil servants such as Carl Brannan and Ian Macdonald had been engineering for the past few years. The strengthening of the Treasury Board and the amalgamation of Macdonald and his economists with the new Department of the Treasury and Economics were introduced as part of the determination to give highest priority to financial management in the government. As Treasury's authority grew, various planning, programming, and budgeting systems were introduced, and economists moved to the centre of government policy-making. The new centralization was reflected in the creation of a Cabinet Committee on Policy Development in January 1968, which replaced the committees on regional development and economics and finance. Robarts chaired the committee, with the treasurer, Charles MacNaughton, as vice-chairman. Its mandate was to advise cabinet 'on fiscal and budgetary policy including the allocation of priorities to expenditure programs and levels of taxation, intergovernmental fiscal relations, regional development, the coordination of employment and manpower policies and generally the development of overall programs and policies which require a coordinated response from government departments.'[11]

One result of these reforms had been to greatly enhance the powers of the treasurer, MacNaughton, who in his department and through his role on the Policy Development Committee now oversaw the whole fiscal program of the government, including federal-provincial negotiations, economic development, and provincial-municipal tax reform. He was effectively John Robarts' lieutenant in a now more hierarchical cabinet. The other members of the Committee on Policy Development – Stanley Randall, William Davis, Allan Grossman, Dalton Bales, and Thomas Wells – were clearly first among the other ministers. Whatever was left of Robarts' chairman-of-the-board approach had largely disappeared.

John Robarts introduced many of these changes in his first major speech to the new session on 28 February 1968. It was a long, detailed address, in the course of which he tried to explain how all the changes in the government's 'horizontal' processing of policies would help it carry out its mandate:

We in government today find ourselves in a virtual maze of inter-related decisions – and I think this is true of any government you wish to look at in any part of the world. We are confronted by multiple demands and by many complex considerations. We have discussed this in the House on other occasions, in terms of the vertical organization of government, in departments, and the increasing characteristic of our problems to be horizontal in nature ... I would say that one of the major problems of the great maze of inter-relationships that face us today is the fact that we must always remember the government is dealing with individuals; individuals who have different expectations; who have changing values; who have varying requirements; who have varying capabilities and varying ambitions and desires as to what they may ultimately ask for from their society and from their government ... At the same time as all these things are going on, any government that has the interest of the people at heart is looking for qualitative improvement as well as quantitative improvement.[12]

Robarts' reminder that governing was about dealing with individuals was part of the premier's personal sense that bureaucrats must never lose sight of the purpose of their work. Not only these remarks, but most of the speech was lost sight of in media reports which highlighted only Robarts' backtracking on French and his attacks on the opposition. In following days most of the prosaic details of government policy and planning were forgotten in legislative debate newly energized by Morton Shulman and other rookie MPPs.

There had been so many recommendations in the Smith Report that the province could not bring in reforms without a systematic evaluation of the package in light of the public's response. MacNaughton had called for briefs on the taxation recommendations, and when more than three hundred of them had descended on him by May 1968 he decided to scrap plans for a white paper and instead have a select committee of the legislature go through the whole issue, complete with public hearings. The committee was established late in May with John White as chairman and Robert Macaulay as senior counsel. It worked frantically towards a mid-September deadline.

In the meantime the broad questions of regional development and regional government were being worked on in two separate departments. Treasury and Economics had inherited the regional development planning function from the old Department of Economics and Development. Early in 1968 cabinet approved a major expansion in the thrust of regional development planning by accepting recommendations to include land use planning, environmental concerns, and transportation planning in the scope of regional development. Soon it was agreed that the whole program would necessarily involve a long-range master plan for Ontario. Robarts indicated just how major the enterprise was going to become when he talked about preparing 'ultimately for the planning of land use in the entire province ... We require a careful set of plans for each of the ten economic regions of the province so that all our governmental activities and expenditures, whatever it may be ... transportation ... power, water, resource development, are all coordinated and directed towards the achievement of specific goals of economic development.'[13].

Through the spring and summer of 1968 Treasury and Economics was hard at work drafting regional economic development plans in consultation with the regional development councils. The drafters soon found themselves working at cross-purposes with civil servants in the Department of Municipal Affairs, now headed by the energetic Darcy McKeough. While the one ministry was worrying about planning for economic development, the other was undertaking planning to change the structure of municipal institutions and adjust municipal boundaries to facilitate the provision of specialized services and inter-municipal coordination. There was enough overlapping and friction that high-level co-ordinating meetings had to be held to work out a memorandum of understanding. The development planners would go ahead with their plans for the province's ten economic regions, and then adjust their boundaries after the municipal government reorganizations had been implemented. The development plans would be 'goals plans,' while community planning, land use, municipal institutions, and procedural questions within government (whatever those were) would be handled in the regional government program. Once the goals plans had been promulgated, the province would allocate its expenditures to support their objectives. But the official land use plans, which would be different, would be prepared by the regional governments (which did not yet exist) under the supervision of the Department of Municipal Affairs. The two departments would co-operate to ensure that the plans did not conflict.[14]

The agreement neatly adjusted territory among bureaucratic angels working out plans on the head of a pin. In the real world the projections of the two sets of planners were bound to clash. They would clash not only with each other, but, more importantly, with the traditional and legal foundations of private property in Ontario. The enthusiasm for planning in the government, particularly Treasury and Economics, was perilously close to being utopian and impossibly interventionist. One of its effects, even before the plans were drawn up, was to apply more pressure in the direction of getting on with regional government. From the planners' point of view it was urgent to get new regional boundaries in place. They were supported in this view by the fact that the Ontario Water Resources Commission, the Department of Education, and the Department of Health were all also proceeding with plans to provide services on the basis of their own sets of regional boundaries. Some co-ordinating had to be done soon by someone with a strong hand.[15]

Robarts was waiting, however, for the recommendations of John White's select committee studying tax reform. White did a yeoman job, bringing in his report on 16 September 1968, a day before it was due. Here at last were the recommendations on which the government was expected to base its reform of the tax system – as well as other reforms, for a chief conclusion of White's committee was that the creation of regional governments be implemented even more quickly than the Smith Committee had suggested.[16]

The challenge of taxation policy was to find the right balance among the three major sources of revenue: the municipally levied property tax, the provincially levied retail sales tax, and the income and corporation taxes which were shared with the federal government. Some suggestions in the Smith report, such as a proposal to increase the tax burden on the province's mining industry, were discarded. There was a general agreement that the two regressive taxes, property and sales, should be broadly extended so that the burden of paying them would be spread as widely as possible to enhance their revenue-raising capacity. Going somewhat further than the Smith Committee, White's select committee urged that the property tax now be collected on all public property, including churches, and the retail sales tax be collected on virtually everything, including food and children's clothing.

How could the inequities of regressive taxation be minimized? White's committee proposed that a tax rebate system, linked to the personal income tax, be implemented to counter the burdens that the sales tax changes would put on low-income earners. Similarly, as Smith had recommended, the province should make direct equalization grants to municipalities with a low fiscal capacity. The aim would be to raise their revenue resources to a level adequate to pay for provincially defined standards of service. To provide for equity in the system across the province, however, it was necessary that the base of the property tax system be modernized by reassessing all property according to its market value.[17]

The government was now inundated with recommendations for tax and municipal reform, none of them particularly relevant to the short-term problem of balancing revenues and expenditures. During the summer of 1968 Charles MacNaughton applied the screws more firmly to his colleagues' spending proclivities, insisting on productivity improvements and percentage cuts in everyone's estimates. Ontario was now using a full range of financial controls, including program budgeting and cost-benefit analysis, but was still short of money. On the very day White brought in his recommendations, cabinet was told by MacNaughton on behalf of the Cabinet Committee on Policy Development that even after cutting its expenditures the government had to raise money by one of three expedients: a 5 per cent surcharge on the income tax coming to the province, removal of the exemptions of the gas tax, or an increase in the retail sales tax. If cabinet decided to change the income tax, the tax collection agreement required it to inform Ottawa by 15 October. Before making a final decision, cabinet agreed that Robarts and MacNaughton should deliver a series of speeches alerting the public to Ontario's financial problems.

The aim was to show how Ontario's attempt to combine financial responsibility with modern social policy was being undermined by a financial squeeze that was substantially Ottawa's fault. In London on 18 September Robarts delivered what some saw as the bluntest speech of his career, predicting an ever-widening gap between provincial revenues and expenditures, and slamming the federal government for trying to impose unwanted and expensive shared cost programs on the provinces while insisting that each level of government should raise its own money:

We cannot tolerate the imposition of spending programs on our already over-burdened facilities which are developed and forced upon us without regard for our capacity to pay and without regard for their effect upon our ability to carry out existing programs. To say that each level of government must willy-nilly go its own way, develop its own programs without regard for others, and tax without regard to taxes levied by other levels of government is, in my opinion, a complete abandonment of responsibility to the individual taxpayer of our country.[18]

If Ottawa persisted in its course, Robarts threatened, Ontario would have no choice but to introduce its own personal income tax, collected separately from Ottawa's, and the governments between them would create for the taxpayer a fiscal nightmare.

The barricades on Parliament Hill did not move. If anything Ottawa became more rigid, as the new finance minister, Edgar Benson, dismissed Ontario's case with the comment that the 'federal taxing power was not designed to make gifts to the provinces.' On 22 October he announced that Ottawa was going to extend for a year the 3 per cent surcharge it had levied on income taxes the year before and add a further 2 per cent surcharge called a social development tax. The provinces would not benefit from these levies because surcharges were not included in the tax-sharing formula. It was instantly clear that the main aim of this new tax was to raise the money to pay for medicare.

Charles MacNaughton was furious, for he had notified Ottawa of Ontario's plan to put its own 5 per cent surcharge on the income tax, but had not yet announced it publicly, and was seeing the initiative pre-empted by Benson. The taxpayer could only take so many punches before reacting wrathfully; now that Ottawa was getting in the first hard blows, Ontario would not dare launch what might be a self-inflicted political knock-out. As well, MacNaughton and Robarts realized that the federal tax-juggling would give Ottawa a great political triumph by making it practically impossible for Ontario to remain out of medicare. As MacNaughton charged:

The federal government, either by implication or direct suggestion, can claim that every income taxpayer in Canada is paying the 2% social development tax as his contribution toward medicare. Ottawa can thus force all provincial governments to participate, since few Canadians will want to pay the tax without receiving the benefit.

By this insidious means, the federal government may believe that it can fulfil quickly its promise to provide subsidized medicare for all citizens of Canada despite the fact that health service is, constitutionally, the sole responsibility of the provinces.[19]

MacNaughton's anger reached its highest pitch at a federal-provincial finance ministers conference on 4 November. In a statement he knew to be 'pretty rough stuff' that he had circulated well in advance to the Toronto papers, MacNaughton charged that

the policies of the federal government during the past four years have, in fact, been leading to a balkanization of the Canadian taxation and political system, a weakening of the financial and political strength of the provincial governments by successive tax increases which have perpetuated the financial imbalance and by the intrusion of a rather disorganized set of federal priorities into areas of provincial jurisdiction. This in turn has loaded the expenditure programs of the provinces with federal priorities and has made the provinces more vulnerable to and dependent upon federal initiatives.[20]

The *Globe and Mail* thought this was the toughest Ontario position vis-à-vis Ottawa since the King-Hepburn feud of 1940. 'Right between the eyes, that's where Charles MacNaughton let them have it.'[21]

Then Ottawa rubbed the provinces' faces in medicare a little more fully by announcing that since more than half of them planned to join the program it was phasing out the existing shared-cost programs for public health, cancer control, and medical research. The effect would be to further increase the burden on non-participating provinces, and even within the system give a higher priority to providing medical services than to laying the foundation for providing them most professionally. Ontario was being joined in its resistance by Quebec, and Robert Stanfield was helping support the provincial cause in the House of Commons, but nothing could be done. On 13 November Charles MacNaughton accused Ottawa of practising economic separatism. The debate, if it could be called that, continued at about this level of acrimony.

In the meantime the people of Ontario were letting Robarts, MacNaughton, John White, and most of the other Conservative MPPs know that they were not interested in paying new taxes on the food they bought, clothing for their children, or their churches' property. On that last subject, for example, Robarts received an 85,000-signature petition demanding that the exemption continue. Everyone's mail was running heavily against the new taxes. Caucus made its unease known to cabinet, and by the end of October had been reassured that church property was sacred.[22] In mid November, stealing a little thunder from an NDP convention with his timing, Robarts held a press conference to announce that children's clothing, food, and church property would not be taxed. The government was responding to the popular will in backing away from its own proposals, but in doing so was close to gutting the results of years of preparation for tax reform. The program for dealing with the fundamental problems of modern Ontario was not unfolding as rationally as the·experts hoped. Because of the political situation on taxes and because of the difficulties of co-ordinating departmental plans, especially between Education and Treasury, plans to issue a white paper responding to the Smith/White recommendations were dropped.

So 1968 was a year of slow progress on the basic, province-wide issues of regional government and tax reform. Despite the lack of substantial achievements, the opposition parties were not noticeably effective in their ongoing attempts to undermine the government. It was not clear what Robert Nixon's Liberals stood for. The New Democrats stood for everything good, but flailed away with so many Shulmanesque roundhouse swings at the government that they had difficulty maintaining their credibility. Then a number of the leading NDPers turned their energies inward, criticizing their leader. Donald MacDonald seemed to be out of touch with the new era of labour militancy, student protest, and 'extra-parliamentary politics' – the kind of politics that James Renwick practised, for example, when he led a group of demonstrators against the Ottawa Board of Control and had to be removed from city hall by the police. It was Renwick, supported by Shulman, Stephen Lewis, and John Brown, among others, who contested MacDonald's leadership at the biannual NDP convention that fall, the first challenge he had faced since assuming office in 1953. MacDonald easily defeated Renwick, but representatives of the new forces in the NDP gained control of the party offices. Not unlike Robarts, MacDonald was starting to seem to be a politician more at home with an Ontario which was beginning to disappear. After the convention, members of the NDP caucus demonstrated their new principles by skipping a session of the legislature to join a picket line. They thought they were going where the action was.

Two major reports released in 1968 showed that the aging government was not as out of touch with the spirit of the times as the opposition thought. Early in the year Mr Justice J.C. McRuer brought in a massive three-volume instalment of the report of his Royal Commission of Inquiry into Civil Rights. Since his appointment in the aftermath of the Bill 99 affair in 1964, McRuer and his staff had conducted a massive examination of the impact of the laws of Ontario on individual rights. They had poked into the powers of commissioners under the Public Inquiries Act, expropriation procedures, compensation for victims of crime, procedures in magistrates' courts, the detention of the mentally ill, the powers of professional bodies, and a hundred and one other areas where the modern state confronted the citizen and his rights.

McRuer found much to complain about in the Ontario government's ways of proceeding and made five hundred recommendations. His complaints did not do the government much harm because it seemed clear that the abuses had crept into the system over many years without anyone being fully conscious of their implications. The government handled McRuer's recommendations in about as effective a way as possible, by moving to implement almost everything he proposed. In April of 1968 Attorney General Wishart sent a letter to all cabinet ministers asking them to review their legislation to ensure it conformed with the recommendations of the McRuer Commission. By 1969 the report was known as the 'bible' of the government, and the minister of justice was planning what would become a massive legislative response to McRuer in 1971. McRuer and his reports (a second part was released in September 1969) were instrumental in the modernization of law and procedures in Ontario as the province passed into an age of high sensitivity to individual rights. The combination of good luck and foresight that the Robarts cabinet had possessed in setting up this royal commission in 1964, well ahead of the full brunt of 1970s concern for individual rights, meant an invaluable legacy to their successors at the end of the decade and on into the next decades.

The second report was submitted by the Provincial Committee on the Aims and Objectives of Education in Ontario Schools, nicknamed the Hall-Dennis Report after its co-chairmen, Mr Justice Emmett M. Hall and Lloyd A. Dennis. Entitled *Living and Learning* and published in a glossy, expensive format, the Hall-Dennis Report was a classic expression of the educational utopianism sweeping North America at the time. Arguing that education went far beyond traditional school subjects into everything involved with 'preparing the child for the world,' and that it ought to protect the child from 'the hazards and frustrations of failure' and avoid 'the lock step structure of past times,' the report included 258 recommendations, ranging from the abolition of grade thirteen and eventually all other grades and examinations to the introduction of free tuition in the universities. In fact William Davis' Department of Education was already liberalizing examination and curricular policy across the province, and in this year the more important substantive issues had to do with creating the new consolidated county boards – a development that Hall-Dennis fully endorsed. Many of the other Hall-Dennis recommendations sparked considerable debate, so much so that the report became a kind of lightning-rod drawing the criticism of people worried that wishy-washy good intentions were replacing standards and values in Ontario education. Many of its recommendations were never implemented. In this sense Hall-Dennis was far less important and effective than McRuer's work. But it was certainly hard to argue that a government which could generate the recommendations in *Living and Learning* was completely out of touch with the mood of young Ontario.

A few Progressive-Conservatives thought the government was out of touch with the mood of the party. Seats and votes had been lost in the 1967 provincial election. The 1968 federal election had been a disaster for the national Progressive-Conservatives, swept aside in young Canada's love affair with Pierre Trudeau and the Liberals. Was the Ontario Conservative party in need of some kind of modernization? Its political leadership, centring on Robarts and his London friends, had been around for quite a long time, and at times seemed narrowly concentrated on their regional base. Perhaps it was becoming even narrower, as in Robarts' recent appointments of Darcy McKeough of Chatham to Municipal Affairs, and John White of London as minister of revenue. Certain foul-ups, such as the unpopular proposal to tax food and churches, seemed to indicate that the Londoners might be out of touch with the popular mood.

Some of their plans for regional government were not very popular either. One of the young Toronto Tories, Alan Eagleson, had tried to get this point across in caucus by opposing the reorganization of Metropolitan Toronto that eliminated the lakeshore communities in his riding, Mimico, New Toronto, and Long Branch. Eagleson lost his battle in caucus and then lost his seat to the NDP in the election. He was not impressed with the political acumen of the party establishment (who, in turn, were not impressed with him), and decided to do something about it by challenging Elmer Bell for the presidency of the Ontario PC Association.

Bell was probably going to have to make a choice between national and provincial politics anyway. He had taken a leading role in the national PC campaign of 1968. Eagleson's open attacks on the party organization as decaying and heading toward a disaster in the next election hastened Bell's decision, prodded by Robarts, to stand aside to allow control to pass to 'more youthful and vigorous hands.' When he announced his intention to retire, other candidates joined the campaign, most of them running as reformers against the party's 'establishment.'

Rumours that Robarts' political goals had been satisfied with the 1967 victory and that he would soon retire added to the stirrings in the Tory party. On 25 October he put an end to them with veiled references to people who 'want my job and they aren't all necessarily in the Opposition ... I'm not really giving much thought to early retirement.'[23] A few days later at a cabinet retreat the ministers agreed to take important steps in reforming the party machinery, including the creation of a new headquarters and the appointment of a full-time paid executive director. Robarts was personally determined to stay in touch with the interests of a new generation, partly because they represented the future, partly because he had always, in one side of his personality, been drawn to the freedom and good times that youth seemed to champion.

On the first night of the Ontario PC annual meeting, John, Norah, and Robin Robarts attended a dance for the Young PCs. Most of the cabinet ministers who were present stood on the sidelines, well away from the crowd, or out in the hall to avoid the noise. John Robarts danced to the rock music of 'Looking Glass.' In a short speech while the musicians took a break, Robarts told the teenagers that his government was considering lowering the drinking and voting ages from twenty-one to eighteen. The next night he performed again, now in his role as the Conservative prime minister accounting for his stewardship. George Drew and Leslie Frost were with him on the platform as Robarts addressed the convention on the theme 'The Challenge of the 1970s.' Among the traditional Tory clichés there was a not bad summing up of Robarts' perceptions of his government's situation:

The challenge of the Forties was to overcome the substantial backlog of development resulting from the Depression ... The challenge of the Fifties was to build what a modern society requires in the way of facilities and services ... The challenge of the Sixties has been to continue this growth to plan and adjust to the effects of technological change and rapid urbanization. These have been discontented, worrisome years for all Canadians. They have been years which have required us to sort out our national aspirations, to help our country come of age, to discard much parochialism and to assess the worth to us of being Canadians. In the midst of much prosperity, we have had to do some agonizing soul searching ...

The overriding challenge of my years as leader of the Government of Ontario has been to ensure the continued strength and unity of Canada. Substantial progress has been made toward this end. I believe we have underway the process which will achieve more ... As I look into the Seventies, it becomes apparent to me that we must turn our attention to the improvement of the quality of the lives we lead ...

To accomplish these broad purposes will require great changes in taxation, in governmental organization, in our approach to regional development and in the bringing into being of methods of control of human activity to a greater degree than we have yet achieved ... As the party of the Seventies, we must be ever more aware, and ever more attuned, to the new pressures and new directions resulting from our growth and increasing maturity as a society.[24]

Alan Eagleson won the party presidency, the first person actively to campaign for and win the position since Drew took office. The pace of organizational change immediately increased. Arthur Harnett, a former radio newsman at CFRB, was appointed director of research for the caucus and shortly became executive director of the party. A few months later Mac King, a Toronto businessman, replaced Harry Price as PC treasurer. In 1969 William Teeter, a pollster who had done some surveys for the party during the 1968 federal election, was hired to monitor public opinion in Ontario as the government's municipal and tax reforms were implemented. Eagleson joined Robarts' political strategy group, which now included Tom Wells, Ernie Jackson, and Eddie Goodman. Robarts was still firmly in charge, and Londoners still effectively ran the Conservative party, especially through Jackson's influence on patronage and throughout the organization. But new hands were in charge of the formal party apparatus, and the new mood of restlessness within the governing party would not dissipate.

'We Cannot All Be Wrong – Can We?'

The Robarts government's program of sweeping reforms was anticipated in the Speech from the Throne opening the 1968-9 session of the legislature. The government was going to initiate regional government 'in various areas of the province where sufficient study has been completed,' would amend the assessment act to improve assessment in accordance with 'certain recommendations' of the Smith and White reports, and would bring in various 'new proposals' for tax reform.[1]

It was not long before Davis realized that a public backlash was building up against the new county school boards. Soon other senior ministers found their proposals either ignored or rejected by the people of Ontario. Much of the reform program was the fulfilment of economists' and administrators' determination to create a modern municipal, tax, and social service structure for the rich, modern province. It was to be a triumph of rationality and planning. Instead, many of the schemes began to come apart from the moment of their introduction, as Ontarians proved intractably committed to such familiar verities as low mill rates and time-honoured municipal boundaries.

Robarts introduced the important new regional development guidelines in a speech to the legislature on 28 November 1968. The province was dedicated to fostering growth by concentrating capital investment in designated urban centres. It would act on the recommendations of regional development plans as they were drafted and refined, within a classification of the regions into those characterized by slow growth, fluctuating growth, or self-sustaining growth. No support would be given to industry locating in self-sustaining growth regions; but long-term economic development aid would be offered to slow growth regions. In that speech Robarts promised to make later, more detailed announcements on the introduction of regional government and a provincial income tax, and continued his war with Ottawa with another blunt attack. He charged that the 'automatic assumption that the federal government, the central government, is the superior power' in Confederation was leading to 'an automatic assumption that our decisions can be made in Ottawa.' This was reducing the provinces to 'branch plants' of Ottawa. It made no sense for Ottawa to insist that the provinces look to their own resources to deal with their financial problems while imposing new financial problems on them in the form of medicare.

Robarts' attack was provoked in part by the strength of political reaction to Ontario's tax reform program. The province had given tax relief to the municipalities before the 1967 election. Now it found itself constantly short of money. It could not afford to bring in one of the centrepieces of tax reform, an income-tax-based tax credit scheme, unless much more revenue came to Ontario from income taxes. The only way to make that happen would be to get more money out of Ottawa, or to introduce Ontario's own personal income tax. This line of reasoning was the basis of the Robarts government's decision to tinker with the tax system through 1969, keep the pressure on Ottawa, and prepare for long-term changes. At all times there would have to be tight spending controls to stretch Ontario's limited revenues as far as possible. Treasury Board and the Cabinet Committee on Policy Development would set priorities. A few weeks later Robarts escalated his rhetoric by charging that Ottawa had precipitated 'one of the most serious confrontations between the provinces and the federal government since the Second World War, indeed during the history of Confederation.'[2]

While Robarts was blasting Ottawa, in an effort to secure the financial basis of his government's reform program, Darcy McKeough, the minister of municipal affairs, unveiled the province's approach to regional government on 2 December. Although he tried to reassure the public that the changes would be gradual and always accompanied by public input, he was making specific and sweeping announcements. Regional government would be introduced in the Ottawa-Carleton area on 1 January 1969, and in the Niagara peninsula and the areas west of Metropolitan Toronto early in 1969. The areas north of Toronto and at the west end of Lake Ontario were next on the province's agenda, to be followed by the Kitchener-Waterloo and Haldimand-Norfolk regions. The amalgamation of Fort William and Port Arthur had just been announced, and legislation would be brought in later in the session to create regional government in the Muskoka District. A local government review was planned for Sudbury and an interdepartmental committee had ben created to review local government throughout northern Ontario. Generally it was planned to design regions around urban centres and to incorporate a population in excess of 150,000 in each regional municipality. The regional governments would be responsible for assessing local property taxes and providing specialized social services. Educational boundaries would not necessarily coincide with regional boundaries.[3]

The third and most critical speech introducing Ontario's reform program was, Charles MacNaughton's budget address on 4 March 1969. Facing television cameras newly installed in the legislative assembly, MacNaughton outlined both short- and long-term tax proposals. For fiscal 1969 the government was determined to balance its budget, exercising severe expenditure restraint in a framework of horizontally established priorities. The priority fields, in which special increases were allowed, were to be education, health, social services, housing, and municipal aid. A large number of minor tax changes, including increases in the tobacco, gasoline, mining profits, and corporate income taxes, as well as extensions of the sales and property taxes, would generate the extra revenue needed to produce a $2 million surplus in a total provincial budget of just under $3 billion.

The province's long-term tax reform program,[4] MacNaughton announced, was to be based on the establishment of a provincial income tax system within the next two years. Once Ontario had its own progressive personal income tax, it would introduce tax abatement programs to ease the burden of the property and sales taxes. Ontario would also introduce its own capital gains tax, at least until Ottawa made up its mind on Carter's recommendation for a national capital gains tax. The policy of tax relief to the municipalities was to continue and be expanded, but these changes depended on other actions being taken on the municipal level. The regional government program had to be implemented to provide the efficiencies and economies necessary to revitalize local government, thus preserving decentralized social services throughout the province. Finally, most aspects of the thrust towards standardized services and provincial equalization grants hinged on there being a common, province-wide measure of property value. The most practical solution, MacNaughton had concluded, was to reassess all property at market value. Ignoring certain reservations about province-wide reassessment in both the Smith and White reports, MacNaughton announced that 'in recognition of the assessment inconsistencies and inequities documented by the Smith Committee,' the provincial government would assume responsibility for the administration of property assessment on 1 July, 1969 in the unorganized portions of northern Ontario and on 1 January 1970 in the rest of the province. It would then 'ensure that the administration and quality of assessment is brought up to a proper level by the end of 1975.' MacNaughton believed reassessment would probably add many new properties to the tax rolls for local government and thus extend the property tax base, ultimately bringing in more money.

Few Ontarians outside of government grasped the full scope of the province's proposals. Press reaction to MacNaughton's budget, for example, concentrated on its implications in the struggle with Ottawa. MacNaughton's tax changes were not the desperate measures Robarts had been predicting, and to some observers it seemed as though the province's ability to produce a balanced budget without more help from Ottawa gave the lie to many of the premier's outbursts.[6] MacNaughton responded to criticisms like this with the comment that 'we couldn't bring in this kind of budget too often or we'd stop development in the province altogether,'[7] but in fact he and his cabinet colleagues were being forced on the defensive. Was not Ontario, which was so angry about medicare, playing exactly

the same game as Ottawa when it proposed to establish its own capital gains tax –
in other words, trying to pressure the other level of government into a new
program? And what about medicare? It was now in place and Ontario was forgoing
approximately $170 million in transfer payments annually by pursuing its own
medical insurance scheme. This money could have been used to avoid cuts to
government programs or to reduce health insurance premiums. Robert Nixon
charged that the Robarts government was pursuing its own policy of 'fiscal
separatism' in its tax and medicare policies.*[8] His party also more vigorously
championed the cause of the province's separate high schools, which were being
hurt by the creation of the French-language secondary schools, and demanded full
separate school funding to grade thirteen.

It happened that Ontario's surrender on medicare was already being negotiated.
Ottawa had just offered a new compromise, which would allow private carriers to
be involved in the provision of the basic medicare plan. It went a considerable way
toward meeting one of Ontario's chief criticisms of the federal plan, and in any
event the financial and perhaps the political costs of staying out of the national plan
were starting to become intolerable. On 17 June 1969, Robarts announced that
Ontario would enter medicare on 1 October. It was hard for him to disguise the fact
that his government had suffered a major, bitter setback after years of battling on
the medicare issue, but it had not been a total defeat. Premiums sensitive to income
and a role for private carriers had been salvaged. They would remain a source of
political controversy for many years.

There were other setbacks and defeats in train. It was all very well to talk the
language of planning and priorities and regional development and tax equity. And
it was certainly true that the advocates of administrative reform had captured
horizontal policy-making. They would sit in Queen's Park and set priorities and
deploy resources according to complex plans and vague guidelines. But what
about the individual, the ordinary Ontarian? What about the local teacher or
municipal clerk or policeman who was worried about his or her job? What about
the local town councillor who was worried about his or her job? Above all, what
about the local taxpayer, whose strongest feelings about the activities of the Ontario
government varied with the size of his tax bill? These Ontarians were neither
impressed by nor interested in the rationality of an administrative revolution in the
province. They were interested in personal security, in *not* having their old Ontario
lives disrupted for the sake of creating some new planner's ideal of regional
government or tax equity.

An undercurrent of resistance to regional government had been gathering

* As usual, there were divided sentiments among the government's Liberally minded critics. While
the Toronto *Star* also trumpeted the 'fiscal separatism' accusations, for example, it was happy to
see Ontario leading the way on the capital gains question: 'When a Conservative government in
Ontario proposes to lead the way to progressive tax reform in Canada, it's time for a Liberal
government at Ottawa to wake up and get moving.'

strength for some years. Open revolt broke out in April 1969, one month after MacNaughton's budget, when the 1969 property tax bills were received across the province. The new county boards of education were levying their first taxes, and they were very high. In many areas of the province property taxes increased by 25 per cent; in a few the tax bill doubled. To a public astonished by revelations of the high salaries that newly appointed local educational bureaucrats were receiving, it seemed obvious that the organizational changes in education had produced the higher costs.

'Each Economy Proposal Seems to Cost Us More,' the Sarnia *Observer* headlined an article:

The *New Jerusalem* of the Ontario Department of Education has sent school taxes soaring from 87 to 130 per cent, with no hint as to where the taxpayers are going to find the added money. What the bureaucrats at Toronto appear to have launched is an entirely new and expensive administrative setup which is going to run to such a height that it could fall under the weight of protest of people who are beginning to demand that they receive something more than promises and new faces crowding around the public trough.[9]

Orillia Township refused to pay its portion of the Simcoe County school board's tax bill. Walpole Township refused to pay its share of the Haldimand-Norfolk increase until both the board and the province had justified it. In the legislature on 16 April Robert Nixon moved want of confidence in the government, charging it with having created 'one of the most serious financial crises in the history of Ontario ... As a direct result of the poorly planned imposition of county boards and the inadequate grant system, communities across this province face a true financial nightmare worse than any that the Treasurer tried to conjure up in his speeches earlier this year.[10] The debate ranged far wider than school boards, as the whole idea of regional government began to be called into question. William Davis fought back on the education issue for the government, putting the best face on the situation, and of course the Liberal motion was defeated. In the privacy of caucus the government's own members reinforced the view that the county board system was causing real trouble.

The development of the problem was a textbook study in the difficulties of imposing sudden 'rationalization' on a complex reality. Many of the old township school boards, which had been doomed from November 1967, had used their last year of life to spend accumulated surpluses on new services or give the money back to the taxpayers through lower mill rates. Both actions neatly hid the reality of rising education costs, as had some local treasurers' habit of working out deals under which municipalities helped cover some expenses properly charged to school boards. The new county boards thus inherited artificially deflated mill rates and local arrangements the remaking of which would cost them a lot of money. Moreover, there were many situations where the pooling of educational costs on a county-wide basis penalized municipalities with inexpensive schools and/or weak assessment bases. The inevitable result was huge tax increases in 1969.

Paul Hickey, a senior civil servant in the Department of Municipal Affairs, had seen the problem coming when he had written to Darcy McKeough in January pointing out that the education mill rates had not increased in 1968 as expected. But he had added that 'there was no way of ascertaining whether there would be a problem or not since the province did not have the information necessary to assess the situation.' Many disbanded local boards had not yet submitted their audited statements. McKeough's response, that 'the matter should be watched carefully,'[11] was an unconsciously ironic comment on the limits of government.

Cabinet decided that it had to increase grants to the municipalities to compensate for the higher taxes. The announcement partially defused the political outcry. But it did so at the cost of making education an exception to the spending restraints in the March budget, and thus having priorities planning upset by a political response to problems. Nor did the planners know how badly restraint had been abandoned, for the old township boards took their time submitting their financial statements. The final bill for increased grants was $84 million.[12] Eventually the government had to act on MacNaughton's earlier warning and impose a ceiling on county school board expenditures.[13]

Public alarm about school boards transferred easily into resistance to the regional government proposals. From the beginning these suffered from guilt through association with the county boards. An editorial in the *Lindsay Post* perfectly captured the sense of concern and the public's desire to slow down:

It appears from current press reports that the new enlarged school areas are having their problems. Many municipalities are being hit hard by increased taxes. It appears for many taxpayers that there will not be any reduced demand nor will the School Boards be able to hold the line ...

Every day we read about the coming of Regional Government. Possibly the officials at Queen's Park should slow this down and take another look. At least to give the new school system a chance to prove itself or otherwise.

The Canadian Taxpayer is getting fed up with continually increasing costs at every level of government. A fair share of these increasing costs are due to costly blunders, generated by people in a hurry to change the old established system. Let's slow down and take a second look now and again.[14]

The regional government experiments were adding to the political backlash in their own right. Almost all of the political changes in the mid-1960s in Metropolitan Toronto had been unpopular with local interests. Now in both the Ottawa-Carleton and the Niagara regional reorganizations there were new disputes over service standards and the property tax load. Costs and taxes were increasing as a result of the reorganizations. As soon as the property tax reassessment legislation was introduced in June, it too became ensnared in the controversy, for the opposition immediately linked assessment at market value with the prospect of further tax increases. Rural sensibilities were further offended as the definition and taxation of farm land under the reassessment program became a matter of instant debate – and this just as the growing environmental movement was beginning to challenge the right of farmers to control and sell their own land.

Government reform programs were now seen as a menace to rural communities. The prospect of regional government or reassessment, even the rumours of either coming to an area, was enough to cause political tremors. It was impossible to discuss the substance of reform proposals which local people equated with higher taxes and the destruction of their communities. The *Lindsay Post* editorial perfectly expressing the conservative attitudes of Ontario society, had been sent to Robarts and McKeough by Leslie Frost. In accompanying letters, Frost warned McKeough about the peril involved if rumours about regional government breaking up Victoria and Haliburton counties were true, and commented in passing that 'Sometimes the matter of government is not pure logic. Confederation itself is an example of this.' To Robarts, Frost offered sound common sense:

I suggest that care be taken in connection with this Regional Government business. It can cause a very considerable political upheaval, particularly in view of the effects of the County Education School Boards ... If the rumours in connection with Victoria and Haliburton were true it would create an unprecedented uproar. I do not think that any such move is necessary. Frankly, sometimes where there is smoke there is fire and there may be more truth than fiction in what the Grits are saying.[15]

The premier had already realized that the reform program had to be put on the back burner. His reply to Frost was a rare personal comment on his government's policies:

The whole matter is very worrisome to me. I think we had a real mistake made in the Department of Education and it certainly accentuated the resentment to the County Boards, and, no doubt, will set back any plan for Regional Government for some time.

I have told Darcy to continue with the Regional Governments we have in the works at the moment but not to undertake any more studies for some time and I have taken great pains to say on any available occasion that we do not, of course, intend to impose Regional Government all across the province. There are many areas where it will not be necessary for a good many years, in my opinion.

I hope that we will be able to straighten out the grant mess within the next year or so. In any event, we are in a position to help a good many of the Boards financially and, in the meantime, I do believe we have squeezed a good deal of fat out of school administration.[16]

Robarts, MacNaughton, and McKeough undertook to explain the reasoning behind the government's proposed reforms to municipal and community leaders through a series of Municipality for Tomorrow conferences (the title, of course, derived from Confederation of Tomorrow). At seventeen of these, held in the summer of 1969, the ministers met with local politicians and community leaders, explained the provincial reform program, and listened to the local concerns. Most of the conferences turned into group therapy sessions. The provincial politicians spent their time reassuring municipal politicians that municipal restructuring was not being imposed across Ontario at present and if and when municipal reform occurred they would have the opportunity to participate in the process. Earlier in the summer Robarts had received a cool reception when he tried to explain the purpose and scope of the municipal, tax, and education reforms to the annual conference of the Ontario Association of Mayors and Reeves. No one seemed to be in a mood to discuss the substance of the provincial reform proposals. The government pressed on as best it could, but at a snail's pace.

And there were regional problems within problems of regional reform. Northern Ontario's affairs, for example, began taking on a momentum of their own after Allan Lawrence took charge of the Ministry of Mines, to which he had been appointed in February 1968. Lawrence was an astute, very competent MPP with a broad range of career experience, including a period of prospecting, and he was a maverick. Although his emotional outburst during the Bill 99 debate had made Robarts reluctant to promote him to cabinet, the premier and Keith Reynolds thought his skills and freshness might be ideal for rebuilding the Conservative party in northern Ontario, where it had fared badly in the 1967 election. Shortly after his appointment, Lawrence began building his and the party's presence in the region with a tour of the north. In May 1969 he announced the convening of a series of northern development conferences, designed 'to bring together responsible leaders in the north in dialogue with people from Queen's Park – not just from this department – to try to resolve some of the long term problems facing the north.'[17]

Lawrence's approach to northern problems was 'horizontal,' in that he wanted to consider them all, but it was to be done through his ministry, not through the government's newly established structures. Lawrence had not participated in the administrative reforms and had little patience with them. In cabinet, for example, he attacked Treasury Board, arguing that its decisions were getting in the way of cabinet's responsibility to establish priorities. Robarts had to mediate Lawrence's disagreements with MacNaughton on the issue. Then Lawrence's northern development conferences, held in the autumn of 1969, led to his compiling a massive list of grievances and concerns. On the basis of these he asked that the mandate of his department be extended so he could co-ordinate the government's approach to the north. After various reviews, Lawrence got his way, his department having its name changed to Mines and Northern Development. As with education, the needs of a politically sensitive ministry had led to another decision to make an exception from the planning process, this time for the affairs of a whole, huge region.

In fact the tension between departmental needs and interests and the horizontal approach to public policy and spending controls was affecting many areas of the public service. Senior, middle, and lower level administrators were resisting new planning and budgeting systems within the government almost as firmly as municipal administrators and taxpayers were resisting municipal and educational and tax reforms imposed on them. There was constant suspicion that the experts in the program review branch of Treasury Board intended to impose structural changes, interdepartmental priority systems, and other management techniques on the existing departmental hierarchies.

Robarts and MacNaughton decided that an influential administrative review body with an ongoing mandate, somewhat on the model of the Ontario Advisory Committee on Confederation, would be the best way of attempting to overcome departmental conservatism. On 20 February 1969 MacNaughton announced the creation of the 'Productivity Improvement Project,' a review of the overall structure of government to be carried out by a committee of businessmen and senior public servants. The members of the committee were not finally appointed until that autumn. John B. Cronyn of London headed a group of influential business members and chaired the committee; the five public servants on it, including Ian Macdonald and Keith Reynolds, were the most powerful in the government. The PIP's steering committee, soon to be transformed into the Committee on Government Productivity, was given authority 'to inquire into all matters pertaining to the management of the Government of Ontario and to make such recommendations as in its opinion will improve the efficiency and effectiveness of the Government of Ontario.' In December 1970 it published the first of a series of reports which would drastically reform the central decision-making structure of the government. Most of its recommendations were designed to strengthen reforms already realized in the strengthening of the Treasury Board, the creation of the Cabinet Committee on Policy Development, and the formation of the Department of Treasury and Economics. The major differences would come in nomenclature and in the creation of cabinet committees under provincial secretaries designed to co-ordinate programs in complementary departments.

Most of these administrative reforms would not be introduced during Robarts' tenure. In fact Robarts himself was increasingly concerned that organizational reform in pursuit of efficiency hampered his ability to maintain personal contact with the affairs of government. He worried that the organizations and offices created in the new administrative state would foreclose his own personal need to communicate with and respond to Ontarians and the Ontario community. The rising bureaucracy was placing a policy filter between himself and the individuals government was supposed to serve.

Robarts tested his rapport with the voters in a by-election in the Middlesex South riding on 18 September 1969. Middlesex South included the eastern suburbs of London and the farmland south and west of the city, and seemed to be an obviously safe Conservative seat. It had been held by the government since 1943. Now, however, both opposition parties poured resources into the campaign, forcing the government to respond. The NDP was particularly vigorous, applying their saturation technique developed earlier in Toronto. They had a surfeit of canvassers, some of them drawn from the thirty-seven thousand steelworkers on strike in Hamilton and Sault Ste Marie that month and the twenty-five thousand other workers laid off because of the steel strike. The NDP workers poured into the riding by the busload, canvassing every house three times during the campaign, attacking the Tories for the size of medicare premiums, higher education taxes, and the county school boards. On 9 September Morton Shulman joined in the fray, telling a rally that the Robarts government was 'old, mean and malicious.' He slashed away with personal attacks on various of the ministers, and then the NDP's gentle candidate, Anglican archdeacon Kenneth C. Bolton, told the rally how politics was 'the way to stick to the Gospel's concern for the poor, the homeless, the hungry and the sick ... and the NDP is the only important opposition.'[19]

The Conservatives sent workers from the London PC Association into Middlesex South to bolster the local organization. On 13 September Robarts and MacNaughton made major appearances, with MacNaughton attacking Morton Shulman and defending regional government. Ontario's insistence on maintaining premiums to help cover the costs of medicare seemed to be the single most commonly raised issue, along with the suspicion, fanned by the opposition, that the federal medicare grants were being diverted to some other purpose. The Liberals echoed many of the NDP concerns, making particular mileage in rural areas with their attack on municipal restructuring.

On by-election day the Conservatives narrowly outpolled the Liberals in the rural areas of the riding. But the NDP swept the London suburbs and beat them both, taking the seat by fourteen hundred votes, with the Liberals a narrow third. The Middlesex South result was a sharp rebuff to the Robarts government's major policies.

At the least it reflected the difficulties Robarts and his ministers were having finding their way in the new political climate of Ontario. They had chosen to steer a course down what had seemed in the early 1960s like a safe political middle – raise standards, modernize services, improve local government – but the people of Ontario did not understand or sympathize with what they were trying to do. In rural Ontario the provincial initiatives had come close to foundering on the rock of local community loyalties, tax resistance, and reaction to the growth of social service establishments. In urban Ontario a whirlpool of sentiment in favour of good things like the environment and animal welfare, and against developers, polluters, reactionary Tories, and the Vietnam war made the reforms seem theoretical. It was hard to see how they could reach the public and have informed political debate on the problems of governing Ontario. In the new television age, images and stereotypes seemed to have replaced substance.

The Robarts government was not quite as out of touch with its constituents as some of its critics suggested, for if the Tories had learned anything over the years it was how to be responsive to short- as well as long-term voter wishes. Such initiatives as the government's decision to lower the voting and drinking age in the province from twenty-one to eighteen were obvious responses to the public mood. So was the decision to give Ontarians, especially Torontonians, a kind of permanent public circus, Ontario Place, to be built on artificial islands next to the Canadian National Exhibition grounds. There had been other successes as well. The Ontario Science Centre was a personal victory for Robarts, and the development of a modern urban presence over the shallow water between Ontario Place and the harbour, as well as an extensive set of provincial parks including Polar Bear Provincial Park, all provided immense satisfaction to Robarts. These additions to the Ontario dream were specific; the reform program was basic to the restructuring of the public sector at all levels in Ontario. No comparable initiative had been launched since 1867. It would have to be chopped into chewable mouthfuls; a first effort had caused the public to choke.

Still, many of the Conservative politicians, including the premier, were sympathetic with the values of the government's critics, sensing that both the urban worries and the rural alarums were rooted in a profoundly conservative concern for the individual and his local community. The problem was how to make the package palatable, how to re-establish the support of the political centre while adjusting public services to harness the technology and realities of the twentieth century. What portion of Conservative policies would go some way toward meeting everyone's concerns without alienating any group irrevocably and without losing the long-term objective? Through most of 1969 the government had failed to find the vital centre. Cabinet had been too influenced by the dreams of the economists and planners, not influenced enough by the simpler, less articulate, and more confused wishes of the people. In the next chapter we will see in more detail how the government and the prime minister managed in a kind of 'last hurrah' to get on top of events again and lead the party effectively toward the new millennium.

The frustrations sometimes took their toll on the premier's patience. Time after time his response to public outcries had been to appoint a commission to inquire into a difficult problem. When Keith Reynolds suggested that public concern about Ontario Hydro's rate increases and other decisions might be met by a royal commission review, Robarts' response was brief: 'No,' he scribbled, '– just another way of providing critics of government with ammo – we cannot all be wrong – can we????'[19]

Entering the Seventies

The crowded political agenda of the late 1960s forced the legislators into ever-lengthening sessions. In 1969 the Ontario legislative assembly sat for 173 days and 81 nights. Two years earlier the strain had taken its toll on the clerk of the assembly, Roderick Lewis, who suffered a heart attack near the end of the session. His plight caused all parties finally to realize that staff reforms were needed. After the 1967 election Robarts appointed Fred Cass, who had done backbench penance for Bill 99, as the new Speaker, with a mandate to reform. Cass appointed an advisory committee of senior civil servants, including Lewis, which recommended the appointment of more staff for the clerk's office and eventually a training program for new servants of the legislature. In the autumn of 1969 members' impatience with the length of debates and sittings finally caused the leaders to agree to time limits on debates. There would be a ninety-hour limit for debate on supply and a five-hour limit for debate on reports from standing committees. In return for opposition acceptance of these limits, the government agreed to make question period more lively by permitting members to ask questions without notifying the Speaker in advance of their substance. The reforms were introduced for a trial period in October, were seen to be popular, and soon became permanent.

Members decided to give themselves adequate accommodation in the buildings where they now spent so much of their time. An all-party committee recommended that the north wing of the legislative building be converted into MPP office space, with each caucus having a floor. In the revival of an institution destroyed generations earlier by the temperance movement, there would be a members' bar in the basement. A 50 per cent pay increase for the MPPs to $18,000 annually capped the transition of Ontario's legislators from the part-time public tribunes of the 1950s to the full-time lawmakers of the 1970s and afterwards.

Question period became the highlight of each day's sitting. John Robarts, who thrived on a challenge, found the development much to his liking, for he enjoyed the cut and thrust of nearly spontaneous debate. Robarts and most other MPPs took much less interest in the succeeding hours of often long-winded and repetitive oratory. Similarly, the members of the press gallery became more selective in their attendance, covering question period and little else except for major policy statements. The press release superseded routine debate in the legislature as a way of transmitting information. The growing research capacity of the opposition parties helped them present their own policy statements and press releases. Except during question period, and during visits from school children, the number of Ontarians present at the debates shrank.

Coverage of Queen's Park events by radio and television had grown to the point of forcing newspaper journalists into a fundamental reconsideration of their role. One of the responses was a growing interest in investigative reporting. Organized wire service coverage of the legislature's proceedings was another way of doing the job while keeping expenses down. With personnel transfers, and the addition of a new type of reporter, the old press gallery corps lost its cohesiveness and much of its old position in the disintegrating Queen's Park 'community.' The passing of the old order was symbolized by the decline of the annual press gallery party, whose skits became more and more slipshod until finally, to no one's regret, it was cancelled in 1967. About the same time, the Toronto *Star* began expressing editorial doubts about the century-long practice of members of the press gallery being 'wined and dined' by the government. Sensitive to charges like this, and not impressed anyway with what seemed like media preoccupation with criticism, Robarts decided to cancel the government's annual reception for the press. A few trusted reporters would occasionally enjoy a briefing from the premier, sometimes over breakfast at the Westbury Hotel. Most had little contact with Robarts, whom they saw as a formal, aloof figure.

To insiders, John Robarts was anything but aloof. In these last years of his premiership he was both increasingly concerned about maintaining contact with individuals and increasingly in personal need of the reassurance that political and social companionship gave him. He liked to keep in touch through small dinner parties, sometimes with backbenchers, sometimes with leaders from the business or cultural communities. Often he combined these occasions with late night visits to the legislature to see how debate was proceeding. The members were not happy at having to sit late into the night – which was Robarts' response to their long-windedness – nor at having the premier drop in to find out how many or how few were actually present. Sometimes members of all parties conspired to get as much business done as possible of an evening and then move adjournment just before 'the boss' returned.

The people around Robarts in the Prime Minister's Department were hard-pressed to stay on top of lengthening sessions, increased governmental and intergovernmental activity, huge increases in the volume of mail, and problems of communication between cabinet ministers and Robarts, the assembly and Robarts, the government and the press, cabinet and cabinet committees, government departments, and cabinet and the public. The retirement of Malcolm McIntyre in March 1969 finally ended the duopoly of executive control in Robarts' office, and Keith Reynolds became both deputy minister and chief executive officer. The cabinet secretariat and the prime minister's executive officers gradually merged, with Hugh Hanson, a recent addition to the Prime Minister's Office after being seconded to the Ontario Committee on Taxation from the Treasury Department, becoming deputy secretary to cabinet and Irene Beatty heading the personal staff as director of administration. Reynolds now was the chief gatekeeper for Robarts, the man through whom cabinet ministers kept in touch with the premier. To keep the office functioning smoothly and on top of things, Reynolds began convening Monday morning staff briefings.

The problem with working in Robarts' office was that the premier wanted his staff kept small and personal. He did not want the office to become a multiplying bureaucracy, accumulating power at the expense of other agencies or departments. Older, simpler ways seemed best. Robarts liked to read his mail for himself, for example, and to review drafts of replies before they were sent. The staff only gradually overcame the premier's hesitation about adopting 'modern' methods of handling a volume of mail which had tripled during his years in office. First they began compiling weekly tallies and summaries of incoming and outgoing mail. Then in January 1969, the office crossed a watershed when an 'auto pen' was installed. It was simply physically impossible for Robarts personally to sign the 2,131 letters answering correspondents on the separate school funding question, or the 4,434 letters on animal welfare. Still, Robarts did not like the idea of the auto pen. When it broke one day he cheerfully took home a box of two hundred letters to be sent to municipal officials in northern Ontario. He returned the box to Reynolds the next morning with a one-word note in a handwritten flourish, 'Done!'

Robarts' life was becoming scheduled, his day moving to the rhythm of the appointments calendar. He did not like the sense that he was losing contact with people and affairs in cabinet. In 1970 he expressed some of these feelings in a letter to a friend:

It might interest you to know that in the last two years I have had two Cabinet Ministers handling the duties of House Leader. The chairing of Cabinet is a duty that I am very reluctant to relinquish.

As the Government has grown it has been necessary to decentralize and deputize more and more work. This inevitably leaves one with the feeling that his total grasp of affairs is becoming less and less and I am afraid this is so.

I have been making a conscious effort to move around this province ... I have been in Windsor, Sarnia, Brantford, St. Catharines, Brampton, Kingston, Ottawa, Whitby – not to mention London plus a whole host of meetings in and around the Metro Toronto area in the last two months. Frankly, it is a type of politicking I enjoy.[1]

In these travels, in his dinner parties, in drinking and relaxing with friends, Robarts seemed to be reaching back to a more traditional kind of politics, the style that he had grown up in and been familiar with (though not always at ease with on formal occasions in the earlier years). When the pressures mounted on his office staff, for example, Robarts would throw a party for them at the Westbury Hotel. Those of his staff who saw the premier sitting with his feet up in his office at the end of a day's work, tying a fishing fly, chatting amiably, were struck by the contrast between this warm man and the public's image of an aloof executive. Bill Rathbun, who worked in the office for many years, reminisced about Robarts' style:

We all took turns on House duty ... He always used to have a staff officer sitting in the Legislature behind the throne when the House was in Session, particularly at nights when he would be out on speeches and so on. He would want to phone back in and say, 'What's going on? What's the progress? Should I drop in?' ... and if he came in he would come over and sit down and say, 'What's been going on? Just give me a quick run through.' ... It was a staff job ... and we all shared it – and it was a unique experience for many people because ... from time to time we had a seconded person from another ministry in for a couple of weeks just getting a feel for what goes on in the Prime Minister's office, ... part of a staff development program, and when we had anyone in on that basis we treated them as a full time staff member and they just went on the roster and some of them ended up having a two-hour chat in his office at 10.00 p.m. just as he put things away and said, 'Let's talk about fishing. Did I ever tell you about that fishing trip on the Sutton?' ... You would be amazed. This man that they had this image of – the Chairman of the Board, cool and aloof – and suddenly he's just a buddy telling them stories and they came away with them.[2]

The sadder, more personal side of this life was Robarts' need for people to be with now that London and his marriage had slid away from being the counterbalance to his political life. Fear and distrust had led Norah to the bottle. John was not much better. The tensions and recriminations at home kept Robarts in his Toronto milieu. Like many Canadian politicians of the seventies and eighties, Robarts was beginning to submerge himself in the political world, making it and its people the centre of both his business and his social life. He still saw a lot of Tim and Robin on weekends, though now often in Toronto; and he got away from the office on occasional fishing trips, often to Polar Bear Provincial Park with Keith Reynolds and Peter Betts. Sometimes on these trips he appeared to be at peace with himself. To other friends who saw him frequently in Toronto he seemed less in charge of his soul during off hours, more dependent on stimulants of one kind or another, ranging from alcohol through the wine of flattery and flirtation. Since 1967 his health had slowly deteriorating as he put on weight – reaching a peak at about 240 pounds – and began to have blood pressure problems. His earlier knee injuries now made walking often painful.

Robarts sometimes made his difficulties worse by refusing to admit that anything was wrong. Early in 1969, for example, he slipped and hurt an ankle. Six weeks, a trip to Europe, and a federal-provincial conference later, Robarts hobbled into a doctor's office and came out with his broken ankle in a cast.

Even in a cast John Robarts still looked like the imperturbable man in charge of Ontario. There were no cracks in his public image, which polls suggested was his party's greatest asset. For insiders, however, there was a gradually developing sense that Robarts was out of control. The pace was grinding him down; as he recalled, even rushing down a hall to a meeting, people would be asking him to make decisions. There was no chance to reflect. It would soon be time for him to go. He knew it too, though sometimes he deluded himself with the thought that some kind of sabbatical would enable him to recuperate and stay on for new challenges.

Sabbatical or not, he was not going to go quite yet. In October 1969 Robarts had a cartilage operation to clear up his knee problem. By December he was free from pain and beginning to feel fit again. He was in a mood to take charge of events, fight back from the disappointments of the preceding spring and summer, and set Ontario's political agenda for the next year. Then, sometime in 1970, he would step aside and pass the torch to one of the bright young men he had brought into his cabinet.

There had been a fair bit of complaining among Conservatives that fall and it was not limited to the youth. Fred Gardiner wrote Leslie Frost:

Something is sadly lacking in the organization of the Conservative Party as I visualize it today. It may be that the Party has been in power for so long that they have become complacent about the present situation ... There were those at one time who thought you moved too slowly but your underlying theory was correct that it takes time for the public generally to accept change and if you endeavour to do it too quickly you will create opposition which may be fatal to what otherwise are in the long run safe and sound solutions to the problems which face us.[3]

Meeting soon after the Middlesex South by-election defeat in September, members of caucus had grumbled about tax reform, county school boards, the medicare premiums, and poor communications within the government. Early in December the annual meeting of the Ontario PC Association was treated to policy discussions in which medicare premiums were again attacked and, much to the delight of the press, Robarts and his minister of health, Tom Wells, were caught offering different explanations of the government's reasons for covering only 90 per cent of the scheduled cost of medical fees. In a kind of choral background to Conservative laments, ten thousand union members and farmers marched on Queen's Park the next morning to protest the medicare premiums.

Robarts would have none of it. In his speech to the PC convention he scolded the delegates for their pessimism and urged members of his party to be active building things rather than destroying them. 'And if we have to march, let's march *for* something, not against something.' The veteran prime minister refused to go over to the defensive: 'I offer no apologies for what we have done, what we are doing, or what we plan to do in the future.'[4]

Robarts supported a number of innovations the new executive had made in the past year. A full-time party director had been appointed, a regional headquarters opened in Windsor, and the Toronto headquarters staff reorganized. At this 1969 meeting Ontario Conservatives agreed to a series of constitutional changes, which included reducing the size of the executive, the creation of a Women's PC Association, the designation of positions for youth on the executive, and provision for the executive to call a leadership convention should the party lose an election. While there was a certain amount of inevitable speculation that the leadership convention proviso signified lack of confidence in Robarts (Alan Eagleson denied this, saying it was just a reflection of similar procedures in other parties), most observers thought the prime minister was easily the paramount figure in the party, however troubled it might be.

Robarts went directly to a constitutional conference in Ottawa, having ended any speculation about Ontario's basic stance by once again attacking Ottawa in his closing speech to the PC meeting. He repeated his concern that Ottawa was preoccupied with Quebec and its problems at the expense of the rest of the country. Ontario did not support the proposals for tax reform outlined in a recent federal white paper responding to the Carter Commission, for they did not deal with the need for co-ordinated federal-provincial tax reform. The federal government, Robarts charged, was using the fiscal imbalance in the country to centralize power in Ottawa. He continued the attack before television cameras at the conference in Ottawa, insisting that the centralist designs of the federal government were preventing tax money from flowing to the provinces where they could be applied to relieve the hard-pressed municipal property taxpayer.[5] His arguments were welcome to at least some of those present: the municipal representatives he had invited to join the Ontario delegation. When Ottawa's conference ended, Robarts announced that Ontario would hold a provincial-municipal conference that spring 'in an attempt to find solutions to the rapidly worsening crisis in the cities.'[6]

Back in the legislature, Robarts was pleased to table the report of the royal commission investigating the collapse of Atlantic Acceptance, and to note that the investigation had so far led to twelve prosecutions and four convictions. So much for criticism that the government's belief in businesses being free to fail did not protect the rights of citizens. In this case the criminal law had done its job, and if that was not enough a massive legislative reform of the laws relating to corporations was already under way to implement the commission's recommendations and prevent repetition of these corporate disasters.

Robarts ended the long session on 17 December with a fighting, partisan speech in which he damned the opposition for sins past and raised the spectre of socialism as the damnation of the future. He labelled the provincial Liberal party's links with its federal counterpart a 'sellout,' while admitting that he had stolen some of their best ideas in the past and would do it again in the future. Tory MPPs were delighted to see their leader in an attacking mood. Robarts' liveliness and the mood of the House were reminiscent of the 'Done!' speech closing the 1963 session. Even Bob Nixon was reported to have enjoyed the show. After Robarts had finished and while they were waiting for the lieutenant-governor, Nixon crossed the floor and wished Robarts and MacNaughton a merry Christmas. The three MPPs relaxed in friendly conversation, ending the legislative history of the 1960s with a moment of the old fellowship.

The provincial Conservatives were heading into the new political era of the 1970s in fairly good organizational shape. Perhaps the most significant innovation during the Eagleson presidency of the party was the acceptance of professional polling to keep in touch with public opinion. The use of polls would increase. Two representatives of the younger element in the party, Eagleson and Wells, had now joined Goodman and Jackson in Robarts' political inner circle, interpreting the meaning of the polls and the state of the party. Robarts' success at bringing younger men into important political positions was one of the hallmarks of his last years of leadership. McKeough, Wells, and Robert Welch had all been given significant cabinet portfolios in 1967; Allan Lawrence had been brought in in February 1968, followed by George Kerr from Burlington and John White in 1969. In February 1970, a few days before the new session began, Bert Lawrence was appointed to succeed Leslie Rowntree as minister of financial and commercial affairs. 'A major cabinet reconstruction has sneaked up on Queen's Park – almost unnoticed,' Eric Dowd of the Toronto *Telegram* wrote:

The cumulative effect already is that Mr. Robarts has now gradually built a Cabinet whose able, mostly young men ... far outshine any comparably sized group on either of the opposition party benches. It has all been so unspectacular and piecemeal that the opposition parties were just beginning to realize yesterday that the Premier, whatever his policy problems, already has a team that would sound well on the hustings.[7]

There was a new tone to the Speech from the Throne at the 24 February 1970 convening of the assembly. The old issues of federal-provincial relations, regional government, and tax reform were hardly mentioned, as the government became much more general and futuristic in describing its intentions. Emphasis was placed on providing a high quality of life for future generations and particularly on the need to preserve the environment. The basic reform programs would be carried on at a slower pace and within the limits of expenditure restraint, for financial responsibility would continue to be a high priority of the Conservative government for

Ontario. Of course the opposition criticized the speech for its vagueness. Robarts agreed, and promised policy statements on specific topics during the session.

Debate was joined almost immediately on Ontario's reaction to the federal government's white paper on taxation. Party president Eagleson had given a blunt speech suggesting that Ontario might enjoy holding an election with the white paper proposals as the central issue. Robarts dismissed the matter as a case of Eagleson speaking for himself, but in fact Ontario's disapproval of federal plans for tax reform would continue to be a source of constant tension for the rest of Robarts' premiership. Using their new computers, Ontario's tax experts were strenuously arguing that Ottawa's proposed tax changes were designed to give it permanently higher revenues. The provinces would suffer. Needless to say, the federal computers came out with different projections.

There was considerable dissatisfaction even among his own caucus during the session with Robarts' insistence on adhering to the government's expenditure ceilings. His and MacNaughton's projections of an imminent 'fiscal nightmare' for Ontario had not materialized, and a number of ministers and members of caucus were more ready than Robarts to see spending increased in response to public pressure. The tension erupted openly on 9 April when a Conservative backbencher, Dr Richard Potter, in a speech to the Associated Nursing Homes of Metropolitan Toronto, made clear his dissatisfaction with the level of government support for nursing homes. Potter charged that his government had become an 'unapproachable, indifferent oligarchy – a clique – that is not listening to its own members in the legislature.'[8] This was a rare surfacing of that undercurrent of resentment that Robarts was out of touch and too dependent on his small circle of London friends.

The communications experts in the government were trying to make sure that he was in touch. Bill Kinmond, who had left the Prime Minister's Office to become Queen's Printer, was busy publishing the first annual index of government services and opening an Ontario Government bookstore. His successor as press secretary, Bill Rathbun, was doing all he could to improve Robarts' relations with the media. It was an uphill battle to persuade the premier that he should do something for the press similar to Donald MacDonald's annual 'bean feed and card party' or Nixon's annual 'apple pie feed' at his farm, for Robarts much preferred seeing small groups of friends to performing at large gatherings of critical or neutral political observers. He had not hosted a function for the press since the liquid party at his home during the 1967 election, and was happy to use media guilt about feeding at the public trough as an excuse not to bother. Rathbun finally convinced him that a private dinner party for the news media, paid for by the party, would be both acceptable and politically astute. It was held at the McMichael Gallery in Kleinburg on 10 June, and for many in the press gallery was the first opportunity they had had to talk informally with the premier.

Fences were also being mended with the municipalities. Robarts' earlier announcement of a provincial-municipal conference had grown out of discussions following the presentation to the government of the annual brief of the Ontario Association of Mayors and Reeves. The other municipal associations in the province had agreed to participate and a joint planning committee had organized the conference, to be held late in April at the new Ontario Science Centre in Toronto. The agenda did not permit direct debate between provincial and municipal spokesmen, but the conference seemed to be a success and led to the creation of a small provincial-municipal committee for further consultation. This group became known as the Provincial-Municipal Liaison Committee, and Robarts agreed that the government would review tax and municipal reform proposals with it before they were implemented. With the municipal associations working toward a common position on issues through their own liaison committee, an institutional-ization of provincial-municipal relations was taking place which, if it worked properly, might minimize political friction between the senior and junior governments. It helped, too, that no new regional government initiatives were imminent. Problems were beginning to well up, however, about the planned future of the Toronto megalopolis.

Generally it seemed that much had been done to put out the brushfires of criticism ignited by the 1969 reform program. There were better relations with the media and the municipalities; there was Lawrence's new approach to northern problems; there were improved procedures in the legislature and in the Prime Minister's Office. The party's polls showed that public reaction to the education, tax, and regional government innovations was beginning to subside, though the concern was still there. If Robarts retired in the spring of 1970, his successor would inherit the new evolutionary form of the reform program and would have the opportunity to respond to the issues that were concerning the urban electorate. Robarts was musing about retiring. He had served almost nine of his ten years, and some of his closest associates felt this might have been the time. As John White later recalled, for example: 'I certainly thought that he should not run again and in fact I thought that he should have retired some months before he did if he was going to retire. I think John could have won another election. But he was really tired out frankly, and I thought he should give the new fellow a good clear year.'[9]

Robarts decided to stay on a bit longer. He monitored the fading public reaction to his reform program and felt he might ride out the storms for a while longer. With a less volatile reaction, his successor could plumb public attitudes more easily. His reflection ended when he learned that Stephen Lewis had launched his campaign to become leader of the NDP. Then, it seemed prudent to sit back and watch how this opposition party's affairs developed. Certainly, too, there was no shortage of pressing business that spring. Just when the municipal and educational situations seemed to have settled down, the new municipal tax bills came in. In many areas there were big increases, creating another round of protest against increasing education costs and the effect of market value reassessment. Farmers were particularly upset; several of their organizations, supported by Bob Nixon, urged a partial withholding of property taxes. They were not finally pacified until the government brought in a major program of tax adjustment and subsidies that fall. These included a direct payment to farm owners of 25 per cent of their property taxes (speculators would not be eligible), a $50 tax rebate to Ontario pensioners receiving the federal income supplement, increased education grants, and provision to ensure that reassessment did not increase the tax burden on residential property. With these changes the government finally parried much of the thrust of rural Ontario's protest against its reforms. In doing so it reduced the Liberals' ability to feed on the discontents of their traditional rural constituency. The one particularly 'Liberal' issue still simmering on a side burner was the question of public support for Roman Catholic secondary schools.

But then there were all the new issues, now centring in urban Ontario and being exploited with increasing effectiveness by the NDP. Concerns about unemployment and pollution control escalated suddenly and dramatically in the spring of 1970. In a climate of intense and rising Canadian nationalism, they came together in opposition to the activities of the multinational corporation, usually American-owned, in the province. These were the new challenges of the 1970s, and the Robarts government, particularly the premier, had very mixed feelings about how to deal with them.

Unemployment was starting to become a problem in the spring of 1970. The federal government was applying Keynesian brakes to an economy which had been running at full speed for several years and was now generating a troublesomely high rate of inflation. But dampening down inflation at a time when the baby boomers were still pouring onto the labour market combined to precipitate a dramatic increase in the numbers of job seekers. By April the unemployment rate exceeded 10 per cent of the labour force in Cornwall and 6 per cent in Niagara Falls, Orillia, Owen Sound, Brantford, London, and Chatham. The existing job creation and other stimulus programs of the provincial government were unable to stop the increase. Robarts and his ministers tried to throw the blame on Ottawa, attacking its restraint policies and its rigidity on tax questions, but made little headway in their dealings with the federal government or in the estimation of a public which expected *every* level of government to do something about unemployment.

The issue began to focus on specific plant closings, particularly the decision of the Dunlop Rubber Company to close its Toronto factory, a shutdown which would throw some six hundred people out of work. The plant was in James Renwick's riding. He demanded that the Ontario government intervene somehow to stop the shutdown. Addressing the legislature on the issue early in March, Robarts bluntly and as a matter of principle refused to intervene:

We do not think it is the function of this government, nor do we think that it is in the best interests of the economy of this province and the development of job opportunities for our people, that we should say to any company that it can or cannot locate or operate in any area it wishes in the province. Nor are we in any position to tell a company that decides that it is uneconomic for it to operate any unit of its operation in this province that it shall continue to operate. Now that is the policy and position of this government as clearly as I can put it, and as I have put it many times before.

When Donald MacDonald pressed him further, Robarts went on:

The basic policy of the government in relation to economic development in the province has been that we provide those things that are best provided by government. Decisions as to what individual businesses are to do are left to them and we are firmly convinced, and always have been, that the fastest way to cut off all economic development in this province would be for the government to attempt to find some means of saying to businesses: 'Thou shalt do this and thou shalt not do that'; and so on.[10]

But the debate did not end, particularly after it was learned that the failure of Ontario Hydro to renew a contract with Dunlop had been one of the events precipitating the plant's closing. Two hundred workers dramatized the fact by picketing Ontario Hydro's head office and then marching to Queen's Park. The premier bent a little in addressing the group, saying he would require firms to notify the government if they intended to close. The Dunlop issue did not recede for several months, with pickets and demonstrators appearing at several political functions to publicize their case. There followed other plant shutdowns. In the legislature Stephen Lewis produced alarming statistics on jobs disappearing almost by the hour in lay-offs and closures, helping create a sense of a provincial economy collapsing. What would the government do about it?

It kept urging those concerned about unemployment to protest to the federal government, whose policies were mostly responsible for the problem. The Ontario government would give priority to industrial retraining, Robarts announced, and of course it backed the efforts of Stanley Randall's Department of Trade and Development to attract industry to Ontario. But politicians could not get into the habit of subsidizing failing or crisis-ridden firms, Robarts reiterated, without opening the floodgates and undermining the free enterprise system. Government could not get into the business of compensating for poor management or artificially maintaining whole industries. It certainly could not urge industries to locate in a province and then deny them the freedom to reduce their work force or close plants. Closures and lay-offs, the premier argued, 'are just cases of management exercising its powers in order to meet the conditions which it is facing. It is very difficult to have foreknowledge of all these matters because they occur, as far as many businesses are concerned, in the normal operation of businesses. Their labour force flows up and down.'[11]

Ontario's environmental protectors also found a specific and highly emotional issue that spring when mercury levels found in fish caught in Ontario caused cramps of public alarm about a major recreational and commercial industry. The federal government banned fishing in Lake St Clair because of the pollution, and the minister of energy and resource management, George Kerr, ordered a number of industrial plants to stop using or discharging mercury. In the legislature Donald MacDonald repeated allegations which had reached him that the Dow Chemical Company had deliberately dumped mercury into Ontario waters at Sarnia after it had been told to stop by the province. Dow, of course, was already a symbol of corporate sin to many of the young because its American parent produced napalm for use in Vietnam. An investigation eventually disproved the charges against Dow, showing the mercury spill was accidental.

The problems of the Lake St Clair fish increased alarm about the much more important Lake Erie fishery, which was undergoing severe economic difficulty. What would governments do to help the fishermen? The Ontario politicians decided to have a fish fry at Queen's Park to reassure potential consumers. MPPs, senior public servants, and members of the press gallery were invited, and major newspapers in the province carried pictures of Robarts and his cabinet colleagues duly eating Lake Erie fish. It was not entirely clear which were the poor fish, however, for the federal government seemed to be willing to go much further than Robarts' men by offering direct financial assistance to the troubled fishermen. This was another case of Robarts being unwilling to see the state get involved in subsidizing an industry to meet a short-term crisis or public misperception.

In a number of speeches that spring Robarts wrestled with the difficult trade-offs between development and the environment, the desirability of economic freedom and the need for controls. On 9 April, for example, he told the Empire Club in Toronto that

only through government action can we deal with many of the extremely large problems which face people today ... We shall have to become accustomed to the idea that there will be controls on our activities. We will not be as free to do as we please with our countryside ... There will be greater control on the use of land ... The people of Ontario will have to submerge immediate, short term interest in favour of those of their grandchildren.[12]

And later that month, addressing the provincial-municipal conference, he was more precise:

While I do not personally relish the idea, I am convinced that we – and by we I mean both the province and the municipalities – must institute very firm controls on some areas of Ontario. Governments may have to forbid certain types of development to prevent pollution, the destruction of the natural beauty of our countryside or the loss of the unique landmarks. Industries may not always be able to establish on locations of their choice.

Housing developments may be prohibited in some areas. There will be stricter controls on economic development. At the same time we must ensure that no municipality will be crippled financially as a result of these restrictions.[13]

Here were the dilemmas facing politicians struggling to find the limits of government's role in a modern economy. Compare these views with Robarts' reluctance to act on the Dunlop closing only a few weeks earlier. In that case a company could not be told for economic reasons where it could locate. But now it could for environmental reasons. On the other hand, as Robarts was maintaining in debates about pollution control legislation, there had to be reasonable limits on pollution control requirements so as not to force companies to shut down and add to the unemployment problem. The premier was personally uncomfortable with the fine shades of these distinctions, and at bottom was becoming deeply concerned about the way in which the modern state was encroaching upon the individual and liberty. In a reflective commencement address at Osgoode Hall that troubled spring, Robarts revealed his conservative concerns:

The increasing demands on the state ... is a development which bothers me greatly ... The biggest challenge we face and which increasingly will be your responsibility as you pursue your law careers is, what are we going to do for individuals in this increasingly state-organized society? ... Every time government regulates some activity it is intruding upon the freedom of action of the individual ... Inch by inch, individual freedoms are being eroded by the constant demands that the government should do something.[14]

Dunlop Rubber, Dow Chemical, and many of the companies that were laying off workers in Ontario were foreign-owned, as were a large number of all the companies in Ontario. The NDP and other critics gradually zeroed in on foreign-owned multinationals as their villains, the causes of both pollution and unemployment, who were being toadied to by the Ontario government in its simplistic policies of attracting industry and investment to the province. Canadians' nationalist fever seemed to be mounting monthly through 1970 as fears about oil companies in the Arctic mingled with perceptions that Canadian culture was being threatened by imported publishers and professors. A self-appointed, Toronto-based Committee for an Independent Canada sprang into existence to ring the alarm bells about the American menace. Suddenly it seemed vitally important to get Canada back from the Americans, and there were many nationalist voices urging tough government action to do it. All three political parties in Ontario gradually became influenced by nationalist sentiments, though on most issues, including pollution and plant closings, it was the NDP that tried to wave the flag most vigorously.

Just as Robarts had never felt the need to defend his patriotism (except, perhaps, when he was accused of provincialism in some of his more bitter squabbles with

Ottawa), now he saw little need to worry about American influence in Canada. Commenting on the issue some years later, he set out what had always been a consistent, common-sense, and very Ontarian position:

I think we've got a strong dominant Canadian personality that isn't going to be altered ... by either the influx here of money or economic and commercial know-how from other countries. That's the reason I don't get fussed up about this problem. At the moment, quite frankly, we are a very appealing place for people from many, many parts of the world ... I think we're very distinctive; I think we're very powerful in our own right ... I've got many, many friends in the United States but they're not taking me over. In the first place they don't want to, and in the second place, I can turn off the television set if it's a great flow of American stuff I'm not interested in ... How many Canadians do you know that want to become Americans? – that are affected by the American capital in this country? I think a lot of them earn a damn good living and are good Canadians working in plants that are there because American capital put them there. Now, what are you going to do? Close those people out? Throw our own people out of work? I don't think management, because the plant happens to be financed from the United States, are trying to brainwash the employees and trying to make Americans out of them. I mean there's something very foolish about this whole argument. It doesn't take into consideration what is the true strength of the Canadian people and that is that we are Canadian people and are not going to change.[15]

Robarts' views were no longer universally held within his party. But he was not nearly as hampered by dissidence as his NDP counterpart, the other long-established provincial leader. By the spring of 1970 it was clear that the gap between Donald MacDonald's moderate democratic socialism and the more activist, nationalist, and radical views of his young turks, personified by Stephen Lewis, was a serious threat to NDP unity. Rather than take the gloves off with his opponents, whom he probably could have beaten, MacDonald decided it was time to go gracefully and announced his resignation in June, paving the way for a leadership convention at which he would not be a candidate.

The NDP leadership fight was between the aggressive, fashionably radical idealism of Stephen Lewis, the son of David Lewis, and the moderate pragmatism of Walter Pitman, who had served as a federal MP before being elected to the Ontario legislature in 1967. Lewis eschewed the quasi-revolutionary orthodoxies of the new nationalist left, as represented by the 'Waffle' faction in the NDP, but his victory over Pitman in the 4 October voting seemed to signal a swing to the political left by the party. The NDP's support for abortion on demand and the nationalization of the energy resources industry, as well as NDPers' constant attacks on American economic imperialism, suggested that the party was about to impose its reality on pragmatic Ontario (except for the unpredictable Morton Shulman, who had neutered himself with charges, subsequently refuted by Mr Justice Campbell Grant, about mafia contacts with the OPP and even a mafia 'contract' being out on Shulman himself). Robarts' worries about the NDP's challenges to his party's handling of economic and environmental issues were eased by the socialists' more aggressive stance. He knew it would not gain the NDP the votes it had to have from the mass of moderate Ontarians.

In the meantime Robarts was facing political fallout from hard choices on fundamental planning issues. On 5 May 1970 the government's determination to deliberately plan the future course of the development of the province reached a culmination at a ceremony attended by more than one thousand municipal representatives where, to the tune of 'A Place to Stand,' Robarts, MacNaughton, and McKeough released the Toronto-Centred Region Plan. Robarts described the document as 'the first broad brush strokes of a regional development policy for the dynamic heart of Ontario.' It considered the future of the entire area within a ninety-mile arc of the centre of Toronto. The plan defined transportation corridors, growth points, green belts, and the future of urban communities for Metropolitan Toronto and a large number of surrounding townships, counties, villages, towns, and cities. Its basic thrust was to encourage growth north and east of Toronto so as to protect the rich farmland of southwestern Ontario. Robarts and his ministers made clear that the planning process involved the imposition of new restrictions on municipal and industrial decision-makers. They urged municipalities to proceed to develop their own plans within the province's plan. Darcy McKeough announced that applications for boundary and zoning changes, which had been held up by his department pending the release of the plan, would be reviewed to make sure the proposals conformed with it. As well, the government invited the public to comment on the plan.

The subsequent reaction illustrated most of the difficulties involved in serious government planning. The Toronto-Centred Region Plan, which had been developed within the Department of Treasury and Economics, crossed the boundaries of five of the ten economic regions of the province. Members of the regional development councils felt their own planning had been in vain and became increasingly outspoken in their reaction against the plan. Municipalities which already had official plans in place found they would have to redo them. There were a host of specific problems. For years developers and speculators had been laying their own plans for future growth in and around Toronto, some of them based on projections contained in earlier official studies and proposals. Now many of the schemes would be frustrated and land values and investments seriously disrupted. Northeast of Toronto, for example, developers had acquired a large parcel of land to build a proposed 'Century City' and seemed to have had government approval in principle for their project. Now it turned out that it would be located in territory reserved for a green belt. Richard Rohmer was the lawyer representing the developers. When reporters asked McKeough if Century City could proceed, he replied 'No way.'[16]

Did that kind of tough statement, and similar comments by Ian Macdonald, mean that the plan was already established as government policy? If so, even the Town Planning Institute of Canada was upset, for it would cause too much disruption. For Chinguacousy Township, for example, the plan set a maximum population target of 250,000 people; but the township had already planned for a population of 560,000 and the Ontario Water Resources Commission had agreed to develop the services necessary to support that population. Then there was the plan's total omission of the airport question. The federal government was proposing to construct a second international airport in the Toronto area. Intense discussions with the province were in progress and their results would have enormous transportation and development implications. And what was going to happen about the proposed Spadina expressway into downtown Toronto, about which a number of vocal community leaders were beginning to agitate?

The trouble with planning was that it led to the politicization of a host of new issues relating to land use and development. Often they were issues in which the interests of developers and those interested in the environment or community stability could not be resolved without a clear loser. In an older, freer society, the market would dictate choices and the resentments of the losers tended to dissipate for lack of a target. Now that planners tried to dictate choices, politicians would be the target of the resentments. In any given debate – over zoning, the Spadina expressway, the location of a Toronto airport, the preservation of the Niagara escarpment – the losers would charge that the government was acting for political reasons, that unprincipled politicians were courting votes or courting campaign funds or both. The flood of briefs reaching the government complaining about the Toronto plan was a preview of an intense debate on planning and development issues that would characterize the early 1970s. In these early discussions Robarts continued to try to explain the absolute necessity for finding a compromise between the controls of planning and the need for freedom and growth.

Leadership on specific issues seemed to be increasingly assumed by Robarts' potential successors in that summer and fall of 1970. Bert Lawrence in Financial and Commercial Affairs had taken the whole realm of corporate affairs in hand, sponsoring important new legislation; he had held a highly visible interprovincial conference on consumer protection that summer, and was becoming a champion of economic nationalism. Allan Lawrence was holding his northern development conferences. Darcy McKeough went to the provincial premiers' conference as Ontario's representative in August 1970. Early in October, with Robarts attending the funeral of the Rt Rev. George Luxton, the Anglican bishop for Huron, in London, Robert Welch, the Conservative House leader, delivered what became known as a 'mini-Throne Speech' on his behalf, outlining the government's response to the property tax difficulties. The new ministers were doing their job and doing it well.

Now that Donald MacDonald had turned his party over to a younger man, Robarts was by many years the oldest leader in the legislature. The Liberal and NDP leaders who had opposed him were all gone. So were those who had contested his bid for the Progressive-Conservative leadership in 1961. John Robarts attended another funeral in October when Kelso Roberts, who had finished second in that race, died after a two-year battle with cancer. The tributes to Roberts in the assembly, stressing his warmth and friendliness toward all members of the legislature, harked back to the days of a Queen's Park community that was passing into history.

'I'm a Has-been'

Violence rocked the Canadian political scene in 1970 when a gang of separatist terrorists kidnapped the British trade commissioner James Cross in Montreal on 5 October, the day before the Ontario legislature opened for a new session, and then Quebec's minister of labour, Pierre Laporte, on 10 October. Within a few days armed soldiers were in the streets of Quebec City, Montreal, and Ottawa, providing security to men and women whose physical safety was imperilled by their having chosen to serve their country in elected office. In Toronto John Robarts' staff insisted that the crisis required better security for the Ontario prime minister and, over Robarts' objections, provided him with a bodyguard. The protector dressed in civilian clothes and masqueraded as a regular staff member.

The occasional crank threats on his life that Robarts had been receiving since 1968 had been ignored. Observing some of the extreme security measures taken to protect American politicians, Robarts had often reflected on the more civilized mood of politics in Canada.[1] Now the idea that physical protection was needed for politicians in a free society cut him to the core. Nor did he believe that the law-breaking was just an isolated case of Quebec's special problems. On 14 October 1970 Queen's Park witnessed its largest demonstration in twenty-five years as organized labour staged a mammoth rally against the government's labour legislation. Outside the legislature after the demonstration Robarts was asked for his views on the Quebec kidnappings. He pulled no punches:

The kidnappings were unfortunate. We fought a war 25 years ago over matters of this sort ... The time has come to stand and fight ... We have overlooked the fact that the large group has rights ... The majority rules.

The law is being broken all the time in these demonstrations ... Police are being hampered and turned into bad guys and that's not right. We've allowed some of our beliefs and institutions to come under attack and now we're paying for it.[2]

Robarts' comments received wide coverage, both inside and outside of Quebec.

His tough attitude anticipated the Trudeau government's firmness in invoking the War Measures Act two days later, shortly before the kidnappers murdered Pierre Laporte. There was negative reaction to Robarts' views from some of those Quebeckers,[3] like Claude Ryan, who favoured conciliating the terrorists. Robarts stood firm, explaining to his legislature that the War Measures Act applied across the country and that he supported it: 'Mr. Speaker, I would simply say that I have a good deal of confidence in the federal government ... and I am quite convinced in my mind that they are not going to abuse the powers that have been given to them by this order in council. I have confidence in their judgment that they considered it necessary or they would not have done it.'

To most members, who loudly thumped their desks in approval, the premier was speaking for decency and order. 'We feel the federal government must do what it needs to do, as must we,' he replied to questioning, 'to ensure that we do maintain our democratic process in this country and we are not ruled by blackmail, and we are not intimidated by terrorization, kidnappings and threats of personal violence to any individuals.'[4] There were scattered demonstrations in Ontario for and against the use of the War Measures Act, but there were none of the abuses of its powers that took place as part of the rooting out of the terrorists in Quebec. An overwhelming majority of Ontarians supported the premier during the October crisis. By mid November he had received 130 letters supporting his stand, four opposing it.

The most volatile issues in Ontario's legislative session that autumn had to do with economic and cultural nationalism, as the NDP sprang to the attack under Stephen Lewis. Robarts had anticipated the new militancy by announcing that his party had shifted its emphasis from promoting increased material production to 'the problems that grow out of materialism – such as pollution, urban crowding and recreation needs.'[5] Some of his ministers, notably Allan Lawrence and William Davis, went considerably further than Robarts in voicing their support for the new nationalist movement. A minor crisis arose that November when an historic Canadian publishing house, the Ryerson Press, was bought by a big American publisher, McGraw-Hill, fanning rumours of more publishing take-overs to come and predictions of the imminent demise of outlets for Canadian writing. Pressure on the government to stop the Ryerson takeover led to a meeting of the premier with the parties involved, but no action. Within a few more weeks, however, pressure from the advocates of Canadian nationalism within the cabinet led to the appointment of a provincial Royal Commission on the Book Publishing Industry. In a plan reminiscent of Frost when he was dealing with his back-benchers in 1955, Robarts asked his friend Richard Rohmer to lead the inquiry. Robarts no longer followed his custom of listening to others, evaluating evidence and setting a course as he had in earlier days. Urged by his friends, he took a harsh position in defence of international flows of capital and against extreme forms of economic nationalism.[6] Publicly, his position contrasted with that of the NDP. In his concluding speech of the session he started with the need to create jobs in Ontario:

We not only have to create enough new jobs to soak up the unemployment; we also have to create enough new jobs to provide meaningful jobs, for the young people for instance who are coming out of our educational system and for people who move into this province from other parts of Canada ... This is an argument and a point of view that should be borne in mind when we start carping about whatever capital it may be that comes into this country to create these jobs in secondary industry ... We do not care, as a government, whether this money comes from the United States, from France, from England, from Germany; we need it here, and we need it to create jobs in this province. That is why our trade missions cover the whole world. In fact we send more trade missions to other parts of the world than we do to the United States. We are not in any way desirous of having American domination of industry in this province. On the other hand, unless the Canadian people can out of their own pockets and their own savings produce the capital to provide these jobs, the jobs are not going to be there.

I just point out to the members opposite, when they start to speak in a theoretical area of keeping the branch plants out of Ontario ... they should relate that to the jobs that will not be there if this does not happen.[7]

Robarts continued to address this theme in his speeches, trying to explain how demands for restrictions on capital, development, land use, and other economic movements had to be balanced against the need for freedom and growth.

He was not having a great impact. The Ontario political arena continued to be swept by gusts of intense public interest on specific issues, the Spadina Expressway, the Niagara escarpment, the location of a new Toronto airport; if one took hold, the subsequent political storm blew masses of demonstrators onto the grounds at Queen's Park. Even the separate school supporters joined the deluge, as some seventeen thousand of them confronted William Davis in Maple Leaf Gardens on 25 October to demand public funding through grade thirteen. Robarts' reflective speeches about finding the appropriate public-private balance in long-term policy were drowned by the political squalls, just as his government's long-term reform programs were being misunderstood and often abandoned, sometimes by ministers within his own cabinet. The government was being judged almost solely on its short-term response to issues, in a divided polity, without substantial public support for or awareness of its goals. As the political buffeting continued, it became increasingly important to prepare the party for the next election, which most observers expected in 1971. Robarts was still the most popular leader in Ontario. He had entered the political fray in opposition to the economic nationalism and more extreme environmental positions of the NDP. The Liberal platform and moderate environmental programs had been incorporated into the Conservative program with the exception of separate schools. As a visible, if tired, leader, he could draw the fire of critics as his potential successors campaigned for public support. In October he asked Jackson and Goodman to book Maple Leaf Gardens for a leadership convention.

An era in the history of London's politics was also passing. John Robarts' generation had held political power in the city for twenty years, the same twenty years in which they became the area's – and for those who had moved on with Robarts, the province's – establishment. Throughout the period London and its region had flourished, and continued to expand in ways that gradually undercut the Robarts Tories' own political base. In 1961 London's population had leaped from 103,000 to 166,000 when the city annexed its surrounding suburbs. By 1967 the population had reached 200,000 and was continuing to grow. Many of the new residents had not been raised in London, and they lived and worked outside the network of companies and families which had been the basis of the old London community. The establishment was still there in London, but the city was far less monolithic, and in a general way 'establishments' – the powerful – were everywhere accorded less respect and deference than a generation earlier.

The population shifts were reflected in the redistributions establishing new constituency boundaries in time for the 1967 provincial and 1968 federal elections. At the provincial level, London North and London South saw their boundaries shifted north and west. Federally, the London constituency was divided into London East and London West. The London Progressive-Conservative Association, Robarts' vehicle for controlling both provincial and federal politics in the city, attempted to adjust to the changes by adding members from those portions of the two Middlesex ridings, now incorporated into the London ridings, and by creating a new zone system of organizing the constituencies now that they no longer coincided with ward boundaries. The changes, however, were the excuse for a number of old party workers to retire to the sidelines. London North and London South had gone their own ways in the 1967 provincial election, as John White had faced an all-out fight and won it, while Robarts took his riding more or less for granted and saw his majority slip. In 1968, London East witnessed the first contested Conservative nomination in the city since 1953 when Gordon Walker, who was supported by John White and many of the young PCs, took on the old guard's candidate, a local contractor and developer, Don Matthews. Matthews won the nomination, and then the London Conservatives lost both seats to the Liberals in the Trudeaumania of that election, their first setback in seventeen years.

Robarts gradually transferred responsibility for his constituency to a younger generation. After the 1967 election he employed a full-time constituency assistant, Don Martyn, to assist him with his political affairs in Toronto and London. By the summer of 1969 Martyn and Fred Jenkins' son, Bill, were working to revitalize London North, while John White and his supporters had their own organization in place in London South. There was a separate organization in London East and none at all in London West, and it was not clear what would be done about the old London PC Association. After considerable discussion, in which Robarts was actively involved, it finally received a new constitution in the autumn of 1969, one which recognized the plurality of riding associations in London and also made room for student PCs at Western and young PCs within the city.

Robarts hoped he could pass the London organization to the younger generation just as he was passing on his government. It was not so easy on the local scene. The four ridings had a tendency to go their own way. John White's London South group was an elected association and was interested in greater riding autonomy. Jenkins in London North was geared to fighting elections, and was interested in greater financial autonomy from the central association. Don Matthews developed a London East association which reflected the local ethnic mosaic and was said to be closer to a mini-United Nations in structure than any of the other organizations. Because there was still no organization in London West, the central executive was able to maintain control of the division of money as between federal or provincial activities.

Except for Robarts and his personal prominence, the central cohesiveness of the organization was gone. The new people, including the teenagers and other young PCs, did not have the old ties and interests. To be sure, the influential organization from John Robarts' early days in London politics, ADSEPA, still existed. But it had aged along with its founders, and its meetings were held at the London Club where members attended in formal dress, enjoyed a formal dinner, and listened to an invited expert deliver a speech on a topic of current interest. Dinners and speakers and formal dress had interesting fundraising possibilities, which Robarts and his new generation of organizers in London North exploited by hosting a $100-a-plate 'Game Dinner' at the London Hunt Club that autumn. But then there was a falling out among the ridings on the division of the funds. And no amount of money could replace the waning political vitality of John Robarts and his generation.

One of Robarts' London friends, Colin Brown, a well-to-do agent for London Life, had more than a little of the old energy. One of his projects was to prod chambers of commerce into organizing an exchange program between London and Quebec City, in the hope of encouraging better national understanding. In 1969 a group of Quebeckers had spent a long weekend visiting London. The second half of Project Lonbec, as it was called, the return visit of Londoners to Quebec, was scheduled for the weekend of 4 December 1970. Robarts had provisionally agreed to take part in the exchange. He probably would not have let it interfere with his retirement planning, but the October crisis suddenly made the tour a symbol of the continued good relations between members of the French and English communities and convinced him to lead the group as Prime Minister of Ontario.

Rumours about Robarts' impending resignation swept Queen's Park during October and November, to be met by the usual coy evasions. Because his standing was so high in the province, higher than that of the other leaders or his party, caucus hoped he would lead them through another provincial election. So did many local Conservative organizers and workers. James Auld and Charles MacNaughton were delegated by caucus to try to persuade Robarts to stay. They could not persuade him. On 12 November MacNaughton added fuel to the speculation at a dinner in Centralia, when, with Robarts present, he referred to his premiership in the past tense.[8]

Robarts joined 150 Londoners for the trip to Quebec City the first weekend in December. During the visit, which he had to interrupt to fly to Lindsay for the funeral of Mrs Leslie Frost, Robarts spoke for national unity, understanding, and tolerance in what some reporters interpreted as a kind of personal summing up. Quebec's Premier Robert Bourassa described him as the English-Canadian leader who best understood Quebec.

At noon on Monday, 7 December, Robarts met with Bill Jenkins and his group of London North organizers at the Holiday Inn. He thanked them for their support in the past, urged them to continue their election planning, and told them he would shortly be announcing his retirement. Robarts then drove to Toronto, called his staff together for a group photograph in the prime minister's office, and told them he was about to retire. The next morning, 8 December, Robarts informed his cabinet and then went to the press conference and made his retirement public.

Robarts began his press conference by stating that he had written Alan Eagleson asking him to proceed with arrangements for a leadership convention. He then gave his reasons for stepping down:

To those who may wonder, as inevitably some people must, why I have chosen this particular time to step down, I can only say that my own personal political philosophy leads me to believe that in the very fast-moving times in which we live government policies and actions need to be continuously reviewed, revised and rethought. I have never believed that any one man or one group had a monopoly on ideas and I firmly believe it is necessary to provide opportunity for new approaches to be made available.

In his letter to Eagleson, he continued:

I have not arrived at the decision to step down ... easily. I am torn by my awareness of the great and loyal support which it has been my great privilege to enjoy during my time as Leader, and my own personal belief that the success of our Party depends on constant rejuvenation from within, and wide opportunity for the members of our Party to participate in the deliberations and responsibilities of governing.

It is over nineteen years since I was first elected ... They have been years of enormous growth and development in Ontario ... They have been filled with exciting activity. They have been years of great accomplishment ... I have received great support from my family and my decision to step down is, in part, influenced by the responsibilities I feel in that direction. May I say that in my view our Party is in good shape, filled with able people prepared and happy to give of themselves.[9]

Robarts announced that he would remain an MPP after stepping aside as premier, but would not seek re-election.

The resignation, which surprised no one, created a wave of eulogies from members of his party and highly flattering assessments from editorial writers. Both opposition leaders praised him, with Stephen Lewis commenting that Robarts probably would have liked to meet him on the hustings 'just to put this young punk in his place.' The Toronto *Star,* which had oscillated for years between its deep-seated Liberalism and its admiration for Robarts, best summed up the public's perception of him in concluding: 'He is a leader of such quality and strength that he will not be easily replaced. He is one of the rare provincial politicians in Canada's history who without ever reaching for federal office, attained the stature of a national statesman.' The newspaper suggested that Robarts be appointed to the Senate.[10]

Robarts left Toronto soon after his announcement for a few days of duck-hunting, but he could not stay away from some of the issues being raised by the way he had chosen to retire. Acting on his earlier request, Jackson and Goodman had gone ahead with the preliminary convention planning, and tentatively booked Maple Leaf Gardens for 10-12 February. They had also worked out a tentative organizational structure for the convention. When this was reported to the executive council of the Ontario PC Association, whose formal job it was to call and organize a convention, Eagleson and a number of other members of council were upset at what seemed like a usurpation of their responsibilities by members of Robarts' inner circle. Perhaps the disagreement would not have happened if Eagleson, who had been a member of Jackson and Goodman's informal committee, had attended its key meeting. But he had to be away on business in New York City that day.

The PC executive council accepted the proposed dates for the convention and took over the planning under Eagleson's supervision. They were not able to prevent rumours of differences between Jackson and the party executive reaching the press, in the form of reports that Jackson and Goodman had set up a private committee to plan the convention before Robarts even announced his resignation, and gossip about 'they' – Robarts' old gang – wanting to rig the convention. Robarts appeared himself at an executive council meeting to explain the situation, and make clear his position that the advance planning had been needed but now it was perfectly appropriate for the council to take over the work. The council was more or less mollified, changed the arrangements slightly to give Jackson less influence at the convention and papered over this last manifestation of the long, lingering resentment of the few sensitive Torontonians toward southwestern Ontario. To counter the rumours Eagleson told the press, 'The convention will be held in a totally democratic manner. Any suggestion that the committees are going to be structured to favour any particular candidate is totally erroneous. It may have appeared before that they were, but it was made clear today that that was not the intention.'[11]

Except for a few minor missteps, none of the ministers who hoped to succeed Robarts had jumped the gun of his resignation. William Davis, who everyone had expected to be the favourite, was the first to declare himself. Davis had so much support from the established powers in the party that stories of attempts to rig the convention got twisted into stories about the Londoners attempting to rig it for Davis so they could perpetuate their power. There was no truth in this. Davis' image as the chosen instrument was further strengthened when Charles Mac-Naughton, Robarts' closest lieutenant, agreed to become his campaign manager. In fact MacNaughton would have given at least tacit support to Darcy McKeough, the most likely successor to Robarts from among the southwesterners, had McKeough made up his mind to enter the race earlier.[12] It was not until the new year, several weeks after Robarts' announcement, that McKeough, Allan Lawrence, Bert Lawrence, and Robert Welch joined Davis in the race.

They criss-crossed the province in a series of all-candidates' meetings. Allan Lawrence soon emerged as the candidate most favoured by those who hoped to stop Bill Davis. Lawrence staked out territory as the enemy of the status quo in the party, pledging, for example, sharply to reduce the proportion of the provincial budget spent (by Davis' department) on education. He tried to mobilize the anti-Robarts 'restlessness' within the party, and to build on both the north's feelings of alienation and the similar sense that had been bothering many Tories in his native Toronto. One of his greatest strengths was the organizing support of Norman Atkins and others connected with the advertising firm of Camp Associates, which had come his way when the Davis group had, in a huge misunderstanding, appeared to reject their support.[13] The most fortunate all-candidates' meeting for Lawrence was the one scheduled for London, which was never held because a great snowstorm shut down all of southwestern Ontario that night. Lawrence had the good luck to be stranded at the same Highway 401 service centre as Robarts (who had been trying to get to London for a farewell dinner in his honour), and received province-wide press coverage of his joining the premier to lead a singsong for stranded travellers.[14] Of all the candidates only Bill Davis had reached London through all the obstacles. Rural Ontario itself was looming as an obstacle to Davis' leadership ambitions, though, as a poll by *Farm and Country* magazine put him on the bottom in respondents' estimation, Lawrence at the top. The anti-Davis whispering campaign was that he might be able to win the leadership but was too colourless, too quiet, to win an election.

Robarts stayed out of the leadership race, adopting a stance which has since become a norm for departing political leaders. He was not unhappy at the prospect of Davis succeeding him, but he and his friends were far less active than the Frost group had been on his behalf in 1961. Robarts had hoped there would be an array of good candidates fighting for his job and was proud of the way the contest developed, with five well-qualified younger men, all of whom he had brought into cabinet, going after the top job. The party seemed in better shape for a leadership transition in 1971 than it had been a decade earlier when he had won the prize after only a couple of years in cabinet. While the candidates went on with their campaigning, Robarts attended to routine housekeeping duties at Queen's Park; his appointment calendar was filled by receptions and farewell meetings with old friends. He stirred up a little political dust in February with some televised comments opposing support for separate high schools on the ground that it could lead to a 'frightful fragmentation of the school system in Ontario.' When he was asked about his disappointments in office, Robarts listed his failure to stop the federal medicare plan and his concern about the effect that the federal tax reform proposals would have on the Ontario economy.[15]

Just before the leadership convention, Robarts went to Ottawa for one last bout of conferencing, a federal-provincial working session on the constitution. He was in a mellow mood, giving cautious approval to federal position papers on a new amending formula and the inclusion of basic human rights in a new constitution. Robarts thought the next full-scale conference, called for Victoria in June, might be pivotal in Canada's quest for constitutional renewal. But he had seen too many pitfalls in these federal-provincial roads to want anyone to get expectations too high.[16] His cautious instinct turned out to be sound, for the Victoria agreement of June 1971 was disowned by Quebec, putting an end to almost four years of televised constitutional discussion in Canada.

On 10 February Robarts registered as a delegate at the leadership convention, which was being held in Maple Leaf Gardens and at the Royal York Hotel. The first night of the convention was all his as eleven hundred party members attended the farewell dinner for John Robarts in the main ballroom of the Royal York. Guests at the head table included George Drew, Leslie Frost, Robert Stanfield, Alan Eagleson, and the premier of New Brunswick, Richard Hatfield. Premiers Joey Smallwood of Newfoundland and Harry Strom of Alberta sent telegrams of best wishes. There was lavish praise from the head table speakers for Robarts' contributions to national unity, and a ten-minute film about his life and work, all televised. Robarts' fifteen-minute speech contained the appropriate thanks to individuals and for the opportunity he had had of leading the province. With Conservative premiers who had governed Ontario through the 1940s, 1950s, and 1960s at the head table, and the Conservative who would be chosen to lead the province in the 1970s somewhere in the audience, the farewell speech played on themes of continuity and change.

Robarts gave no signals to the audience, endorsing the five candidates from his cabinet as 'my boys – brought into the cabinet by me, men with whom I have worked closely and intimately.' His speech was interrupted by ovation after ovation. When Robarts had finished, Alan Eagleson presented him with a box wrapped in white. Robarts asked if it was a picture of Eagleson's star client, Bobby Orr. It was a brass plaque engraved 'Smooth Sailing Forever.' Eagleson explained that the Conservative party would outfit Robarts' new 31-foot sailboat.

John and Norah Robarts were onlookers, sometimes sitting with Drew or Frost, during the chaotic ballotting on Friday night. (The foul-up was caused when the voting machines that the up-to-date party had hired for the occasion could not be made to work.) On the fourth ballot William Davis beat Allan Lawrence by the surprisingly small margin of 812 votes to 768. Having had access to the private bar in Maple Leaf Gardens all evening, Robarts was in easy form shortly after 2 AM on Saturday when he appeared on stage with the candidates to congratulate the winner. 'I've achieved my objective,' he told the audience, 'I'm a has-been.'[17]

Robarts had delegated most of the routine jobs involved in engineering the changeover. On 16 February he and Davis met and settled on 1 March for the swearing-in ceremony. After their meeting Robarts travelled to London for the rescheduled farewell dinner there. Many of his old friends attended and, as in the old days, they partied well into the night. Then they had been young and hopeful; now they were the elite of the community. This was Robarts' last London function as prime minister.

He met his cabinet for the last time in Toronto on 18 February. With Davis taking a short holiday in Florida, the other ministers gathered at Carman's Restaurant for a formal reception organized by John Yaremko and Keith Reynolds in Robarts' honour. They were all potential 'has-beens.'

On 21 February Robarts gave Rosemary Spiers of the Toronto *Star* an interview in which he said, 'I am a product of my times exactly, and my time is finished.'[18] On 1 March Robarts and his cabinet submitted their resignations to Lieutenant-Governor W. Ross Macdonald in a private ceremony. They proceeded to the legislature where Reynolds, as secretary to the cabinet, swore in the new prime minister. His years as premier over, John Robarts sat lost in thought near Davis at the clerk's table.

'My Time Is Finished'

Did John Robarts' premiership end when he turned over the office to William Davis on 1 March 1971? Or did the real end come almost eight months later, on 24 October, when the Ontario Progressive-Conservative party won its ninth successive provincial general election, increasing both its share of the popular vote and its number of seats? Biographers of William Davis will properly credit the new man with a whirlwind of legislative activity in the spring of 1971; with having quickly developed his own image as a highly competent, trustworthy leader; and with the political good sense to have made use of the Atkins-Camp group from Allan Lawrence's organization, who in turn revolutionized Ontario elections with their modern (and expensive) methods, giving birth to the 'Big Blue Machine.' Still, it was John Robarts who had set the stage for the transition, leaving the Progressive-Conservative players in excellent health as a political troupe of remarkable skills and longevity, capable of putting on a new show at short notice and sweeping away the other companies in town.

Robarts remained an MPP after resigning the premiership. He attended the official opening of the legislature on 31 March 1971, sitting at the extreme end of the front bench nearest the Speaker. This was his last day in the assembly. He wanted to avoid any appearance of standing in the new prime minister's way in the House, and he also found that as a private member at Queen's Park he had nothing to do but sort his papers and look at the walls of his office.

At one of the farewell parties Robarts' staff presented him with a mock guide for the return to private life. It included instructions on how to buy bus tickets, ride a bus, park a car, and use a telephone book. It was almost as though Robarts was returning to the strange world of civilian life, as he had at the end of World War II. He would have to make a sharp transition to a new style of life, to new roles.

The idea of staying in politics as a gracefully aging Ontario statesman, or perhaps going to Ottawa as a senator, never appealed to him. During a visit to the House of Commons in Ottawa one day, Robarts had watched an elderly backbencher struggling to gain the attention of the Speaker, and repeatedly failing because he was no longer agile enough to rise before his younger colleagues. The image remained etched in his mind as his likely fate if he tried to remain a legislator.[1] He had never intended to make a career out of politics or government anyway; his profession was the law. He had served his time in politics, and now he intended to resume practising law. At fifty-four he was at least a decade from retirement age, and his experience in government meant there would be a host of new professional opportunities and challenges available to him back in private life.

Norah Robarts and many of John's friends thought that leaving Queen's Park would mean spending much less time in Toronto. Surely he would come back to London and pick up the threads of his law practice and his family life, somewhat like Cincinnatus returning to his plough. But of course he would come back covered in glory and would enjoy a final decade as the leader of the London social, political, and legal establishment. Perhaps he would be available from time to time for special provincial or national duties.[2]

They did not understand how thoroughly John had become entwined in the larger world of Toronto. Nor did they realize the extent to which London as a regional centre had become entwined in the web of power radiating out from Toronto, as many of its leaders assumed positions of significance in the political and bureaucratic affairs of the provincial capital. As premier John had played in a major political league; now he expected that his legal and business contacts would continue to be of provincial and national, perhaps international importance. For Robarts and several others of his generation, including businessmen-politicians like Ernie Jackson, London without the challenges of politics had the status of a minor league town. It was a nice place to live in, but during the week you went down the road to Toronto to do your business. Besides, Robarts liked the life of Toronto. He was unwilling to settle into the role of the local boy home from the wars with his medals, who patches things up with his neglected wife and settles down and vegetates.

Norah *had* been neglected during the later years of prime ministership, and John did hope that their marriage could be mended and saved. Partly for that reason, he agreed that the family home would remain in London, that he would establish a professional presence there and play a role in London society. He would commute to Toronto during the week for the business he had to do there. The arrangement continued the compartmentalization that had been the pattern of Robarts' life since entering provincial politics. Some days he would live in his London role, other days in his Toronto one. Knowing how he had gradually lost the ability to play these parts concurrently during his political years, Robarts was sceptical about the likelihood of the arrangement working out. Privately he decided to give the situation two years. If he was not happy with London and his marriage at the end of that period he would leave.[3]

Robarts joined two law firms: Robarts, Betts, McLennan and Flinn in London; Stikeman, Elliott, Robarts and Bowman in Toronto. So many invitations were pouring in to serve on the boards of corporations that Robarts asked Jim Gillies of the York University business school to prepare a list of the benefits and privileges accompanying each directorship. While Gillies was doing this, Robarts accepted two offers because of personal connections. One was to serve on the board of Reed, Shaw, Stenhouse Limited, an insurance brokerage and consulting company of which Ernie Jackson was a vice-president. Second, he agreed to join the board of the Canadian Imperial Bank of Commerce, the company his father had served. Later in the spring of 1971 he also joined the board of Bell Canada.

John and Norah spent a considerable amount of time travelling and enjoying themselves in 1971, then he was ready to settle down to private life after relinquishing his seat in the October election. The following year he commuted busily from London to Toronto, playing both of the planned roles. Almost immediately he found himself in great demand in Toronto and, as in the past, Norah continued to be reluctant to be more than a token commuter. Often Robin Robarts filled in for her at Toronto social functions, the good-looking young redhead with John causing quite a stir in corporate circles. Robarts' sailboat, the *Trillium,* had been fitted out by that summer and there was good family sailing off Grand Bend. Life seemed a bit more relaxing than during the governing days, and John seemed to be adjusting.

That fall, however, he began to feel increased pressure as he undertook more and more corporate and legal work. By 1973 Robarts had expanded his directorships to include the boards of Abitibi Paper, Commonwealth Holiday Inns of Canada, Metropolitan Life Insurance Company, and Power Corporation. He also was chancellor of the University of Western Ontario. His directorships introduced him to global business issues, new social circles, and even new recreational outlets, such as the salmon streams of Anticosti Island. Although his positions still represented a balance between London and Toronto, the pull was increasingly towards the metropolis. He seemed constantly in demand in both cities, and could hardly arrive in Toronto before he was needed in London, or vice versa.

Robarts was ambivalent about this hectic pace of life, complaining about it even as he found himself enjoying being at the centre of the 'action' in legal and business circles just as he had come to enjoy being at the centre of government.[4] He was considerably overweight, driving his blood pressure and his constitution close to their limits, skimping again on the London side of his life, and jeopardizing the future of the family. Some observers wondered if he was not being driven by a need to make money, for his pension as a former premier was not particularly generous.

The problem was not money. His blind trust was returned the day after the 1971 election. It had been well invested and amounted to approximately $350,000. Moreover, the income from his corporate and legal positions was found to be substantial. As Harry Price, who understood the corporate world, commented,

'John is making money so quickly he won't know how to spend it.' To others, Robarts remained poor. Possibly as a habit from his childhood, he husbanded his resources. For example, just before he announced his retirement as Prime Minister of Ontario, Robarts wrote his daughter:

You wrote concerning living in residence when you go to university. I am prepared to consent to this and to finance it, but once again it gets back to your plea for money. It doesn't grow on trees. There is a limited amount of it available and I can only spend each dollar once and if you want some of these things that you mention, I guess you will have to plan for them because sometimes the well runs dry.[5]

Robarts' drive was rooted in his search for personal challenge, challenge not available as an organizational cog. The excitement, the power, the diversity of social life attracted him to Toronto again, like a moth to light.

In March 1973, two years to the month after their discussions leading to the London-Toronto arrangement, John proposed to Norah that they move to Toronto. It was an offer made in unhappiness and uncertainty, for Robarts was not confident that his wife would or could make the adjustment. Without the encouragement and commitments she needed from John, Norah was no more willing to move to Toronto than she had ever been.[6] They both had drinking problems, and they fought frequently. He was not sure they could or even wanted to continue living together.

When Norah declined to move, John decided to go his own way. The break was not abrupt, but starting that spring he spent more and more time in Toronto, New York, and London, England. He found fulfilment in these cities, partly in association with men exercising corporate power (which had many similarities to the comradeship of politics), partly in the after-hours lifestyle he had first begun during the war. Accompanied part of the time by Jackson, Robarts was moving into a crowd of talented, urbane, and powerful individuals, jetting from a reception at the Rothschilds in England to a Rockefeller function in New York, participating in international economic decisions that made Ontario politics seem parochial by comparison and London's business affairs almost incestuous.

The challenge and the stakes led him to increase his Toronto business and political commitments. At the same time, his friends in government, concerned about his financial wellbeing, proposed his name as chairman of a provincial Royal Commission on Metropolitan Toronto. The Metropolitan Council had been advocating a review of local government structures and processes. With his interests and experience, Robarts would be an ideal appointment. William Davis, who had not made much use of Robarts until this time, acceded and personally asked him to chair the commission, which was established in September 1974. Robarts then persuaded Richard Rohmer to serve as the commission's counsel, oversaw the preparation of background papers by a research staff, and conducted two major rounds of public hearings, at which Rohmer took the leading role, in the spring and fall of 1975. In the course of their investigation, Robarts and Rohmer visited England and Europe. Consideration of the evidence and the drafting of recommendations went on through 1976. As it did, Robarts' personal life continued its rapid evolution.

During evenings in Toronto, John liked to relax in a pub, enjoy the music and the people. On 15 August 1973, he asked two ladies to join him for a drink at his table at the Bombay Bicycle Club, on the second floor of the old Massey mansion on Jarvis Street. When he and Katherine Sickafuse, one of the ladies, began verbal sparring, she was either unaware of, or refused to be impressed by, Robarts' past.[7] She became a challenge. They continued to meet, seeing each other frequently over the next two years.

Katherine was a divorcée who had left her husband in 1968. Twenty-eight years John's junior, she was twenty-eight when they met. A small-town girl from Rome, New York, she had completed her nurse's training at Mercy Hospital in Buffalo before accepting a job as an inspector of nursing homes for the Ontario government in early 1973. Katherine had one daughter, Kimberly, who lived with her.

News of their liaison got back to London, disturbing many in Robarts' circle. Norah would not consider a divorce, and most of their London acquaintances rallied to her support, seeing John as irresponsible at best, a 'damn fool' at worst.[8] Despite these criticisms and personal interventions by his brother Robert, John would not end a relationship that had opened avenues of emotion and satisfaction long closed by the failure of his marriage to Norah.

During their courting, John warned Katherine that London would not welcome, or even accept, her. His warnings went unheeded. John finally took the initiative in divorcing Norah. Attended by Tim and Robin Robarts and Kimberly Sickafuse, on 22 August 1976, Katherine and John were married at her parents' home in Rome, New York. Her parents, the Kwasniewskis, were egalitarian, unpretentious folk who had little in common with the visitors from Ontario. There was no mixing of the more volatile and effervescent Europeans with the more withdrawn London visitors. After the wedding, John and Katherine were left to bridge the gap.

Katherine became John's companion as well as his wife. Unlike Norah and many other wives of Robarts' generation who left the men to do men's things on their own, Katherine was happy to go hunting and fishing with him. John carried the ice, champagne, and clams as the newlyweds set out down logging trails north of Katherine's house in Rome to catch brook trout. On Saturdays they cooked gourmet dishes together late into the evening, or talked in the kitchen with Katherine working while John sat in his rocking chair. There were hunting trips together at Griffith Island, an elite club off the Bruce peninsula in Georgian Bay. They both enjoyed a lively Toronto social life, the gracious aspects of it along with the much less formal funny side. There were times when they seemed to be living in a fairy-tale world, John as a late middle-aged Prince Charming, Katherine as his princess. They were in love and enjoying themselves, but also at times exceeding the social tolerance of their fellows.

The worrisome side of the idyll was John's chronic high blood pressure and the extra weight he was carrying. Despite their love of good cooking, Katherine managed to help him stick to a diet and through 1976 he shrank back to his football weight of about 180 pounds. His blood pressure came under control and by early 1977 it had returned to normal, making it possible for him to stop medication. That year the Robarts moved into a house in Rosedale. John had put London behind him. He found the corporate world exciting and agreeable, and on this second time around he and Katherine were a part of the social and cultural milieu, and the privacy, that Toronto offered. Robarts had turned his back on many aspects of the post-premier role most people had expected him to play. He and Katherine were finding a new, freer identity in Toronto.

Politics returned to claim a share of his life in the summer of 1977. The November 1976 election of René Lévesque's Parti Québécois had brought the national unity question, which had so concerned John Robarts in 1967, back to prominence with a vengeance. One of Prime Minister Trudeau's responses to the PQ challenge was to commission a special Task Force on Canadian Unity to review the character of the Canadian federation and publicize the views and visions Canadians had of and for their country. He asked Robarts to serve as co-chairman of the task force with Jean-Luc Pepin, the dynamic Quebec Liberal politician who was temporarily out of elected office and undertaking a variety of jobs for the government.

Robarts found Trudeau's invitation difficult to handle. He could probably make time to do the job, for the Royal Commission on Metropolitan Toronto had almost finished its work, and the force of a call to serve the country was almost irresistible. On the other hand, for the first time in years his private life was a source of satisfaction. Undertaking the task force duty would mean re-enlisting in a major theatre of Canadian politics. Robarts had been drawn away from his first marriage by the challenge of government, and he did not want to make the same mistake twice. In later interviews he talked about being haunted by Santayana's comment, 'Those who do not remember the past are condemned to repeat it.'[9]

After lengthy discussions with Katherine, Robarts finally agreed to serve on the task force. Not the least of his reasons was the opportunity it gave him to articulate the vision of Canada he had championed as premier of Ontario – a decentralized federation which tolerated a regional diversity that included the uniqueness of Quebec. In appointing Robarts to the task force, Trudeau would not be getting another centralizer in the Liberal mode. Robarts also looked forward to working with the personable Pepin (no Liberal ideologue either, for that matter) whom he had recently come to know better through their membership on the boards of Canada Steamship Lines and Power Corporation.

The work on Metropolitan Toronto was completed quickly. Rohmer had wanted the 126 recommendations they were making to be released in digestible packages roughly paralleling the background papers published earlier by the commission. Robarts argued that the report should contain all of the recommendations and be released as a single package. So it became a wide-ranging document, packed with recommendations, all of which, however, were based on fundamental approval of the Toronto experiment in metropolitan government. Most of Robarts' suggestions were for improvements in the process of governing, such as better inter-metropolitan communication and the election of regional councillors. The report was released on 4 July 1977, and had little immediate impact. With its release, Robarts left the commission behind him, believing his job was done and his advice tendered. Referring back to Leslie Frost as the best adviser he ever had, he often commented: 'He gave his advice and then left you free to accept or reject it.'[10]

The day after the royal commission report was released, Prime Minister Trudeau announced that Robarts and Pepin would be the co-chairmen of the task force studying national unity. The seven-member group would tour the country listening to Canadians' views on the strengths and weaknesses of the federation, then present their findings to the government and to the country.

The demanding schedule of public hearings took Robarts away from home for long periods that summer and autumn. His dieting ended, his drinking continued, his weight and blood pressure soared. Just as the task force was picking up momentum in August, Tim Robarts, John's adopted son, committed suicide at the age of twenty-one. The young man had become a casualty of the drug culture of his generation. John Robarts was devastated by his son's death, which brought him face to face with his personal failures, his own mortality, and the question of a continuing purpose in life. He internalized his grief, managing to keep it out of the task force, his law practice, and his life at home. But he found it hard to see a continuing point in controlling his weight and his drinking. Katherine tried to warn him that his excesses would kill him. Like Norah before her, it had no effect. John just said that would be his problem, not hers. Robarts had lost his future. He played a mediating, but low-profile, role on the task force.

The task force hearings brought out an incredible diversity and strength of feeling about Canada and its future. At times the clash of opinion was agonizingly painful to witness, as Canadians hardly seemed to be talking about the same country. Eventually Robarts and Pepin agreed that a necessary first step toward understanding was to suggest a common vocabulary, some kind of common denominator, to participants in a debate who flung around words as symbols of good and evil. The quest for terms in which to talk about Canada became the focus of their preliminary work.

Robarts seized all the time he could to be back in Toronto with Katherine. Their life together was both lively and iconoclastic. Tension over health was forgotten as they participated in the formal rituals of Canada's highest social circles: the round of dinners and parties and receptions for governors general, premiers, former premiers, all the members of the corporate and cultural elite. But they also sometimes deliberately thumbed their noses at convention. At one notable Castle Society costume party in Toronto, for example, Katherine had found authentic circus costumes for the pair. She went as a slightly clad showgirl, plumed tail and all. Her husband was dressed as a perfect clown, from his rainbow Afro wig and bulbous nose down to his mismatched floppy shoes. The Robartses enjoyed themselves at the affair; others thought the costumes were too good, that even at a costume party a former prime minister of Ontario and his wife ought to preserve some of the trappings of dignity.

In October 1978 John and Katherine sent out unsigned formal announcements to a select group of their friends reading,

> On the occasion of their resurrection
> The Count and Countess Dracula
> will pay you a visitation.
> Please remove all holy water, religious artifacts
> and vessels from your home.

That Hallowe'en night they rented a hearse and costumes and went from house to house inviting their friends to join them in the back of the hearse for champagne. They were still in costume at Sabatino's Restaurant at the end of the evening. Doing it all in straight face and trying to preserve their anonymity, the Robarts caused a considerable stir.

The Robarts-Pepin task force completed its work in late 1978 and published its findings in three reports: *A Future Together* in January; *Coming to Terms* in February; and *A Time to Speak* in March 1979. It was surprisingly detailed and sweeping in recommending the major components of a new constitution for Canada, one which would create a considerably more decentralized country, and yet a country whose central government would have more power to ensure such national priorities as the free flow of labour and capital from province to province. Close scrutiny of the structure of *A Future Together* reveals a number of themes redolent of Ontario's views on dominion-provincial relations during the Robarts years, most notably proposals for better mechanisms to ensure consultation and co-operation between the dominion and the provinces in national policy-making. Far more than was recognized at the time, the Robarts-Pepin recommendations reflected the view of Canadian unity through pluralism[11] that John Robarts had championed in his ten years as prime minister of the nation's most powerful province.

The co-chairmen were a study in contrasts. Pepin, the colourful, forceful and lively federal leader, pored through the background studies and took an aggressive stance in public meetings. Prodding and probing, struggling with the material, he eclipsed his colleague who listened and synthesized what he heard. The contrast extended to substance where Robarts still felt that although constitutional structures could be changed, a necessary prerequisite was the 'will' to make the country work. His stance was a loud echo of the Confederation of Tomorrow conference and found its way explicitly into the text of the report alongside the constitutional prescriptions.

The vision was no more acceptable to a federal Liberal government in 1979 than Robarts' views had been in 1960 or earlier. Publication of the report sparked a sharp round of intense and often critical discussion of its proposals. Then they were largely neglected in the federal elections of 1979 and 1980 and in the debate on the Quebec referendum held in April 1980. Perhaps the task force's greatest value had been in the function of its hearings as a kind of national safety-valve, permitting people and groups to express their feelings in a time of national uncertainty and tension.

His public service completed, Robarts returned to the law, his corporate responsibilities, a second university position as chancellor of York University, and his wife. He was overweight, back on medication for his blood pressure, and unwilling or unable to slow down the pace of his life. He still retained a certain amount of contact with Ernie Jackson, Keith Reynolds, and a few friends who had moved into business from politics and government. But the old London group had disappeared. Once, in 1976, they had held a reunion in Toronto to relive past glories, but after that they had gone their own ways. John Robarts' life centred about his home, Robin, his new wife and daughter, and his fishing and hunting trips with Katherine and their friends. In May 1981, Norah died suddenly in London.

On 6 August 1981 Katherine and John joined Frank Moores and his wife on a trout-fishing expedition in Labrador arranged for them by Brian Mulroney, then president of the Iron Ore Company of Canada. They flew into a company fishing camp on a Thursday. The best of everything was laid on for the group and, as expected, the fishing was excellent. On Saturday John commented to Katherine that he was having a hard time keeping his balance and found casting difficult. He kept slipping on the rocks. As the party was preparing to leave on Sunday, he was unusually upset, looking everywhere for glasses he had somehow lost. That evening as John walked upstairs in his Toronto home, his leg buckled. He assumed that it was more cartilage trouble and he would have to have this knee fixed much as the other one had been handled earlier. By Monday the trouble seemed to have cleared up, the normal pace of life took over, and the incidents were forgotten.

That Wednesday John attended a Metropolitan Life board meeting in New York and then went on to Houston for meetings in his capacity as chairman of Reed, Shaw, Stenhouse. En route to Houston he suffered a stroke. When he phoned Katherine, who had been ill, from his hotel room to say he had arrived safely and to inquire about her own health, she realized something was wrong and quizzed him about his condition. She demanded that he summon the hotel doctor. After some urging and a call directly to the doctor, John was examined and sent to Twelve Oaks Hospital on Katherine's insistence.[12] By this time Ernie Jackson had learned of John's illness through his corporate connection and immediately took charge. Robarts suffered a second stroke after being admitted to Twelve Oaks, and was transferred to the Plaza del Oro Hospital for more specialized treatment.

Back in Toronto Katherine waited for news. There was none. She finally called Jackson and learned that John had been moved to the specialized hospital. Upset, she made arrangements to go to Houston, and arrived there with Robin on Friday. The doctors were confident, but also concerned. They urged her to act as if nothing was wrong, so that John would not become too disturbed about his condition. He was not to read newspapers or become upset.[13] By Friday evening the doctors knew that Robarts had suffered a left hemiplegia with dysphasia, which meant he had lost some control of his left side, including his arm and leg, and was slurring his speech. The attack was directly attributable to his high blood pressure and a clogged anterior cerebral artery. He seemed to be responding well to medication, but would have to stay in hospital for some time.

Katherine stayed in Houston to look after John. But Ernie Jackson and Robert Robarts were also there, and in the tense atmosphere surrounding the sick man in hospital the latent animosities between the old friends and relations and the new wife led to sharp clashes and misunderstandings. Everyone's primary concern, of course, was John and his health. On Monday, 17 August, Robarts was taken off the critical list, and on 12 September he was transferred to the Toronto General Hospital.

By October John was starting to realize how serious his stroke had been. While the doctors were satisfied with his slow progress toward recovery, and Katherine knew enough about the situation to be patient, John gradually became frustrated and angry at his body's failure to respond. That anger was not his alone. Katherine knew she had to challenge him lest he lose the will to live. She also suffered like any spouse at the chronic incapacity of her mate. Occasionally that frustration erupted in public, causing bystanders to assume there was tension in the marriage and that his wife was harsh and intolerant. The deeper emotions of love and pain were buried from view.

As winter approached, John's speech simply would not clear up; co-ordination did not come back to his arm and leg. Exercises like whittling, which were suggested to improve his co-ordination, seemed an absolute waste of time to the former premier. Robarts' frustration at his inability to control even his own body resulted in periods of deep depression. Had he become incapable of participating in life? Was it worth continuing? These questions, with their suicidal overtones, frightened Katherine, who had been urged by the doctors to keep him challenged precisely to stave off such moods.

Don Martyn and Hugh Hanson offered to help with the rehabilitation by taking their former boss out for walks and the occasional lunch. That winter they devoted many hours to their friend and stayed with him one week while Katherine took time off to recuperate. All three of them worked hard encouraging Robarts to stick to his physiotherapy routines and trying to rebuild his self-confidence. By spring Keith Reynolds had joined the group. They were pleased with his progress, but John was still sensitive about his speech and afraid to speak in public. Hanson and Martyn took him to the West Indies for a week to give him a change of environment and help him gain strength. On his return Robarts attempted his first speech since the stroke. The slight slurring of his words was noticeable to his audience, but on the whole John was more sensitive to and alarmed about his limitations than his audience. Among the people around him, who could not avoid each other now that John was sick, there was continuing friction and disagreement about the best way to handle his day-to-day progress.

During February and March of 1982 John began going into the office during the day. He lunched with an increasing circle of relatives and acquaintances, including Robin and Keith Reynolds. At home Katherine applied considerable pressure to keep him occupied and interested in his recovery. In the outside world he found it deeply frustrating to be unable to rise to his old level. In June John asked Richard Rohmer, who had not been entangled in any of the differences surrounding Robarts' personal life, to make him a new will. Rohmer and Katherine would be co-executors of his estate. With this first step taken toward arranging his affairs, Robarts became even more morose. His friends and Katherine struggled to help him pull out of his depression, but with limited success. He once remarked to Katherine that he was giving himself a year to recover from the stroke.[14]

Martyn and Hanson took Robarts sailing in the summer of 1982, but he was not co-ordinated enough to control the boat. His demands on himself exceeded the reasonable. His frustration made him increasingly difficult to live with and continued the downward spiral of depression and introversion. In September he sold his boat.[15] On Thanksgiving weekend John and Katherine took their annual hunting trip to Griffith Island. John managed to shoot one or two birds, but in doing so caught and injured his hand on the gun mechanism. The accident and the blood preoccupied him. At home on Sunday, he found his arm was bruised from the gun's recoil. John decided he could no longer hunt.

Robarts was determined to stay in control of his life. Insecure in his position, the gulf between his wife – whom he loved dearly – and his friends – who had shared the major portion of his life – provided disjointed reference points in a pattern that no longer seemed to make sense to him. There were no roles left that Jack could play. The drive pent-up inside a weakened body, the road closed, the past denied, and love tainted with the awareness that he would not be a vibrant contributor, Robarts saw only one way of staying in charge to the end. Early on Monday morning, 18 October 1982, Jack Robarts went into the bathroom and took his life.[16]

John Robarts' suicide shattered everyone around him. He had always been the man in charge. He had always represented a sense of order, even as his private life was coming apart in tatters. Robarts' state funeral was formal. Archbishop Garnsworthy, speaking for those who knew him as a public figure, had agreed that the service should be in St Paul's Church. In his homily, he remembered Robarts for his generosity in serving his province and his country, and for his vision of Canada as 'a land of rich mosaics and of varied cultures.' His emphasis was well placed, especially in light of Robarts' struggle over Trudeau's call for him to serve on the task force. Despite his concern for his second marriage, he had responded.

The burial ceremony was private. Afterwards, his friends created memorials to John Robarts: a medical research centre at the University of Western Ontario, and a centre to study Canadian federalism at York University. The people who had loved John Robarts were left to reconstruct their lives.

If one steps further back from his personal life, Robarts was a successful prime minister of Ontario. From a party point of view, Robarts' achievement was primarily to hold onto power through a difficult decade and pass his mantle smoothly to his successor, Bill Davis. When the complete history of Ontario's Tory dynasty is written, much will be made of the enormous personal and ideological differences between the early Conservative premiers and the later ones. The distance between George Drew and William Davis was very great, as was the distance between the Ontarios they governed and the kind of governments they ran. In this perspective, John Robarts appears as the transitional premier. Drew and Frost used the same political machine and many of the same political methods. When John Robarts took over the leadership in 1961 he brought a new group of Conservatives to power in the party and the province, created a new machine and new methods, and provided the second generation of PC dominance. Always with that remarkable continuity, of course, for when Robarts left a decade later the two leading contenders, Davis and Allan Lawrence, were the men who had managed the Macaulay and Roberts campaigns. With Davis' victory and his quick use of Lawrence people, the Robarts group left the scene, giving way to the third generation.

The transition had been not only from one Conservative philosophy to another, but from old Ontario and its politics to a new Ontario and a new political game. John Robarts began his career in the rural-dominated, personal government of Leslie Frost, with its eight-week sessions and the simple departmentalized structure of government and the civil service. When Robarts left power, Ontario had an administratively centralized, management-oriented governing system capable of processing the volume of work and conflicting demands generated by modern, technologically based urban society.

Emphasis on that shift in administrative technique as the dominant characteristic of the Robarts years in Ontario leads easily into a characterization of John Robarts as the consummate management man in Ontario's political history – the administrative reformer, the chief executive officer, the businessman-planner, the non-politician, the non-ideologue. There is much truth in this view of Robarts and his years, for it may well be that the modernization of the Ontario government, along with municipal and social services throughout the province, was the most important legacy of his premiership, quite apart from his legacy to his party. Nor is there any doubt that Robarts' personal style of governing was less ideological and emotional than George Drew's, less instinctive than Leslie Frost's, less political and poll-oriented than William Davis'. But the management-man image of Robarts is also inadequate, or superficial, in failing to incorporate the ways in which Robarts was a conservative product of his times. His was a political style deeply rooted in a cluster of traditionally conservative attitudes about man and society and government, a conservatism which by the end of his time in government left him often troubled by the situation he was passing on to Davis.

Robarts was a product of his generation of Londoners. They were shaped by their regional upbringing to believe in many of the values of the rural Ontario society that they had grown up in; but they were urban and cosmopolitan enough to be able to adjust to the pace and mores of the rapidly changing postwar society. More important, they were products of the depression and Hitler's war, a generation of young Canadians who entered the late 1940s with a desire to build careers and families, to get on with the business of living. Those of them who went into politics, as Robarts did, looked on it as secondary, a part-time calling, less important than the development of their private affairs. Governing and government had a distinct, limited place in their lives. They wanted to keep it in its place, both in preserving the realm of their personal privacy, and in their business and professional careers, where the free marketplace seemed to them to be the appropriate arena for entrepreneurial energies and individual initiative leading to the creation of personal and community wealth. They were Tories in their sense that the realm of government was only one limited aspect of a much richer, diverse community life.

Robarts' dislike of politics in and of itself was partly rooted in this determination not to give himself over to government, and perhaps partly rooted in an older Tory disdain for the grubbery and pandering of the unprincipled 'professional' politician. He went into government to get on with governing, not to make a career out of politics, and the way in which these attitudes blended with his wartime experience as a naval officer had much to do with the creation of his managerial style.

It was not the style of today's professional manager or of the rootless managerial politicians who were beginning to spring up during his own time and became as common as weeds in Canada during the next decade. John Robarts always had a deeply conservative sense of being at the head of a complex society, a community whose institutions – schools, municipalities, companies, and professions – had been built up over the generations and ought not to be tampered with unnecessarily. If they could be left alone, leave them alone. It happened, though, that the need to give Ontarians modern social services made a large amount of tampering with established institutions necessary during the Robarts years, so much so that his governments seemed at times to be committed to the demolition of deeply cherished institutions. Where was Robarts the conservative then?

The answer is that he was to be found in the *process* by which the course of reform was determined. The key to understanding this process is Robarts' much misunderstood habit of responding to political issues by launching special studies, inquiries, or royal commissions. The aim of these investigations was to produce an understanding of a situation as it really existed, not as politicians and/or the media thought it existed. Was the problem real? If it was, something would have to be done about it. But perhaps a close study by experts – perhaps several studies by people with differing expertise or experience – would reveal it was not, and if that was the case there was no reason not to maintain the status quo. When governments rushed to prescribe action in situations they did not understand, they risked making problems worse, risked being out of touch with their voters, risked falling into the bad habit of unnecessarily interfering with other people's freedoms, and risked developing their own insatiable appetite for growth beyond reasonable and proper bounds.

The distinctiveness of Robarts' approach was often manifest in his clashes with the Liberal style of policy-making in Ottawa during his premiership. In the early years Robarts had to defend Ontario's carefully prepared pragmatic approach to pensions in the teeth of Ottawa's announcement that it was going to introduce a politically glamorous pension plan before it had any idea of the costs, details, or even the need for its proposals. In the long, bitter, and losing fight against medicare, Robarts faced the same Liberal propensity to work from a theoretical assumption of social need. Ottawa was determined to impose its approach to medical insurance on all of Canada, complete with a set of fixed ideological presuppositions about how medical service *ought* to be delivered. Robarts could not understand what was so objectionable about the way they *were* being delivered in Ontario; he saw no reason to slash through the network of public and private insurers who were serving both high- and low-income earners; and he thought the cheapness and efficiency of Ontario's system should count as important reasons for keeping it in existence. Finally, Robarts was never an enthusiast for remaking Canada's constitution. He saw no need to waste time figuring out how the Canadian reality should be reorganized on the basis of new first principles. Far better to get on with adjusting the machine where it was breaking down, which usually seemed to be in the area of revenue allocation, and to do it through co-operative arrangements worked out by real people talking to each other, not grandstanding politicians mouthing idealistic abstractions. Robarts lost much of this battle too.

Indeed, by the end of his tenure he was starting to have to face up to the possibility that his approach to government had reached its limits. The negative reaction to the great reform program – the county boards, regional government, assessment at market value, horizontal policy-making in government – suggested that Robarts and his ministers, despite their instincts, had lost touch with the complex reality 'out there,' had become too enamoured of the abstractions and the plans of the new technocrats they had brought into their government. They had not been conservative enough.

Still, the situation was manageable, as the government proved in simply slowing down the pace of change, band-aiding open wounds with grants and subsidies, and (as in the second round of administrative reorganization) proceeding more carefully along better-scouted trails. The more serious problems being posed for Robarts and his generation involved those areas of provincial life where it seemed impossible to avoid a sharp clash within their own conservative principles. Robarts knew that his government's responsibility to future generations required tough anti-pollution legislation, for example, entailing in some cases a major expansion of government controls on industry. His government brought in the controls and he worried about the trade-offs involved. Similarly, the preservation of farm land and green belts and other public spaces in the Toronto-Centred Region Plan seemed necessary for the community's future health, but the extreme intrusion of big government into private and local decision-making necessary to make the plans effective documents was offensive to Robarts' conservative instincts. He was not sure how to resolve this dilemma. Throughout his premiership he had been firm in resisting demands that economic hardship or corporate mismanagement should spark major government intrusions into the private economic sector. By the end he was resisting a current of economic nationalism in his own party in insisting that it was important to keep the Canadian border and the international flow of goods and capital as open as possible. The reforming side of Robarts had not hesitated to change organizations and use the powers of government in directions helpful to the people of Ontario. By the end of his tenure, even his personal style of being less concerned with the machinery and more with the people reflected his conservative sense that the process of governing was starting to interfere with the real business of personal relations. Politicians had to remember that they were people, working with people. And in any community it was individual people, not governments, who bore final responsibility for their destinies.

The dilemmas and misgivings and personal problems toward the end of his leadership did not mar the fact that John Robarts had been a highly successful prime minister of Ontario. His success had been demonstrated at the polls, and it existed in the up-to-date institutions and modern government and healthy party he left behind him. Robarts had succeeded because his policies had been precisely in tune with the connotations of his party's name: they had been progressive and conservative. The government had stayed in touch with the mass of its supporters on the centre-right of the Ontario political spectrum. Sometimes it had jumped out a bit ahead of their desires. Other times it had had to scramble a bit to catch up. But it had never been very far out of contact. Nor had it been handicapped by anything approaching serious scandal.

As prime minister, John Robarts had contributed sound management abilities, including a particularly well-developed ability to work with people, to the achievements of his government. More than this, his personal image had developed remarkably during his years in office. The somewhat colourless chairman of the board of the earlier 1960s changed almost imperceptibly into the gravel-voiced elder statesman, the national figure who commanded enormous personal respect and trust. The foundation of both images had been the young naval officer who knew that the officer's role while on duty was to be calm and controlled and in charge no matter what happened. Especially when leadership was required, Robarts had had to retain an internal sense of order.

Appendices

A / The Ontario Cabinet

	First elected	*Portfolio*
*Leslie M. Frost	1937	Premier
Charles Daley	1943	Labour
William A. Goodfellow	1943	Agriculture
Louis P. Cecile	1948	Public Welfare
*William J. Dunlop	1951	Minister without Portfolio
William K. Warrender	1951	Municipal Affairs
James N. Allan	1951	Treasurer
W.M. Nickle	1951	Planning and Development
A. Kelso Roberts	1943	Attorney General
Bryan L. Cathcart	1945	Travel and Publicity
Thomas Ray Connell	1951	Public Works
Matthew B. Dymond	1955	Health
J. Wilfrid Spooner	1955	Lands and Forests
Frederick M. Cass	1955	Highways
John Yaremko	1951	Provincial Secretary
Robert W. Macaulay	1951	Energy Resources, second vice-chairman, Ontario Hydro
†James A. Maloney	1956	Mines
George C. Wardrope	1951	Reform Institutions
John P. Robarts	1951	Education
John Root	1951	Minister without Portfolio
Allan Grossman	1955	Minister without Portfolio
Leslie Rowntree	1956	Transport
William Stewart	1957	Minister without Portfolio

*Not in Robarts' cabinet
†Deceased; not in Robarts' cabinet

ROBARTS' FIRST CABINET

	First elected	Portfolio
John P. Robarts		Premier
A. Kelso Roberts		Attorney General
*Charles Daley		Minister without Portfolio
William A. Goodfellow		Highways
Louis P. Cecile		Public Welfare
*William K. Warrender		Labour
James N. Allan		Treasurer
William M. Nickle		Minister without Portfolio
Bryan L. Cathcart		Travel and Publicity
T. Ray Connell		Public Works
Matthew B. Dymond		Health
J. Wilfrid Spooner		Lands and Forests
Frederick M. Cass		Municipal Affairs
John Yaremko		Provincial Secretary
Robert W. Macaulay		Energy Resources
		Commerce and Development
George C. Wardrope		Mines
H. Leslie Rowntree		Transport
Allan Grossman		Minister without Portfolio
William A. Stewart		Agriculture
Charles S. MacNaughton	1958	Minister without Portfolio
Irwin Haskett	1959	Reform Institutions
†James Auld	1954	
†William G. Davis	1959	
†John R. Simonett	1959	

*Not in new cabinet of 25 October 1962
†Added on 25 October 1962

ROBARTS' CABINET OF 25 OCTOBER 1962

	First elected	*Portfolio*
John P. Robarts		Premier
A. Kelso Roberts		Lands and Forests
*William A. Goodfellow		Minister without Portfolio
‡Louis P. Cecile		Public Welfare
James N. Allan		Treasurer
*Bryan L. Cathcart		Travel and Publicity
T. Ray Connell		Public Works
Matthew B. Dymond		Health
J. Wilfrid Spooner		Municipal Affairs
§Frederick M. Cass		Attorney General
John Yaremko		Provincial Secretary
*Robert W. Macaulay		Energy Resources
		Commerce and Development
George Wardrope		Mines
H. Leslie Rowntree		Labour
Allan Grossman		Minister without Portfolio
		(Reform Institutions)
William A. Stewart		Agriculture
Charles S. MacNaughton		Highways
Irwin Haskett		Reform Institutions
		(Transport)
James A.C. Auld		Transport
		(Travel and Publicity)
William G. Davis		Education
J. Richard Simonett		Minister without Portfolio
		(Energy)
†Stanley J. Randall	1963	(Economics and Development)

*Retired after 1963 election
†Added after 1963 election
‡Retired in cabinet shuffle of 24 November 1966
( )Portfolio in post-1963 election shuffle
§Resigned after Bill 99 disruption, 1964

ROBARTS' CABINET PRE-1967 ELECTION

	First elected	Portfolio
John P. Robarts		Premier
§James N. Allan		Minister without Portfolio
#T. Ray Connell		Public Works
#Matthew B. Dymond		Health
‡J. Wilfrid Spooner		Municipal Affairs
John Yaremko		Public Welfare
‡George C. Wardrope		Mines
#H. Leslie Rowntree		Financial and Commercial Affairs
Allan Grossman		Reform Institutions
William A. Stewart		Agriculture and Food
Charles S. MacNaughton		Provincial Treasurer
Irwin Haskett		Transport
James A.C. Auld		Tourism and Information
William G. Davis		Education and University Affairs
J. Richard Simonett		Energy and Resources Management
Stanley J. Randall		Economics and Development
†Arthur A. Wishart	1963	Justice and Attorney General
†George E. Gomme	1959	Highways
*René Brunelle	1958	Lands and Forest
*Dalton A. Bales	1963	Labour
*Robert S. Welch	1963	Provincial Secretary
*Thomas L. Wells	1963	Minister without Portfolio
W. Darcy McKeough	1963	Minister without Portfolio
‖ Fernand Guindon	1957	
‖ Allan F. Lawrence	1958	

*Joined cabinet in shuffle of 24 November 1966
†Joined cabinet in 1964 or 1965
‡Left cabinet after defeat in 1967 election
§Retired after 1967 election
‖ Added after 1967 election
Retired in 1969 or early 1970

ROBARTS' CABINET 1970

	First elected	Portfolio
*John P. Robarts		Premier
John Yaremko		Social and Family Services
Allan Grossman		Correctional Services
William A. Stewart		Agriculture and Food
Charles S. MacNaughton		Treasury and Economics
*Irwin Haskett		Transport
James A.C. Auld		Tourism and Information
William G. Davis		Education and University Affairs
*J. Richard Simonett		Public Works
*Stanley J. Randall		Trade and Development
*Arthur A. Wishart		Justice and Attorney General
*George E. Gomme		Highways
René Brunelle		Lands and Forests
Dalton A. Bales		Labour
Robert S. Welch		Provincial Secretary
Thomas L. Wells		Health
W. Darcy McKeough		Municipal Affairs
Fernand Guindon		Minister without Portfolio
Allan F. Lawrence		Mines
†John H. White	1959	Revenue
‡George A. Kerr	1963	Energy and Resources Management
§A.B.R. Lawrence	1963	Financial and Commercial Affairs

*Retired in the 1971 election
†Joined cabinet 10 October 1968
‡Joined cabinet 5 June 1969
§Joined cabinet 5 February 1970

B / Ontario Legislative Assembly
Length of Sessions, 1958-71

1958	3 February to 27 March
1959	27 January to 26 March
1960	26 January to 12 April
1960–1	22 November to 16 December; 24 January to 29 March
1961–2	22 November to 15 December; 20 February to 18 April
1962–3	27 November to 19 December; 5 February to 3 April; 17 April to 26 April
1963	29 and 30 October
1964	15 January to 8 May
1965	20 January to 14 April; 27 April to 22 June
1966	25 January to 6 April; 18 April to 8 July
1967	25 January to 22 March; 4 April to 15 June
1968	4 February to 11 April; 22 April to 23 July
1968–9	19 November to 20 December; 4 February to 3 April; 15 April to 27 June; 30 September to 17 December
1970	24 February to 19 March; 31 March to 26 June; 6 October to 13 November
1971	30 March to 28 July. Dissolved on 13 December

C / Ontario Election Results

	PC	L	Lib-Lab	CCF/NDP	LPP	Total
1937	23	64		1 (UFO)	2	90
1943	38	16		34	2	90
1945	66	11	3	8	2	90
1948	53	13	1	21	2	90
1951	79	7	1	2	1	90
1955	84	11	–	3	–	98
1959	71	22	–	5	–	98
1963	77	24	–	7	–	108
1967	69	27	1	20	–	117
1971	78	19	1	19	–	117

VOTES

	% of voters	# of voters	% of Votes Cast		
			PC	L	NDP/CCF
1937	70.2	2,238,030	40	51	5
1943	57.88	2,269,895	36	31	32
1945	71.49	2,469,960	44	30	22
1948	67.02	2,623,281	41	30	27
1951	64.59	2,750,709	48	32	19
1955	60.61	2,905,760	49	33	17
1959	58.89	3,196,801	46	37	17
1963	62.07	3,437,834	48	35	16
1967	65.65	3,685,755	42	32	26
1971	73	4,485,000	44.5	27.75	27.15

SOURCE: For 1937 to 1967, John Wilson and David Hoffman, 'Ontario: A Three Party System in Transition,' in M. Robin, *Canadian Provincial Politics*, 1st ed. (Scarborough: Prentice-Hall 1972). For 1971, *Report* of Chief Electoral Officer for Ontario

Notes

CHAPTER 1: 'WHO'S JOHN?'

1 Marion attended elementary school in London before following Catherine to Branksome Hall. After she graduated, she returned to London briefly. In 1952 she married B.E. Floyd and moved to Toronto.
2 After Catherine graduated, she trained as a registered nurse at Toronto General Hospital. Shortly after her graduation, she married O.N. Eaton, and although she maintained close ties with the family, she moved to California in the early 1940s. She thus leaves the story at this point.
3 Their paths continued to diverge, Robert graduating from high school after grade twelve and following his father in banking, while John continued on to university with his goal set on studying the law like Unk.
4 Public Archives of Ontario (PAO), J.P. Robarts Personal Papers, JPR to parents, 31 Oct. 1940
5 Ibid., 4 Aug. 1940
6 Ibid., 25 Sept. 1940
7 Ibid., 31 Oct. 1940
8 Ibid., 30 Mar. 1941 (misdated 1940 by JPR)
9 Ibid.
10 Ibid., 3 May, 1944
11 Ibid., 30 Mar. 1944
12 Ibid., 26 Nov. 1944

CHAPTER 2: LONDONERS

1 For the history of London and area, see Armstrong and Brock, 'The Rise of London: A Study of Urban Evolution in Nineteenth-Century Southwestern Ontario,' in Armstrong, Stevenson, and Wilson, eds, *Aspects of Nineteenth Century Ontario;* Miller, *A Century of Western Ontario;* Baker, *The Rise and Progress of London.*

2 London *Free Press,* 9 Dec. 1948
3 PAO, RG 3, L.M. Frost Papers, General Correspondence, Box 106, File 183G, Manross to Frost, 5 July 1949
4 Interview with JPR
5 Interview with William Heine
6 Privileged interview
7 Interview with JPR and Frederick Jenkins
8 Interview with F. Jenkins
9 PAO, RG 3, L.M. Frost Papers, General Correspondence, Box 164, File 223-G, G. Reid to Frost, 20 Oct. 1951; privileged interviews
10 One of the first cobalt bomb units was unveiled by Leslie Frost at London's Victoria Hospital earlier that year.
11 London *Free Press,* 23 Nov. 1951, and earlier for details about the campaign

CHAPTER 3: A PART-TIME JOB

1 PAO, RG 3, L.M. Frost Papers, General Correspondence, Box 168, 239-G, H.M. Robbins to Frost, 2 Sept. 1958; ibid., Subject Files, Box 20, 'Policy on Questions to all Cabinet Ministers' from L.R. McDonald. For a description of the executive organization of the Ontario government, see Schindeler, *Responsible Government in Ontario,* chap. 3.
2 PAO, RG 3, L.M. Frost Papers, Subject Files, Box 20, 'Legislative Assembly Requests for Information 1952-8'
3 Interviews with Alex Jeffery and Dr S. Floyd Maine
4 PAO, RG 3, L.M. Frost Papers, General Correspondence, Box 56, File 105, Macaulay to Frost, 24 Jan. 1955
5 Ibid., Frost to Macaulay, 2 Dec. 1959
6 Ibid., Macaulay to Frost, 9 Mar. 1955
7 London *Free Press,* 2 May 1955
8 Ibid., 21 May, 7 and 8 June 1955
9 Interviews with Robert W. Mitchell and F. Jenkins
10 PAO, RG 3, L.M. Frost Papers, General Correspondence, Box 105, 182-G, Macaulay to Frost, 19 Jan. 1956
11 Ibid., Subject Files, Box 34, Toll Roads 1954-5
12 Although the report did not recommend Highway 401 explicitly, it recommended a super-highway crossing the interior of southwestern Ontario. Its proposal combined with the offer of the federal government to cover most of the cost of a Trans-Canada Highway to provide the ingredients for the system of super-highways designed by the Department of Transport over the next decade. C.S. MacNaughton, with early experience as minister of highways and as a member of a Cabinet Committee on Provincial Transportation Policy in the early 1960s, understood the significance of the integration of all aspects of transportation policy in one depart-

ment. Eventually, the umbrella extended to economic development and land use policy in the late 1960s. MacNaughton, in fact, gave up the offer to serve as provincial treasurer in the Davis administration to nurture the new Ministry of Transportation and Communications. Interview with Charles S. MacNaughton

13 Stewart was offered the Transport portfolio but declined, stating that he would prefer another portfolio when it came available. A shocked Leslie Frost told him that he was the first backbencher to turn down an offer to enter cabinet. Stewart later accepted a minister without portfolio position and undertook to assist William Goodfellow in Agriculture. His close relationship with Goodfellow later was a significant factor when Goodfellow agreed to nominate Robarts in the leadership convention of 1961.

14 Manthorpe, *The Power and the Tories,* 60

CHAPTER 4: THE CROSSROADS

1 PAO, RG 3, L.M. Frost Papers, General Correspondence, Box 163-G, Letters from Members File, 16 Jan. 1958. See also ibid., Subject File, Box 20, Legislative Assembly Requests for Information, 1952-8

2 PAO, RG 3, L.M. Frost Papers, General Correspondence, Box 168, 239-G, J.P. Robarts 1952-9, JPR to Frost, 19 Jan. 1959

3 Ibid., Memo for Hon. W. Nickle from Attorney General A.K. Roberts, 17 Aug. 1955

4 Cameron, *Schools for Ontario,* 198; interviews with William McHugh, JPR, and Harold Walker

5 Ontario Legislative Assembly, *Proceedings,* 28 Mar. 1960, pp. 1828-32

6 PAO, RG 2, P. 3, Temporary Box 482, Canadian Vocational Training, 7-9, p. 1308; see also, Dupré et al., *Federalism and Policy Development,* 69-70.

7 PAO, RG 3, L.M. Frost Papers, General Correspondence, Box 82-G, Re Technical and Vocational Training Agreement 1961, Frost to File, 18 May 1961

CHAPTER 5: GOING FOR THE LEADERSHIP

1 Toronto *Telegram,* 9 Feb. 1971

2 *Globe and Mail* (Toronto), 30 Sept. 1961

3 Interview with H. Price

4 Interview with F. Gardiner; A.K. Roberts, 'Thirty Years of Ontario Political Action' (Toronto: Private edition 1969), 127 (hereafter cited as Memoirs)

5 Ab Shepherd noted the campaign had cost $8,000 before the convention itself and Londoners had raised $8,400. But the cost which would be incurred during the convention period had Robarts' organizers worried. With the increased support from Toronto, the campaign actually showed a surplus. Some quotes went as high as $35,000.

6 *Globe and Mail,* 18 Oct. 1961

7 Ibid., 20 Oct. 1961; Sault Ste Marie *Star,* 19 Oct. 1961; Kingston *Whig Standard,* 19 Oct. 1961

8 Interview with John White
9 Interviews with Hon. William G. Davis and David B. Weldon. Also, both Macaulay and Roberts had reserved ballrooms at the Park Plaza for a victory celebration after the convention.
10 Toronto *Telegram,* 25 Oct. 1961
11 Roberts, *Memoirs,* 127-8
12 Interview with Robert Macaulay; Toronto *Telegram,* 25 Oct. 1961

CHAPTER 6: THE ROBARTS STYLE

1 Privileged interviews; interview with Colonel Douglas B. Weldon, Harry Price and JPR
2 Interview with JPR
3 Letter from R. Macaulay to A.K. McDougall, July 1978
4 Interviews with JPR and Don Collins. The recommendations are found in PAO, RG 3, Robarts, General Correspondence, Box 285, 'Org-Personnel PM's Dept., Jan.-Dec. 65.'
5 For background to the organized crime issue and the government's response, see A.K. McDougall, 'Policing in Ontario: The Occupational Dimension to Provincial Municipal Relations' (PH.D. thesis, University of Toronto, 1971).
6 Cited in ibid., 215
7 *Report* of the Attorney General's Committee on the Enforcement of the Law Related to Gambling (Morton Report), 1961, p. 127
8 OLA *Proceedings,* 7 Dec. 1961, pp. 251-3
9 Letter from R. Macaulay to A.K. McDougall, July 1978
10 PAO, RG 4, A-G. Box 38, A.K. Roberts to JPR, 11 Dec. 1961
11 Windsor *Star,* 26 Jan. 1962; *Globe and Mail,* 26 Jan. 1962
12 OLA *Proceedings,* 20 Feb. 1962, pp. 514-5
13 Ibid., 30 Nov. 1961, pp. 125-7
14 Interviews with R. Macaulay and James Allan .
15 *Globe and Mail,* 7 May 1962; Toronto *Telegram,* 9 May 1962
16 PAO, RG 3, Robarts, General Correspondence, Box 418, H.H. Walker to McIntyre, 24 April 1962; for a longer discussion of these reforms, see Schindeler, *Responsible Government,* 59-61.
17 PAO, RG 3, Robarts, Personal Correspondence, Macaulay to Robarts, 11 Sept. 1962
18 Ibid., General Correspondence, Box 363, Ontario Development Corporation, Nov. 61-Dec. 64 and Ontario Development Corporation 1961-1964
19 Ibid., By-Elections File, 448, 24 Oct. 1968
20 Interviews with JPR and Irene Beatty

CHAPTER 7: 'DONE!'

1 PAO, RG 3, Text File, JPR Speech to Canadian Club, Montreal, Jan. 1962; Ottawa *Citizen,* 8 Feb. 1962

2 *Globe and Mail,* 2 June 1962
3 PAO, RG 3, Robarts, Text File, JPR Speech at Royal York Hotel, 5 Oct. 1962
4 See John P. Robarts, Personal Papers, Series 4-3, 'Diefenbaker, John, 1965-7.'
5 London *Free Press,* 6 Feb. 1963
6 Toronto *Star,* 22 Feb. 1963
7 PAO, RG 3, Robarts, Personal Correspondence, Press Gallery, 25 Mar. 1963
8 Toronto *Star,* 20 Apr. 1963. Reprinted with permission – The Toronto Star Syndicate
9 *Globe and Mail,* 1 May 1963
10 PAO, RG 3, Robarts, Personal Correspondence, JPR to Pearson, 22 Apr. 1963
11 Ibid., Robarts, Statements-Speeches, Speech in Quebec City, 15 June 1963

CHAPTER 8: FIGHTING GRITS

1 PAO, RG 3, Robarts, Personal Correspondence, JPR to Pearson, 18 July 1963
2 Ibid., Robarts, General Correspondence, Box 478, Robarts Statement, 26 July 1963
3 *Globe and Mail,* 27 Aug. 1963
4 Ibid., 25 Aug. – 2 Sept. 1963
5 Interviews with E. Westendorp, E. Bell, E. Jackson, W. Kinmond, and H. Latimer
6 *Globe and Mail,* 6 Sept. 1963
7 LaMarsh, *Memoirs of a Bird in A Gilded Cage,* 84-5
8 Elmer Bell, 'Election Saga,' unpublished account of his role as Robarts' front man in the 1963 provincial election
9 PAO, RG 3, Box 488, Federal-Provincial Conference, 9-10 Sept. 1963
10 LaMarsh, *Bird in a Gilded Cage,* 85; *Globe and Mail,* 11 Sept. 1963
11 PAO, RG 3, Robarts, Press Releases, 11 Sept. 1963
12 *Globe and Mail,* 13 Sept. 1963
13 E. Bell, 'Election Saga'

CHAPTER 9: 'TERRIBLE LEGISLATION': BILL 99

1 PAO, RG 4, A-G. Files 1964, 607-8 Legislative Assembly
2 Ibid., RG 3, Robarts, Personal Correspondence, Macaulay to Robarts, 8 Oct. 1963
3 Interviews with JPR, E. Westendorp, R. Rohmer, E. Jackson, W. Kinmond, and I. Beatty
4 Edwards, *Law Officers of the Crown,* chaps. 9 and 10
5 For the Ontario Police Commission and other details of the Bill 99 affair, see McDougall, 'Policing in Ontario.'
6 PAO, RG 4, 1963, A-G. Files, Memo Collins to Robarts, 18 Oct. 1962
7 Interviews with Eric Silk, D. Collins, D.C. MacDonald
8 *Globe and Mail,* 26 Oct. 1962; Toronto *Telegram,* 21 Dec. 1963; *Globe and Mail,* 11 Jan. 1964
9 PAO, RG 4, 1963, A-G. Files, Box 72, Cass to JPR, 29 Oct. 1963

10 Ontario Police Commission, *Report on Crime,* 31 Jan. 1964, pp. 127-36
11 PAO, RG 4, 1965, A-G. Files, 757 re Bill 99
12 Ibid., and *Report on Crime,* 124
13 PAO, RG 4, 1965, A-G. Files, 757
14 Ibid.
15 Ibid., 1964, A-G. Files, Legislative Proposals for 1964, Police Act, File 608
16 Interview with F. Cass
17 *Canadian Annual Review,* 1964
18 *Maclean's,* 4 July 1964
19 *Canadian Annual Review,* 1964; OLA *Proceedings,* 20 Mar. 1964, p. 1865
20 Interviews with JPR, Kinmond, Cass
21 OLA *Proceedings,* 20 Mar. 1964, p. 1838
22 Interviews with JPR, Kinmond, Cass
23 PAO, RG 3, Robarts, General Correspondence, Box 33, 'Police Act, Mr. Robarts File,' Frost to JPR, 22 Mar. 1964
24 OLA *Proceedings,* 23 Mar. 1964, p. 1863
25 Ibid., 1864
26 Ibid., 1886
27 Ibid., 1907
28 Ibid.
29 PAO, RG 3, Robarts, Personal Correspondence, 'Resignations File,' 23 Mar. 1964
30 Ibid., Robarts, General Correspondence, Box 33, McIntyre to Robarts and att., 25 Mar. 1964
31 Order-in-council, 21 May 1964

CHAPTER 10: MODERNIZING THE GOVERNMENT

1 For background to these issues, see Perry et al., *Financing Canadian Federation;* also Foot, *Provincial Public Finance in Ontario.*
2 PAO, RG 3, Robarts, General Correspondence, Box 488, 'Federal-Provincial Conference, Nov. 26-29, 1963
3 Toronto *Telegram,* 13 Dec. 1963
4 PAO, RG 3, Robarts, Personal Correspondence, Robarts to Pearson, 14 Feb. 1964. See also, PAO, RG 3, Robarts, General Correspondence, Box 478, 'Canada Pension Plan Nov. 61-Oct. 64' for a broader review of the issue.
5 LaMarsh, *Bird in a Gilded Cage,* 130: used by permission of The Canadian Publishers, McClelland & Stewart Ltd., Toronto
6 PAO, RG 3, Robarts, General Correspondence, Box 489, Communiqué, 2 Apr. 1964
7 Ibid., Federal-Provincial Conference, 31 Mar.-2 Apr. 1964
8 Ibid.
9 Schindeler, *Responsible Government in Ontario,* 126-7

10 See Appendix B for the actual change in the length of sessions. Note that with Macaulay's departure, fall sittings also ended.
11 PAO, RG 3, Robarts, General Correspondence, Box 285, Memo Collins to Robarts, 29 July 1964
12 Interviews with H. Ian Macdonald and George Gathercole
13 PAO, RG 3, Robarts, General Correspondence, Box 471, Hogan-Rohmer, 14 Sept. 1964
14 Interview with JPR
15 PAO, RG 3, Robarts, General Correspondence, Box 405, Regional Development 1966
16 Interview with H. Ian Macdonald. See also, PAO, RG 3, Robarts, General Correspondence, Box 356, 'Economic Research-Reorg. of Economic Division 1965.'
17 Ibid., Reynolds to JPR, 16 June 1965. For the formation of the cabinet committe, see ibid., Box 392, Economics and Finance
18 Ibid., Brannan to Reynolds, 15 Dec. 1965; and for general background, see ibid., Boxes 406 and 407
19 Ibid., Box 367, 'Ontario Economic Council,' W.H. Cranston to JPR, 25 July 1966
20 Ibid., Statements-Press Releases, 9 Nov. 1967
21 Ibid.

CHAPTER II: TENDING THE GOLDEN GOOSE

1 For the development of this corporation from Macaulay's initiatives until it comes to fruition under Randall, see PAO, RG 3, Robarts, General Correspondence, Box 358, 'Housing General Nov 61-Dec 65.'
2 Bank of Canada, 'Annual Report of the Governor to the Minister of Finance for the Year 1965' (Ottawa, 28 Feb. 1966), 3
3 OLA, Select Committee on the Municipal Act and Related Acts, *Reports 2-5* (Toronto, 1964-5)
4 PAO, RG 3, Robarts, Box 406, Cabinet Committee Meeting, Minutes, 3 Mar. 1966; Advisory Committee on Regional Development, First Meeting, 16 Dec. 1966
5 *Financial Post,* 9 Feb. 1962
6 OLA *Proceedings,* 21 Feb. 1964, pp. 964ff
7 PAO, RG 3, Robarts, General Correspondence, Box 119, Goodman to JPR, 6 Aug. 1964
8 Ibid., RG 4, Plans for A-G.'s Department, Box 10, 30 June 1964, p. 4
9 Ibid., RG 3, Robarts, General Correspondence, Box 119, Kimber to JPR, 6 Aug. 1964
10 Royal Commission to Investigate Trading in the Shares of Windfall Oils and Mines Ltd., Sept. 1965, pp. 61-5
11 PAO, RG 3, Robarts, General Correspondence, Box 119, Report, Kimber to JPR, 6 Aug. 1964
12 Ibid., Statements-Press Releases, Press Release, 4 Aug. 1964

13 Ibid., General Correspondence, Box 119, 'Royal Commission of Inquiry – Windfall Nov 61-Dec 65'

14 Ibid., Goodman to JPR, 6 Aug. 1964

15 Ibid., Statements-Speeches, Statement by Hon. John P. Robarts, 8

16 Ibid., General Correspondence, Box 119, Kelly to JPR, 4 June 1965; reply 15 June 1965

17 OLA *Proceedings,* 16 Mar. 1966, p. 1581

18 *The Cooperatives Loans Act,* RSO 1960, c. 67

19 Mr Justice C. Grant, 'Fame Inquiry,' *Report,* Aug. 1965, pp. 105, 110, 113

20 *Report* of the Royal Commission Appointed to Inquire into the Failure of Atlantic Acceptance Corporation Ltd., 12 Sept. 1969, pp. 8-9

21 Ibid., 1-2

22 PAO, RG 3, Robarts, General Correspondence, Box 118, Kimber to Rowntree, 9 Aug. 1965

23 Ibid.

24 *Report* of the Royal Commission Appointed to Inquire into the Failure of Atlantic Acceptance Corporation Ltd., 1072, 1074

25 PAO, RG 3, Robarts, General Correspondence, Box 118, Registrar to Attorney General, 16 July 1965

26 Interview with JPR

27 *Report* of the Royal Commission Appointed to Inquire into the Failure of Atlantic Acceptance Corporation Ltd., 1080-81

28 Ibid.; announcement by A.A. Wishart, 27 July 1965. McCutcheon thus was approached behind the scenes by Price and agreed to help Lawson when asked. The overlap in communications is typical. Note also that McLaughlin and Frost were on the board of Victoria and Grey which eventually took over British Mortgage and Trust.

29 PAO, RG 3, Robarts, General Correspondence, Box 118, Macdonald to Gordon, 30 July 1965; reply, 17 Aug.

30 Interview with JPR

31 PAO, RG 3, Robarts, General Correspondence, Box 118, Robarts to H.J. McLaughlin, 10 Sept. 1965

32 Ibid., Bray to Kimber, 26 July 1965; Kimber to Rowntree, 9 Aug. 1965

33 Ibid., Box 113, McRuer to Wishart, 1 Dec. 1965; Wishart to JPR, 9 Dec. 1965; JPR to Wishart, 17 Dec. 1965

34 Ibid., Box 119, JPR to Wishart, 13 Oct. 1965

35 OLA *Proceedings,* 5 July 1966, p. 5622

36 Ibid., 16 Mar. 1966, p. 1583

37 PAO, RG 3, Robarts, General Correspondence, Box 113, Statement by Attorney General, 2 Dec. 1966. (Note the consistency with Robarts' position on the 'FAME' request.)

38 House of Commons, *Debates,* 19 Dec. 1966, p. 11286

39 Ibid., 11289-90
40 PAO, RG 3, Robarts, General Correspondence, Box 113, Statement, Wishart re Prudential Finance Corporation, Queen's Park, 21 Dec. 1966
41 For illustrations, see ibid., Box 115, 'Federal Provincial Securities Legislation Jan 66-Dec 66.'

CHAPTER 12: THE FACES OF FEDERALISM

1 Interview with JPR; also PAO, RG 3, Robarts, General Correspondence, Box 489, Federal-Provincial Conference, 31 Mar.-2 Apr. 1964
2 PAO, RG 3, Robarts, General Correspondence, Box 288, 'Premiers Conference 1964'
3 Ibid., Box 490, Pearson to JPR, 19 Aug. 1964
4 Federal-Provincial Conference, September 1964, *Proceedings, passim.;* communiqué, 2 Sept. 1964. See PAO, RG 3, Robarts, General Correspondence, Box 490 for the Summary of Proceedings prepared by Robarts' advisers as well.
5 PAO, RG 3, Robarts, General Correspondence, Box 490, 'Meeting re Federal-Provincial Conference,' 24 Sept. 1964
6 Ibid., Robarts, Statements-Speeches, CCAB Convention, Niagara Falls, 13-14 Oct. 1964
7 Ibid., Robarts, Personal Correspondence, Pearson to JPR, 3 Nov. 1964
8 Toronto *Telegram,* 4 Nov. 1964
9 Ibid., 5 Nov. 1964
10 OLA *Journals,* 1965, pp. 66-70
11 House of Commons, *Debates,* 18 Mar. 1965, pp. 12505-6
12 London *Free Press,* 19 Mar. 1965
13 PAO, RG 3, Robarts, General Correspondence, Box 491, 'Federal-Provincial Conference, July 18-22 1965,' Proceedings of Planning Meeting, 7 May 1965
14 Ibid.
15 Toronto *Telegram,* 21 July 1965; Toronto *Star,* 27 July 1965
16 PAO, RG 3, Robarts, General Correspondence, 'Folder on "Special Meetings",' Proceedings of the Meeting re Medicare, 14 Sept. 1965
17 Toronto *Star,* 13 Sept. 1965
18 Toronto *Telegram,* 2 Oct. 1965
19 Ibid., 8 Oct. 1965
20 PAO, RG 3, Robarts, Statements-Speeches, Seminar of Ontario and Quebec Editors, 8 Oct. 1965. See also, ibid., General Correspondence, Box 467, 'Ontario Advisory Committee on Confederation 1965-1966.'
21 Lubor Zink, in Toronto *Telegram,* 2 Dec. 1965
22 Letter from Rt Hon. John G. Diefenbaker to A.K. McDougall, 3 June 1977
23 PAO, RG 3, Robarts, Statements-Speeches, Text of Luncheon Address to Canadian Club, Montreal, 17 Jan. 1966
24 OLA *Proceedings,* 11 Feb. 1966, p. 456

25 Toronto *Telegram,* 3 Aug. 1966; Toronto *Star,* 4 Aug. 1966
26 PAO, RG 3, Robarts, General Correspondence, Box 492, Statements by Hon. Mitchell Sharp and John P. Robarts to the Tax Structure Committee
27 Ibid., Box 138, 'Medical Insurance-Ont. Participation, Jan-Dec 66'
28 Toronto *Star,* 16 Sept. 1966
29 A.K. Roberts, *Memoirs,* 180
30 PAO, RG 3, Robarts, General Correspondence, Box 492, text of speech by Hon. Mitchell Sharp
31 Ibid., Box 493, 'Federal-Provincial Conference on Taxation, Oct. 1966'
32 Toronto *Telegram,* 28 Oct. 1966
33 Ibid.
34 Coates, *The Night of the Knives,* 36; interviews with Jackson, Bell and JPR. See also, John P. Robarts Personal Papers. Series 4-3, 'Diefenbaker, John, 1965-7.'
35 Interview with JPR
36 Toronto *Star,* 15 Nov. 1966. Reprinted with permission – The Toronto Star Syndicate
37 Coates, *Night of the Knives,* 42-3

CHAPTER 13: CENTENNIAL: TURNING FIFTY

1 See Appendix A.
2 PAO, RG 3, Robarts, Personal Correspondence, 'Pearson,' Pearson-Robarts, 25 Jan. 1967; also ibid., General Correspondence, Box 443, Robarts-Pearson, 1 Feb. 1967 and att.
3 For a report on the seminar of 13-15 Jan. 1967 in Kingston, see PAO, RG 3, Robarts, General Correspondence, Box 466, 'Ontario Advisory Committee on Confederation, Jan.-July 67,'
4 House of Commons, *Debates,* 27 Jan. 1967, p. 12331
5 OLA *Proceedings,* 1 Feb. 1967, p. 149; PAO, RG 3, Robarts, General Correspondence, Box 443, 'Confederation of Tomorrow Conference,' JPR to Pearson, 1 Feb. 1967
6 For this interplay, see ibid., 'Confederation of Tomorrow Jan.-Apr. 67.'
7 Interview with W. Kinmond
8 Interviews with JPR and C.S. MacNaughton
9 Interview with JPR
10 PAO, RG 3, Robarts, General Correspondence, Box 35, Shulman to Wishart, 3 Apr. 1967
11 See the *Report* of the Royal Commission to Investigate Allegations relating to Coroners' Inquests, 1968 for details of the incident.
12 Toronto *Telegram,* 11 Apr. 1967
13 PAO, RG 3, Robarts, General Correspondence, Box 443, Results of a Meeting in Ottawa on 3 May 1967, undated
14 Ibid., Memo Macdonald to JPR, 5 May 1967; House of Commons, *Debates,* 10 May 1967, p. 55

15 *Globe and Mail,* 11 May 1967; OLA *Proceedings,* 18 May 1967, pp. 3566-71

16 PAO, RG 3, Robarts, Personal Correspondence, 'Pearson,' JPR to L.B. Pearson, 9 June 1967; Pearson to JPR, 15 June 1967. See also, the exchange of letters in ibid., Box 504, 'Pearson,' especially 1 Feb. 1967.

CHAPTER 14: CENTENNIAL: CONFEDERATION OF TOMORROW

1 PAO, RG 3, Robarts, Statements-Speeches, Address at Expo 67, 5 Aug. 1967, p. 7

2 Ibid., 5 Sept. 1967, pp. 1-2

3 *Canadian Annual Review,* 1967

4 Toronto *Star,* 29 Sept. 1967

5 Sudbury *Star,* 5 Oct. 1967; Toronto *Telegram,* 3 Oct. 1967; London *Free Press,* 5 Oct. 1967

6 PAO, RG 3, Robarts, Statements-Speeches, Oct. 1967, p.2

7 For a detailed analysis of the results, see Wilson and Hoffman, 'Ontario: A Three-Party System in Transition,' in Robin, *Canadian Provincial Politics.*

8 The posturing had its effect. See Toronto *Telegram* and *Globe and Mail,* 21 Nov. 1967

9 For a review of the preparations for the Confederation of Tomorrow conference, including the preliminary provincial consultations of which the Regina speech marked a final instalment, see PAO, RG 3, Robarts, General Correspondence, Boxes 443 and 444. For federal reservations, see ibid., Box 445. The *Proceedings* of the conference were published separately by the Advisory Committee on Confederation in 1968.

10 PAO, RG 3, Robarts, Statements-Speeches, 27 Nov. 1967

11 *Globe and Mail,* 29 Nov. 1967

12 Ibid., 29, 30 Nov. 1967

13 *Globe and Mail,* Toronto *Telegram,* Vancouver *Sun,* Montreal *Star,* 30 Nov. 1967

14 Interview with JPR

15 PAO, RG 3, Robarts, Statements-Speeches, 27 Feb. 1968

16 Ibid., 17 May 1968, Statement at Queen's Park

CHAPTER 15: NEW MOOD, OLD ISSUES

1 OLA *Proceedings,* 6-7 Mar. 1968, pp. 502-18, 539-54

2 Ibid., 29 Feb. 1968, pp. 332-3

3 Ibid., 340

4 Ibid., 11 Apr. 1968, p. 1865

5 See Bibliography for the resultant Local Government Reviews.

6 Ontario, Minister of Education, *Annual Report,* 1967, p. 9

7 Toronto *Telegram,* 15 Nov. 1967

8 House of Commons, *Debates,* 10 Nov. 1967, p. 4214

9 MacNaughton Papers, Speeches, MacNaughton to the Ministers of Finance and Pro-

vincial Treasurers, 16 Nov. 1967. See also House of Commons, *Debates*, 20 Nov. 1967, p. 4434

10 *Canadian Annual Review*, 1968, p. 125

11 PAO, RG 3, Robarts, General Correspondence, Box 451, 'Executive Council Jan 68-Dec 68,' JPR Memo, 22 Jan. 1968

12 OLA *Proceedings*, 28 Feb. 1968, pp. 302-3

13 Ibid., 306-7

14 For a review of this, see PAO, RG 3, Robarts, General Correspondence, Box 410, 'Regional Development – Regional Govt. Jan-Dec 1968,' Memorandum from McKeough, and Department of Treasury and Economics, Background Papers for Cabinet, 'The Relationship between Regional Government, Regional Development, the Smith Report and Other Provincial Issues,' 28 Aug. 1968, pp. 4-5.

15 Ibid. The problem was a major issue at the cabinet 'retreat' in August 1968.

16 The short deadline and the recommendation that the Prime Minister's Department be responsible for regional government contained a touch of 'We made *our* deadline; let's see what *you* can do.' Interview with John White.

17 *Taxation in Ontario:* The Report of the Select Committee of the Legislature on the Report of the Ontario Committee on Taxation (White), 16 Sept. 1968, especially 3-4, 118, 149

18 PAO, RG 3, Robarts, Statements-Speeches, 17 Sept. 1968

19 MacNaughton Papers, Text of Speech, Charles S. MacNaughton, 24 Oct. 1968

20 PAO, RG 3, Robarts, Statements-Speeches, 4 Nov. 1968

21 *Globe and Mail*, 5 Nov. 1968

22 Toronto *Telegram*, 25 Oct. 1968

23 PAO, RG 3, Robarts, Statements-Speeches, 25 Oct. 1968

24 Ibid., Text of Speech to Annual Convention, 3 Nov. 1968

CHAPTER 16: 'WE CANNOT ALL BE WRONG – CAN WE?'

1 OLA *Proceedings*, 19 Nov. 1968, p. 4 and Ontario, Department of the Prime Minister, *Design for Development*, Phase II, 1968

2 OLA *Proceedings*, 28 Nov. 1968, p. 235

3 *Design for Development*, Phase II

4 The short-term proposals were contained in 'A Fiscal Framework for the Future.' The long-term proposals were set out in 'The White Paper on Tax Reform.' Both were components of the 1969 budget.

5 Ontario Budget Statement, 1969

6 Toronto *Star*, 6 Mar. 1969 (Anthony Westall) and Hamilton *Spectator*, 5 Mar. 1969

7 MacNaughton Papers, Speech, 7 Mar. 1969

8 OLA *Proceedings* 10 Mar. 1969, p. 2036

9 Sarnia *Observer*, 8 Apr. 1969

10 OLA *Proceedings*, 16 Apr. 1969, p. 3171

11 PAO, RG 3, Robarts, General Correspondence, Box 234, Healey-McKeough, 6 Jan. 1969
12 Davis had a difficult time defining the magnitude of the problem: OLA *Proceedings,* 24 Apr. 1969, pp. 3505-6. The result is found in the Ontario Budget, 1970-1, p. 15.
13 See MacNaughton's statement in OLA *Proceedings,* 24 Apr. 1969, pp. 3507-8.
14 *Lindsay Post,* 5 Apr. 1969
15 PAO, RG 3, Robarts, Personal Correspondence, 'Education Dept. of, General,' Frost to Robarts, 2 May 1969
16 Ibid., JPR to Frost, 6 May 1969
17 OLA *Proceedings,* 13 May 1969, p. 4360
18 London *Free Press,* 10 Sept. 1969
19 PAO, RG 3, Robarts, General Correspondence, Box 34 'Hydro,' Reynolds to Robarts, 3 Nov. 1969

CHAPTER 17: ENTERING THE SEVENTIES

1 PAO, RG 3, Robarts, Personal Correspondence, Robarts to Beverley Matthews, 9 June 1970
2 Interview with William Rathbun
3 John P. Robarts, Personal Papers, Series 4-3, L.M. Frost 1969, Gardiner to Frost, 26 Sept. 1969
4 PAO, RG 3, Robarts, Statements-Speeches, OPCA Annual Meeting, 6 Dec. 1969
5 Ibid., Federal-Provincial Conference, 8 Dec. 1969
6 Toronto *Telegram,* 11 Dec. 1969
7 Ibid., 6 Feb. 1970
8 Toronto *Star,* 10 Apr. 1970
9 Interview with John White
10 OLA *Proceedings,* 9 Mar. 1970, p. 341
11 Ibid., 14 Apr. 1970, p. 1468
12 PAO, RG 3, Robarts, Statements-Speeches, Empire Club (Toronto), 9 Apr. 1970
13 Ibid., Provincial-Municipal Conference, 22 Apr. 1970, pp. 9-10
14 Ibid., Law Society of Upper Canada, 19 Mar. 1970
15 Interview with JPR
16 *Globe and Mail,* 30 Dec. 1970

CHAPTER 18: 'I'M A HAS-BEEN'

1 Robarts' most extreme reaction to oppressive security resulted from his experience at the tenth anniversary of the opening of the St Lawrence Seaway in northern New York State. After the ceremony, he literally raced back to Ontario and the peace of Upper Canada Village. Interviews with JPR and Rathbun

2 *Ottawa Journal,* 15 Oct. 1970
3 Toronto *Star,* 15 Oct. 1970
4 OLA *Proceedings,* 16 Oct. 1970, pp. 5097-5100
5 Toronto *Star,* 3 Oct. 1970
6 Interview with JPR. See also, for example, William Davis in OLA *Proceedings,* 6 Oct. 1970, p. 4661.
7 OLA *Proceedings,* 13 Nov. 1970, p. 6552
8 Toronto *Star,* 27 Nov. 1970
9 PAO, RG 3, Robarts, General Correspondence, Box 470, JPR to Eagleson, 8 Dec. 1970
10 London *Free Press,* 8 Dec. 1970; Toronto *Star,* 9 Dec. 1970
11 Toronto *Telegram,* 11 Dec. 1970; Guelph *Mercury,* 15 Dec. 1970; Eric Dowd, *Ottawa Citizen,* 16 Dec. 1970; Jonathan Manthorpe, *Globe and Mail,* 17 Dec. 1970; D.O'Hearn, Woodstock *Sentinel Review,* 17 Dec. 1970
12 Interview with MacNaughton
13 For a review of this story, see Manthorpe, *The Power and the Tories,* chaps. 7-10.
14 The incident received extensive press coverage. For example, see *Globe and Mail,* 27 Jan. 1971.
15 Toronto *Star,* 4 Feb. 1971; Toronto *Telegram,* 4 Feb. 1971
16 *Globe and Mail,* 10 Feb. 1971
17 Interviews with JPR, R. Spiers, and personal observation
18 Toronto *Star,* 21 Feb. 1971

CHAPTER 19: 'MY TIME IS FINISHED'

1 Interview with JPR
2 Interview with Norah Robarts
3 Conversations between the author and JPR
4 Ibid.
5 John P. Robarts Personal Papers, Series 4-3, Investment Portfolio
6 Interview with Robin Robarts
7 Interview with Katherine Robarts
8 Interview with Colonel D.B. Weldon
9 Interview with JPR
10 Ibid.
11 Task Force on Canadian Unity, *A Future Together* (January 1979), 6, 21
12 Interview with Katherine Robarts
13 Ibid.
14 Ibid.
15 He received the final payment in early October 1982.
16 Interview with Katherine Robarts. For Katherine's memories of this period and the suicide, see the Toronto *Star,* 20 Oct. 1983.

Bibliography

PRIMARY SOURCES

The substance of this book rests primarily on documents held in the Ontario Archives and material generated by interviews given by many of the people involved in this period of Ontario's history.

The Ontario Archives has organized its holdings by department. The record sets for the departments of Treasury and Economics, Treasury, Economics and Development, Trade and Development, Education, and the Attorney General were used extensively and are referred to by the appropriate access code in the notes. In addition, the prime minister's papers are divided. His personal papers are maintained with the private collections, while personal correspondence, notes, or appointment books kept at Queen's Park are found in a personal papers collection under the Prime Minister's Department. This comprises the RG 3 collection referred to in the notes. Useful information is also to be found in the papers of Leslie Frost, Charles MacNaughton, and William Stewart. Other records used extensively were the Minutes of the Ontario Progressive-Conservative Association from 1948 to 1971 and the Minutes of the London Progressive-Conservative Association from 1958 to 1971.

John Robarts provided lengthy and precise comments on issues and events as the story took form. Over the last ten years, his family, friends, and colleagues have given freely of their time to confirm facts or clarify vague references. Robert and Eleanor Robarts have been generous enough to review the family Bible time and time again as well as to sort through family records.

Keith Reynolds kindly lent me his oral diary for the late 1960s while he served as deputy minister for the Prime Minister's Department and secretary to the cabinet, provided interviews, and reviewed part of the text. Throughout, the only person who refused to be interviewed was John Diefenbaker, who in the mid-1970s commented that he had nothing good to say about John Robarts.

The following people granted lengthy interviews:

James Allan
James Auld
Walter Baker
Ben Baldwin
Irene R. Beatty
Elmer Bell
Stuart Carver
Frederick Cass
Donald J. Collins
Reginald H. Cooper
Ted Dampier
William G. Davis
A. Rendall Dick
Richard Dillon
J. Stefan Dupré
Tom Eberlee
T. Ray Farrell
Geno Francolini
George Gathercole
Reva Gerstein
Walter Gordon
William C. Heine
Ernest G. Jackson
Alex Jeffery
Fred Jenkins
William Jenkins
William Kinmond

Hugh Latimer
A.B.R. (Bert) Lawrence
Roderick Lewis
Robert Macaulay
Donald C. MacDonald
H. Ian Macdonald
David McFadden
William McGuffin
Mary McHugh
William McHugh
Charles MacNaughton
S. Floyd Maine
Don Martyn
Robert W. Mitchell
Robert Nixon
Farquhar Oliver
Claude Pensa
Clarence Peterson
Harry Price
James Ramsay
Stanley Randall
William Rathbun
J. Keith Reynolds
Eleanor Robarts
Katherine Robarts
Norah Robarts

Robert Robarts
Robin Robarts
Tim Robarts
Richard Rohmer
Ann Rudd
D.S. (Bill) Rudd
Albert H. Shepherd
Eric Silk
Rosemary Spiers
Michael Starr
Don Stevenson
William Stewart
Dale Thomson
Peter Venton
Gordon Walker
Harold Walker
David Weldon
Col. Douglas B. Weldon
Clare Westcott
Eugene Westendorp
John H. White
Peter G. White
Benson Wilson
Eric Winkler
John Wintermeyer
Arthur Wishart

SECONDARY SOURCES

Government Reports: Canada
Royal Commission on Health Services (Hall). *Report*. Ottawa: Queen's Printer
  1964–5
The Amendment of the Constitution of Canada. Ottawa: Queen's Printer 1965
Royal Commission on Taxation (Carter). *Report*. Ottawa: Queen's Printer
  1966–7
Task Force on Canadian Unity. *A Future Together*. Ottawa, January 1979; *Coming to
  Terms*. Ottawa, February 1979; *A Time to Speak*. Ottawa, March 1979
Federal-Provincial Conference, 1963, Ottawa, 26–29 November 1963. *Report of Pro-
  ceedings*. Ottawa: Queen's Printer 1964
Federal-Provincial Conference, Quebec, 31 March–1 April 1964. *Proceedings*. Ottawa:
  Privy Council Office 1968

Federal-Provincial Conference, Charlottetown, 31 August–2 September 1964. *Proceedings*. Ottawa: Privy Council Office 1968

Federal-Provincial Conference, Ottawa, 24–28 October 1966. *Proceedings*. Ottawa: Privy Council Office 1968

Federal-Provincial Conference of Ministers of Finance and Provincial Treasurers, Ottawa, 1968. *Proceedings*. Ottawa: Queen's Printer 1969

Federal-Provincial Rural Development Agreement, 12 May 1970. Federal-Provincial Rural Development Agreement 1970–75: ARDA. Department of Regional Economic Expansion 1971

Government Reports: Ontario

Advisory Committee on Confederation. Background Papers and Reports. 3 vols. *The Confederation Challenge*. Toronto 1967

Advisory Committee on Confederation. The Confederation of Tomorrow Conference. *Proceedings*. Toronto 1968

Attorney General's Department. Committee on Enforcement of the Law Relating to Gambling (J.D. Morton). *Report*. Toronto 1961

Attorney General's Department. Committee on Securities Legislation (J.R. Kimber). *Report*. Toronto 1965

Committee on Government Productivity (Cronyn Committee). *Reports 1–10*. Toronto 1970–3

Committee on the Healing Arts. *Report*. Toronto 1970

Committee on the Organization of Government in Ontario (Walter Gordon). *Report*. Toronto 1959

Committee on Taxation (L.J. Smith). *Report*. Toronto 1967

Ontario Economic Council. *The Evolution of Policy in Contemporary Ontario*. Toronto 1974

Ontario Economic Council. *Government Reform in Ontario: A Report*. Toronto 1969

Ontario Economic Council. *Municipal Reform: A Proposal for the Future*. Toronto 1971

Ontario Economic Council (D.K. Foot). *Provincial Public Finance in Ontario*. Toronto 1972

GO-Transit. *Government of Ontario Transit: A New Approach to Urban Transportation*. Toronto 1968

Ontario Law Reform Commission. *Reports 3, 3A*. Toronto: Department of the Attorney General 1965–6

Medical Services Insurance Committee (J.G. Hagey). *Report*. Toronto 1964

Municipal Affairs. Haldimand-Norfolk Study. *Towards a New System of Local Government*. Toronto 1972

Municipal Affairs. Hamilton-Burlington-Wentworth Local Government Review Commission (Steele). *Report and Recommendations*. Hamilton 1964

Municipal Affairs. Lakehead Local Government Review (Hardy). *Report and Recommendations*. 11 Mar. 1968

Municipal Affairs. Muskoka District Local Government Review (Paterson). *Report*.
Gravenhurst 1968–9

Municipal Affairs. Niagara Region Local Government Review (Mayo). *Report*. Toronto
1966

Municipal Affairs. Ottawa, Eastview and Carleton County. Local Government Review
(M. Jones). *Report*. Toronto 1965

Municipal Affairs. Oshawa Area Planning and Development Study. *The Regional
Development Concept Plan*. Oshawa 1971

Municipal Affairs. Oxford Area Local Government Study. *Final Report*. Woodstock
1973

Municipal Affairs. Peel Halton Local Government Review (Plunkett). *Report*. Toronto
1966

Police Commission. *Report to the Attorney General on Organized Crime, January 31,
1964*. 1964

Prime Minister. *Design for Development, Phase I, April 5, 1966*. Toronto 1966

Prime Minister. *Design for Development, Phase II, December 2, 1968*. Toronto 1968

Prime Minister. *The Ontario Foundation Tax Plan, 1964*. Toronto 1963

Prime Minister. *Responsible Taxation: The Ontario Approach ...* Toronto 1969

Ontario Securities Commission (D.S. Beatty). *Report* on Financing of Mining Exploration and Development Companies. Toronto 1968

Royal Commission on Atlantic Acceptance (H.S. Hughes) *Report*. Toronto 1969

Submission to the Royal Commission on Banking and Finance. Ottawa 1962

Royal Commission of Inquiry into Civil rights in Ontario (McRuer). 3 vols. *Reports*.
Toronto 1968–71

Royal Commission on Crime (Roach). *Report*. Toronto 1963

Royal Commission under the Designation FAME Inquiry. *Report*. Toronto 1965

Royal Commission of Inquiry into Labour Disputes (Ivan Rand). *Report*. Toronto 1968

Commission on the Legislature (Dalton Camp). 5 vols. *Reports*. Toronto 1973–5

Royal Commission on Metropolitan Toronto (Goldenberg). *Report*. Toronto 1965

Royal Commission on Metropolitan Toronto (Robarts). *Report*. Toronto 1977

Commission of Inquiry re Ontario Provincial Police. *Report*. Toronto 1970

Royal Commission to Investigate Trading in the Shares of Windfall Oils and Mines Ltd.
(A. Kelly). *Report*. Toronto 1965

Resources for Tomorrow Conference. *Resources for Tomorrow*. Ottawa 1961–2

Department of Treasury and Economics. Metropolitan Toronto and Region Transportation
Study. Toronto 1967–8

Department of Treasury and Economics. *Report* of the Central Ontario Lakeshore Urban
Complex Task Force. Toronto 1974

Department of Treasury and Economics. *Regional Planning and Development: A Policy
to Implement the Toronto-Centred Region Development Concept*. Toronto: Municipality of Metropolitan Toronto 1971

Books

Armstrong, F.H. et al. *Aspects of Nineteenth-Century Ontario*. Toronto: University of Toronto Press 1974

Baker, S. *The Rise and Progress of London*. London: Hayden Press 1924[?]

Bothwell, Robert. *Lester Pearson: His Life and World*. Toronto: McGraw-Hill/Ryerson 1978

Bothwell, Robert, Ian Drummond, and John English. *Canada Since 1945: Power, Politics, and Provincialism*. Toronto: University of Toronto Press 1981

Bothwell, Robert and William Kilbourn. *C.D. Howe: A Biography*. Toronto: McClelland and Stewart 1979

Cameron, David M. *Schools for Ontario: Policy-making, Administration and Finance in the 1960s*. Toronto: University of Toronto Press 1972

Camp, Dalton. *Gentlemen, Players and Politicians*. Ottawa: Deneau 1979

Caplan, Gerald Lewis. *The Dilemma of Canadian Socialism: The CCF in Ontario*. Toronto: McClelland and Stewart 1973

Chandler, Marsha A. and William M. Chandler. *Public Policy and Provincial Politics*. Toronto: McGraw-Hill/Ryerson 1979

Coates, Robert C. *The Night of the Knives*. Fredericton: Brunswick Press 1969

Colton, Tim. *Big Daddy: Frederick G. Gardiner and the Building of Metropolitan Toronto*. Toronto: University of Toronto Press 1980

Desbarats, Peter. *René: A Canadian in Search of a Country*. Toronto: McClelland and Stewart 1976

Diefenbaker, John George. *One Canada*. 3 vols. Toronto: Macmillan of Canada 1975–7

Dupré, J. Stefan et al. *Federalism and Policy Development: The Case of Adult Occupational Training in Ontario*. Toronto: University of Toronto Press 1973

Edwards, J.Ll.J. *Law Officers of the Crown*. London: Sweet and Maxwell 1964

Elkins, D.J. and R. Simeon. *Small Worlds: Parties and Provinces in Canadian Political Life*. Toronto: Methuen Company of Canada 1980

Feldman, Lionel and M. Goldrick. *Politics and Government of Urban Canada: Selected Readings*. Toronto: Methuen Company of Canada 1969

Gordon, Walter. *A Political Memoir*. Toronto: McClelland and Stewart 1977

Granatstein, J.L. *The Politics of Survival: The Conservative Party of Canada 1939–1945*. Toronto: University of Toronto Press 1967

Hogan, G. *The Conservative in Canada*. Toronto: McClelland and Stewart 1963

Horowitz, Gad. *Canadian Labour in Politics*. Toronto: University of Toronto Press 1968

LaMarsh, Judy. *Memoirs of a Bird in a Gilded Cage*. Toronto: McClelland and Stewart 1968

Lewis, David. *The Good Fight: Political Memoirs 1909–1958*. Toronto: Macmillan of Canada 1981

MacDonald, Donald C. *The Government and Politics of Ontario*. Rev. ed. Toronto: Van Nostrand Reinhold 1980

McRoberts, Kenneth and Dale Postgate. *Quebec: Social Change and Political Crisis.* Rev. ed. Toronto: McClelland and Stewart 1980

Manthorpe, Jonathan. *The Power and the Tories: Ontario Politics – 1943 to the Present.* Toronto: Macmillan of Canada 1974

Martin, Paul. *A Very Public Life.* Ottawa: Deneau 1983

Miller, Orlo. *A Century of Western Ontario: The Story of London.* Westport, Conn.: Greenwood Press 1949

Nelles, Henry Vivian. *The Politics of Development: Forestry, Mines & Hydro-Electric Power in Ontario, 1849–1941.* Toronto: Macmillan of Canada 1974

Newman, Peter C. *The Distemper of Our Times: Canadian Politics in Transition, 1963–1968.* Toronto: McClelland and Stewart 1968

– *Renegade in Power: The Diefenbaker Years.* Toronto: Carleton Library 1973

Pearson, Lester B. *Mike: The Memoirs of the Rt. Hon. Lester B. Pearson.* Vol. 1. Toronto: University of Toronto Press 1972; Vol. 2. Edited by John A. Munro and A.I. Inglis. Toronto: University of Toronto Press 1973; Vol. 3. Edited by John A. Munro and A.I. Inglis. Toronto: University of Toronto Press 1975

Perry, J.H. et al. *Financing Canadian Federation.* Toronto: Canadian Tax Foundation 1967

Plunkett, Thomas J. *Urban Canada and Its Government.* Toronto: Macmillan of Canada 1968

Provencher, Jean. *René Lévesque: Portrait of a Québécois.* Translated by David Ellis. Don Mills: PaperJacks 1977

Quinn, Herbert F. *The Union Nationale: Quebec Nationalism from Duplessis to Lévesque.* 2d ed. Toronto: University of Toronto Press 1979

Roberts, A. Kelso. *Thirty Years of Ontario Political Action.* Toronto: Private edition 1969

Robin, Martin. *Canadian Provincial Politics.* 1st ed. Scarborough: Prentice-Hall 1972

Schindeler, F.F. *Responsible Government in Ontario.* Toronto: University of Toronto Press 1969

Shulman, Morton. *Member of the Legislature.* Don Mills: Fitzhenry & Whiteside 1979

Simeon, Richard. *Federal-Provincial Diplomacy: The Making of Recent Policy in Canada.* Toronto: University of Toronto Press 1972

Smiley, D.V. *Canada in Question.* 2d ed. Toronto: McGraw-Hill/Ryerson 1976

Stevens, Geoffrey. *Stanfield.* Toronto: McClelland and Stewart 1973

Thomson, Dale. *Louis St. Laurent, Canadian.* Toronto: Macmillan of Canada 1967

Trudeau, P.E. *Federalism and the French Canadians.* Toronto: Macmillan of Canada 1968

Whitaker, R. *The Government Party.* Toronto: University of Toronto Press 1977

Articles

Beecroft, Eric. 'Regional Government and Public Finance,' *Canadian Forum* 47 (1967), 201–3

Bell, E. 'An Election Saga.' Unpublished 1963

Bryden, Kenneth. 'Executive and Legislature in Ontario: A Case Study on Governmental Reform,' *Canadian Public Administration* 18, no. 2 (Summer 1975)

Calvert, John. 'The Ontario Development Corporation,' *Canadian Forum* 51 (1971), 23–8

Courchene, Thomas J. 'Federal-Provincial Tax Equalization: An Evaluation,' *Canadian Journal of Economics* 6 (1973), 483–502

Cronyn, J.B. 'Management of Government: A Reappraisal,' *Business Quarterly* 38, no. 2 (Summer 1973), 56–64

Etchen, A. 'Some Impressions Arising from the First Year of Operation of the Ontario Development Agency,' *Ontario Economic Review* 12 (1964)

– 'Government Reorganization and TEIGA,' *Ontario Economic Review* 11 (1973)

Fleck, J.D. 'Restructuring the Ontario Government,' *Canadian Public Administration* 16, no. 1 (Spring 1973), 55–68

Grossman, Lawrence S. '"Safe" Seats: The Rural-Urban Pattern in Ontario,' *Canadian Journal of Economics and Political Science* 29 (1963), 367–71

Jacek, H. et al. 'Federal Provincial Integration in Ontario Party Organization,' paper presented to the Canadian Political Science Association 1970

Leduc, Lawrence et al. 'The Role of Opposition in a One-Party Dominant System: The Case of Ontario,' *Canadian Journal of Political Science* 7 (1974), 86–100

Macdonald, H. Ian. 'The Solemnization of an Institutional Marriage,' *Ontario Economic Review* 7 (1969)

McKeough, W. Darcy. 'Urban Policies in the Making – Ontario,' *Community Planning Review* 20, no. 2 (1970), 11–13

Martin, Joe. 'The Role and Place of Ontario in the Canadian Confederation,' Ontario Economic Council 1974

Morton, Desmond. 'The Reform of Taxation and Government Structure in Ontario,' *Ontario Economic Review* 7 (1969), 3–9

– 'Ontario, 1975: 'Reflections on the Tory Decline,' *Canadian Forum* 56 (1975), 8–10

Smiley, Donald V. 'The McRuer Report; Parliamentary Majoritarian Democracy and Human Rights,' *Journal of Canadian Studies* 5 (1970), 3–10

White, John. 'Fiscal Policy Management and Tax Sharing Reform,' *Ontario Economic Review* 11 (1973), 3–6

Willis, John. 'Report of the Committee on the Organization of Government in Ontario,' *University of Toronto Law Journal* 14 (1961), 103–7

Wilson, John M. 'The Election That Never Was,' *Canadian Forum* 47 (1967), 169–71

Wilson, John and David Hoffman. 'The Liberal Party in Ontario Politics,' *Canadian Journal of Political Science* 3 (1970), 177–204

Index

Abitibi Paper 263
Administration of justice 118, 190, 210
ADSEPA 18, 19, 25–7, 38, 59, 66, 255
Allan, Harry 36
Allan, James 51, 56, 60, 63–5, 68, 70–1, 76–7, 86, 88, 91, 107, 113, 139, 170, 178, 207
Apps, Syl 109
Arnup, J.D. 146
Atkins, Norman 258, 261
Atlantic Acceptance 151–6, 239
Atomic energy 41, 49
Attorney general 76, 91, 115, 117, 119, 122, 124, 155, 156, 158, 209
Auld, James 40, 42, 44, 50, 59, 61, 91, 98, 104, 121, 122, 189, 256

Baby boom 52, 87, 183, 205, 206, 221, 243
Backbench evenings 36, 40, 44, 45, 46, 134
Bagwell, George 28
Baldwin, Ben 59
Bales, Dalton 178, 213
Banff, Alberta 3, 4
Bassett, John 76
Beal Technical School, London 29
Beatty, Irene 82, 92, 122, 236
Beck, Sir Adam 16, 20

Beckett, Hollis 85, 86, 210
Bell Canada 263
Bell, Elmer 23, 58, 59, 60, 68, 71, 77, 103, 106–10, 140, 168, 175, 182, 220
Bennett, W.A.C. 197
Benson, Edgar 216
Bettam, A.E. 22
Betts, Peter 36, 237
Bickle, E.W. 58
Bill 99, 114–15, 118–26, 128, 133, 147, 155, 161, 185, 219, 230
Bill of Rights 186, 188, 196, 200
Blackburn, Walter 51
Blackwell, Leslie 18
Bolton, Kenneth C. 232
Bourassa, Robert 201, 256
Braden, Harold 15, 17
Bradford, Norman 22
Brannan, C.E. 89, 138, 212
Branksome Hall, Toronto 5, 7
Brantford *Expositor* 193
Brett, Earl 3, 4
Brett, Florency May Stacpoole. *See* Robarts, Florency May
HMS *Britannia* 188
British Mortgage and Trust 152–7, 160, 292
Brockville, Ontario 40, 44

Brown, Colin 255
Brown, Hugh 138
Brown, John 193, 195, 218
Brunelle, René 178
Bullbrook, James 195

Cabinet (Ontario) 221, 233, 236
Cabinet Committee on Economics and
 Finance 212
Cabinet Committee on Policy Develop-
 ment 212, 216, 224, 231
Cabinet Committee on Regional Develop-
 ment 212
Cabinet shuffles: (1958) 49; (1959) 58;
 (1961–2) 71, 277, 278; (1962) 279;
 restructuring (1966) 137, 178, 212,
 213; (1967) 240; (1968) 240; (1969)
 230, 235, 236, 240; (1970) 240
Calder, Campbell 17, 24, 25, 28, 30, 110
Camp, Dalton 86, 174, 175, 182, 258,
 261
Canada Assistance Plan 167
Canada, centennial 114, 163, 177, 185,
 188ff
Canada Pension Plan. See Pension plans
Canada Trust 153
Canadian Annual Review 110
Canadian Bar Association 146
Canadian Broadcasting Corporation 121,
 184
Canadian Imperial Bank of Commerce
 263. See also Imperial Bank
Canadian Industrial Supply Company 51
Canadian Institute of Public Opinion 98
Canadian Oil Companies 145, 146
Canadian Securities and Exchange Com-
 mission 160
Capital gains tax 225
Capital markets 142, 151, 247, 252, 253
Carrothers, Fox, Robarts, and Betts 23,
 36, 50
Cartier, Frank 194

Carver, Stuart 9, 10, 18
Cass, Fred 63, 76, 91, 116–22, 124–6,
 145, 146, 147, 234
Cathcart, Brian 104
Cecile, Louis 178
Century City 248
Chapman, J. Ronald 21, 22, 23
Charlottetown, PEI 163
Chateau Laurier Hotel, Ottawa 175
Chautauqua troupe 6
Chedoke Expressway 91
'Chicago Gang' 112–13, 125
Children's Aid Society 193
Chinguacousy Township 249
Civil Service Commission (Ontario) 116
Cobalt bomb 286
Collective bargaining (Public Service) 89,
 95
Collins, Donald J. 42–3, 45, 48, 77, 83,
 89, 116, 134–5, 140
Committee for an Independent Canada 246
Committee of Economic and Financial
 Advisers 138–9
Committee on Government Productivity
 231
Committee on the Organization of the
 Government of Ontario 89
Common, W.B. 146
Commonwealth Holiday Inns of Canada
 263
Confederation of Tomorrow conference
 174, 177–80, 185–90, 193ff, 198, 200,
 211, 269
Connell, Ray 63
Conservatism 10, 18, 23, 43
Conservative party. See Progressive-
 Conservative party
Constituency boundaries 85, 86
Constitutional amendment 163–9, 199,
 259
Constitutional reform 163–4, 176, 179,
 196–201, 239, 259, 269

Consumer protection 114, 18, 143, 146, 147, 154–9

CCF 17, 14, 51; London campaign (1951) 28, 29, 30; provincial campaign (1951) 28; provincial campaign (1955) 41

Co-operative federalism 102

ss *Corinthia* 161

Cornell, Ward 52, 66, 194

Cotnam, H.B. 185

County school boards 211, 220, 223, 227, 229, 238

Cowling, Alfred 40

Croden, John 51

Cronyn, John B. 231

Cross, James 251

Cudney, J.R. 108–9

Currie, James H. 38

Daley, Charles 'Tod' 76, 91

Daley, Pat 28, 30

Dalgleish, Oakley 58, 64, 78

Dampier, Ted 19

Davis, William 91, 100, 198, 213, 220, 223, 227, 252–3, 258, 260–1, 264, 272–3

Dawson City, Yukon 3

Day, Ruth 24

de Gaulle, Charles 189, 197–8

Delta Upsilon Fraternity 9, 17, 19, 25, 27, 51

Democratic Party convention (1960) 66

Denison Mines Limited 152–3

Dennis, Lloyd 219–20

Dennison, W. 177

Department of the Attorney General 97, 116, 118, 147, 155–6, 178

Department of Economics and Development 86, 96, 113, 135–7, 144–5, 214

Department of Education 52–3, 56, 77, 87, 90–1, 114, 211, 215, 220, 227, 229

Department of Energy and Resources Management 113–14

Department of Financial and Commercial Affairs 156, 158, 159, 178, 240, 249

Department of Health 89, 215

Department of Highways 76, 178

Department of Insurance 115, 147, 155

Department of Labour 44, 54, 55, 76, 89, 178

Department of Lands and Forests 98, 178

Department of Mines 76, 230

Department of Mines and Northern Development 230

Department of Municipal Affairs 76, 214, 228

Department of the Prime Minister (Ontario) 83, 114, 119, 134, 206–7, 235–6, 237

Department of Provincial Revenue 139

Department of Public Welfare 178

Department of Reform Institutions 104

Department of Trade and Industry 244

Department of Transport 45, 47, 87, 91, 104

Department of Travel and Publicity 104, 121

Department, Treasury 136–8

Department of Treasury and Economics (Ontario) 139, 212, 214–15, 231, 248

Depositor protection 155, 159–60

Design for Development 137, 145, 211, 223, 248

Diefenbaker, John G. 46–7, 51, 63, 66, 68, 78, 88–9, 93–8, 131, 143, 145, 159, 163, 165–70, 174–5, 178, 183, 191

Dillon, Richard 27, 53

Disclosure requirements (financial) 146, 154

Dow Chemical Company 245

Dowd, Eric 240

Downer, Rev. A.W. 39, 68, 70, 84

Drew, George 17, 23, 25, 31, 37, 39, 40, 43, 46, 77, 85, 94, 145, 192, 221, 259, 260, 272, 273; 22-point platform 17
Dunlop Rubber Company 243–4, 246
Dunlop, William J. 53
Dunnville, Ontario 207
Duplessis, M. 132
Dwyer, William 38
Dymond, Matthew 62, 68, 70, 89, 91, 170

Eagleson, R. Alan 112–13, 220–2, 239–41, 256–9
Eaton, Catherine Brett 4, 5, 7
Eberlee, Tom 78, 87
Economic advisers 135, 137, 138, 139, 144
Economic development 76, 86–90, 93–6, 114, 129, 137, 142–5, 167, 192, 198, 214, 223, 244–5, 252–3
Economic nationalism 246–7, 252
Education 90, 114, 143, 209, 211, 219, 220, 226–8, 232, 258
Education grants 55, 56, 90, 95, 96, 162, 168–73, 190–1, 196, 243, 253
Elgin County 16, 29
Emergency Measures Organization 115
Empire Club, Toronto 66, 245
Environmental protection 190, 206, 214, 245, 246, 275
Equalization grants 129, 130, 171–4, 215, 225
Exeter, Ontario 23, 71, 77, 182
Expenditure policy 89, 138, 139, 168, 170, 173, 177, 178, 210, 212, 213, 224, 225, 228, 231, 241
Expo '67 177, 187–9

Facer, R.W. 26–7
Fairfield Corporation, Owen Sound 96
Fanshawe Dam, London 29
Faribault, Marcel 171

Farm and Country 258
Farmers Allied Meat Enterprises Co-operative (FAME) 150–1, 156–7
Farmland 206, 229
Farm tax rebate 242–3
Farrell, Ray 114
Favreau, G. 164
Fearman, F.W. 150–1
Federal elections: (1953) 37, 38, 39; (1962) 88; (1963) 95; (1965) 168–70; (1968) 201, 222
Federal-provincial conference on education (1960) 55
Federal-provincial conference on pensions (September 1963) 106–7
Federal-provincial conferences: (July 1963) 101–2; (November 1963) 129; Quebec (March–April 1964) 128, 131–2, 162; Charlottetown (September 1964) 163; (July 1965) 167; (October 1966) 172–4, 179; (July 1967) 188–9; (February 1968) 196, 200; (December 1969) 239; Victoria (1971) 201, 259
Federal-provincial relations 44, 93, 98, 99, 102, 128, 130–8, 142, 154, 156–60, 164–80 passim, 186, 196, 199, 212–26 passim, 243, 245, 269
Financial community 142–5, 151, 154–60, 244
Financial Post 145
Fiscal policy 17, 90, 95, 96, 114, 130, 138–9, 142–4, 162, 164, 168, 170–3, 209, 224–6, 231, 241
Flag 164–5
Ford, Arthur 18, 20
Ford, Gordon 18
French-Canadian nationalism 129, 168–73, 189, 197, 252
French-language education 190–1, 198, 211
Front de libération du Québec (FLQ) 251
Frost, Cecil 16, 17

Frost, Leslie 17, 20, 23, 25, 26, 28–34, 39–45, 48–52, 55–8, 62, 64–6, 68, 71, 72, 75–9, 82, 83, 88, 94, 102, 104, 106, 108, 123–4, 135, 139, 142, 154, 170, 192, 209, 210, 221, 229, 238, 252, 256, 259–60, 267, 272–3
Fulton, Davie 163, 165

Galt, Ontario 3, 4, 5, 7, 10
Gammage, Bill 19
Gardiner, Fred 17, 58, 64–5, 78, 238
Garnsworthy, Archbishop Lewis 272
Gathercole, George 33, 58, 77, 90, 135–6, 139–40
Gilbride, Gordon 19, 21–6, 37, 38, 42
Gillies, J. 263
Globe and Mail (Toronto) 58, 59, 62, 64, 67, 80, 98, 121–2, 126, 186, 198, 217
Goldenberg, Carl 87–8, 100
Gomme, George 178
Goodall, Alan J. ('Unk') 4, 6, 7, 8
Goodall, Edith ('Auntie') 4, 7
Goodfellow, William 64, 76, 287
Goodman, Edwin 10, 78, 146, 149–50, 170, 222, 240, 254, 257
Gordon, H. Glen 46
Gordon, Walter 106, 154–6
GO Transit 190
Goudy, Bill 19
Government reorganization 76, 89, 95, 114, 116, 127–41 *passim*, 147, 155–6, 161, 177, 195, 205, 209, 212–14, 218, 221, 224–6, 228, 231, 233, 236, 238, 272–3
Graham, General Howard 147
Grand Bend, Ontario 75, 76, 77, 119, 177, 182
Grant, Mr Justice Campbell 151, 155
Granton, Ontario 64
Greer, Harold 80, 84, 103–4
Gregory, Wilfred D. 152–3

Griesinger, W. 46
Griffith Island 265, 271
Grosart, Allister 46–7, 94
Grossman, Allan 64, 76, 88, 104, 105, 213
Grossman, Larry 67
Guelph, Ontario 17

Haldimand-Norfolk 224
Hall Commission (on health insurance) 162
Hall-Dennis Report 219–20
Hall, Mr Justice Emmett 161, 219
Halpenny, Ernest G. 38, 43–4, 46–7, 50, 53, 59, 63, 67, 154
Hamilton, Ontario 15, 51, 91
Hanover, Ontario 107
Hanson, Hugh 236, 271
Harnett, Art 222
Harris, Walter 154
Harvison, C.W. 80, 117
Haskett, W. Irwin 76, 104
Hatfield, Richard 259
Hawkins, Chris 27
Health insurance 89, 94–5, 97, 161, 162, 166–72, 184, 196, 212, 217–18, 224–6, 232, 238, 259
Hepburn, Mitchell 16, 29, 39, 41, 45
Hickey, Paul 228
Highway 401 286
Hogan, George 78, 135–6
Hospital expenditures 114
Hotel London 18, 110, 194
Housing policy 212
Howe, C.D. 37
Hughes, Mr Justice S. 152, 155–6
Human Rights Code 78, 86
Hunter, Peter 178

Imperial Bank 3, 4, 7, 19
Imperial Council of Shriners, Atlantic City 19

Inflation 184, 192, 210, 243
Insider trading 145–8, 156
Insurance companies 184
International Conference on Regional
  Development and Economic Change
  144
Interprovincial conference (1964) 148
Interprovincial conference on consumer
  protection 249
Interprovincial relations 89, 101, 130–3,
  156, 162, 171, 174
Iron Ore Company of Canada 269
Ivey, Mrs Charles Sr 18
Ivey, Peter 18, 19

Jackson, Ernest G. 42, 44, 46, 50–3, 59,
  61–5, 67, 71, 77, 78, 83–5, 88, 99,
  103, 106, 108, 140, 175, 182, 189, 191,
  222, 240, 254, 257, 262–4, 269–70
Jeffery, Alex 20, 28, 37
Jenkins, Fred 19, 21, 24–7, 37–9, 43, 50,
  51, 53, 59, 62, 65–7, 69, 194, 254
Jenkins, William A. 21
Jenkins, William Jr 255–6
Job, Louisa 3
Johnson, Allan 22
Johnson, Daniel 131, 171–4, 179, 197–9,
  200, 201
Johnson, Lyndon 151
Jolliffe, Edward 28, 31, 41

Kefauver, Senator Estes 79
Kelly, A. 150
Kelly, Phillip T. 46
Kennedy, Robert 79
Kennedy, Colonel T.L. 38
Kerr, George 240, 245
Killingsworth, J. Stewart 22
Killoran, Cam 9, 15, 18–19, 23, 36
Kimber Committee (Attorney general's
  committee on securities regulation)
  146–9, 155

Kimber, J.R. 135, 146, 148, 150 154
King, W.L. Mackenzie 9, 15, 18, 19
King Edward Hotel 39, 72
King George VI 34
King, Mac 222
Kinmond, William 63, 67, 83, 98, 103,
  109, 114, 122–3, 195, 241
Kitchener-Waterloo, Ontario 224

Labatt's Breweries 22
Labour Management Committee (London) 22
Lake Erie fishery 245
Lakehead 192, 224
LaMarsh, Judy 99, 102–8 passim, 132,
  168, 192
Laporte, Pierre 131, 251–2
Latimer, Hugh 46, 58, 78
Lavergne, Gordon 103
Law Reform Commission, Ontario 118,
  126, 147
Lawrence, A.B.R. (Bert) 103, 240, 258
Lawrence, Allan 124–6, 230, 240, 249,
  252, 258, 260–1, 272
Law Society of Upper Canada 119, 146
Lawson, H.R. 152–3, 292
Leadership campaign (1961) 59–67,
  70–1, 287
Leal, Allan 146
Le Droit (Ottawa) 99
Lee, Paul 103
Leighton, Jack 69
Lesage, Jean 86, 93–4, 100, 102, 128–33,
  163, 166–72 passim
Lévesque, René 132, 197, 266
Lewis, Major Alex 33
Lewis, David 159
Lewis, Roderick 33, 112, 133, 234
Lewis, Stephen 184, 218, 242, 244, 247,
  252, 257
Liberal Club (University of Western
  Ontario) 18
Liberal party (federal) 98, 99, 105, 192

Liberal party (London) 20, 28, 30, 37, 42, 103, 194, 254

Liberal party (Ontario) 17, 20, 40, 42, 51, 80, 81, 84, 105, 125, 163, 184, 195, 208, 218, 253; Middlesex by-election 232

Lindsay, Ontario 17, 104

Lindsay *Post* 228, 229

Liquor Control Board of Ontario 17, 76, 104, 105

Loans and Trusts Act 156, 159–60

London, Ontario 4, 7, 10, 15–17, 19–21, 23, 161, 181, 254; annexation 34, 36

London and Suburban Planning Board 22, 23, 49

London Central Collegiate 9, 17

London Club 51, 59, 255

London Concrete Machinery 21

London constituencies 42, 110

London *Free Press* 18, 22, 30, 32, 51, 52

London Hunt Club 9, 14, 19, 59, 255

London Life Insurance Company 108, 255

'London mafia' 39, 43, 59, 67

London Municipal Council 22

London municipal election (1950) 22

London PC Association 21, 24, 37, 38, 43, 50, 52, 53, 232, 254, 255, 260

London Printing and Lithographing Company 26

London-Quebec exchange 255–6

London YMCA 42

Lord's Day (Ontario) Act 208

Luxton, Rt Rev. George 249

Macaulay, Leopold 34

Macaulay, Robert 34–6, 39, 40, 44–5, 47, 49, 51–2, 54, 59, 61–73 *passim*, 76, 77, 79, 81–2, 86–98 *passim*, 103, 113, 135, 137, 143, 163, 184, 188, 214, 272

Macdonald, Judge B.J.S. 115–22

MacDonald, Donald C. 41, 42–3, 51, 54, 79, 84–5, 100, 104, 110, 113, 119, 123–6, 184, 185, 193, 195, 207, 218, 241, 244–5, 247, 249

Macdonald, H. Ian 136–40, 180, 186, 190, 200, 212, 231, 248

Macdonald, Sir John A. 59

Macdonald, Lieutenant-Governor W. Ross 260

Macdonnell, J.M. 17

MacDougall, Frank 134

Mackay, Lieutenant-Governor J. Keiller 27, 96

MacLeod, Alex 100

MacMillan, George and Viola 148

MacNaughton, Charles S. 62–3, 76–8, 139, 141, 178, 180, 182, 190, 210, 213–18, 224–5, 227–8, 230–2, 240, 241, 248, 256, 258

MacOdrum, Charles G. 40

Maine, Dr S. Floyd 37

Makarchuk, Mac 193, 195

Maloney, James 49

Manning, E. 198

Manross, Park 19

Mapledoram, Clare 46

Maple Leaf Gardens, 254, 257, 259

Martyn, Don 254, 271

Matthews, Donald 254–5

McAllister, Fred G. 26

McConnell, James 65

McCormick, C. Garfield 14

McCormick, Norah. *See* Robarts, Norah McCormick

McCutcheon, Senator Wallace 153–4, 156

McDonald, Lorne R. 33

McGraw-Hill 252

McHugh, William 54–5

McIntyre, W. Malcolm 33, 58, 77–8, 80, 83, 114, 126, 134, 236

McKenzie, Alex D. 17, 33, 40, 46–7, 50, 58–9, 63, 77–8, 83, 140

McKeough, Darcy 178, 214, 220, 224, 228–30, 240, 248–9, 258
McLaughlin, H.J. 154
McMaster University, Hamilton 91
McRuer, J.C. 126, 146, 155, 219
McTavish, L.R. 33
Media relations 82–3, 110, 114, 119, 122, 178, 195–200, 235, 238, 241
Mercy Hospital, Buffalo 265
Metropolitan Life Insurance Company 263, 269
Metropolitan Toronto 142, 190, 192, 210, 220
Metropolitan Toronto and Region Transportation Study 114, 139
Middlesex North 28
Milligan, R.P. 126
Mimico, Ontario 192, 220
Mining 145, 147, 149, 155
Mitchell, R.W. 38–9, 43, 47, 53
Montreal 16, 93
Moores, Frank 269
Morton, J.D. 79, 80
Mowat, Farley 206
Mulroney, Brian 269
Municipal Development and Loan Fund 101–2, 113
Municipal reform 89, 96, 191, 205, 209–11, 214, 223, 230, 248
Municipality for Tomorrow conference 230

National economy 130, 162, 163, 169
National Housing Act 192
National Life Assurance Company 152–3
National unity 100, 165, 167, 169, 190, 194, 259, 266
New Democratic Party 59, 104, 107, 126, 159, 184, 185, 192–3, 195, 206–7, 218, 220, 232, 242, 246–8, 252
New Toronto 192, 220
New York Stock Exchange 147

Niagara 99, 105, 224
Niagara escarpment 16, 190, 206, 249, 253
Nickle, W.F. 40, 64, 91
Nixon, Harry 42, 84
Nixon, Robert 84, 184, 192–3, 208, 218, 226, 227, 240, 241, 243
North American General Insurance Company 158
Northern Ontario 87, 224, 230
Northern development conferences 230, 249
Northern Ontario Natural Gas 46–7, 51, 146

October crisis (1970) 251, 255
Offshore resources 166
Old London community 8–9, 16, 18, 20, 24, 26, 110, 111, 154, 254, 262, 265, 269
O'Leary, Grattan 63
Oliver, Farquhar 41, 113, 123, 124
Ontario Advisory Committee on Confederation 136, 179, 190, 195, 200, 231
Ontario Arts Council 95, 96
Ontario Association of Mayors and Reeves 230, 241
Ontario budgets: (1967) 180; (1969) 224–5
Ontario by-elections: (1962) 78, 84–5; (Huron Bruce) 91, 97; (Middlesex South) 232, 238
Ontario cabinets: 75–7, 91; (1961) 81–2; (1963) 104; (1966) 178; (1967 restructuring) 137, 140; Cabinet Committee on Economics and Finance 137–40; Cabinet Committee on Planning and Priorities 139; Cabinet Committee on Regional Development 145; (1969) 226
Ontario Civil Service Commission 89
Ontario Committee on Taxation 90, 96,

139, 162, 177, 183, 190, 210–15, 223, 225, 236

Ontario Deposit Insurance Corporation 159

Ontario Development Fund 89–90, 96, 143, 145, 151

Ontario Economic Council 86, 103, 138, 140, 144–5

Ontario elections: (1951) 25, 26, 29, 30; (1955) 40–2, 111, 221; (1959) 51–2; (by-elections, 1962) 78, 84–5; (1963) 91, 93, 98, 102–12, 146; (by-election, 1964) 163–4; (1967) 177–9, 183, 190–5, 220, 230, 254; (by-election, 1969) 232; (1971) 261, 263

Ontario Flue Cured Tobacco Marketing Board 150

Ontario Foundation Tax Plan 90, 96, 129

Ontario Heritage Foundation 178

Ontario hospital insurance 62

Ontario Human Rights Commission 100. See also Human Rights Code

Ontario Hydro 16, 49, 77, 87–8, 135, 153, 207, 233, 244

Ontario Law Reform Commission 146

Ontario legislature (1951) 25, 31, 32, 79; MPPS 32, 40, 112, 114, 134, 181, 206–8; support services 32, 112, 133–5; timetable 33, 133, 156, 178, 180–1, 183, 234, 282; committee restructuring 133, 227, 234; changing environment 185, 193–4, 208, 213, 218–19, 234, 250; French language 200–1; House leader 236; chief whip 208

Ontario legislature committees: on Air Pollution 40; Legal Bills 36, 40, 124, 126; on Motor Vehicle Titles 40; on Municipal Law 34, 144; Select Committee on Consumer Credit 114, 146–7, 155–6; Select Committee on Tax Reform 132–3, 215, 223; on Toll Roads 40, 42–5, 49

Ontario Medical Services Insurance Plan. See Health insurance

Ontario Medical Association 89

Ontario Municipal Association 90

Ontario Northland Railway 85

Ontario Pension Advisory Committee 102, 107–8, 135

Ontario Place 233

Ontario Police Commission 80–1, 115–24, 126, 147, 209

Ontario PC Association 33, 39, 59, 67, 77, 103, 140, 165, 174, 220, 221, 238, 239, 257

Ontario Provincial Police 79, 80, 115–20, 209

Ontario-Quebec newspaper editors seminar 168–9

Ontario-Quebec relations 93–4, 98, 101, 102, 105, 128–9, 131, 162, 167–9, 172, 179, 180, 218, 252, 256

Ontario, redistribution 85–6, 96–7

Ontario Research Foundation 86

Ontario, royal commissions: on the Book Publishing Industry 252; Inquiry into Civil Rights 126, 207, 219–20; on the Construction Industry 87; on Metropolitan Toronto 264–5, 267; on Organized Crime 80, 82, 86, 97–8, 104, 108–9, 116–17; Inquiry into Windfall Oils and Mines 148–50

Ontario sales tax 58, 59

Ontario Science Centre 233, 241

Ontario Securities Commission 97, 115, 118, 145–8, 152, 155–6, 158

Ontario Water Resources Commission 48–50, 52, 53, 215, 249

Orange Order 24

Organized crime 58, 79–82, 84, 88, 105, 108, 113–25 passim, 146, 208, 247–8

Organized labour 41, 87, 184, 192, 238, 251

Oriental Band 19, 27, 38, 42, 67

Osgoode Hall 10, 14, 15, 35, 146, 246
Ottawa-Carleton 224
Ottawa *Journal* 63

HMS *Palomares* 13
Park Plaza Hotel, Toronto 67, 69, 72
Parti Québécois 266
Patrick, Tom 36
Pearson, Lester B. 75, 95, 98, 99, 101–2,
    105, 106, 128, 130–1, 162–74 *passim*,
    179, 185–8, 196, 197, 199
Pension plans 89, 95, 97, 99, 101–2,
    105–8, 128–35, 162, 164, 196
Pepin, Jean-Luc 266
Peterson, Clarence 42
Pitman, Walter 247
Polar Bear Provincial Park 233
Policy process reform 135, 138–40, 212,
    223, 233
Pollution 190, 192, 206, 243, 245, 275
Port Huron 19
Port Maitland 206
Port Stanley 4, 6
Porter Commission 145–7
Porter, Dana 145, 158
Potter, Richard 208, 241
Power Corporation 263, 266
Powers of inquiry 188, 120–1, 219
Press gallery 42, 63, 80, 82–4, 100,
    119–20, 122, 131, 235
Price, Bud 156
Price, Harry 17, 44, 50, 64, 65, 70, 72,
    75, 78, 84, 90, 94, 154, 222, 263, 264,
    292
Prime Minister's Office 32, 33, 75, 77,
    82, 91–2, 92, 113–14, 119, 122, 134,
    139
Prince Philip 188
Privy Council of Canada 185, 188
Productivity Improvement Project 231
Progressive-Conservative Association of
    Canada 135, 174

Progressive-Conservative Association
    (University of Western Ontario) 18
Progressive-Conservative party; caucus
    (Ontario) 33–5, 85, 88, 112, 120,
    125–6, 133–4, 140; federal 16–17, 23,
    38, 43, 46, 88, 95, 168, 170, 182–3,
    191; London 19, 20, 21, 24–8, 30,
    37–9, 42–3, 69, 111, 154, 194–5, 254,
    256
PC party provincial organization 17, 20,
    34, 39; 1951 campaign 28; 1955 cam-
    paign 46; 1961 leadership campaign
    59–67, 70, 71, 72; 1962 Robarts 84,
    88; 1963 94, 95, 103, 105–7, 110; chief
    whip 133, 208; 1967–70 190, 192,
    194–5, 220–3, 238–9, 246, 272; 1971
    leadership 257–60
Property assessment 223, 225, 228–9,
    242–3
Property tax 227–8, 242–3
Provincial Institute of Trades 55–6
Provincial-Municipal conference 239,
    242, 245
Provincial-Municipal Liaison Committee
    242
Prudential Finance 158–60, 184, 193, 207
Public Inquiries Act 119
Public Service Act 1962 89

Quebec City 128
Quebec: Quiet Revolution 86, 93–4, 100,
    128; referendum 269; separatism 99–
    100, 132, 198, 251
Quebec Election (1966) 171
Queen Alexandria Hospital Association 59
Queen Elizabeth 185, 188
'Queen's Park on the Thames' 140–1, 178,
    220, 222, 241, 257–8
Queen's Printer 241
Queen's University, Kingston 64, 66

Ramsay, James 86, 188–90, 195

Rand, Mr Justice Ivan 184
Randall, Stanley J. 103, 113, 138, 144, 175, 213, 244
Rasminsky, Louis 144
Rathbun, William 195, 237, 241
Reaume, Arthur 105–6, 111
Reed, Shaw, Stenhouse 263, 269
Reform program, reaction 223, 226–7, 229, 231–2, 242
Regional development 45, 95, 137, 144, 166, 211, 213–15, 223, 248–9
Regional development councils 145, 248
Regional government 114, 144, 191, 192, 205, 210, 214–16, 218, 220, 223–32 *passim*
Regional water supply 23, 49
Registrar of Loans and Trust Companies 153
Reid, Gordon 20, 24, 29
Reilly, Leonard 208
Reilly, Peter 121
Renwick, James 164, 184–5, 243
Reynolds, Dr J. Keith 134, 135, 138–41, 171, 186, 231, 233, 236, 237, 260, 269, 271
Roach, W.D. 82, 86, 97, 117
Robarts, Andrea (niece) 36
Robarts, Betts, McLennan, and Flinn 262
Robarts, Catherine Brett (step-sister) 4, 5, 7
Robarts, Eleanor (sister-in-law) 23, 36
Robarts, Ethel (McIrvine) 7, 11
Robarts, Florency May (Stacpoole Brett) 3, 4
Robarts, Herbert (father) 3, 4, 5, 7, 8, 13, 15, 24, 25, 119
Robarts, John Parmenter
– CAREER: early life 5–7; education 7–9; university 9; war service 10–14; marriage 14; legal career 6, 10, 15, 19, 35–6, 44–9 *passim*, 161, 207, 262–3, 269; municipal politics 21–3; provincial nomination 24–5; election campaign 26–30, 32; backbencher 34–5, 40, 43, 45–8, 261; toll roads committee 40, 43, 45; Ontario Water Resources Commission 49; education portfolio 52–6, 87, 90, 211; leadership campaign 59–63, 71, 78, 82, 85–8, 122–3, 143; first cabinet 75–82 *passim*, 88, 91; prime minister 71–2; reorganization of office 77, 82–3, 86, 91, 98, 117, 128, 133–40, 156, 177–8, 236; economic initiatives 89, 90, 129, 137–9; Bill 99 114–25; British Mortgage and Trust bailout 153; provincial rights 86, 93, 94, 102, 130, 133; centennial 186–7; Confederation of Tomorrow conference 185–7, 197, 199; constitutional reform 173, 197–8, 201; fiscal reform program 209; county school boards 227–8; health insurance 168, 170, 179–83; transition of power 231, 238, 240, 242, 254–64 *passim*; retirement 255–7, 260; directorships 263–4; second marriage 256–9; stroke 269–7; death 271–2
– CHARACTER: gambling 8–10; role-playing 6, 14, 34, 38–9, 45, 50, 52, 83, 109; discipline 5, 7–8, 11, 27–8, 52, 140, 267, 272, 276; domestic relationships 36–7, 48–50, 53, 61, 119, 161, 177, 187, 262–7, 270–1; attitude to health 180–2, 263, 270–1; approach to money 13, 14, 48–9, 75–6, 177, 263–4; relations with press 83, 97–8, 178, 235, 241–2
– POLITICAL IDEAS AND POLICIES: leadership style 9, 29, 49–50, 53–4, 66–7, 72, 75–94 *passim*, 98–100, 105–7, 123–7, 149, 160, 192–3, 199–200, 220–2, 233, 234–40, 254–5, 259–61, 272–6; individual freedom 66, 246–7, 251–2; government reform 88–9, 91,

139, 150, 212, 214, 216, 221, 272–5;
views on federalism 162, 167–74
passim, 223–6, 256, 266–9, 274;
organizational approach 133–41
passim, 209–14, 222–6, 229, 231, 233,
248
Robarts, Katherine (Kwasniewski
Sickafuse) 265–71
Robarts, Marion (half-sister) 7, 21, 285
Robarts, Norah (McCormick) 8, 9, 11,
14, 17, 19, 21, 25–6, 35–6, 48, 50,
61, 67–72, 75, 161, 180–2, 188, 221,
237, 260, 262–5, 267, 269
Robarts, Robert George (brother) 4–5, 8,
10–12, 19, 21, 36, 110, 194, 270
Robarts, Robin (daughter) 36, 50, 161,
182, 187, 188, 221, 237, 264, 269,
270, 271
Robarts, Timothy (son) 37, 161, 182, 187,
237, 267
'Robarts Plan' 54–7, 60, 62, 64, 72, 143
Robbins, Harold 34, 58
Roberts, A. Kelso 60, 62–4, 66–72, 76,
79, 81–2, 86, 88, 91, 98, 115–17,
122–4, 173, 178, 209, 250
Robertson, Gordon 186
Robichaud, Louis 198
Roblin, Duff 174, 191, 197
Rochdale College, Toronto 206
Rohmer, Richard 64, 69, 114, 122–3,
134, 140, 153–4, 248, 252, 264–5,
267, 271
Root, John 49
Rowe, Lieutenant-Governor Earl 188
Rowntree, Leslie 99, 107, 159, 178, 207,
240
Royal Canadian Mounted Police 80, 117,
120, 209
Royal Commission on Health Services
161, 164
Royal Commission on Taxation 162, 190,
212, 225

Royal Military College, Kingston 188
Royal York Hotel, Toronto 33, 39, 44,
58, 72, 87, 88, 121, 195, 259
Rudd, D.S. 'Bill' 66, 107–8
Rural consolidation 114, 224
Rush, Allan 22, 23, 38
Ryan, Claude 252
Ryerson Press 252

St John the Evangelist Church, London 14
St Joseph's Hospital, London 26
St Laurent, Louis 75
St Lawrence Seaway 28, 41
St Paul's Church, Toronto 272
Sales tax 84, 85, 94
Sarnia *Observer* 227
Securities regulation 135, 145–8, 155–6,
158–9, 207, 239
Senate reform 196
Separate schools 191, 226, 236, 253, 259
Sharp, Mitchell 158, 171, 173, 174, 196
Shell Oil Company 145
Shepherd, Ab 62, 65, 69
Shortreed, Bill 22, 25–6
Shulman, Morton 184–5, 193, 195,
207–8, 213, 218, 232, 247, 248
Silk, Eric H. 116, 119
Simonett, J.R. 91, 113
Singer, Vernon 120
Smallwood, Joey 198, 259
Smith, Jack 180
Smith, Lancelot 96, 190, 210
Sopha, Elmer 58
Spadina Expressway 249, 253
Speirs, Rosemary 260
Spooner, Wilfrid 195
Stacpoole, Florency May. *See* Robarts,
Florency May
Stanfield, Robert 183, 191, 196, 218, 259
Starr, Michael 55, 56
Steel Company of Canada 192
Stevenson, Don 186

Stewart, William 47, 62–4, 76, 91, 150
Stikeman, Elliott, Robarts, and Bowman 262
Strom, H. 259
Stronach, Gordon 194
Sudbury *Star* 193, 224

Takeover bids 146
Task Force on Canadian Unity 266–9
Tax reform 89, 95, 132–3, 164, 171, 177, 190, 191, 205, 209, 210–18 *passim*, 223–5, 228–9, 238, 241, 259
Tax Structure Committee 162, 164, 170–1, 173–4, 180
Technical and vocational training 52–6, 143, 174, 244
Teeter, William 222
Templeton, Charles 163
Texas-Gulf Sulphur company 147–8
Thatcher, Ross 172, 198
Thomas, Fletcher S. 46
Thomas, William 63
Thompson, Andrew 125, 164, 184
Thompson, Jack 38
Thomson, Walter 25, 28, 29, 31
Timmins, Ontario 147, 148
Toronto, Ontario 10, 15, 16, 20, 34, 41, 50, 58, 77, 262, 264, 265
Toronto-centred region 248, 249, 275
Toronto *Star* 25, 29, 30, 63, 97, 98, 103, 110, 175, 198, 226, 235, 257, 260
Toronto Stock Exchange 145, 147, 148, 156
Toronto *Telegram* 69, 76, 165, 178, 240
Town Planning Institute of Canada 249
Trans-Canada Highway 41
TransCanada Pipeline 44
Treasury Board, Ontario 89, 138–9, 173, 212, 224, 230–1
Treasury Department, Ontario 33, 138, 139

Trudeau, P.E. 186, 200, 201, 220, 252, 266, 267
Trust Companies Association of Canada 153

Unemployment 76, 143, 243, 253
Union Nationale 93, 171
US Securities and Exchange Commission 147
University of Western Ontario 8, 9, 10, 15, 17, 38, 51, 54, 87, 263, 272
University of Windsor 87

Varsity Arena, University of Toronto 66
Victoria and Grey Trust Company 153–5, 157, 292
Victoria Hospital, London 23
Vimy Branch, Royal Canadian Legion 19, 26, 27, 38, 42

Walker, Gordon 194, 254
Wardrope, George 65, 68–70, 76, 195
War Measures Act 252
Warrendale Treatment Centre 193
Warrender, William Kenneth 64, 76, 91
Waterloo University 87
Webster, William 17, 20, 24–7, 30
Welch, Robert 178, 240, 249, 258
Weldon, David 53, 61, 62, 66, 68, 69
Weldon, Colonel Douglas 20, 24, 61
Wells, Thomas 178, 213, 222, 238, 240
Wenige, George 22
Wentworth County Council 91
Westbury Hotel 46, 50, 67, 68, 72, 75, 78, 235, 237
Westcott, Clare 86
Westendorp, Eugene 18, 25, 26, 27, 30, 78, 84, 106
Western Ontario PC Association 20, 23, 24, 41, 59, 62
White, Harry 63

White, John 51, 52, 66–7, 72, 81, 110,
  126, 133–4, 140, 194, 208, 214–15,
  218, 220, 240, 242, 254, 255
Wilson, Dr J. Cameron 21–2
Willis, George 9, 10, 18
Windfall Mines 148, 155–6
Wingham *Advance* 63
Winnipeg, Manitoba 3, 4
Wintermeyer, John 51, 52, 79, 80–2, 84,
  85, 87, 97–100, 103–11, 116, 207,
  208
Wishart, A.A. 126, 147–8, 150–1,
  155–6, 158–9, 165, 185, 219
Walker, H.H. 89

Women's Bureau 114
Workmen's Compensation Board Hospital
  207

Yaremko, John 47, 178, 193, 260
Yorkdale Shopping Centre, Toronto 193
York Trust and Savings Corporation
  159
York University 263, 269, 272
Yorkville, Toronto 206
Young, Colonel E.J. 33, 34, 45–7, 53,
  58, 77, 135, 139, 140
Young PC Association 78, 85, 221, 254,
  255